PINOLE

maison ikkoku 7

STORY AND ART BY RUMIKO TAKAHASHI

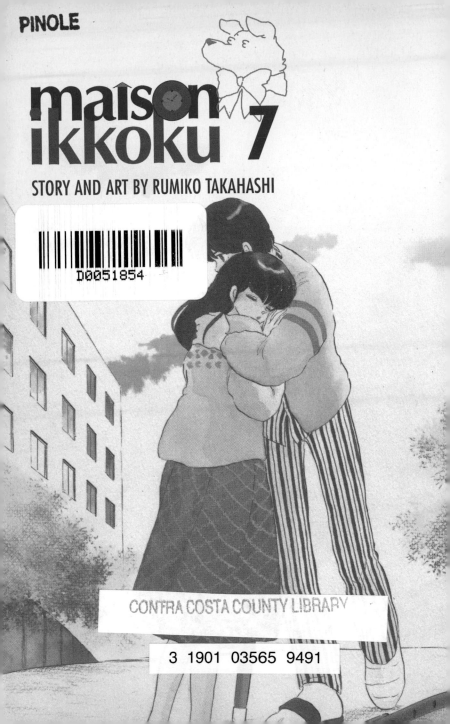

D0051854

CONTRA COSTA COUNTY LIBRARY

3 1901 03565 9491

TABLE OF CONTENTS

PART ONE
FAREWELL ON PLATFORM 18

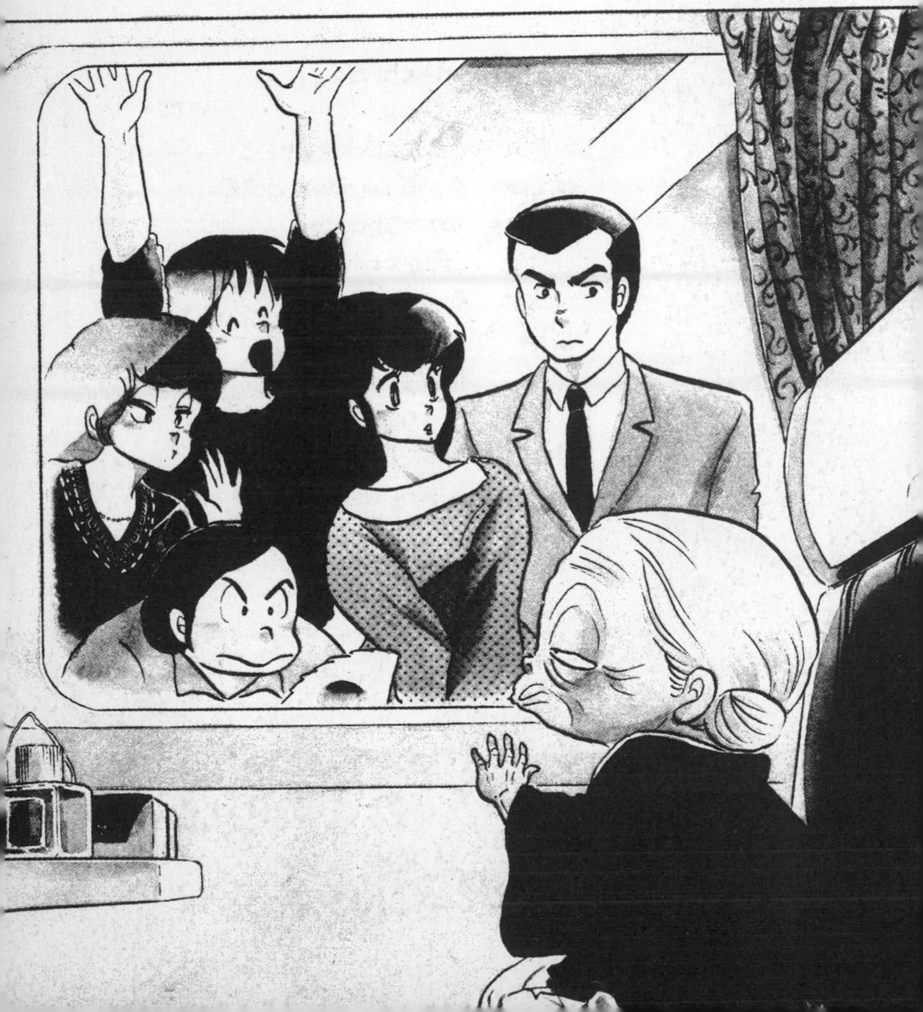

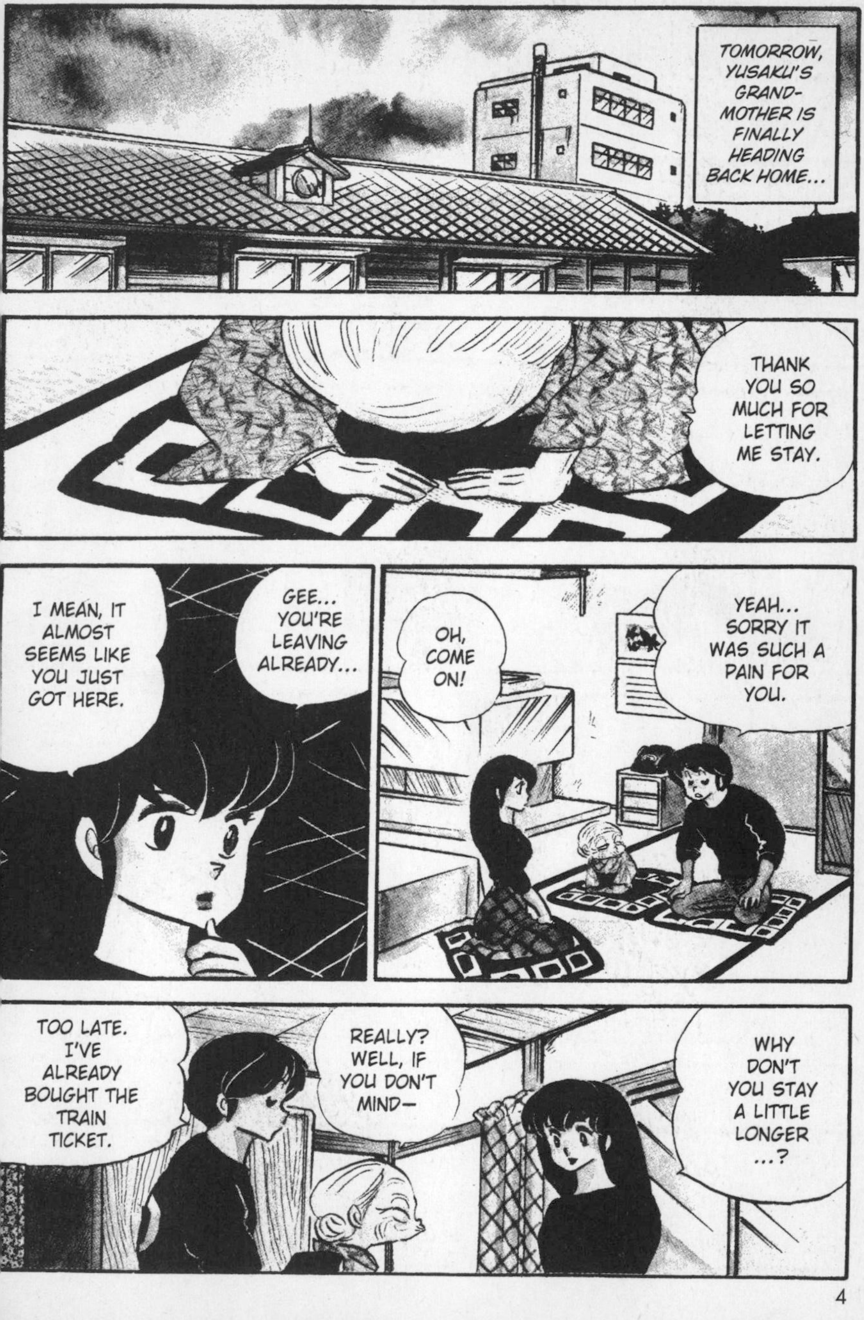
TOMORROW, YUSAKU'S GRAND-MOTHER IS FINALLY HEADING BACK HOME...
THANK YOU SO MUCH FOR LETTING ME STAY.
YEAH... SORRY IT WAS SUCH A PAIN FOR YOU.
OH, COME ON!
GEE... YOU'RE LEAVING ALREADY...
I MEAN, IT ALMOST SEEMS LIKE YOU JUST GOT HERE.
WHY DON'T YOU STAY A LITTLE LONGER ...?
REALLY? WELL, IF YOU DON'T MIND—
TOO LATE. I'VE ALREADY BOUGHT THE TRAIN TICKET.

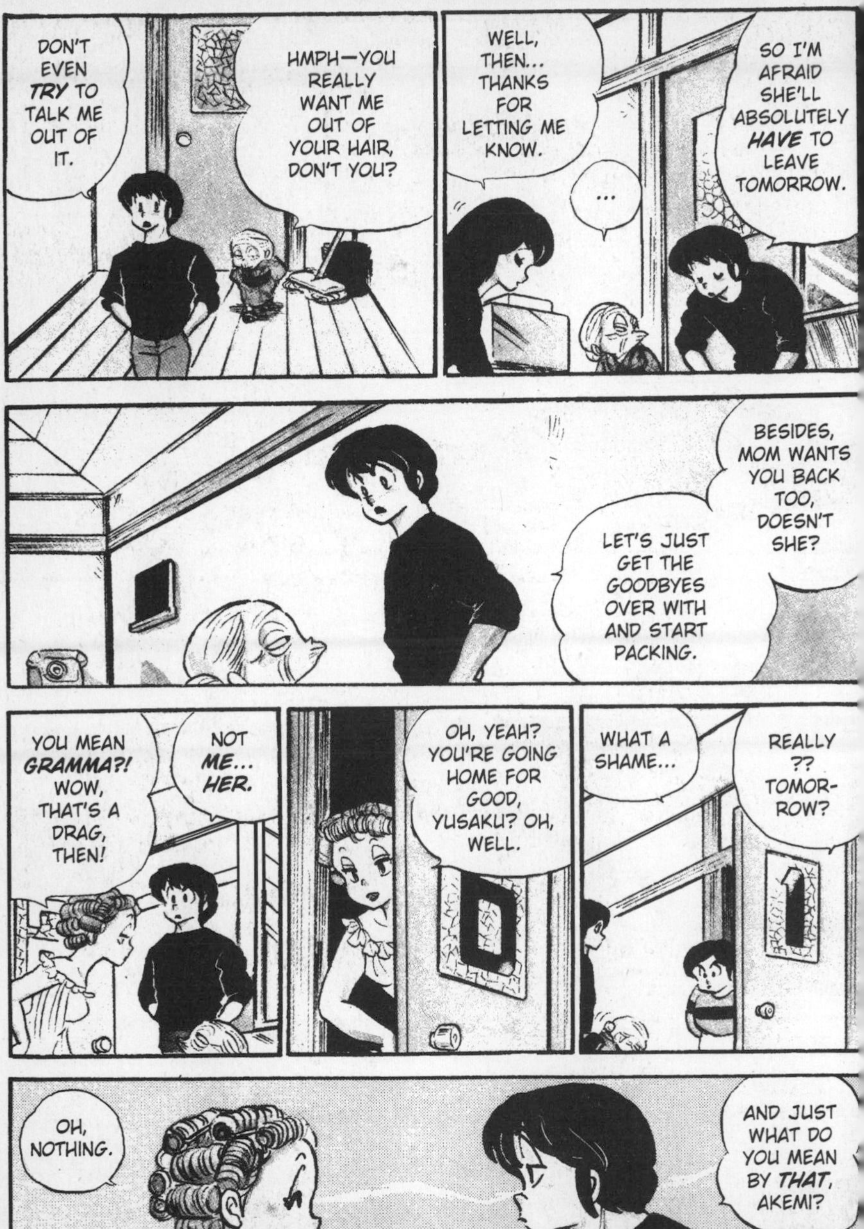
SO I'M AFRAID SHE'LL ABSOLUTELY HAVE TO LEAVE TOMORROW.
WELL, THEN... THANKS FOR LETTING ME KNOW.
...
HMPH—YOU REALLY WANT ME OUT OF YOUR HAIR, DON'T YOU?
DON'T EVEN TRY TO TALK ME OUT OF IT.
BESIDES, MOM WANTS YOU BACK TOO, DOESN'T SHE?
LET'S JUST GET THE GOODBYES OVER WITH AND START PACKING.
REALLY ?? TOMOR-ROW?
WHAT A SHAME...
OH, YEAH? YOU'RE GOING HOME FOR GOOD, YUSAKU? OH, WELL.
NOT ME... HER.
YOU MEAN GRAMMA?! WOW, THAT'S A DRAG, THEN!
AND JUST WHAT DO YOU MEAN BY THAT, AKEMI?
OH, NOTHING.

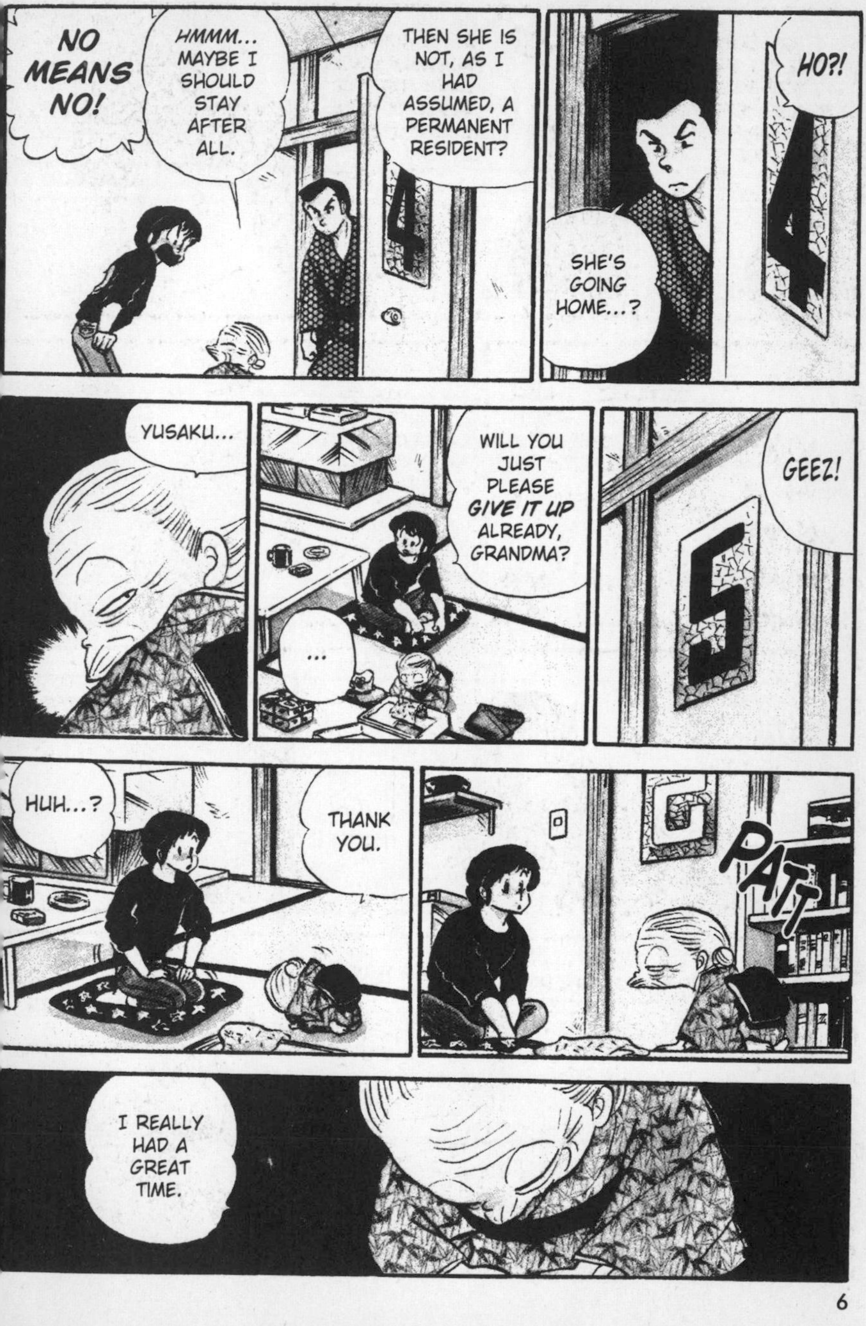
HO?!
SHE'S GOING HOME...?
THEN SHE IS NOT, AS I HAD ASSUMED, A PERMANENT RESIDENT?
HMMM... MAYBE I SHOULD STAY AFTER ALL.
NO MEANS NO!
GEEZ!
WILL YOU JUST PLEASE *GIVE IT UP* ALREADY, GRANDMA?
...
YUSAKU...
PATT
THANK YOU.
HUH...?
I REALLY HAD A GREAT TIME.

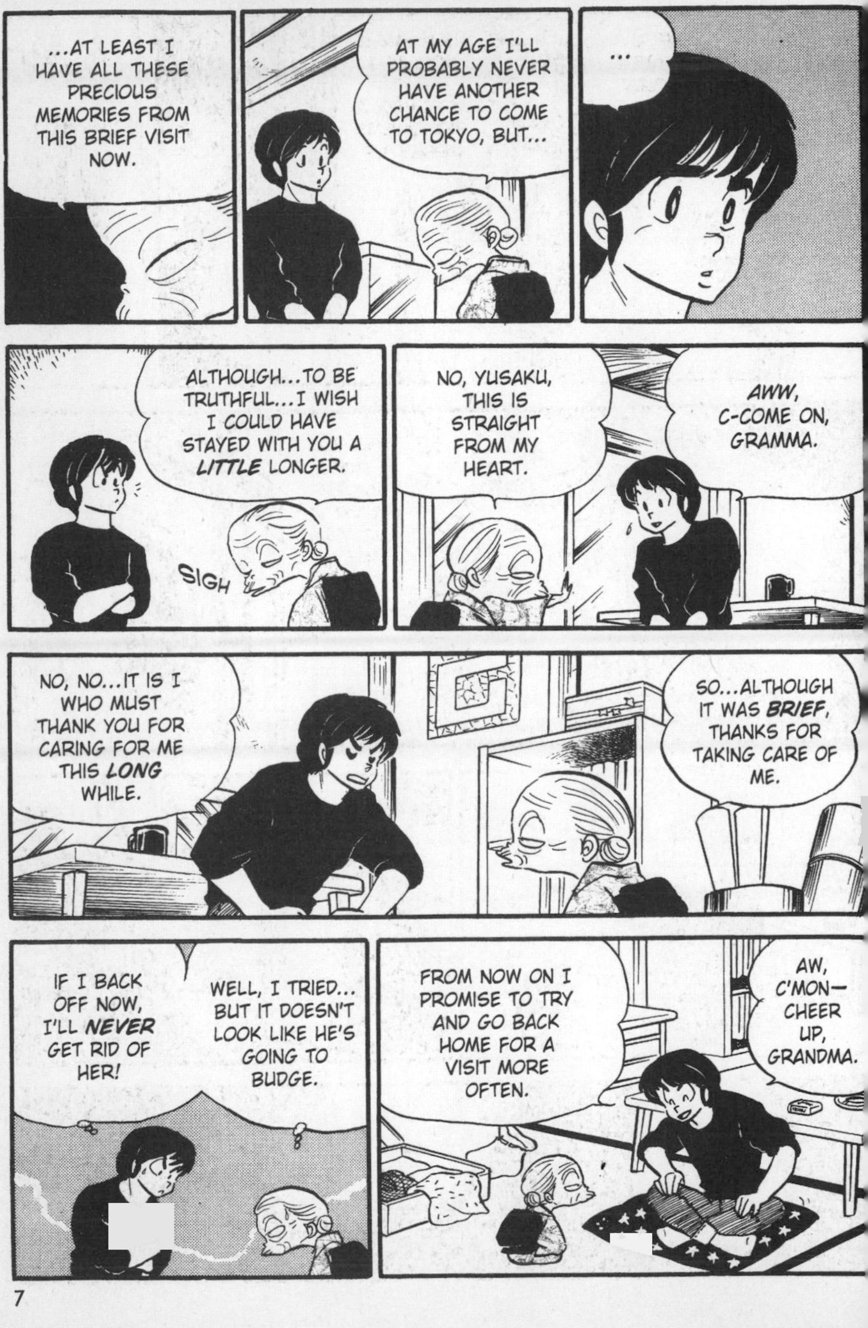
...
AT MY AGE I'LL PROBABLY NEVER HAVE ANOTHER CHANCE TO COME TO TOKYO, BUT...
...AT LEAST I HAVE ALL THESE PRECIOUS MEMORIES FROM THIS BRIEF VISIT NOW.
AWW, C-COME ON, GRAMMA.
NO, YUSAKU, THIS IS STRAIGHT FROM MY HEART.
ALTHOUGH...TO BE TRUTHFUL...I WISH I COULD HAVE STAYED WITH YOU A LITTLE LONGER.
SIGH
SO...ALTHOUGH IT WAS BRIEF, THANKS FOR TAKING CARE OF ME.
NO, NO...IT IS I WHO MUST THANK YOU FOR CARING FOR ME THIS LONG WHILE.
AW, C'MON—CHEER UP, GRANDMA.
FROM NOW ON I PROMISE TO TRY AND GO BACK HOME FOR A VISIT MORE OFTEN.
WELL, I TRIED... BUT IT DOESN'T LOOK LIKE HE'S GOING TO BUDGE.
IF I BACK OFF NOW, I'LL NEVER GET RID OF HER!

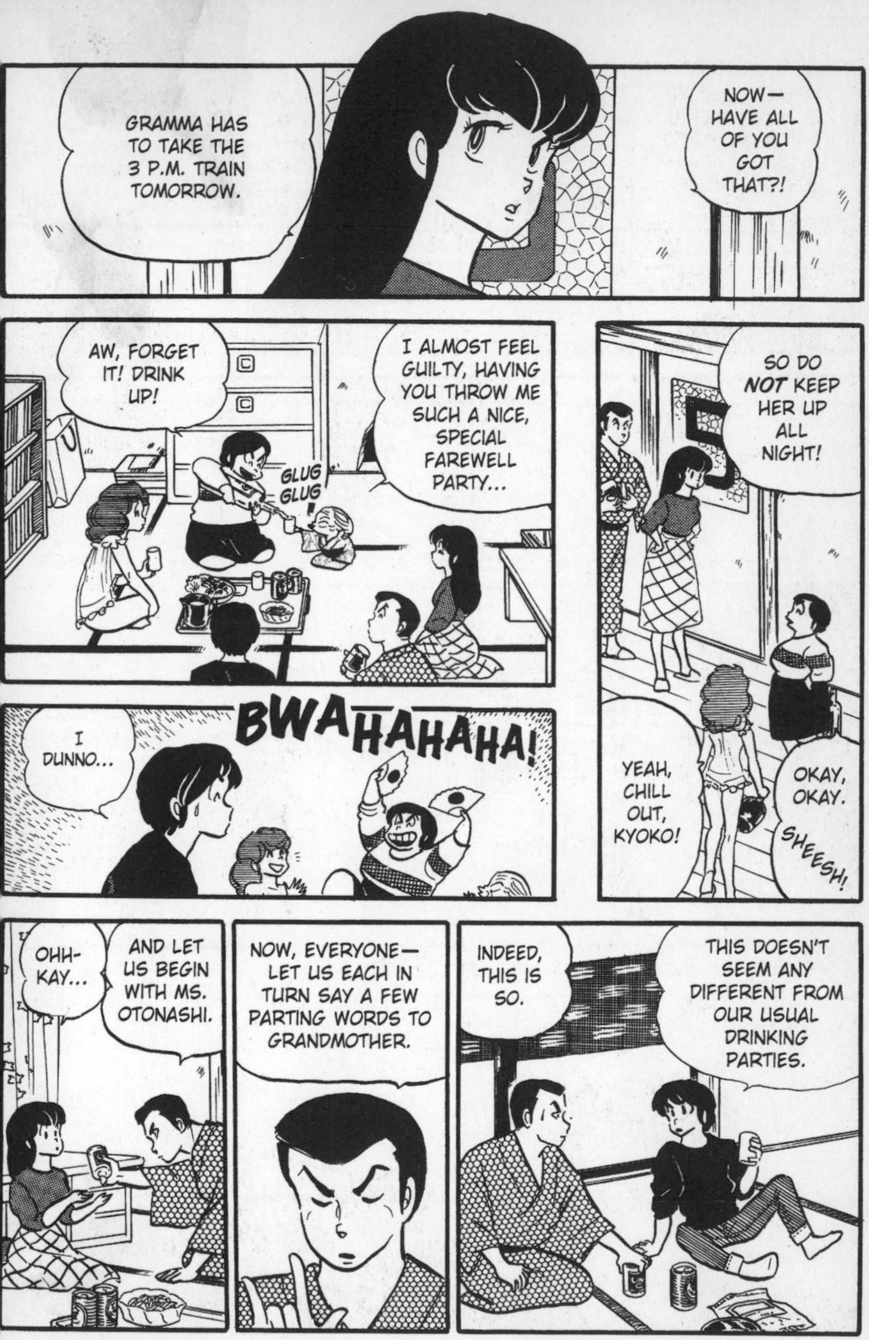
NOW—HAVE ALL OF YOU GOT THAT?!
GRAMMA HAS TO TAKE THE 3 P.M. TRAIN TOMORROW.
SO DO **NOT** KEEP HER UP ALL NIGHT!
OKAY, OKAY.
SHEESH!
YEAH, CHILL OUT, KYOKO!
I ALMOST FEEL GUILTY, HAVING YOU THROW ME SUCH A NICE, SPECIAL FAREWELL PARTY...
AW, FORGET IT! DRINK UP!
GLUG GLUG
BWAHAHAHA!
I DUNNO...
THIS DOESN'T SEEM ANY DIFFERENT FROM OUR USUAL DRINKING PARTIES.
INDEED, THIS IS SO.
NOW, EVERYONE—LET US EACH IN TURN SAY A FEW PARTING WORDS TO GRANDMOTHER.
AND LET US BEGIN WITH MS. OTONASHI.
OHH-KAY...

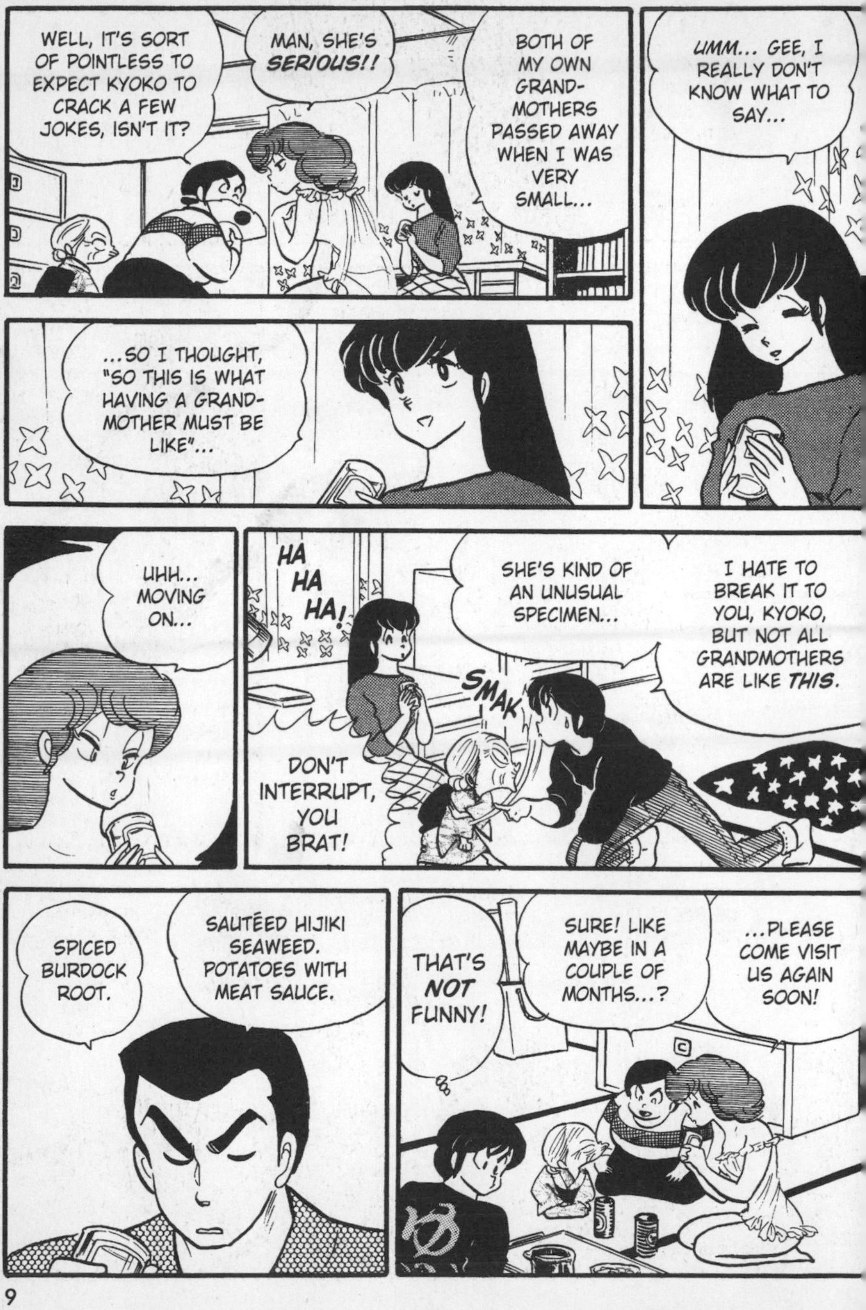
UMM... GEE, I REALLY DON'T KNOW WHAT TO SAY...
BOTH OF MY OWN GRAND-MOTHERS PASSED AWAY WHEN I WAS VERY SMALL...
MAN, SHE'S *SERIOUS!!*
WELL, IT'S SORT OF POINTLESS TO EXPECT KYOKO TO CRACK A FEW JOKES, ISN'T IT?
...SO I THOUGHT, "SO THIS IS WHAT HAVING A GRAND-MOTHER MUST BE LIKE"...
I HATE TO BREAK IT TO YOU, KYOKO, BUT NOT ALL GRANDMOTHERS ARE LIKE *THIS*.
SHE'S KIND OF AN UNUSUAL SPECIMEN...
HA HA HA!
SMAK
DON'T INTERRUPT, YOU BRAT!
UHH... MOVING ON...
...PLEASE COME VISIT US AGAIN SOON!
SURE! LIKE MAYBE IN A COUPLE OF MONTHS...?
THAT'S *NOT* FUNNY!
SAUTÉED HIJIKI SEAWEED. POTATOES WITH MEAT SAUCE.
SPICED BURDOCK ROOT.

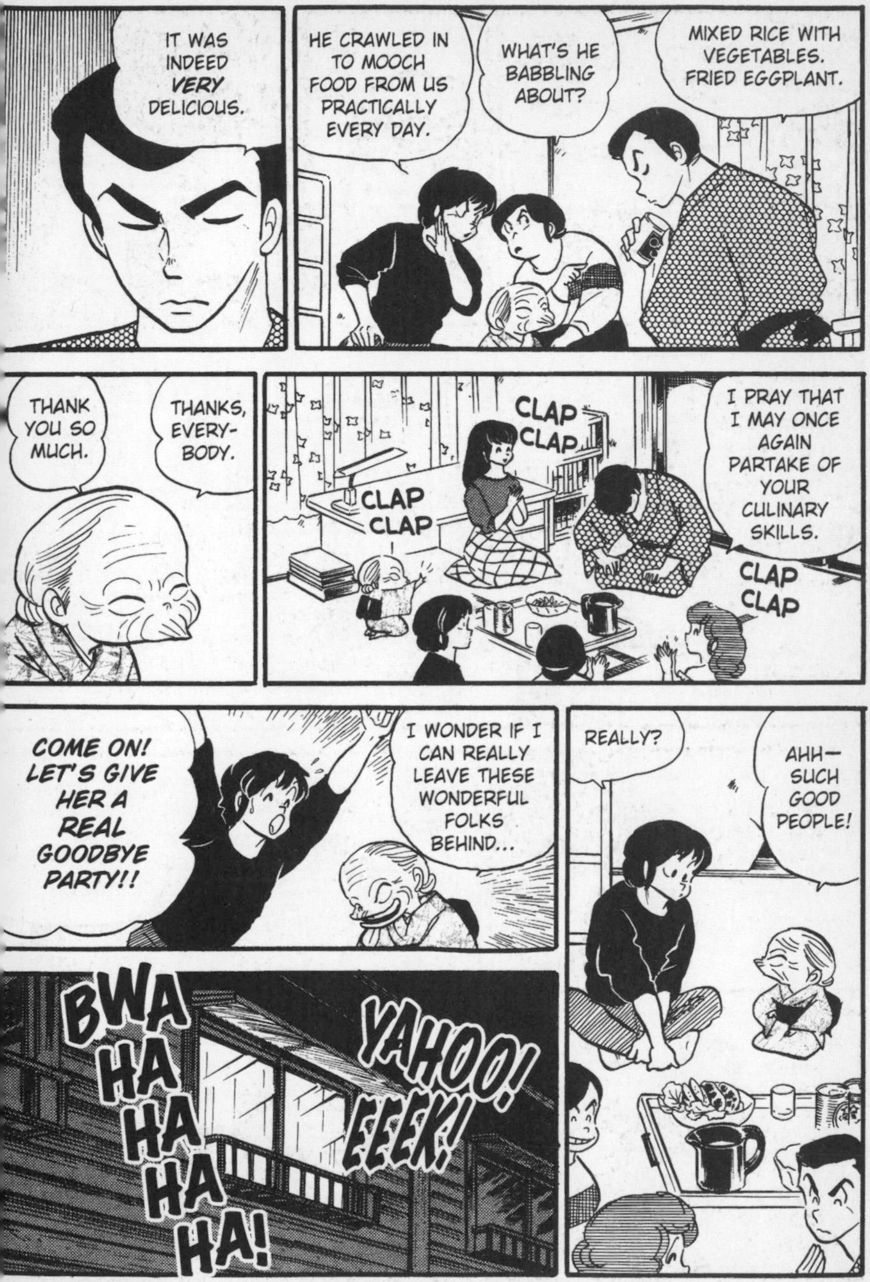
MIXED RICE WITH VEGETABLES. FRIED EGGPLANT.
WHAT'S HE BABBLING ABOUT?
HE CRAWLED IN TO MOOCH FOOD FROM US PRACTICALLY EVERY DAY.
IT WAS INDEED VERY DELICIOUS.
I PRAY THAT I MAY ONCE AGAIN PARTAKE OF YOUR CULINARY SKILLS.
CLAP CLAP
CLAP CLAP
CLAP CLAP
THANKS, EVERY-BODY.
THANK YOU SO MUCH.
AHH— SUCH GOOD PEOPLE!
REALLY?
I WONDER IF I CAN REALLY LEAVE THESE WONDERFUL FOLKS BEHIND...
COME ON! LET'S GIVE HER A REAL GOODBYE PARTY!!
YAHOO! EEEK!
BWA HA HA HA HA HA!

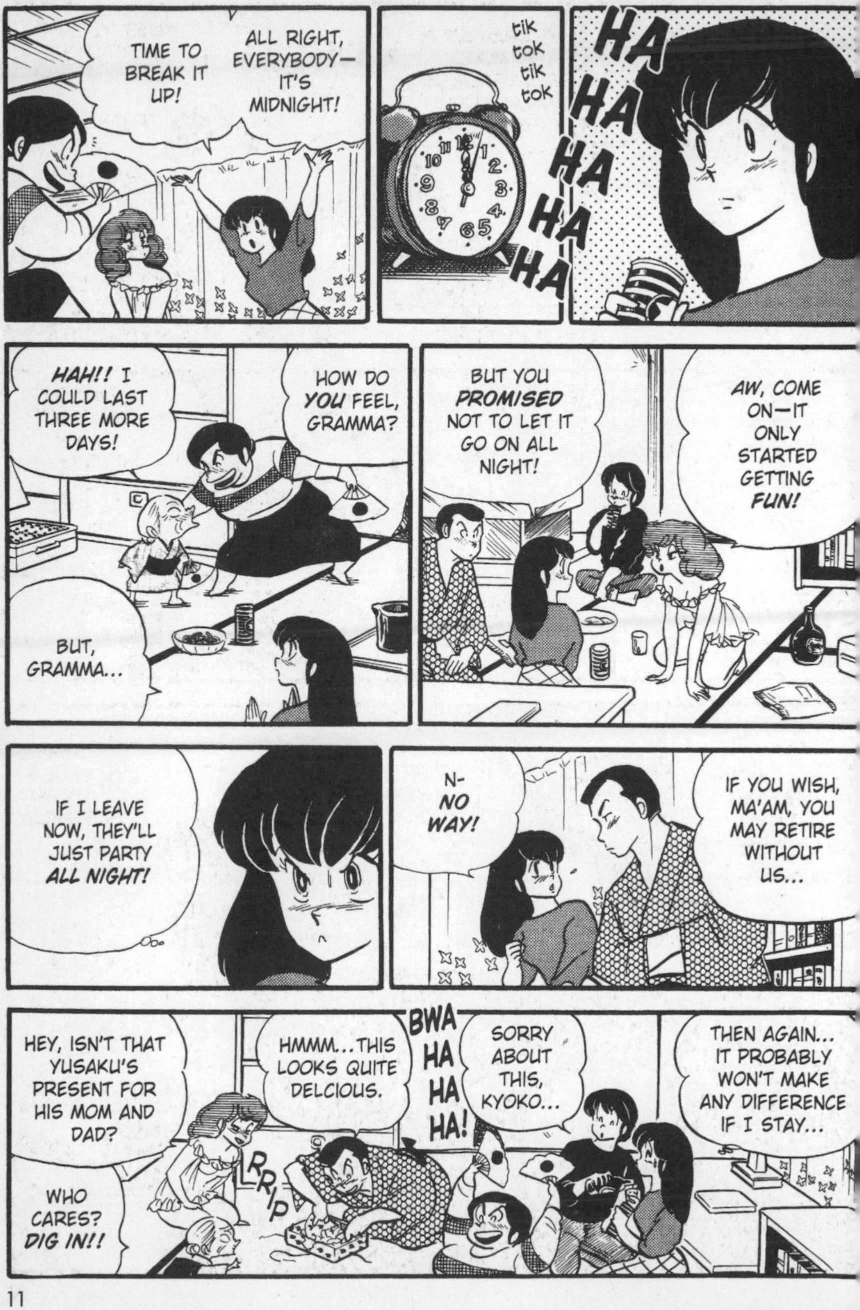
HA HA HA HA HA
tik tok tik tok
ALL RIGHT, EVERYBODY—IT'S MIDNIGHT!
TIME TO BREAK IT UP!
AW, COME ON—IT ONLY STARTED GETTING FUN!
BUT YOU PROMISED NOT TO LET IT GO ON ALL NIGHT!
HOW DO YOU FEEL, GRAMMA?
HAH!! I COULD LAST THREE MORE DAYS!
BUT, GRAMMA...
IF YOU WISH, MA'AM, YOU MAY RETIRE WITHOUT US...
N- NO WAY!
IF I LEAVE NOW, THEY'LL JUST PARTY ALL NIGHT!
THEN AGAIN... IT PROBABLY WON'T MAKE ANY DIFFERENCE IF I STAY...
SORRY ABOUT THIS, KYOKO...
BWA HA HA HA!
HMMM...THIS LOOKS QUITE DELCIOUS.
RRIP
HEY, ISN'T THAT YUSAKU'S PRESENT FOR HIS MOM AND DAD?
WHO CARES? DIG IN!!

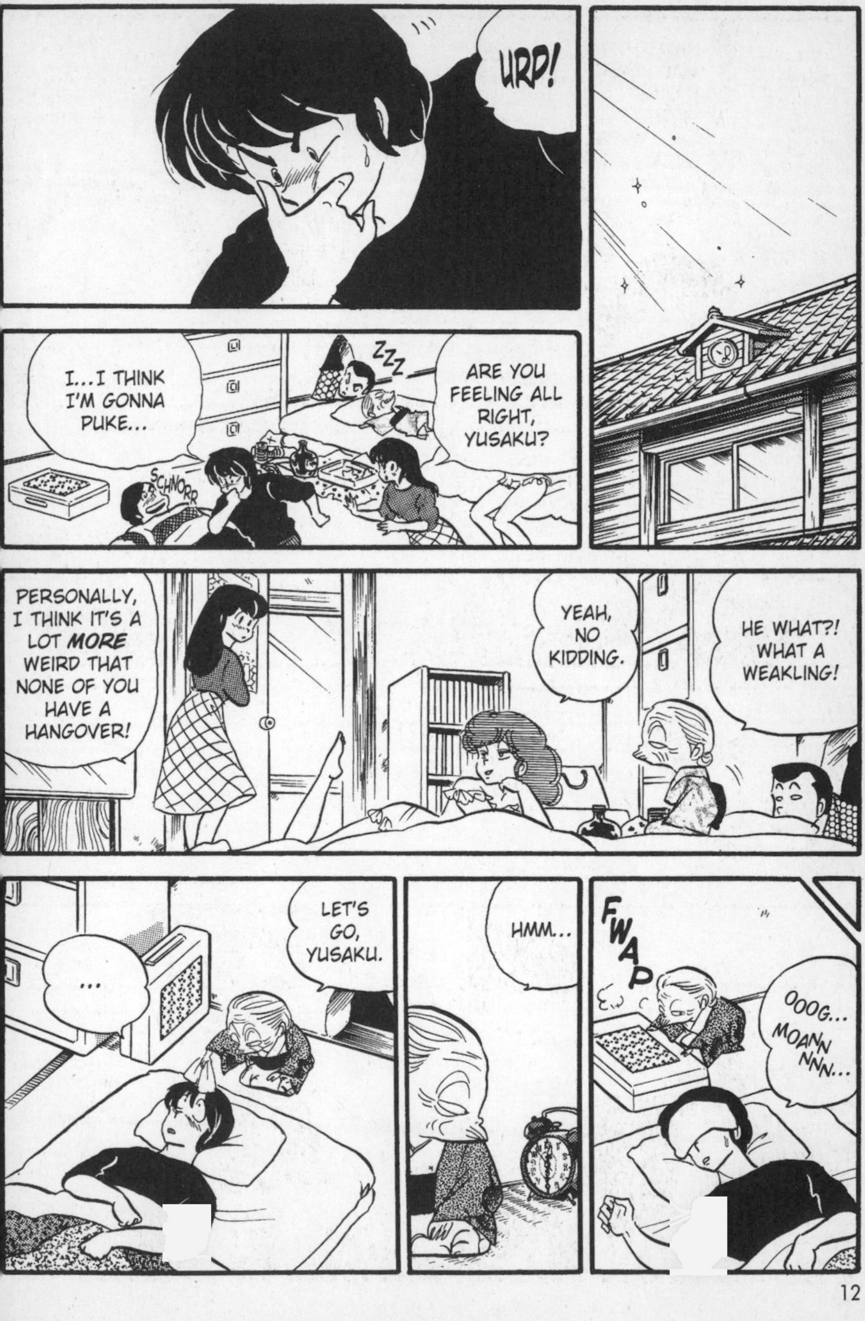
URP!
ARE YOU FEELING ALL RIGHT, YUSAKU?
ZZZ
I...I THINK I'M GONNA PUKE...
SCHNORR
HE WHAT?! WHAT A WEAKLING!
YEAH, NO KIDDING.
PERSONALLY, I THINK IT'S A LOT MORE WEIRD THAT NONE OF YOU HAVE A HANGOVER!
OOOG... MOANN NNN...
FWAP
HMM...
LET'S GO, YUSAKU.
...

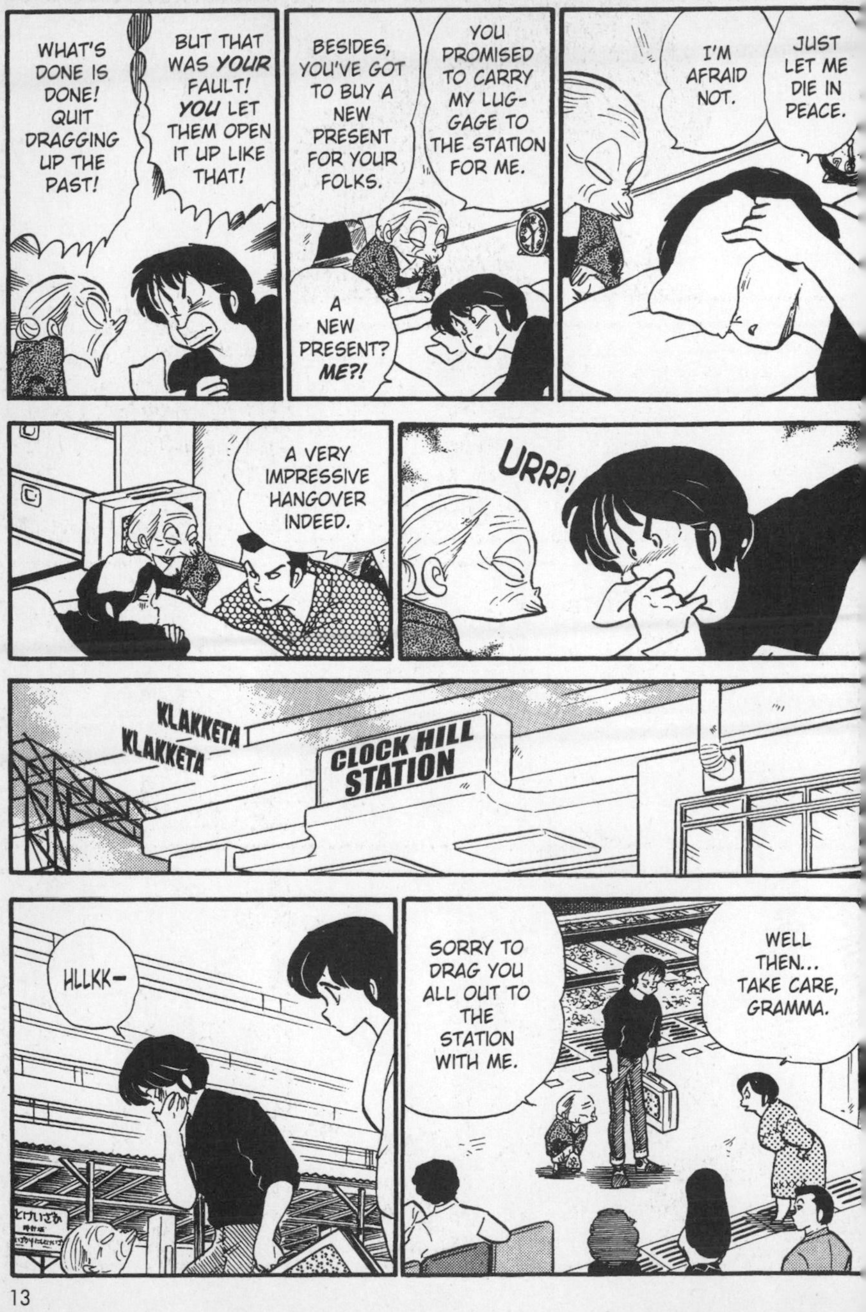
JUST LET ME DIE IN PEACE.
I'M AFRAID NOT.
YOU PROMISED TO CARRY MY LUGGAGE TO THE STATION FOR ME.
BESIDES, YOU'VE GOT TO BUY A NEW PRESENT FOR YOUR FOLKS.
A NEW PRESENT? ***ME?!***
BUT THAT WAS ***YOUR*** FAULT! ***YOU*** LET THEM OPEN IT UP LIKE THAT!
WHAT'S DONE IS DONE! QUIT DRAGGING UP THE PAST!
URRP!
A VERY IMPRESSIVE HANGOVER INDEED.
CLOCK HILL STATION
KLAKKETA
KLAKKETA
WELL THEN... TAKE CARE, GRAMMA.
SORRY TO DRAG YOU ALL OUT TO THE STATION WITH ME.
HLLKK—

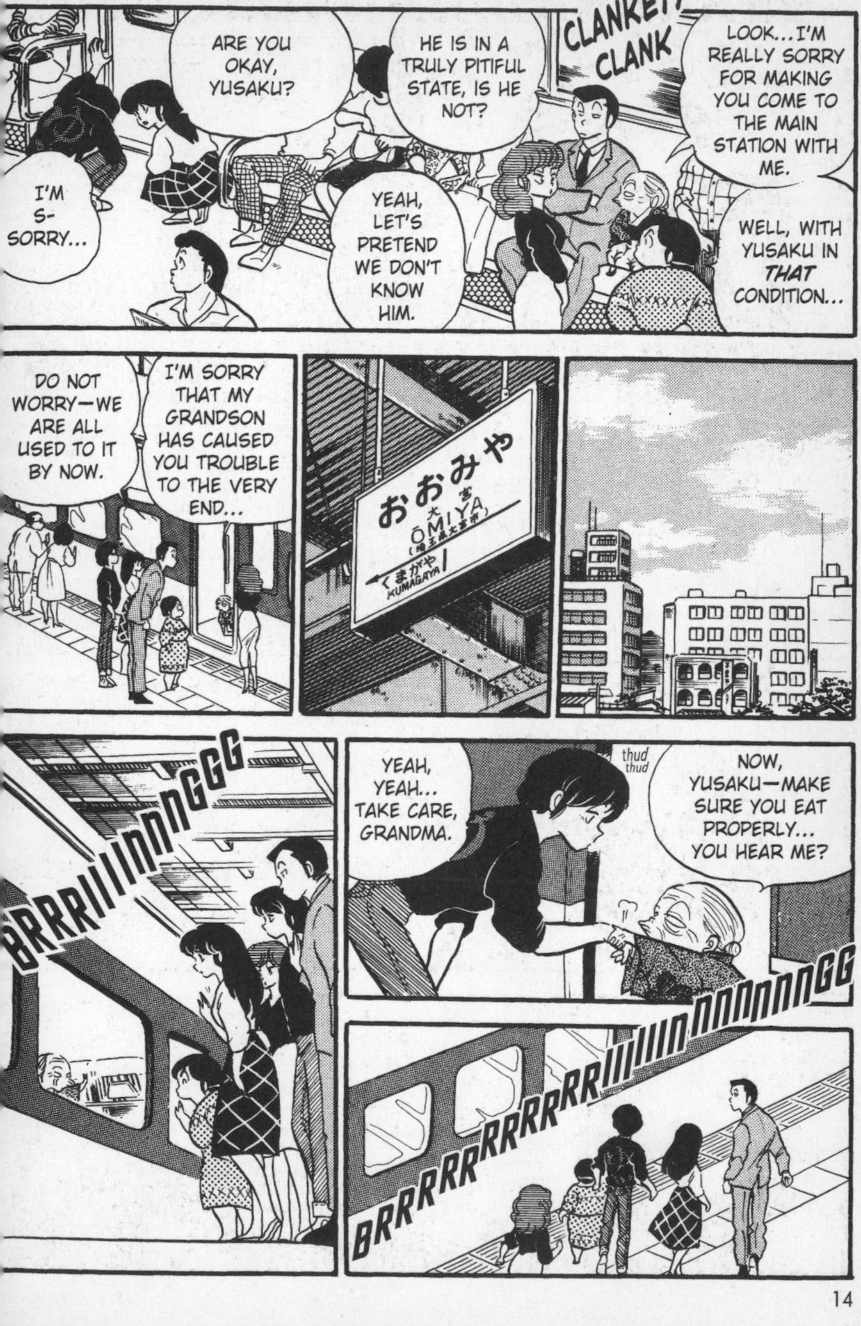
CLANKETY CLANK
LOOK...I'M REALLY SORRY FOR MAKING YOU COME TO THE MAIN STATION WITH ME.
WELL, WITH YUSAKU IN *THAT* CONDITION...
HE IS IN A TRULY PITIFUL STATE, IS HE NOT?
YEAH, LET'S PRETEND WE DON'T KNOW HIM.
ARE YOU OKAY, YUSAKU?
I'M S-SORRY...
おおみや
ŌMIYA
くまがや
KUMAGAYA
I'M SORRY THAT MY GRANDSON HAS CAUSED YOU TROUBLE TO THE VERY END...
DO NOT WORRY—WE ARE ALL USED TO IT BY NOW.
NOW, YUSAKU—MAKE SURE YOU EAT PROPERLY... YOU HEAR ME?
thud thud
YEAH, YEAH... TAKE CARE, GRANDMA.
BRRRRRRRRRRRRIIIIIINNNNNNNGG
BRRRIIIINNNGGG

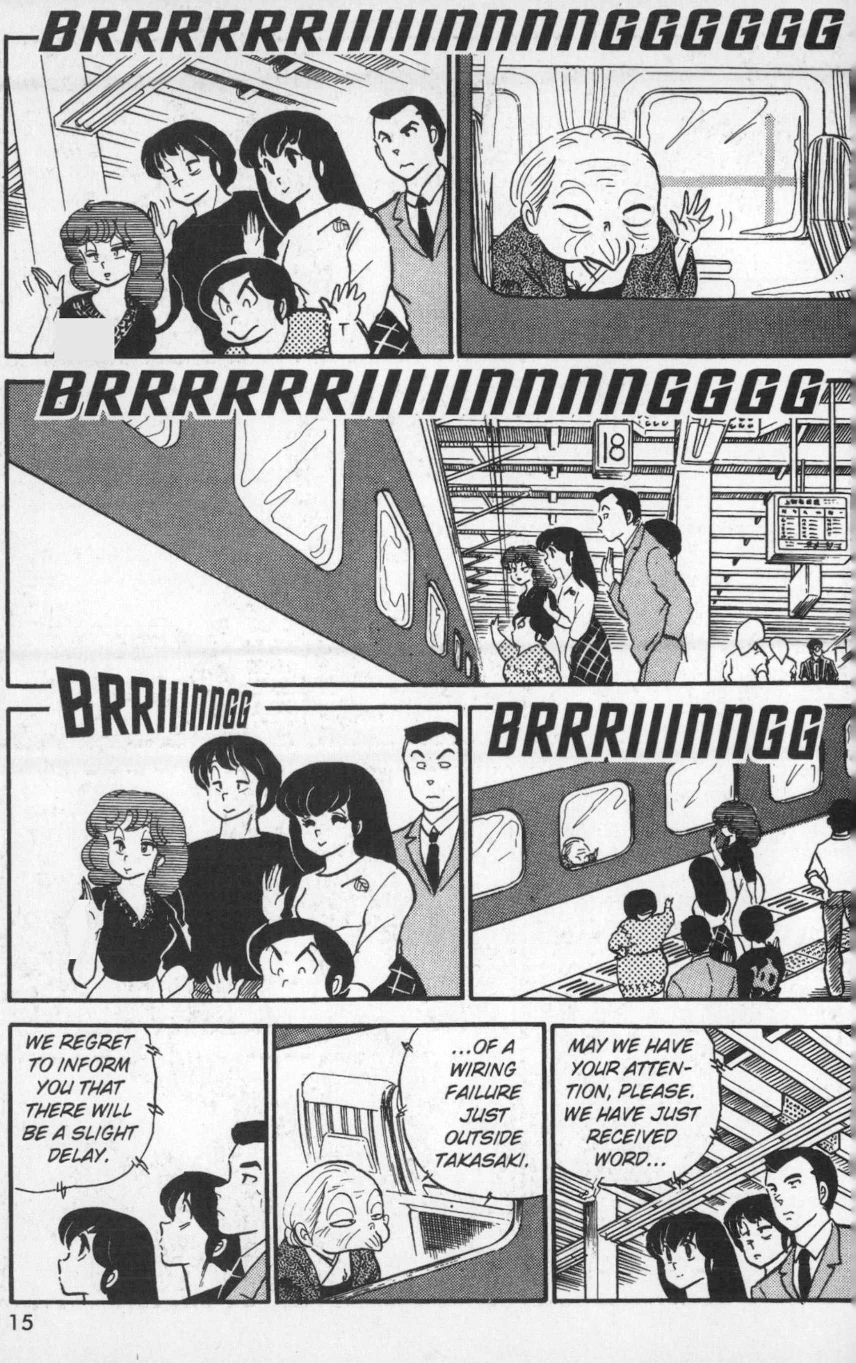
BRRRRRRIIIIINNNNGGGGGG
BRRRRRRIIIIINNNNGGGG
BRRRIIINNGG
BRRIIINNGG
MAY WE HAVE YOUR ATTENTION, PLEASE. WE HAVE JUST RECEIVED WORD...
...OF A WIRING FAILURE JUST OUTSIDE TAKASAKI.
WE REGRET TO INFORM YOU THAT THERE WILL BE A SLIGHT DELAY.

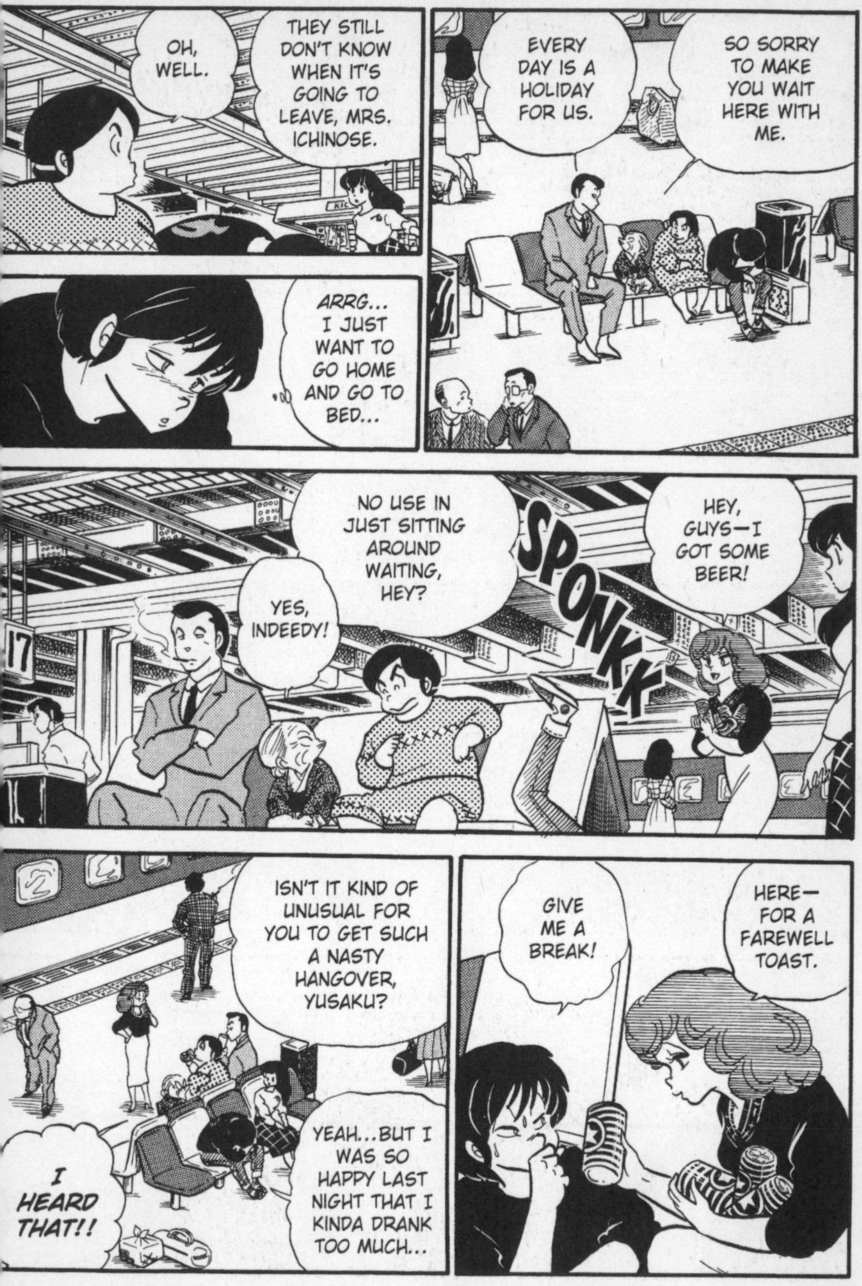
SO SORRY TO MAKE YOU WAIT HERE WITH ME.
EVERY DAY IS A HOLIDAY FOR US.
THEY STILL DON'T KNOW WHEN IT'S GOING TO LEAVE, MRS. ICHINOSE.
OH, WELL.
ARRG... I JUST WANT TO GO HOME AND GO TO BED...
HEY, GUYS—I GOT SOME BEER!
SPONKK
NO USE IN JUST SITTING AROUND WAITING, HEY?
YES, INDEEDY!
HERE— FOR A FAREWELL TOAST.
GIVE ME A BREAK!
ISN'T IT KIND OF UNUSUAL FOR YOU TO GET SUCH A NASTY HANGOVER, YUSAKU?
YEAH...BUT I WAS SO HAPPY LAST NIGHT THAT I KINDA DRANK TOO MUCH...
I HEARD THAT!!

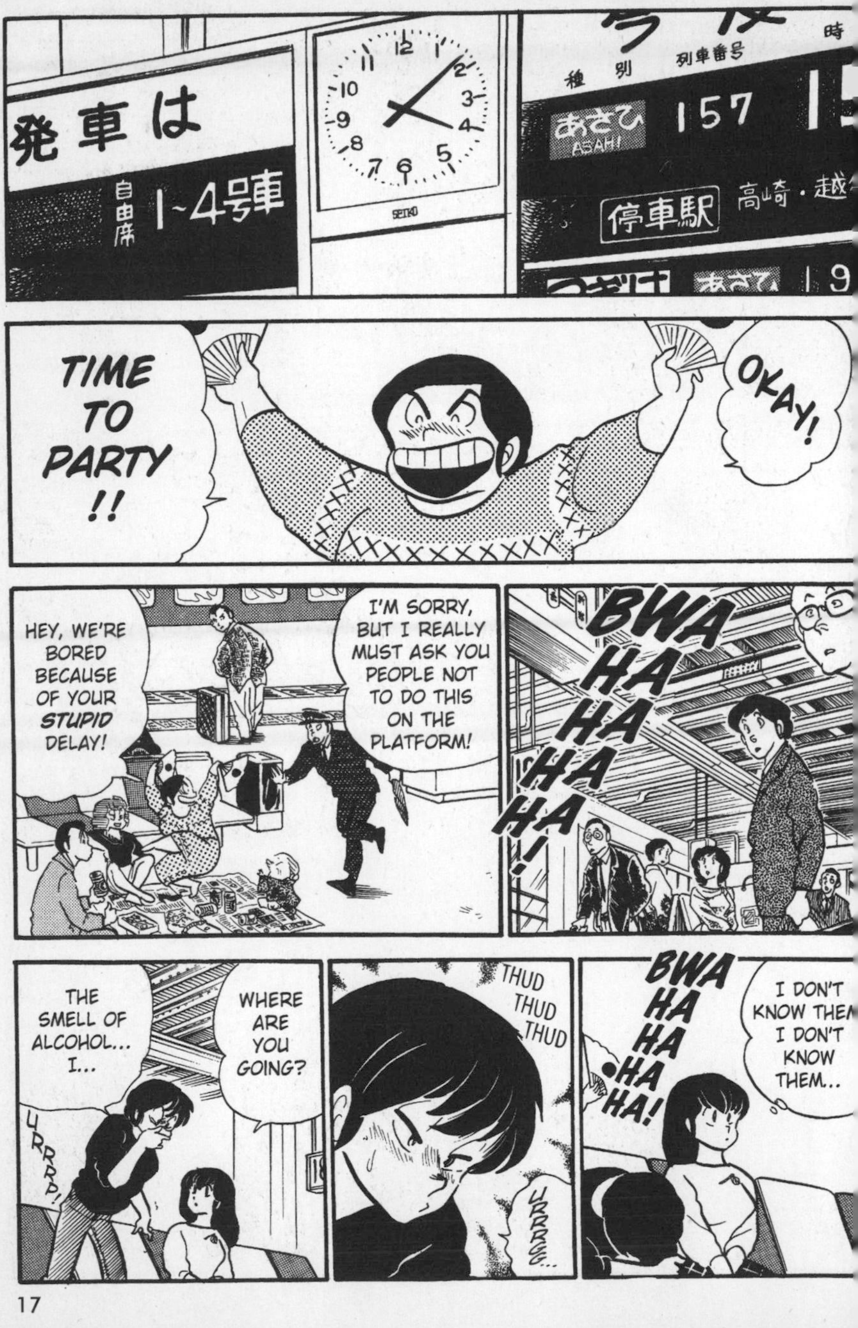

時
種別 列車番号
あさひ
ASAHI
157
停車駅
高崎・越
つぎは
あさひ
19
発車は
自由席
1~4号車
SEIKO
OKAY!
TIME TO PARTY!!
BWA HA HA HA HA HA!
I'M SORRY, BUT I REALLY MUST ASK YOU PEOPLE NOT TO DO THIS ON THE PLATFORM!
HEY, WE'RE BORED BECAUSE OF YOUR *STUPID* DELAY!
I DON'T KNOW THEM I DON'T KNOW THEM...
BWA HA HA HA HA HA!
THUD THUD THUD
URRRGG...
WHERE ARE YOU GOING?
THE SMELL OF ALCOHOL... I...
URRRP!

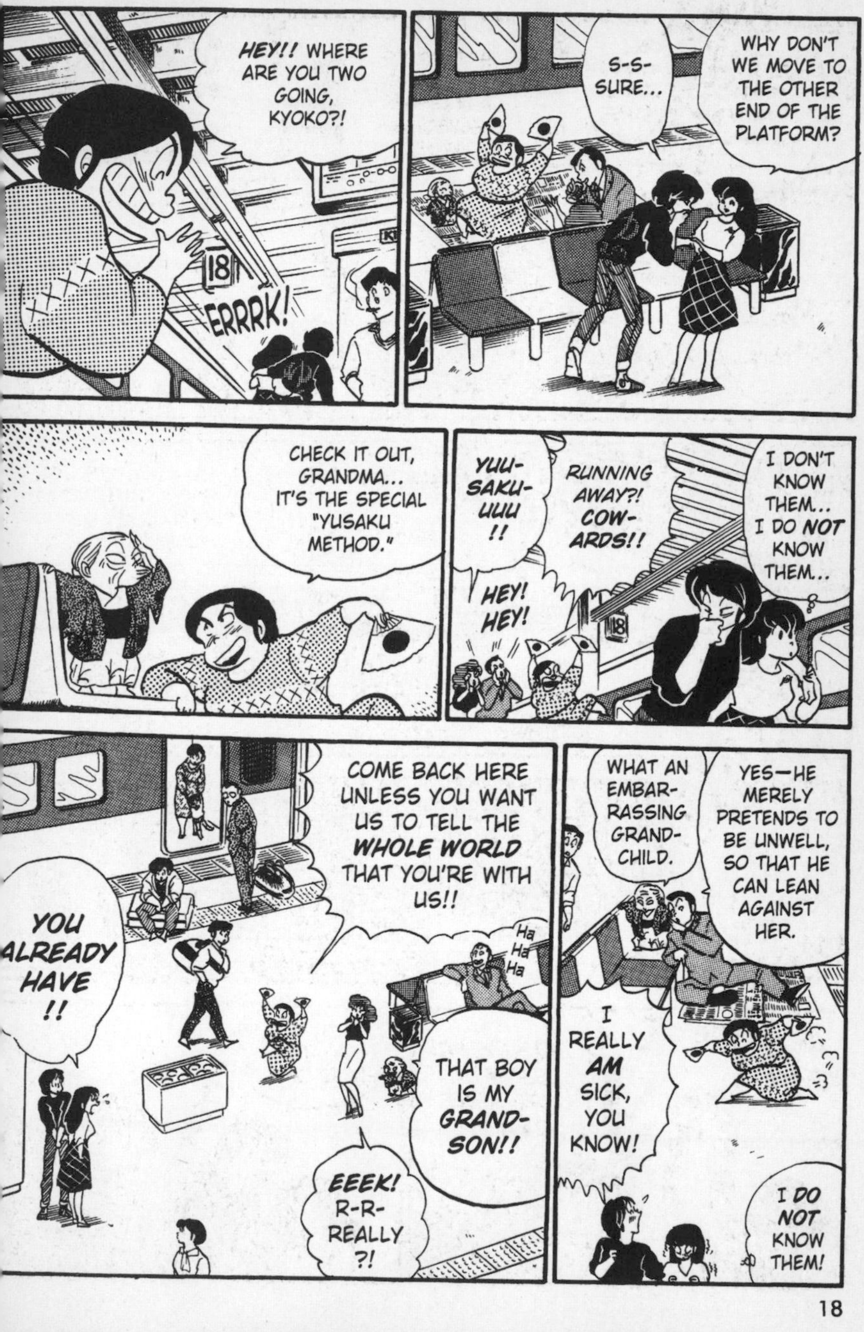
WHY DON'T WE MOVE TO THE OTHER END OF THE PLATFORM?
S-S-SURE...
HEY!! WHERE ARE YOU TWO GOING, KYOKO?!
18
ERRRK!
I DON'T KNOW THEM.. I DO NOT KNOW THEM..
RUNNING AWAY?! COWARDS!!
YUU-SAKU-UUU!!
HEY! HEY!
18
CHECK IT OUT, GRANDMA... IT'S THE SPECIAL "YUSAKU METHOD."
YES—HE MERELY PRETENDS TO BE UNWELL, SO THAT HE CAN LEAN AGAINST HER.
WHAT AN EMBARRASSING GRANDCHILD.
I REALLY AM SICK, YOU KNOW!
I DO NOT KNOW THEM!
COME BACK HERE UNLESS YOU WANT US TO TELL THE WHOLE WORLD THAT YOU'RE WITH US!!
Ha Ha Ha
YOU ALREADY HAVE!!
THAT BOY IS MY GRANDSON!!
EEEK! R-R-REALLY?!

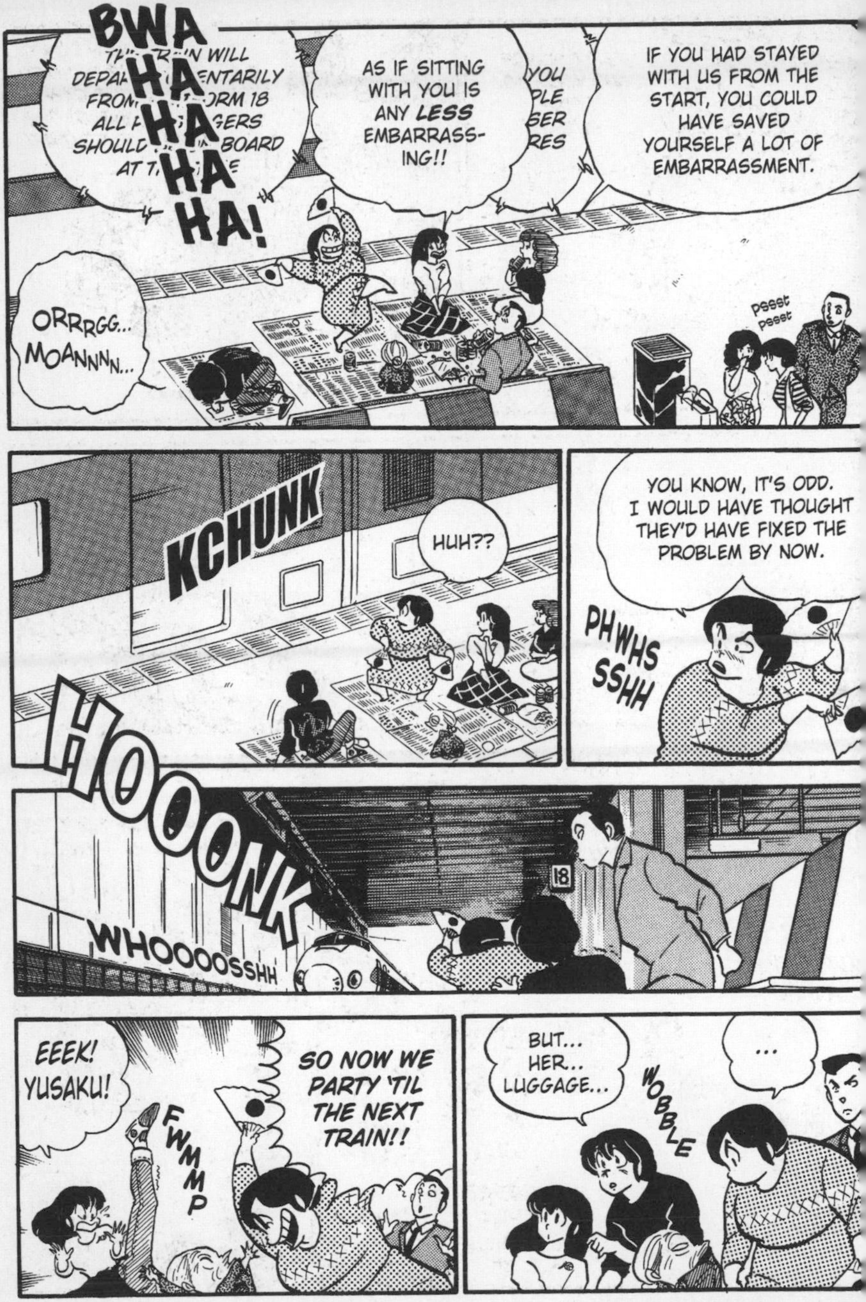
IF YOU HAD STAYED WITH US FROM THE START, YOU COULD HAVE SAVED YOURSELF A LOT OF EMBARRASSMENT.
AS IF SITTING WITH YOU IS ANY LESS EMBARRASSING!!
BWA HA HA HA HA HA!
pssst pssst
ORRRGG... MOANNNN...
YOU KNOW, IT'S ODD. I WOULD HAVE THOUGHT THEY'D HAVE FIXED THE PROBLEM BY NOW.
PHWHS SSHH
HUH??
KCHUNK
HOOOONK
WHOOOOSSHH
...
BUT... HER... LUGGAGE...
WOBBLE
SO NOW WE PARTY 'TIL THE NEXT TRAIN!!
FWMMP
EEEK! YUSAKU!

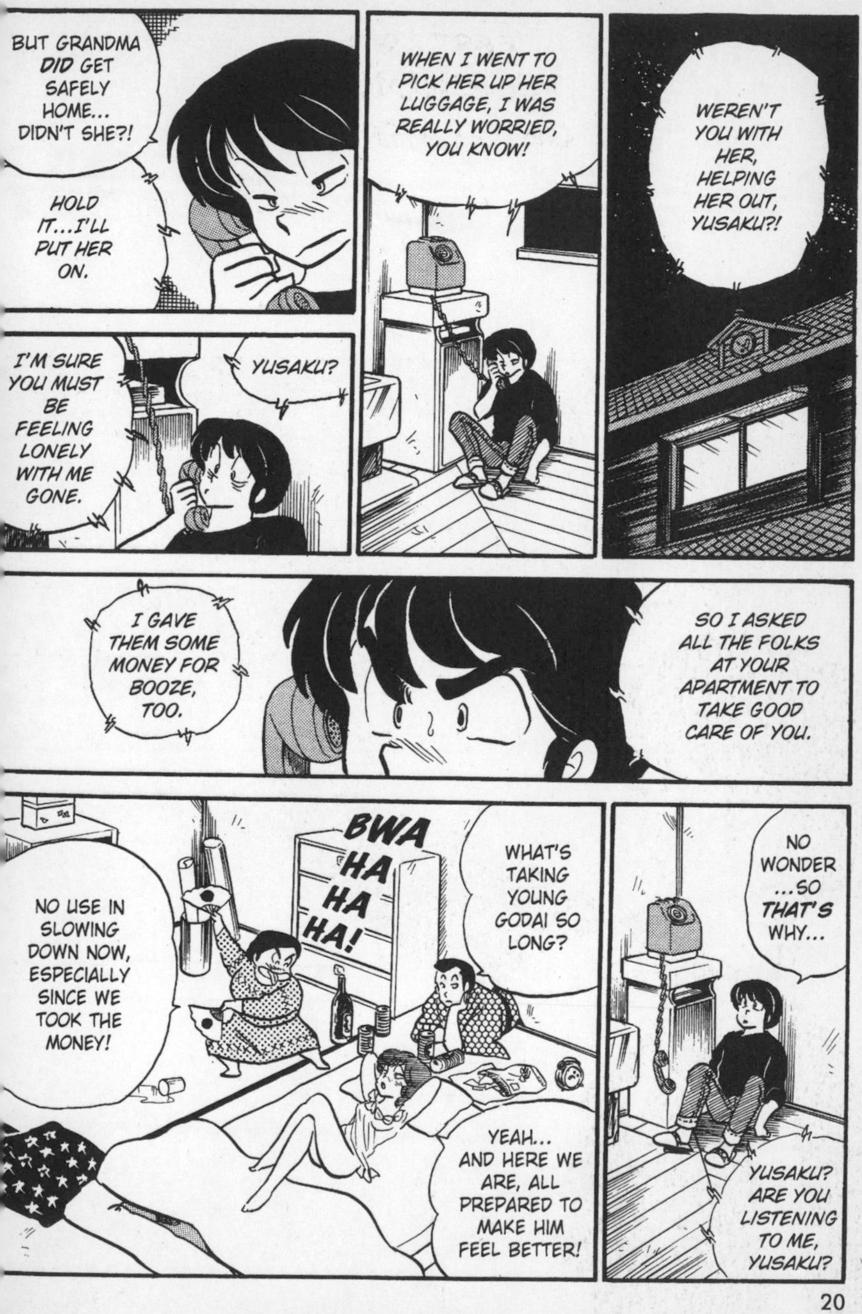
WEREN'T YOU WITH HER, HELPING HER OUT, YUSAKU?!
WHEN I WENT TO PICK HER UP HER LUGGAGE, I WAS REALLY WORRIED, YOU KNOW!
BUT GRANDMA DID GET SAFELY HOME... DIDN'T SHE?!
HOLD IT...I'LL PUT HER ON.
YUSAKU?
I'M SURE YOU MUST BE FEELING LONELY WITH ME GONE.
SO I ASKED ALL THE FOLKS AT YOUR APARTMENT TO TAKE GOOD CARE OF YOU.
I GAVE THEM SOME MONEY FOR BOOZE, TOO.
NO WONDER ...SO THAT'S WHY...
YUSAKU? ARE YOU LISTENING TO ME, YUSAKU?
WHAT'S TAKING YOUNG GODAI SO LONG?
BWA HA HA HA!
NO USE IN SLOWING DOWN NOW, ESPECIALLY SINCE WE TOOK THE MONEY!
YEAH... AND HERE WE ARE, ALL PREPARED TO MAKE HIM FEEL BETTER!

PART TWO
MR. ICHINOSE GETS LAID OFF

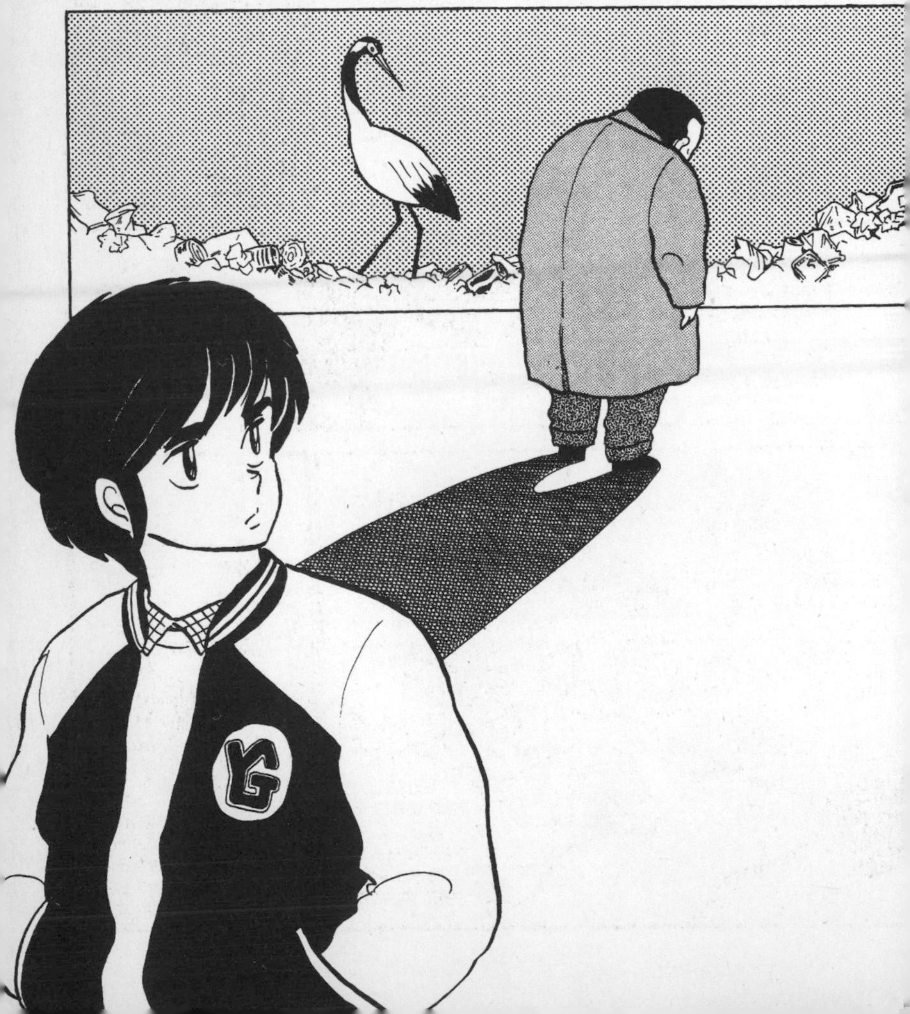

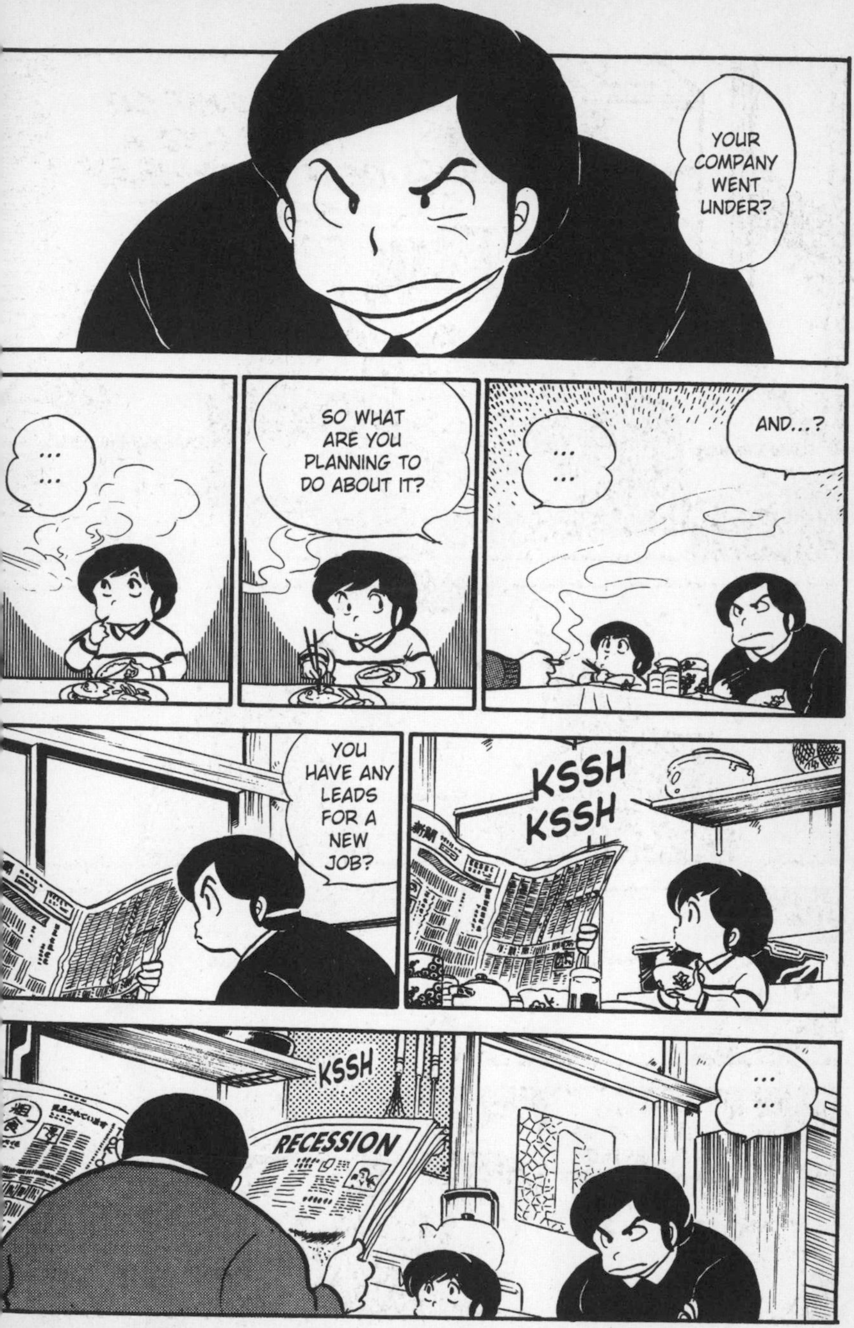
YOUR COMPANY WENT UNDER?
AND...?
... ...
SO WHAT ARE YOU PLANNING TO DO ABOUT IT?
... ...
KSSH KSSH
YOU HAVE ANY LEADS FOR A NEW JOB?
... ...
KSSH
RECESSION

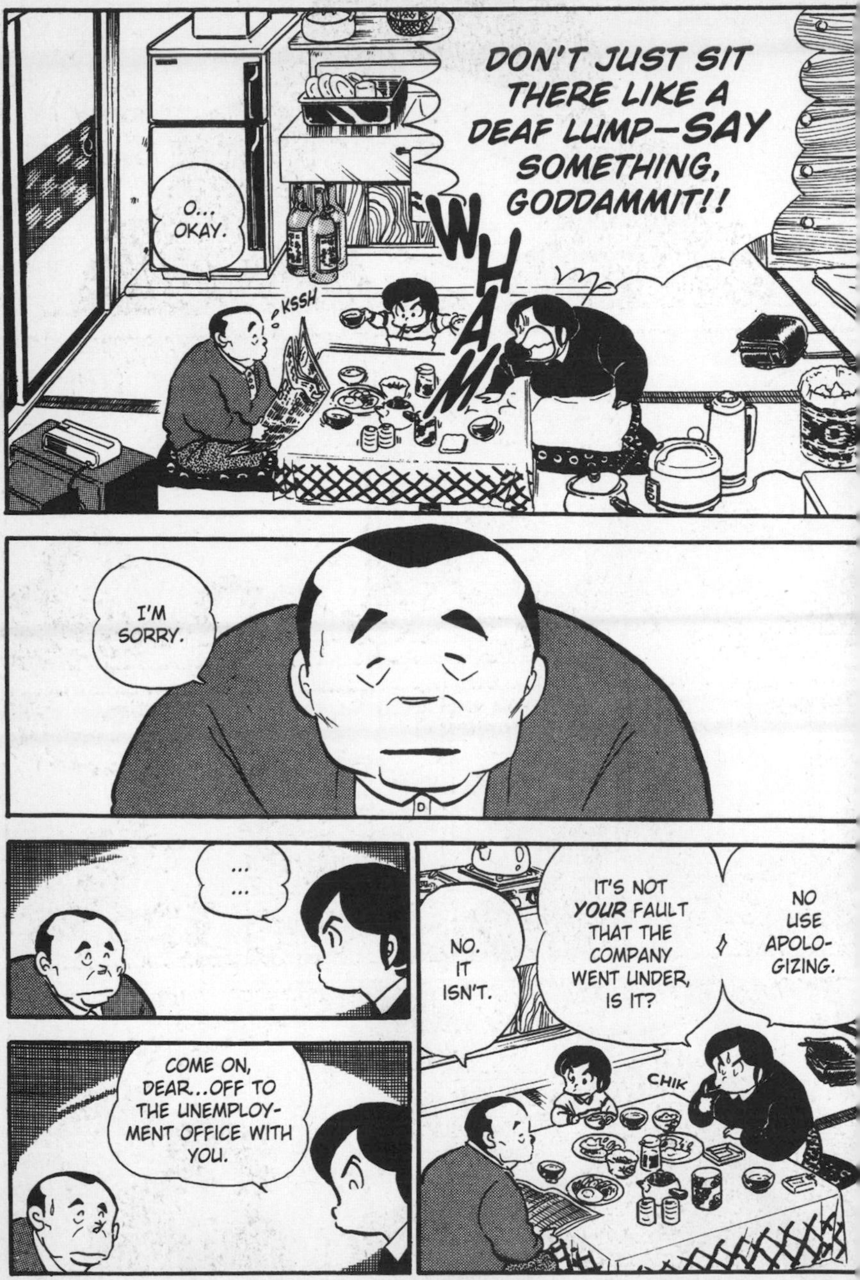
DON'T JUST SIT THERE LIKE A DEAF LUMP—SAY SOMETHING, GODDAMMIT!!
WHAM
O... OKAY.
KSSH
I'M SORRY.
NO USE APOLO-GIZING.
IT'S NOT *YOUR* FAULT THAT THE COMPANY WENT UNDER, IS IT?
NO. IT ISN'T.
CHIK
...
...
COME ON, DEAR...OFF TO THE UNEMPLOY-MENT OFFICE WITH YOU.

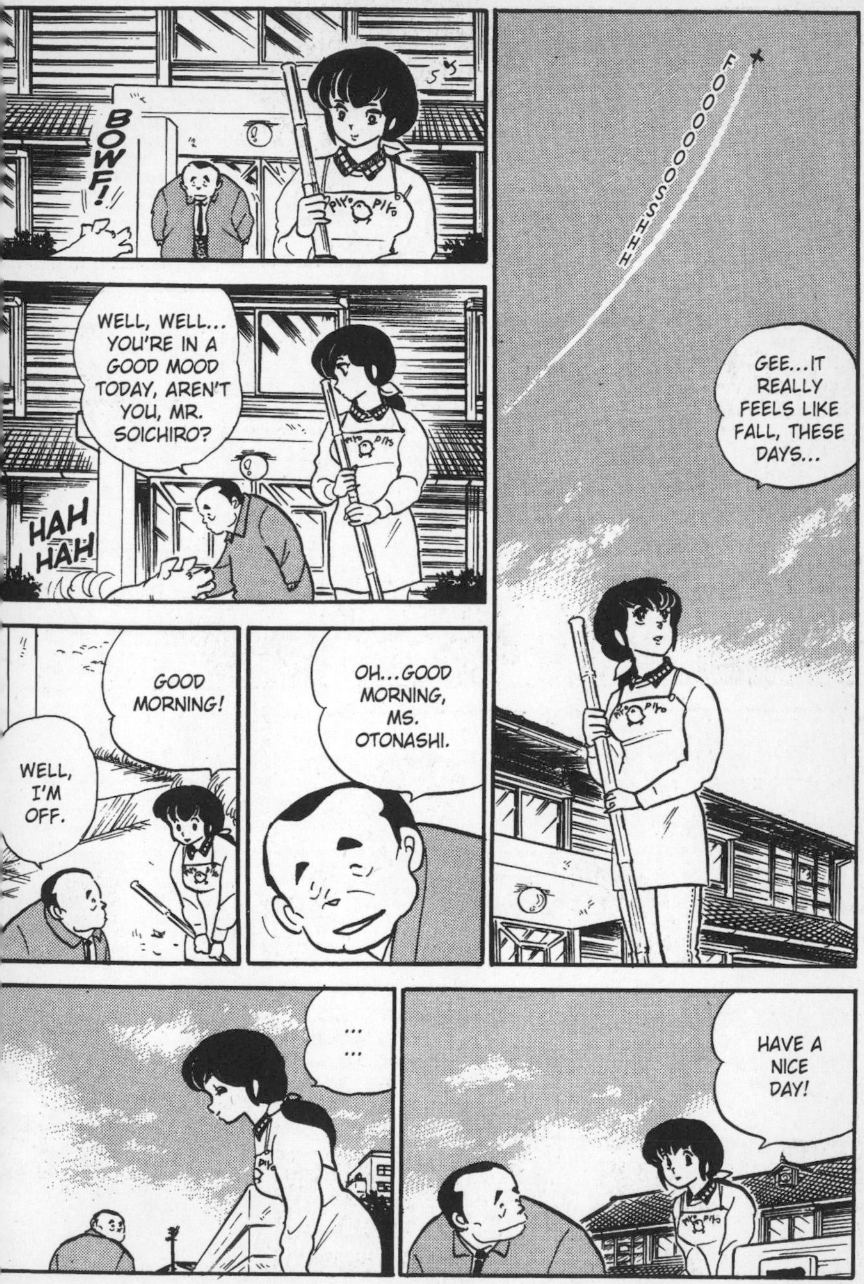
FOOOOOOOOSSHHHH
GEE...IT REALLY FEELS LIKE FALL, THESE DAYS...
BOWF!
WELL, WELL... YOU'RE IN A GOOD MOOD TODAY, AREN'T YOU, MR. SOICHIRO?
HAH HAH
OH...GOOD MORNING, MS. OTONASHI.
GOOD MORNING!
WELL, I'M OFF.
HAVE A NICE DAY!
... ...

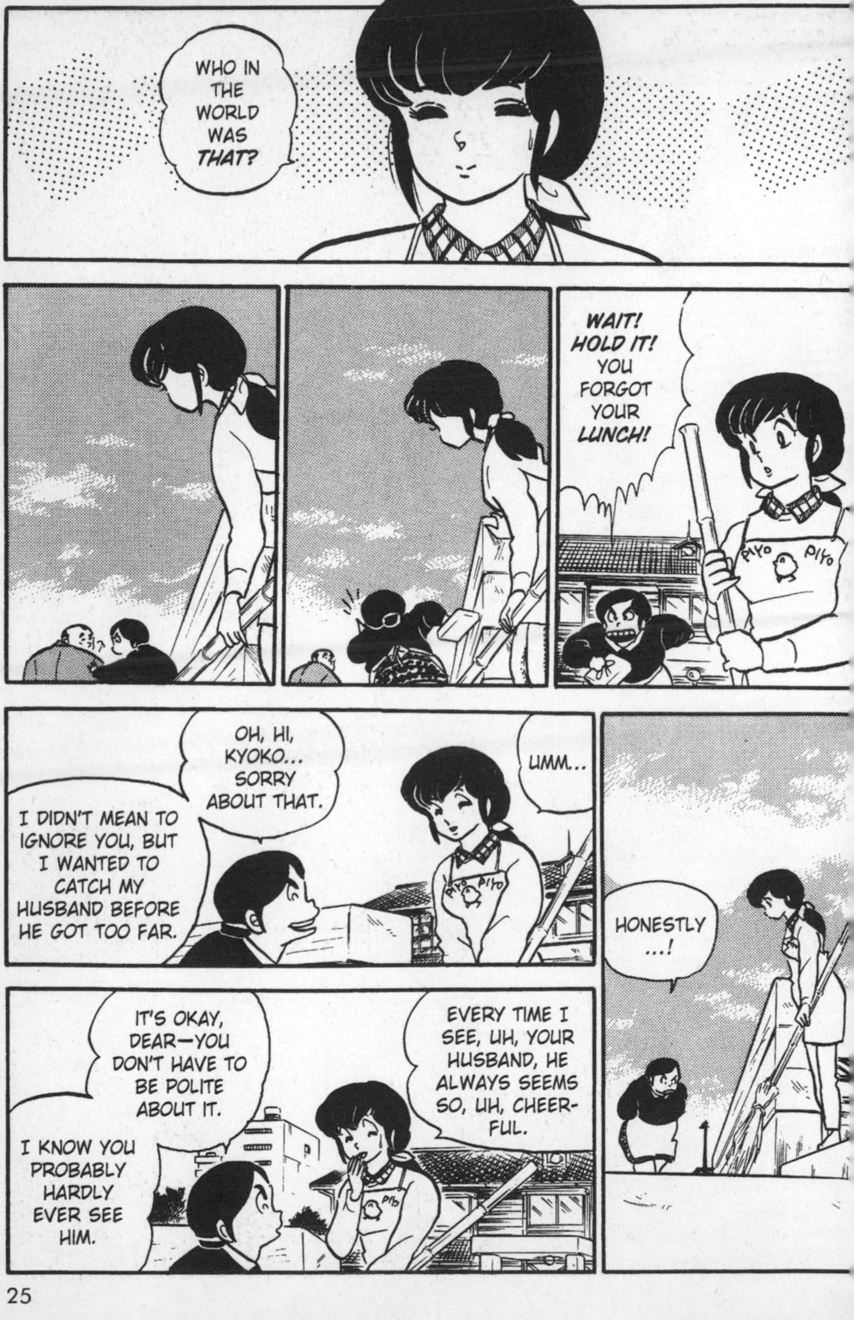
WHO IN THE WORLD WAS *THAT?*
WAIT! HOLD IT! YOU FORGOT YOUR *LUNCH!*
HONESTLY ...!
UMM...
OH, HI, KYOKO... SORRY ABOUT THAT.
I DIDN'T MEAN TO IGNORE YOU, BUT I WANTED TO CATCH MY HUSBAND BEFORE HE GOT TOO FAR.
EVERY TIME I SEE, UH, YOUR HUSBAND, HE ALWAYS SEEMS SO, UH, CHEER-FUL.
IT'S OKAY, DEAR—YOU DON'T HAVE TO BE POLITE ABOUT IT.
I KNOW YOU PROBABLY HARDLY EVER SEE HIM.

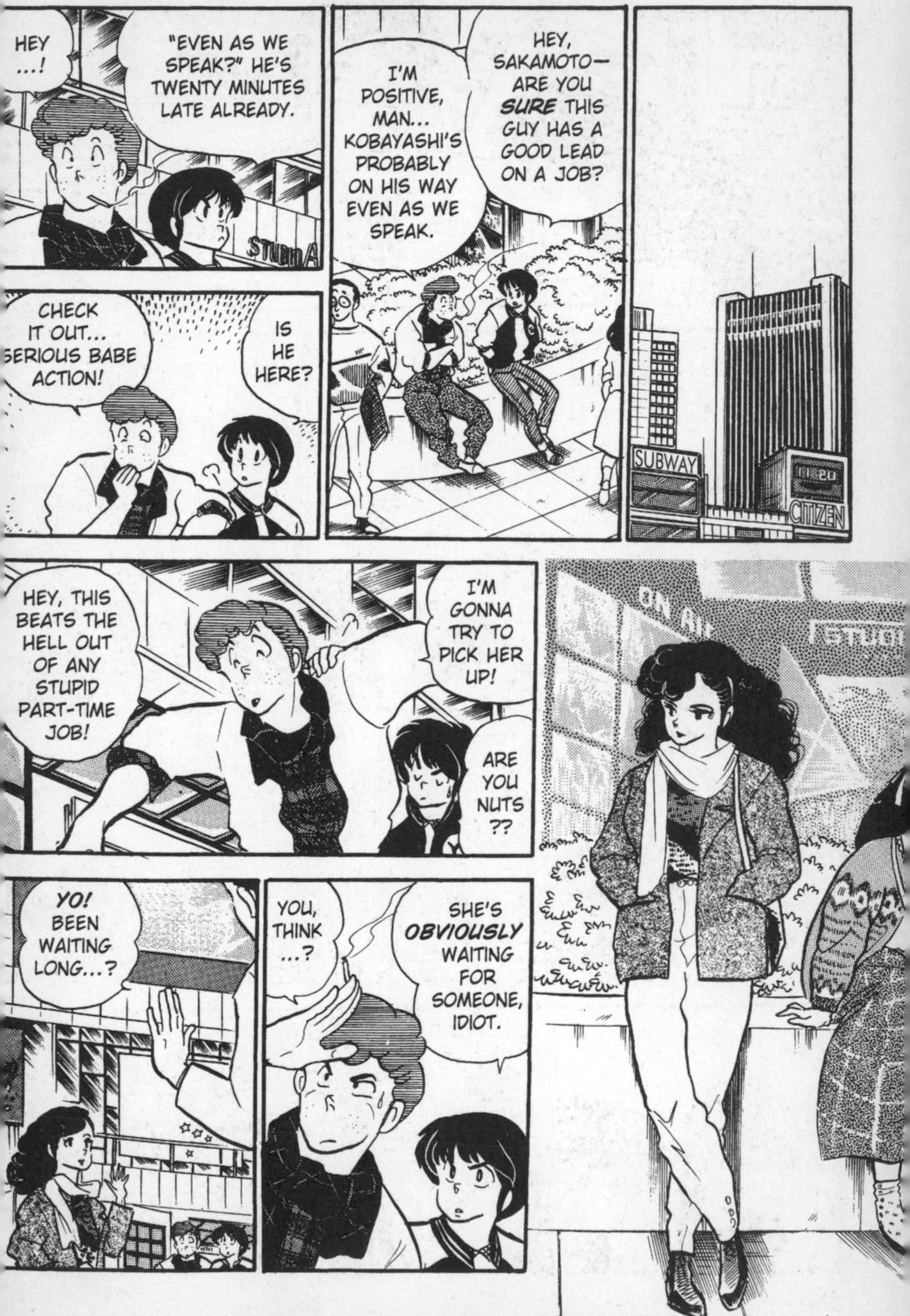
SUBWAY
11:20
CITIZEN
HEY, SAKAMOTO— ARE YOU ***SURE*** THIS GUY HAS A GOOD LEAD ON A JOB?
I'M POSITIVE, MAN... KOBAYASHI'S PROBABLY ON HIS WAY EVEN AS WE SPEAK.
"EVEN AS WE SPEAK?" HE'S TWENTY MINUTES LATE ALREADY.
HEY ...!
IS HE HERE?
CHECK IT OUT... SERIOUS BABE ACTION!
I'M GONNA TRY TO PICK HER UP!
ARE YOU NUTS ??
HEY, THIS BEATS THE HELL OUT OF ANY STUPID PART-TIME JOB!
SHE'S ***OBVIOUSLY*** WAITING FOR SOMEONE, IDIOT.
YOU, THINK ...?
YO! BEEN WAITING LONG...?

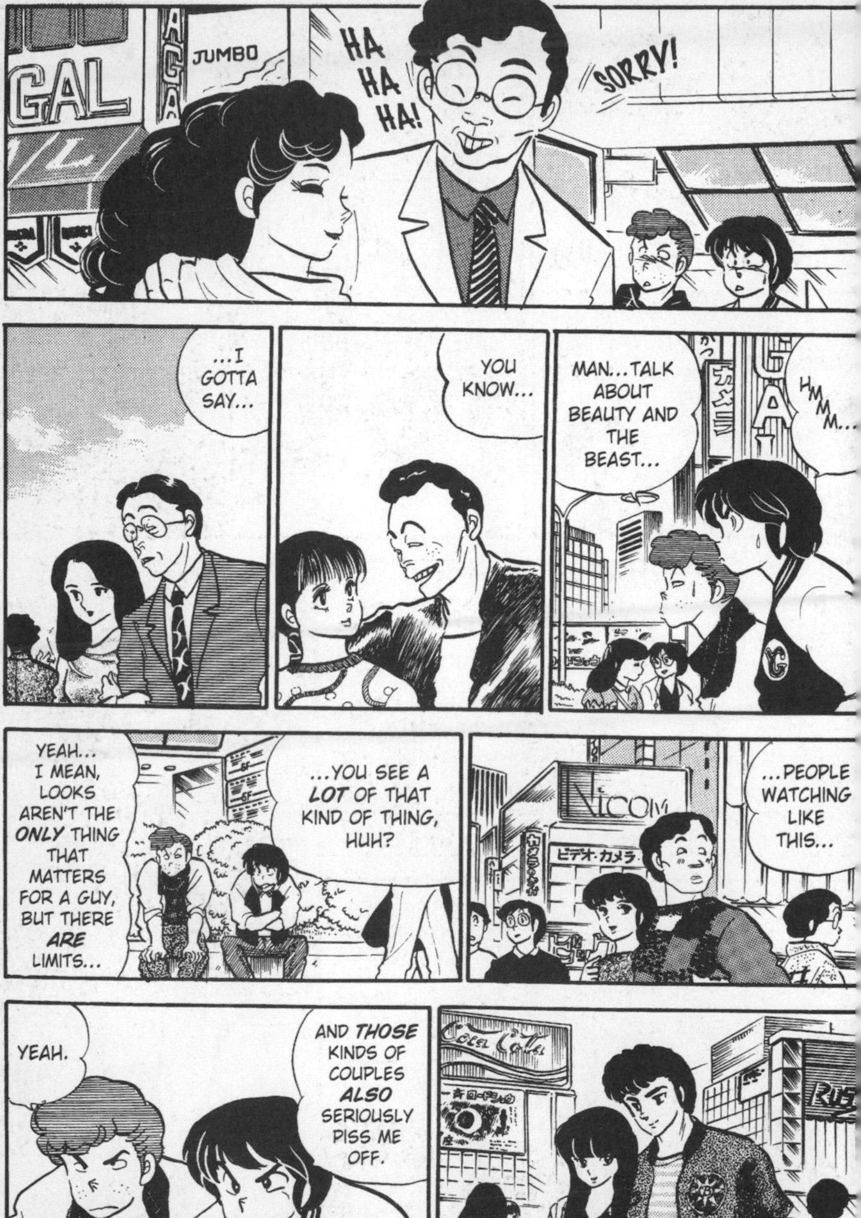
SORRY!
HA HA HA!
JUMBO
GAL
HMMM...
MAN...TALK ABOUT BEAUTY AND THE BEAST...
YOU KNOW...
...I GOTTA SAY...
...PEOPLE WATCHING LIKE THIS...
NICOM
ビデオ・カメラ
...YOU SEE A *LOT* OF THAT KIND OF THING, HUH?
YEAH... I MEAN, LOOKS AREN'T THE *ONLY* THING THAT MATTERS FOR A GUY, BUT THERE *ARE* LIMITS...
AND *THOSE* KINDS OF COUPLES *ALSO* SERIOUSLY PISS ME OFF.
YEAH.

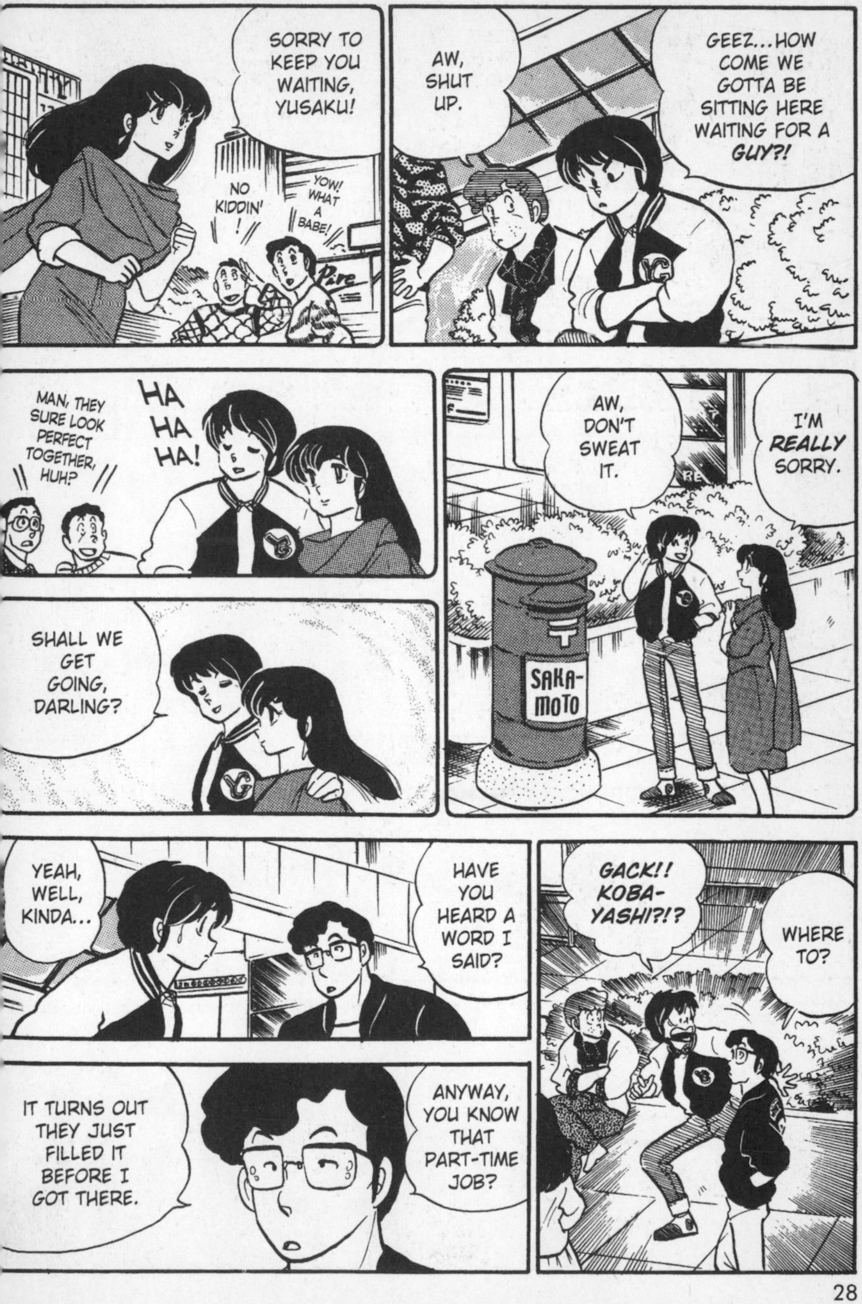
GEEZ...HOW COME WE GOTTA BE SITTING HERE WAITING FOR A GUY?!
AW, SHUT UP.
SORRY TO KEEP YOU WAITING, YUSAKU!
YOW! WHAT A BABE!
NO KIDDIN'!
I'M REALLY SORRY.
AW, DON'T SWEAT IT.
SAKA-MOTO
HA HA HA!
MAN, THEY SURE LOOK PERFECT TOGETHER, HUH?
SHALL WE GET GOING, DARLING?
WHERE TO?
GACK!! KOBA-YASHI?!?
HAVE YOU HEARD A WORD I SAID?
YEAH, WELL, KINDA...
ANYWAY, YOU KNOW THAT PART-TIME JOB?
IT TURNS OUT THEY JUST FILLED IT BEFORE I GOT THERE.

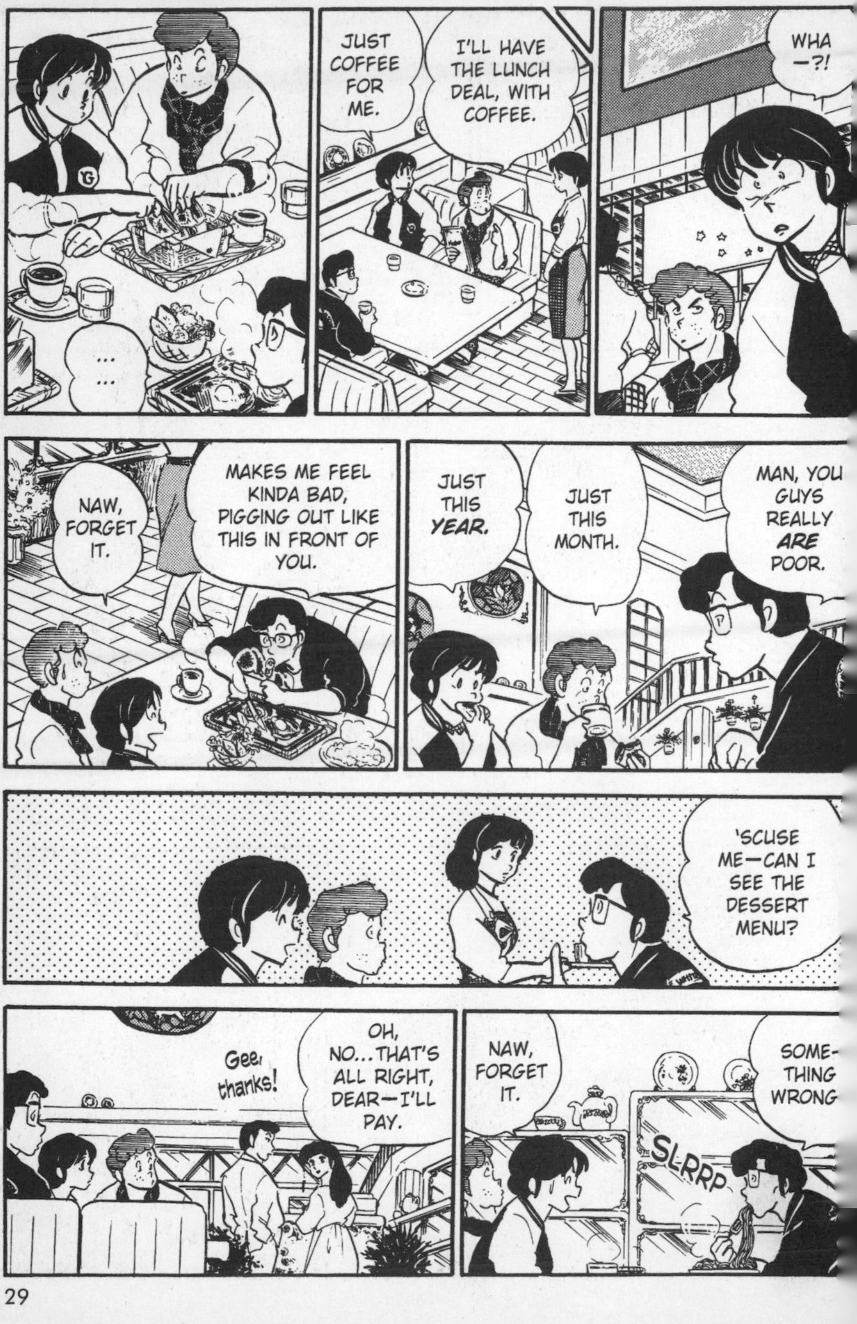
WHA—?!
I'LL HAVE THE LUNCH DEAL, WITH COFFEE.
JUST COFFEE FOR ME.
... ...
MAN, YOU GUYS REALLY ARE POOR.
JUST THIS MONTH.
JUST THIS YEAR.
MAKES ME FEEL KINDA BAD, PIGGING OUT LIKE THIS IN FRONT OF YOU.
NAW, FORGET IT.
'SCUSE ME—CAN I SEE THE DESSERT MENU?
SOME-THING WRONG
SLRRP
NAW, FORGET IT.
OH, NO...THAT'S ALL RIGHT, DEAR—I'LL PAY.
Gee, thanks!

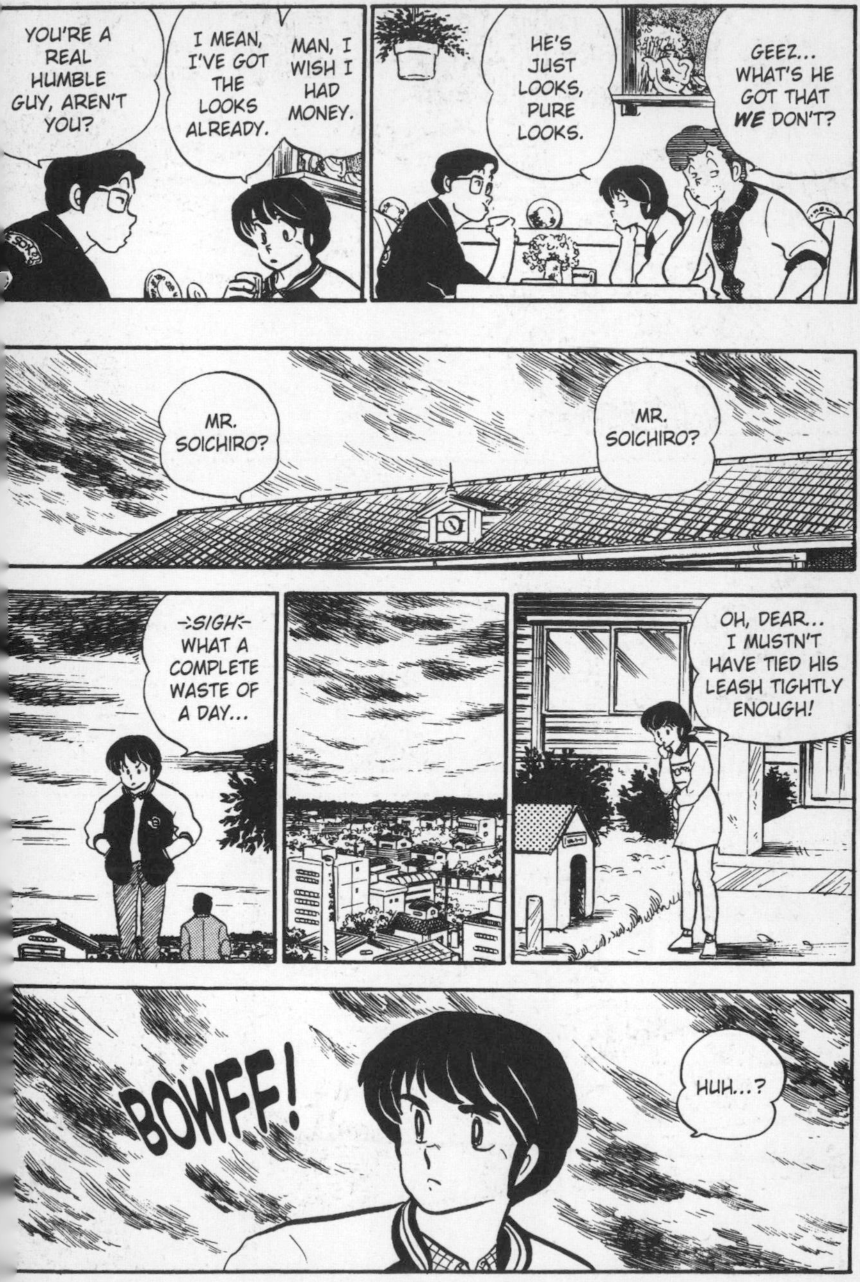
GEEZ... WHAT'S HE GOT THAT WE DON'T?
HE'S JUST LOOKS, PURE LOOKS.
MAN, I WISH I HAD MONEY.
I MEAN, I'VE GOT THE LOOKS ALREADY.
YOU'RE A REAL HUMBLE GUY, AREN'T YOU?
MR. SOICHIRO?
MR. SOICHIRO?
OH, DEAR... I MUSTN'T HAVE TIED HIS LEASH TIGHTLY ENOUGH!
SIGH WHAT A COMPLETE WASTE OF A DAY...
HUH...?
BOWFF!

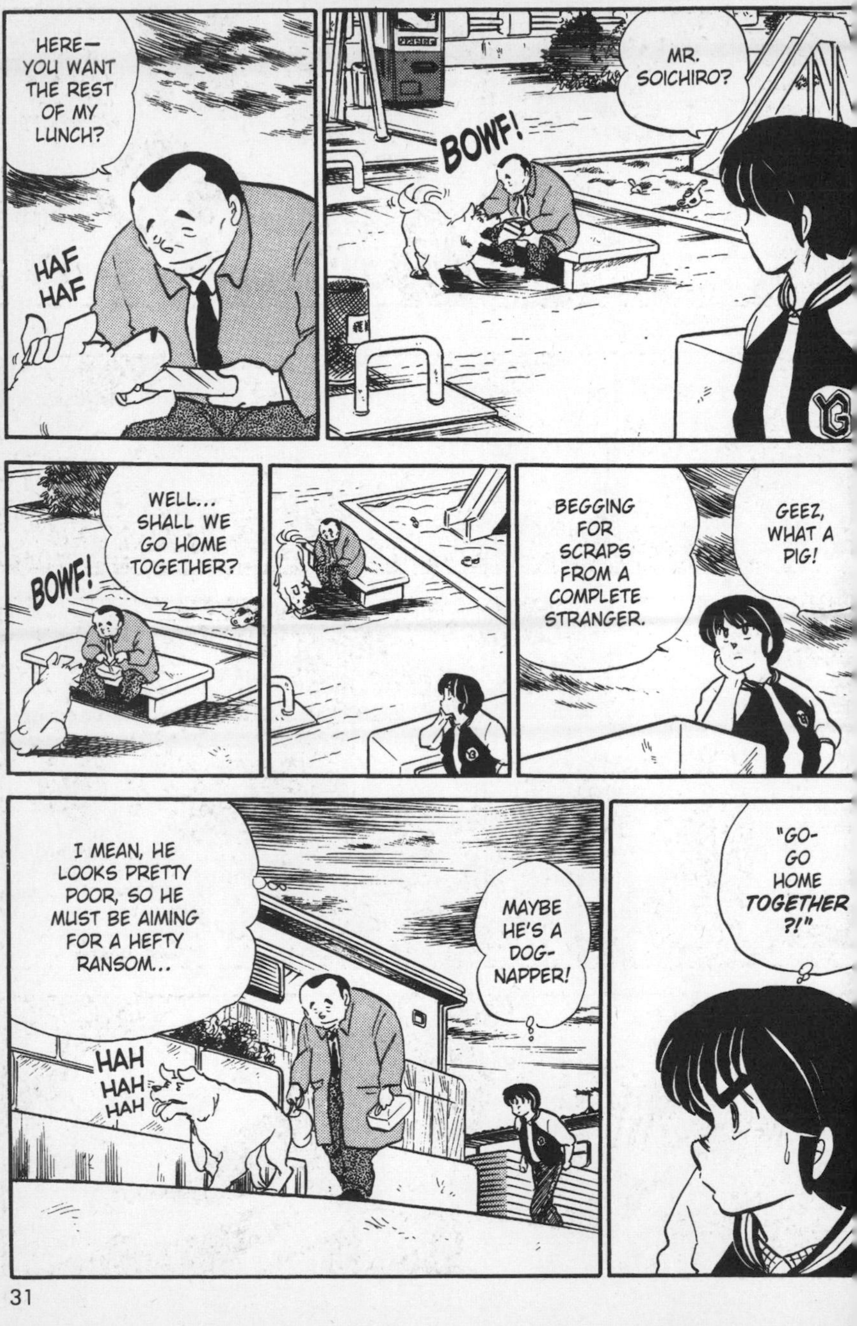
MR. SOICHIRO?
BOWF!
HERE— YOU WANT THE REST OF MY LUNCH?
HAF HAF
GEEZ, WHAT A PIG!
BEGGING FOR SCRAPS FROM A COMPLETE STRANGER.
WELL... SHALL WE GO HOME TOGETHER?
BOWF!
"GO-GO HOME TOGETHER?!"
MAYBE HE'S A DOG-NAPPER!
I MEAN, HE LOOKS PRETTY POOR, SO HE MUST BE AIMING FOR A HEFTY RANSOM...
HAH HAH HAH

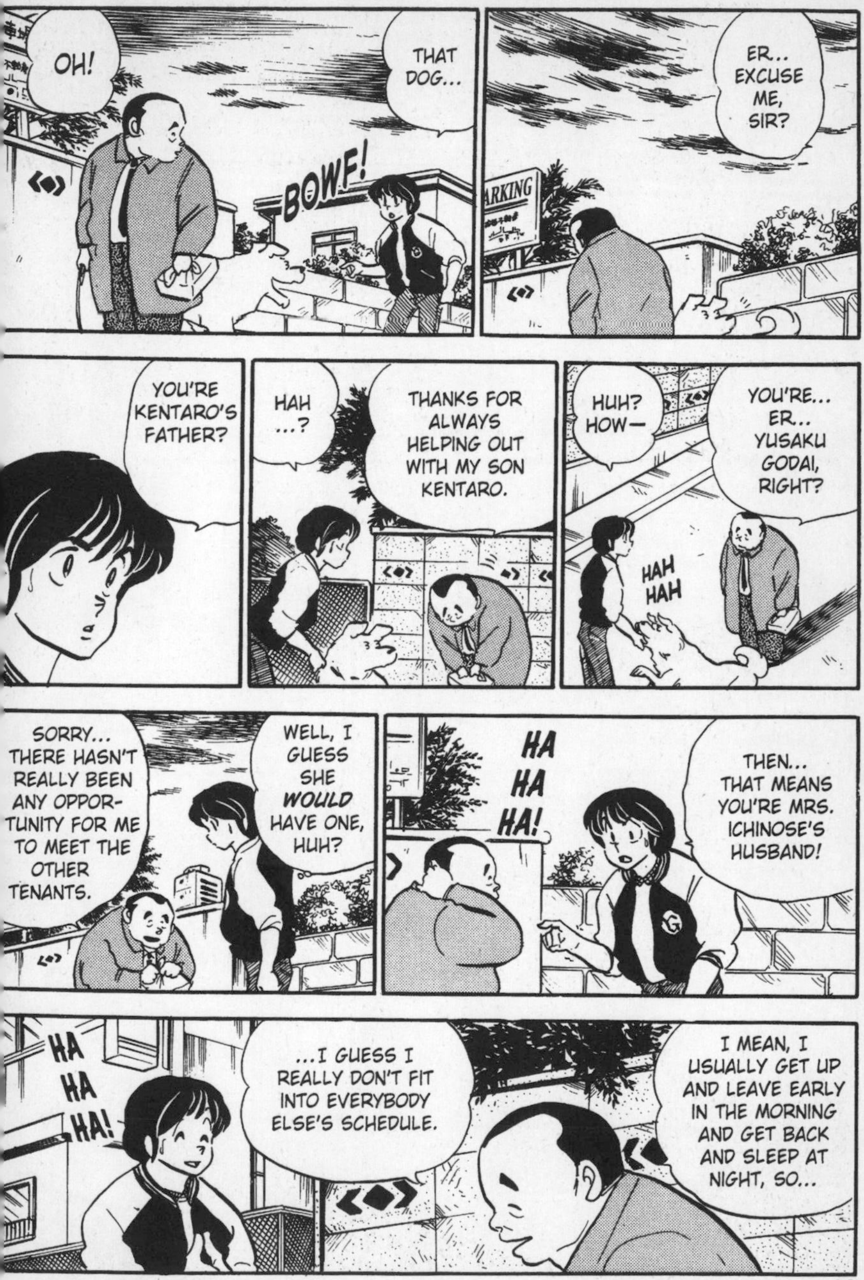
ER... EXCUSE ME, SIR?
THAT DOG...
OH!
BOWF!
YOU'RE... ER... YUSAKU GODAI, RIGHT?
HUH? HOW—
HAH HAH
THANKS FOR ALWAYS HELPING OUT WITH MY SON KENTARO.
HAH ...?
YOU'RE KENTARO'S FATHER?
THEN... THAT MEANS YOU'RE MRS. ICHINOSE'S HUSBAND!
HA HA HA!
WELL, I GUESS SHE *WOULD* HAVE ONE, HUH?
SORRY... THERE HASN'T REALLY BEEN ANY OPPORTUNITY FOR ME TO MEET THE OTHER TENANTS.
I MEAN, I USUALLY GET UP AND LEAVE EARLY IN THE MORNING AND GET BACK AND SLEEP AT NIGHT, SO...
...I GUESS I REALLY DON'T FIT INTO EVERYBODY ELSE'S SCHEDULE.
HA HA HA!

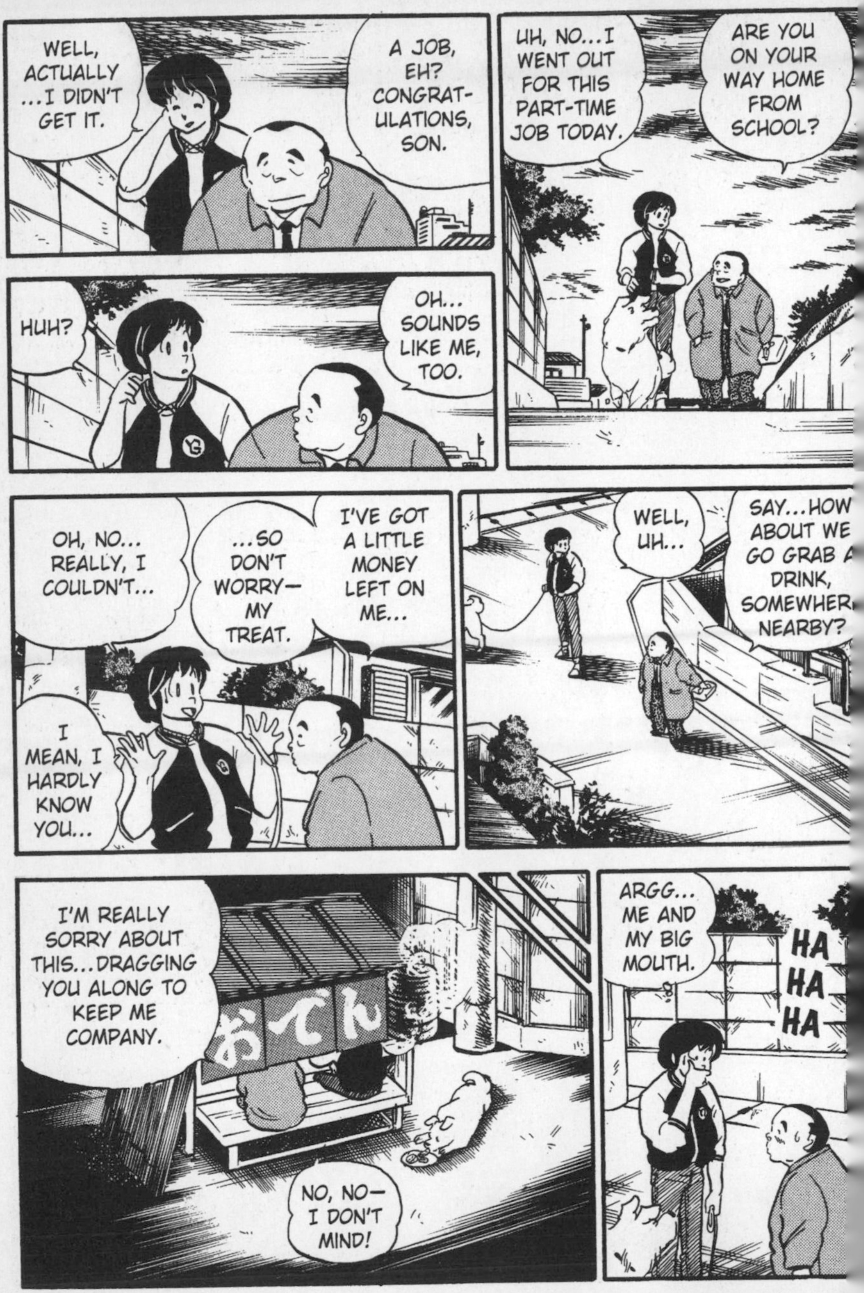
ARE YOU ON YOUR WAY HOME FROM SCHOOL?
UH, NO...I WENT OUT FOR THIS PART-TIME JOB TODAY.
A JOB, EH? CONGRAT-ULATIONS, SON.
WELL, ACTUALLY ...I DIDN'T GET IT.
OH... SOUNDS LIKE ME, TOO.
HUH?
SAY...HOW ABOUT WE GO GRAB A DRINK, SOMEWHER NEARBY?
WELL, UH...
I'VE GOT A LITTLE MONEY LEFT ON ME...
...SO DON'T WORRY—MY TREAT.
OH, NO... REALLY, I COULDN'T...
I MEAN, I HARDLY KNOW YOU...
ARGG... ME AND MY BIG MOUTH.
HA HA HA
I'M REALLY SORRY ABOUT THIS...DRAGGING YOU ALONG TO KEEP ME COMPANY.
おでん
NO, NO— I DON'T MIND!

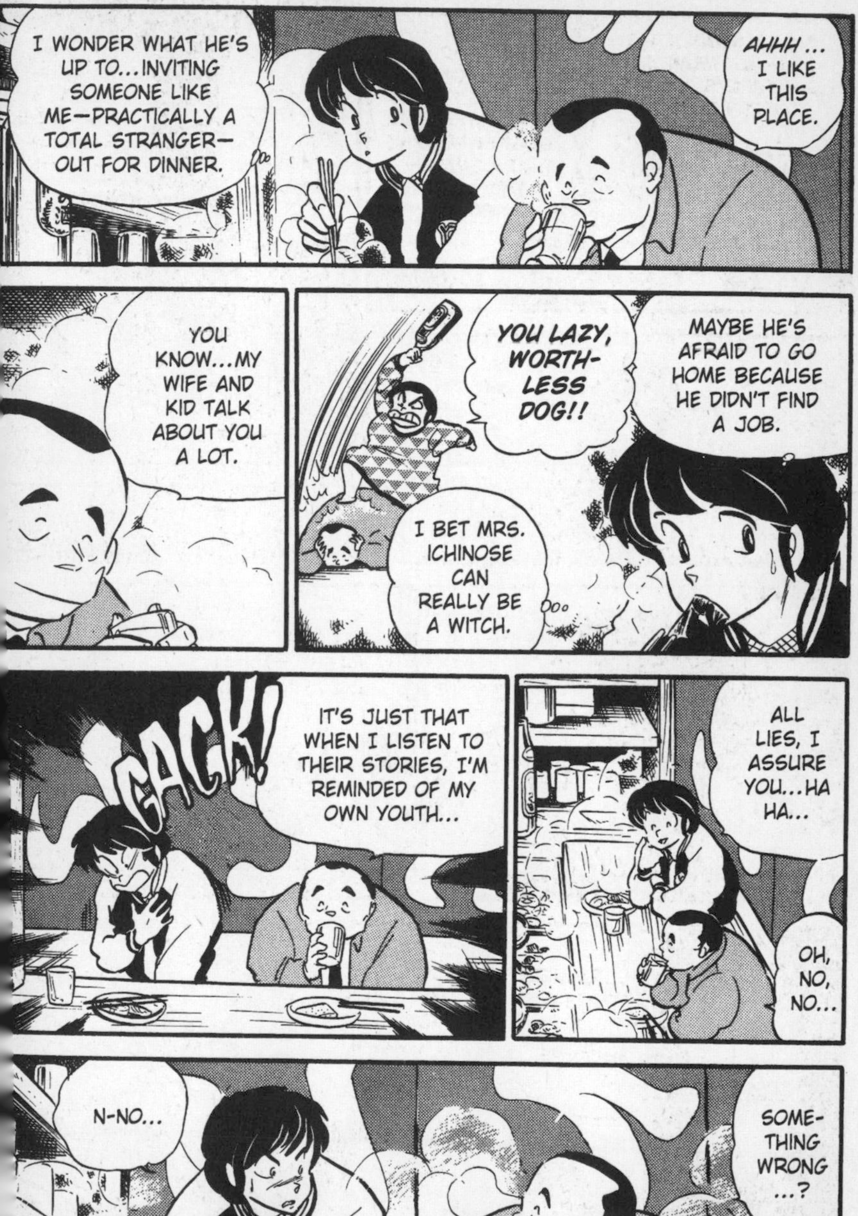
AHHH... I LIKE THIS PLACE.
I WONDER WHAT HE'S UP TO...INVITING SOMEONE LIKE ME—PRACTICALLY A TOTAL STRANGER—OUT FOR DINNER.
MAYBE HE'S AFRAID TO GO HOME BECAUSE HE DIDN'T FIND A JOB.
YOU LAZY, WORTHLESS DOG!!
I BET MRS. ICHINOSE CAN REALLY BE A WITCH.
YOU KNOW...MY WIFE AND KID TALK ABOUT YOU A LOT.
ALL LIES, I ASSURE YOU...HA HA...
OH, NO, NO...
IT'S JUST THAT WHEN I LISTEN TO THEIR STORIES, I'M REMINDED OF MY OWN YOUTH...
GACK!
SOMETHING WRONG...?
N-NO...

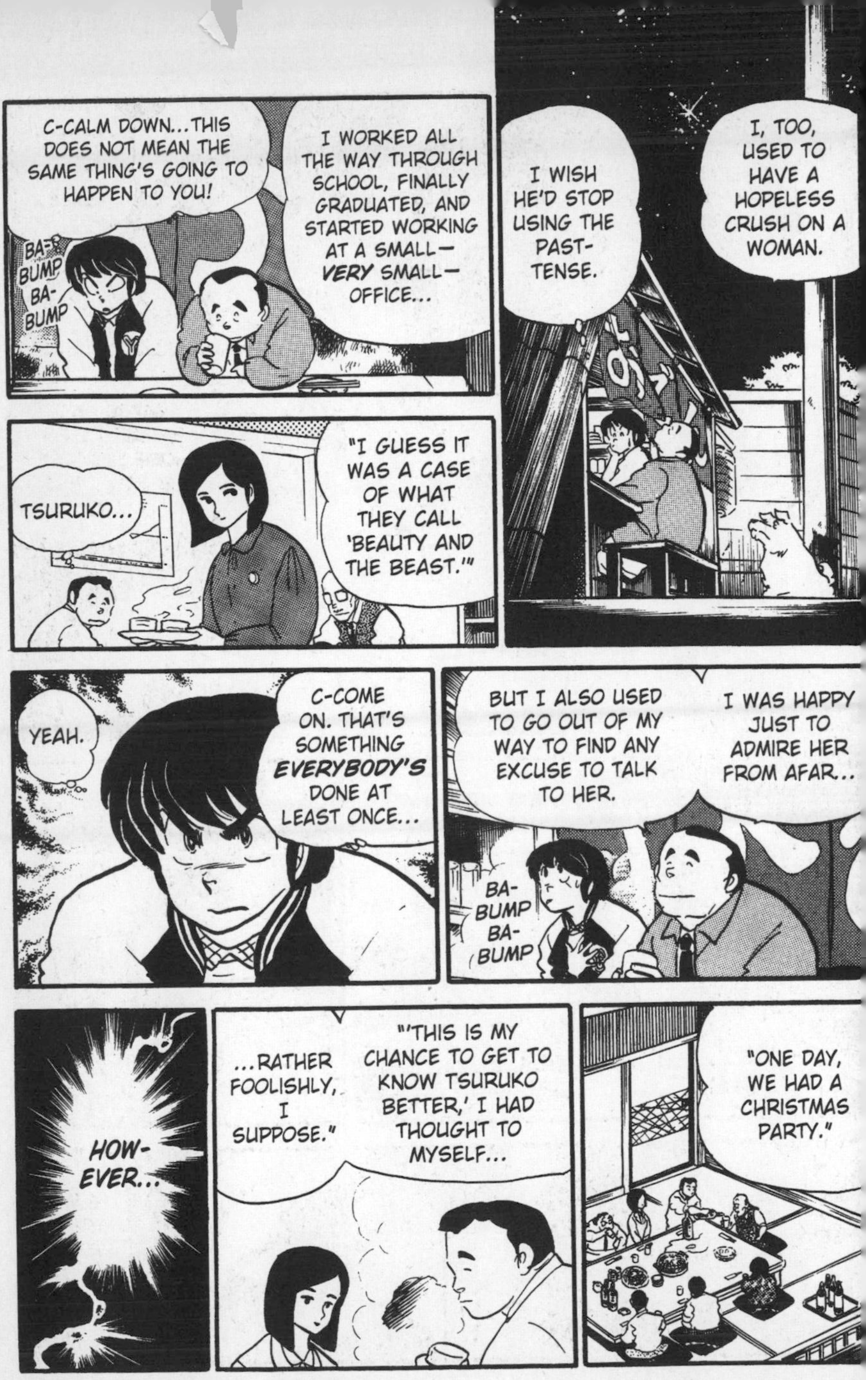
I, TOO, USED TO HAVE A HOPELESS CRUSH ON A WOMAN.
I WISH HE'D STOP USING THE PAST-TENSE.
I WORKED ALL THE WAY THROUGH SCHOOL, FINALLY GRADUATED, AND STARTED WORKING AT A SMALL— *VERY* SMALL— OFFICE...
C-CALM DOWN... THIS DOES NOT MEAN THE SAME THING'S GOING TO HAPPEN TO YOU!
BA-BUMP BA-BUMP
"I GUESS IT WAS A CASE OF WHAT THEY CALL 'BEAUTY AND THE BEAST.'"
TSURUKO...
I WAS HAPPY JUST TO ADMIRE HER FROM AFAR...
BUT I ALSO USED TO GO OUT OF MY WAY TO FIND ANY EXCUSE TO TALK TO HER.
BA-BUMP BA-BUMP
C-COME ON. THAT'S SOMETHING *EVERYBODY'S* DONE AT LEAST ONCE...
YEAH.
"ONE DAY, WE HAD A CHRISTMAS PARTY."
"'THIS IS MY CHANCE TO GET TO KNOW TSURUKO BETTER,' I HAD THOUGHT TO MYSELF...
...RATHER FOOLISHLY, I SUPPOSE."
HOW-EVER...

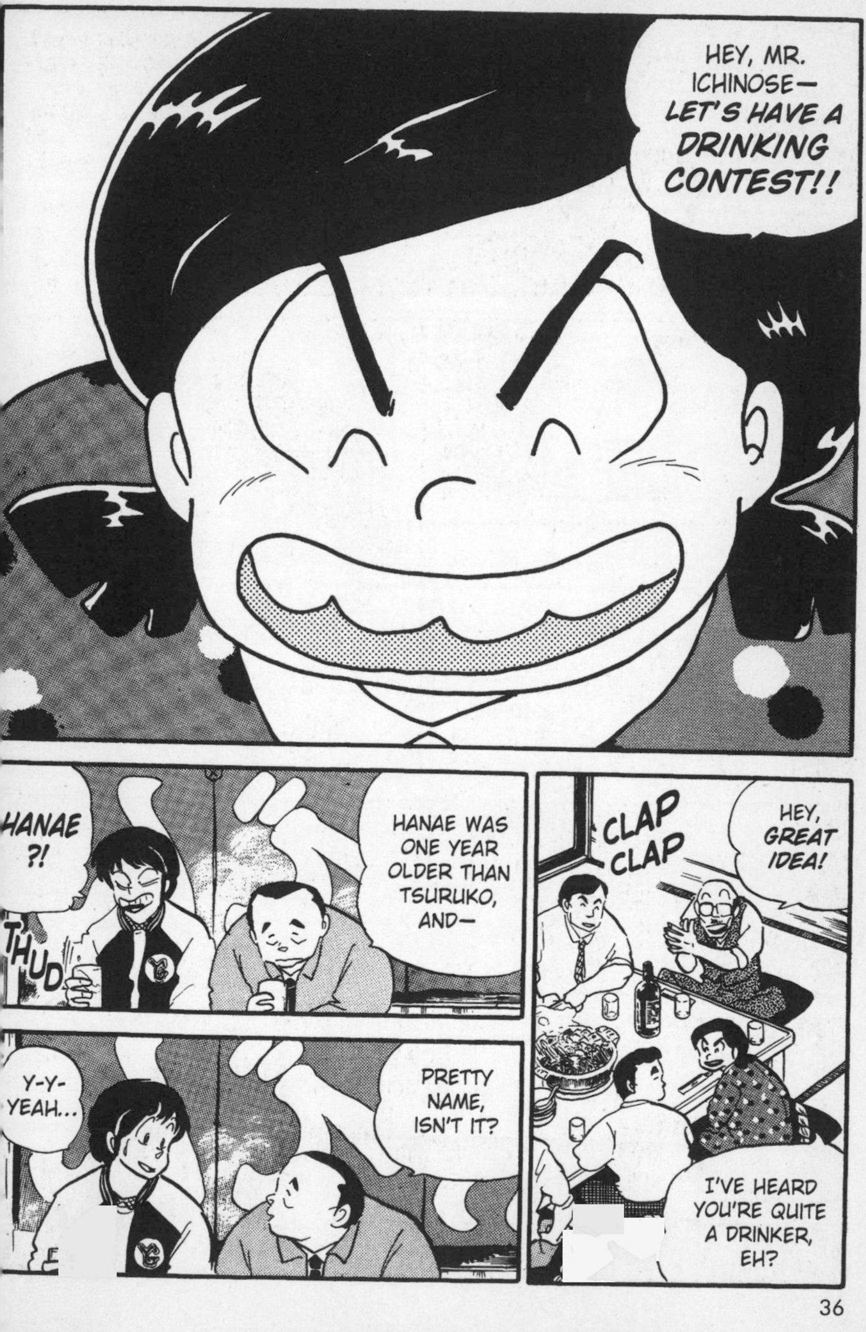
HEY, MR. ICHINOSE— LET'S HAVE A DRINKING CONTEST!!
CLAP CLAP
HEY, GREAT IDEA!
I'VE HEARD YOU'RE QUITE A DRINKER, EH?
HANAE WAS ONE YEAR OLDER THAN TSURUKO, AND—
HANAE ?!
THUD
PRETTY NAME, ISN'T IT?
Y-Y-YEAH...

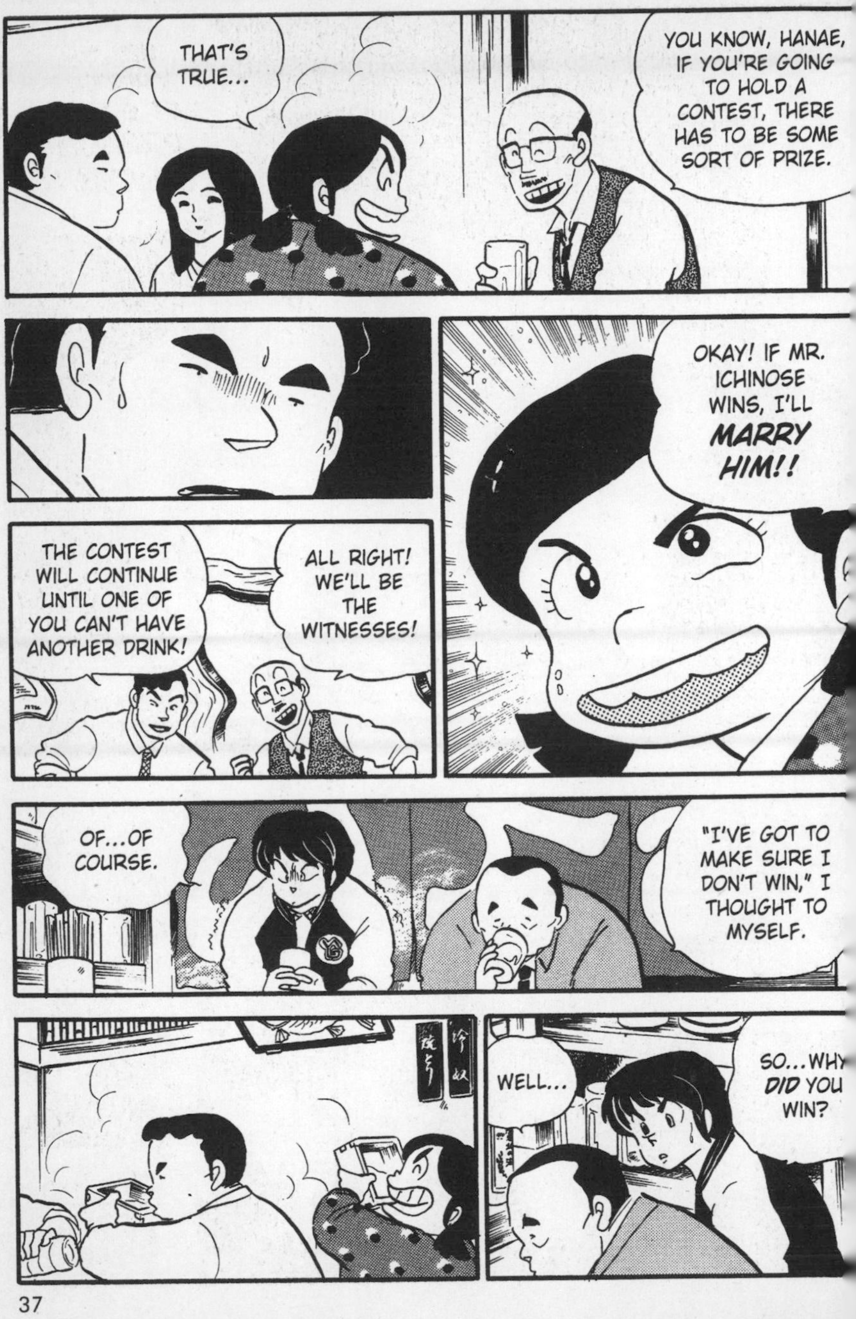
YOU KNOW, HANAE, IF YOU'RE GOING TO HOLD A CONTEST, THERE HAS TO BE SOME SORT OF PRIZE.
THAT'S TRUE...
OKAY! IF MR. ICHINOSE WINS, I'LL *MARRY HIM!!*
ALL RIGHT! WE'LL BE THE WITNESSES!
THE CONTEST WILL CONTINUE UNTIL ONE OF YOU CAN'T HAVE ANOTHER DRINK!
"I'VE GOT TO MAKE SURE I DON'T WIN," I THOUGHT TO MYSELF.
OF...OF COURSE.
SO...WHY *DID* YOU WIN?
WELL...

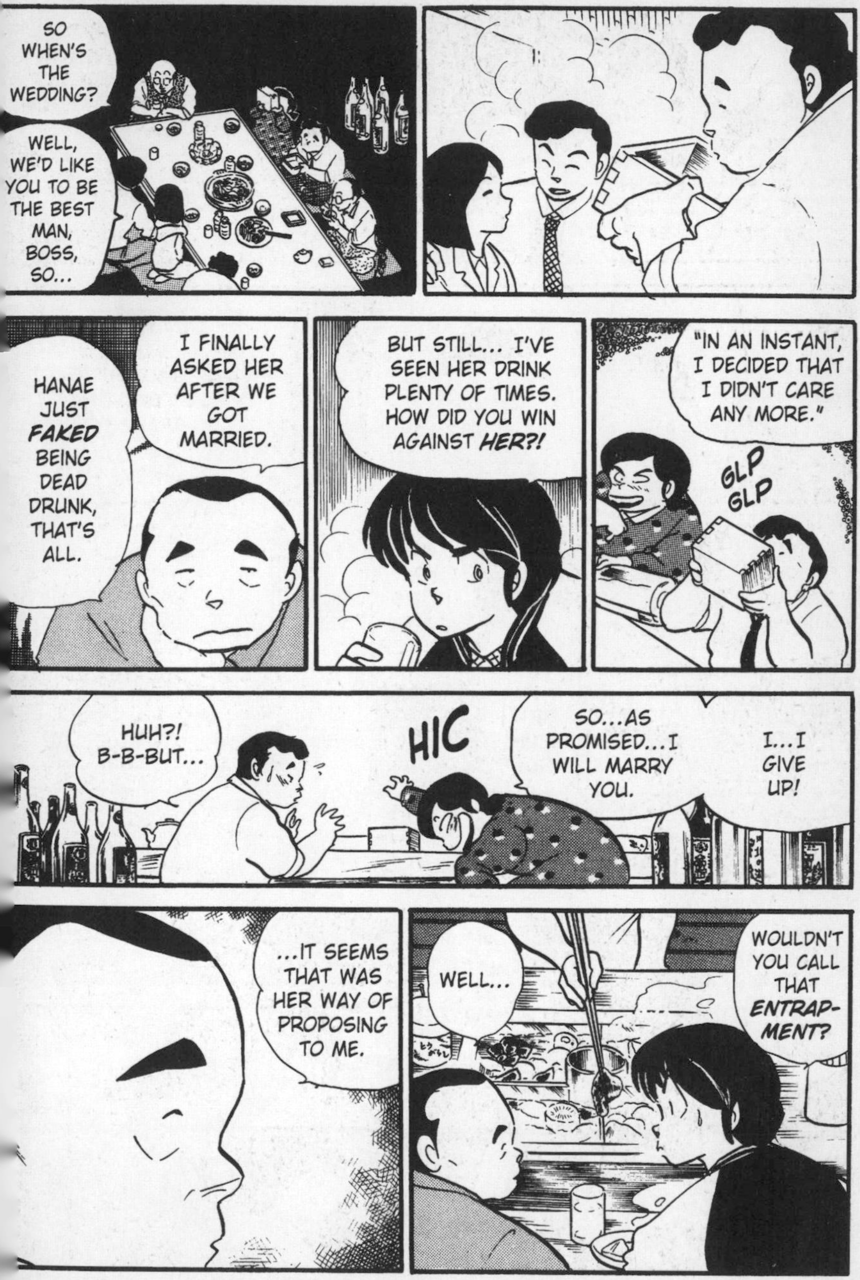
SO WHEN'S THE WEDDING?
WELL, WE'D LIKE YOU TO BE THE BEST MAN, BOSS, SO...
"IN AN INSTANT, I DECIDED THAT I DIDN'T CARE ANY MORE."
GLP GLP
BUT STILL... I'VE SEEN HER DRINK PLENTY OF TIMES. HOW DID YOU WIN AGAINST *HER?!*
I FINALLY ASKED HER AFTER WE GOT MARRIED.
HANAE JUST *FAKED* BEING DEAD DRUNK, THAT'S ALL.
I...I GIVE UP!
SO...AS PROMISED...I WILL MARRY YOU.
HIC
HUH?! B-B-BUT...
WOULDN'T YOU CALL THAT *ENTRAPMENT?*
WELL...
...IT SEEMS THAT WAS HER WAY OF PROPOSING TO ME.

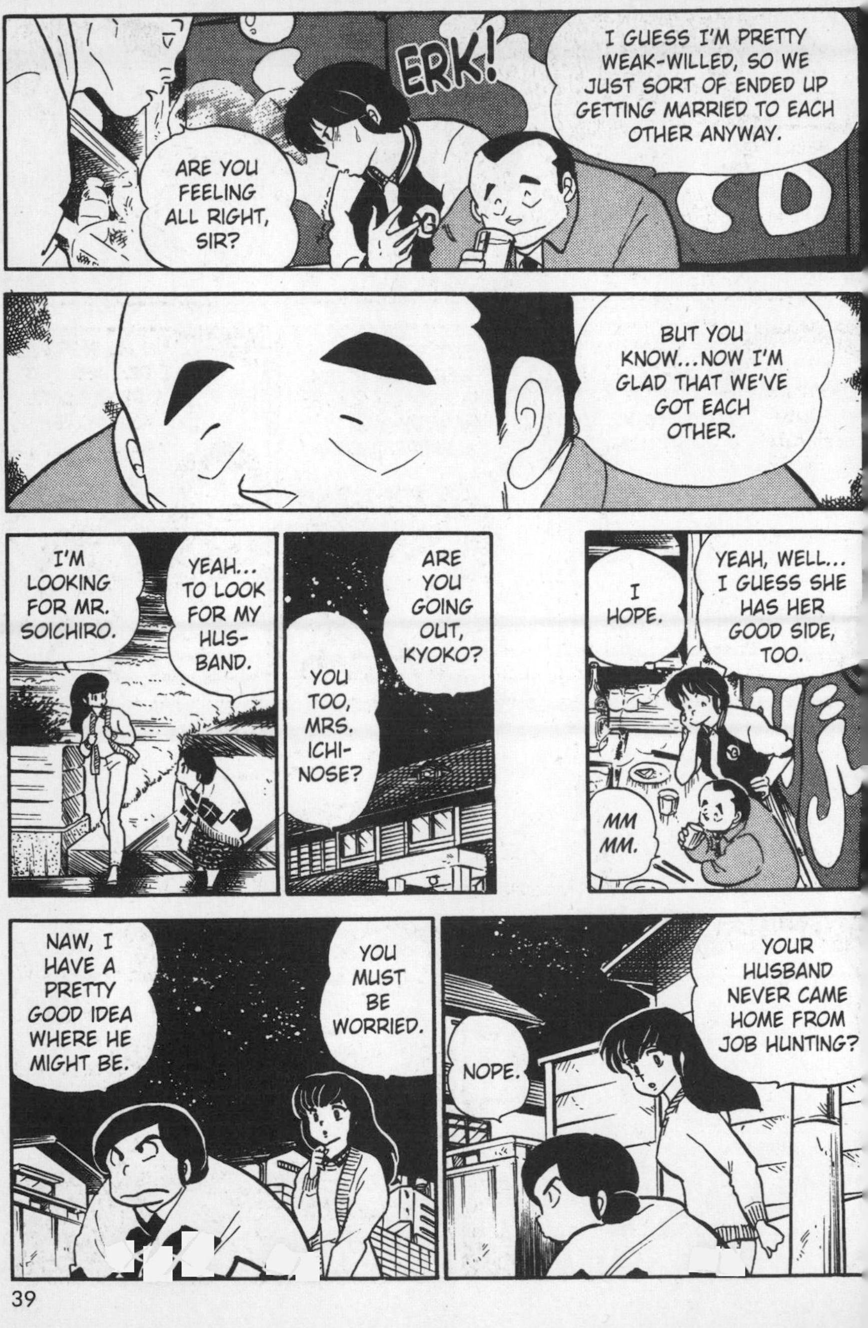

I GUESS I'M PRETTY WEAK-WILLED, SO WE JUST SORT OF ENDED UP GETTING MARRIED TO EACH OTHER ANYWAY.
ERK!
ARE YOU FEELING ALL RIGHT, SIR?
BUT YOU KNOW...NOW I'M GLAD THAT WE'VE GOT EACH OTHER.
YEAH, WELL... I GUESS SHE HAS HER GOOD SIDE, TOO.
I HOPE.
MM MM.
ARE YOU GOING OUT, KYOKO?
YOU TOO, MRS. ICHINOSE?
YEAH... TO LOOK FOR MY HUSBAND.
I'M LOOKING FOR MR. SOICHIRO.
YOUR HUSBAND NEVER CAME HOME FROM JOB HUNTING?
NOPE.
YOU MUST BE WORRIED.
NAW, I HAVE A PRETTY GOOD IDEA WHERE HE MIGHT BE.

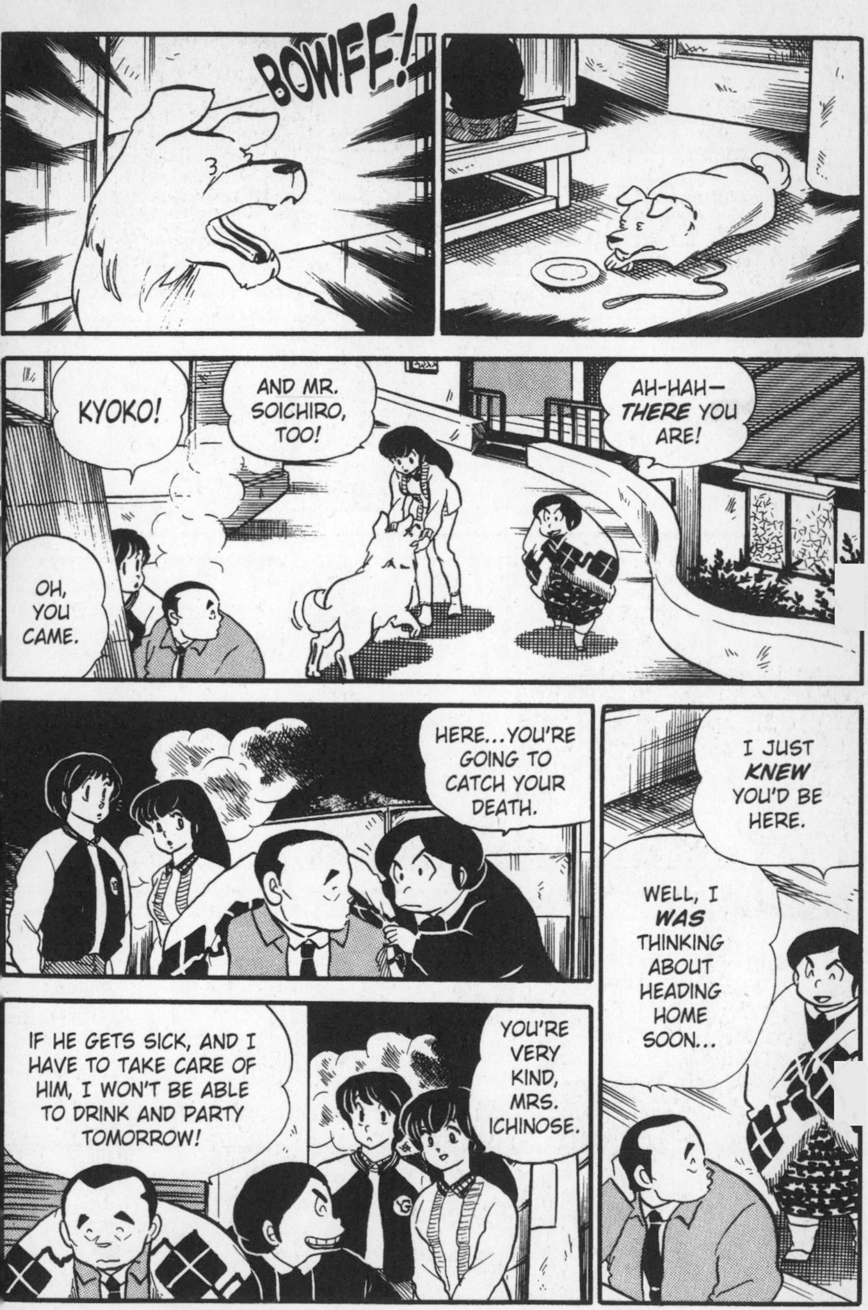
BOWFF!
AH-HAH—THERE YOU ARE!
AND MR. SOICHIRO, TOO!
KYOKO!
OH, YOU CAME.
I JUST KNEW YOU'D BE HERE.
WELL, I WAS THINKING ABOUT HEADING HOME SOON...
HERE...YOU'RE GOING TO CATCH YOUR DEATH.
YOU'RE VERY KIND, MRS. ICHINOSE.
IF HE GETS SICK, AND I HAVE TO TAKE CARE OF HIM, I WON'T BE ABLE TO DRINK AND PARTY TOMORROW!

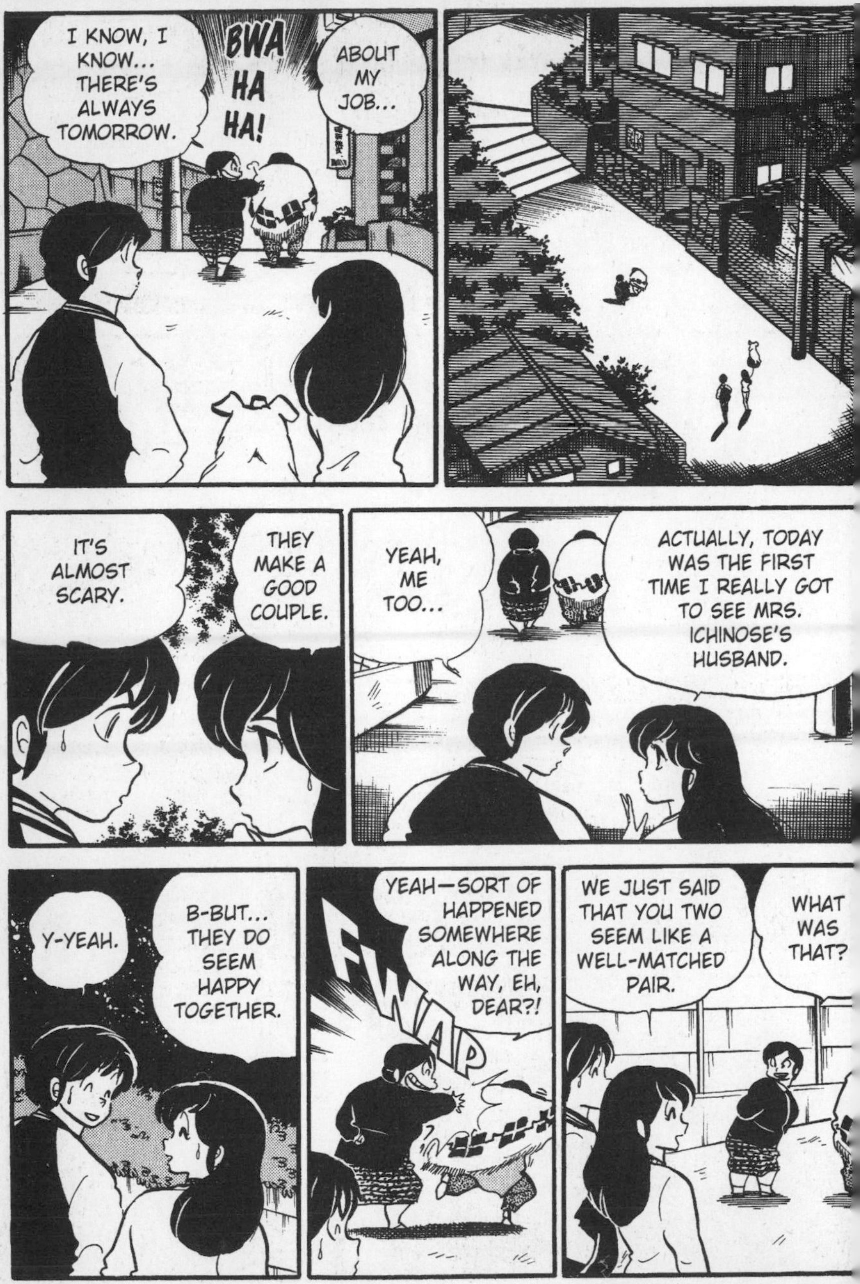
ABOUT MY JOB...
BWA HA HA!
I KNOW, I KNOW... THERE'S ALWAYS TOMORROW.
ACTUALLY, TODAY WAS THE FIRST TIME I REALLY GOT TO SEE MRS. ICHINOSE'S HUSBAND.
YEAH, ME TOO...
THEY MAKE A GOOD COUPLE.
IT'S ALMOST SCARY.
WHAT WAS THAT?
WE JUST SAID THAT YOU TWO SEEM LIKE A WELL-MATCHED PAIR.
YEAH—SORT OF HAPPENED SOMEWHERE ALONG THE WAY, EH, DEAR?!
FWAP
B-BUT... THEY DO SEEM HAPPY TOGETHER.
Y-YEAH.

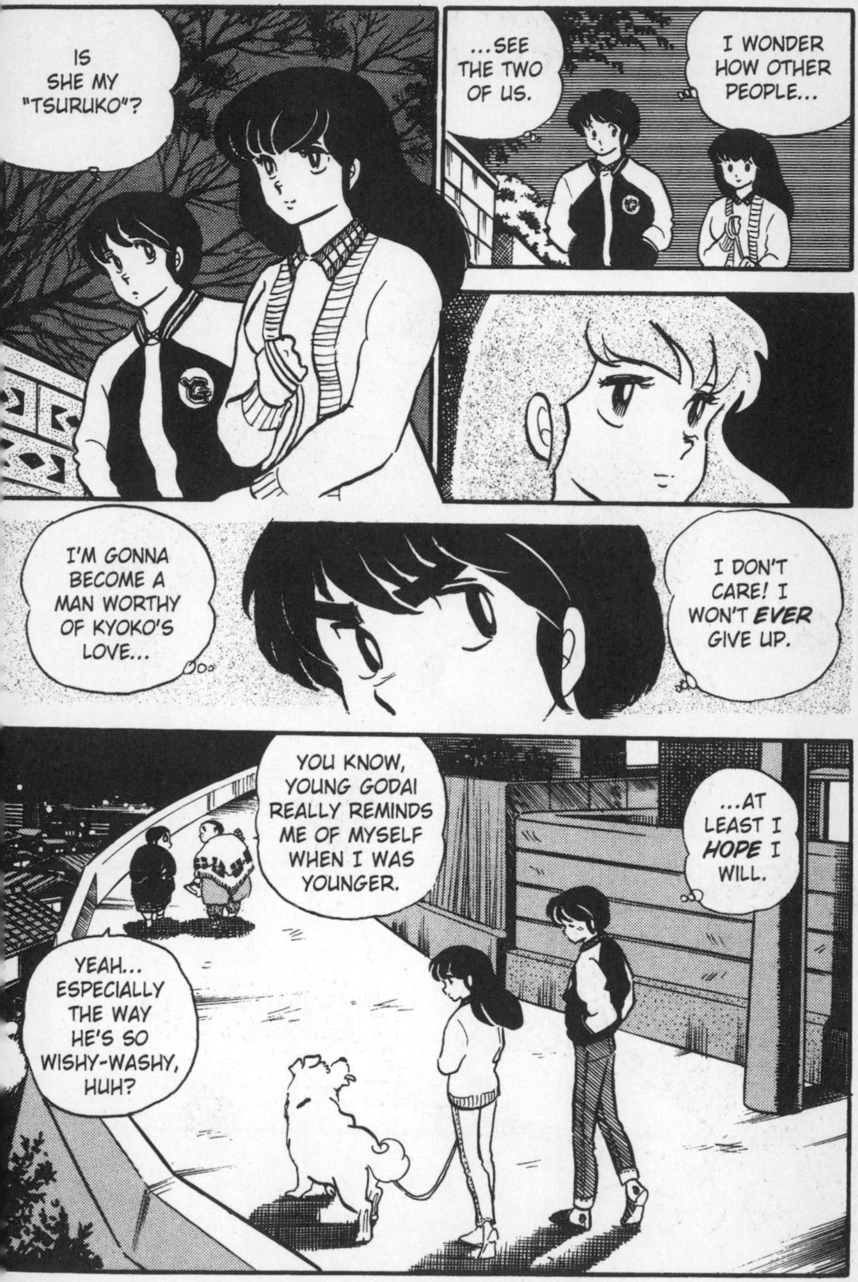
I WONDER HOW OTHER PEOPLE...
...SEE THE TWO OF US.
IS SHE MY "TSURUKO"?
I DON'T CARE! I WON'T ***EVER*** GIVE UP.
I'M GONNA BECOME A MAN WORTHY OF KYOKO'S LOVE...
...AT LEAST I ***HOPE*** I WILL.
YOU KNOW, YOUNG GODAI REALLY REMINDS ME OF MYSELF WHEN I WAS YOUNGER.
YEAH... ESPECIALLY THE WAY HE'S SO WISHY-WASHY, HUH?

PART THREE
RUN, ICHINOSE, RUN!

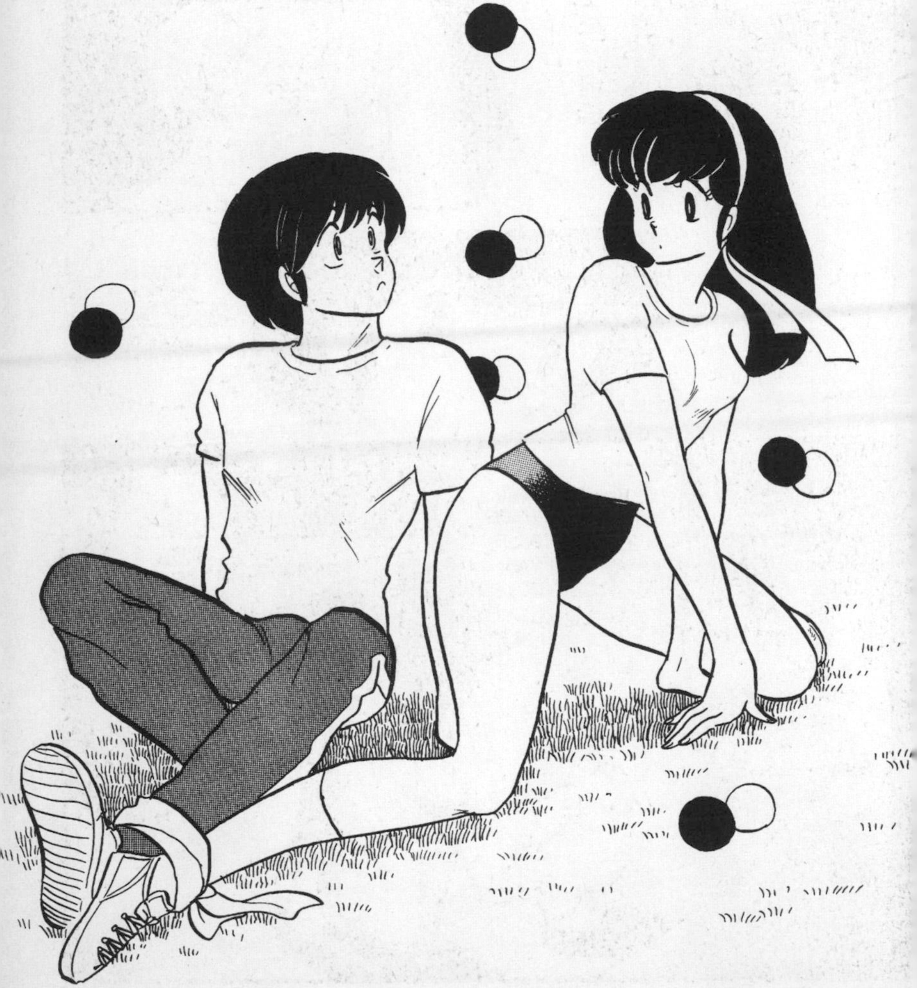

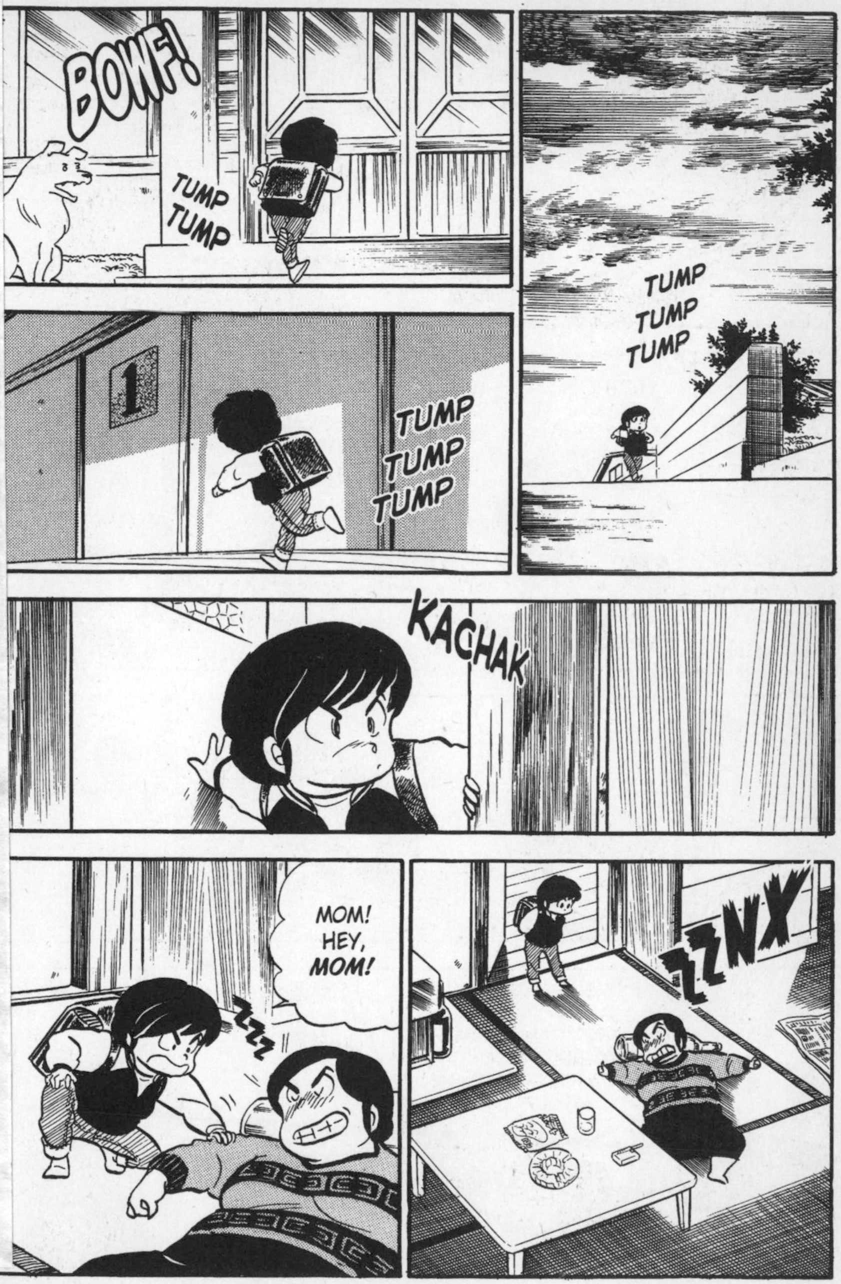
TUMP
TUMP
TUMP
BOWF!
TUMP
TUMP
TUMP
TUMP
TUMP
KACHAK
ZZZNX
MOM!
HEY,
MOM!
ZZZ

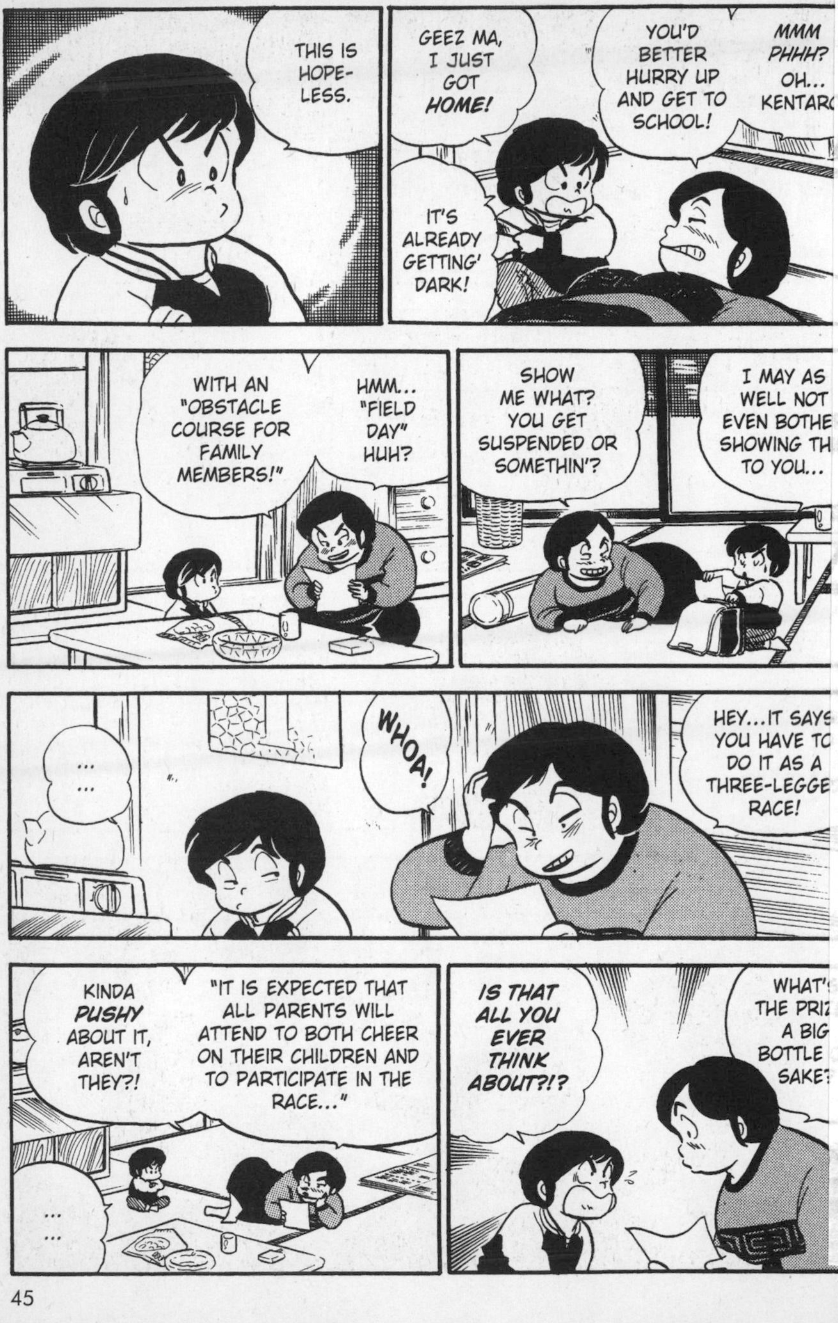
MMM PHHH? OH... KENTARO
YOU'D BETTER HURRY UP AND GET TO SCHOOL!
GEEZ MA, I JUST GOT HOME!
IT'S ALREADY GETTING' DARK!
THIS IS HOPE-LESS.
I MAY AS WELL NOT EVEN BOTHE SHOWING TH TO YOU...
SHOW ME WHAT? YOU GET SUSPENDED OR SOMETHIN'?
HMM... "FIELD DAY" HUH?
WITH AN "OBSTACLE COURSE FOR FAMILY MEMBERS!"
HEY...IT SAYS YOU HAVE TO DO IT AS A THREE-LEGGE RACE!
WHOA!
... ...
WHAT'S THE PRIZ A BIG BOTTLE SAKE?
IS THAT ALL YOU EVER THINK ABOUT?!?
"IT IS EXPECTED THAT ALL PARENTS WILL ATTEND TO BOTH CHEER ON THEIR CHILDREN AND TO PARTICIPATE IN THE RACE..."
KINDA PUSHY ABOUT IT, AREN'T THEY?!
... ...

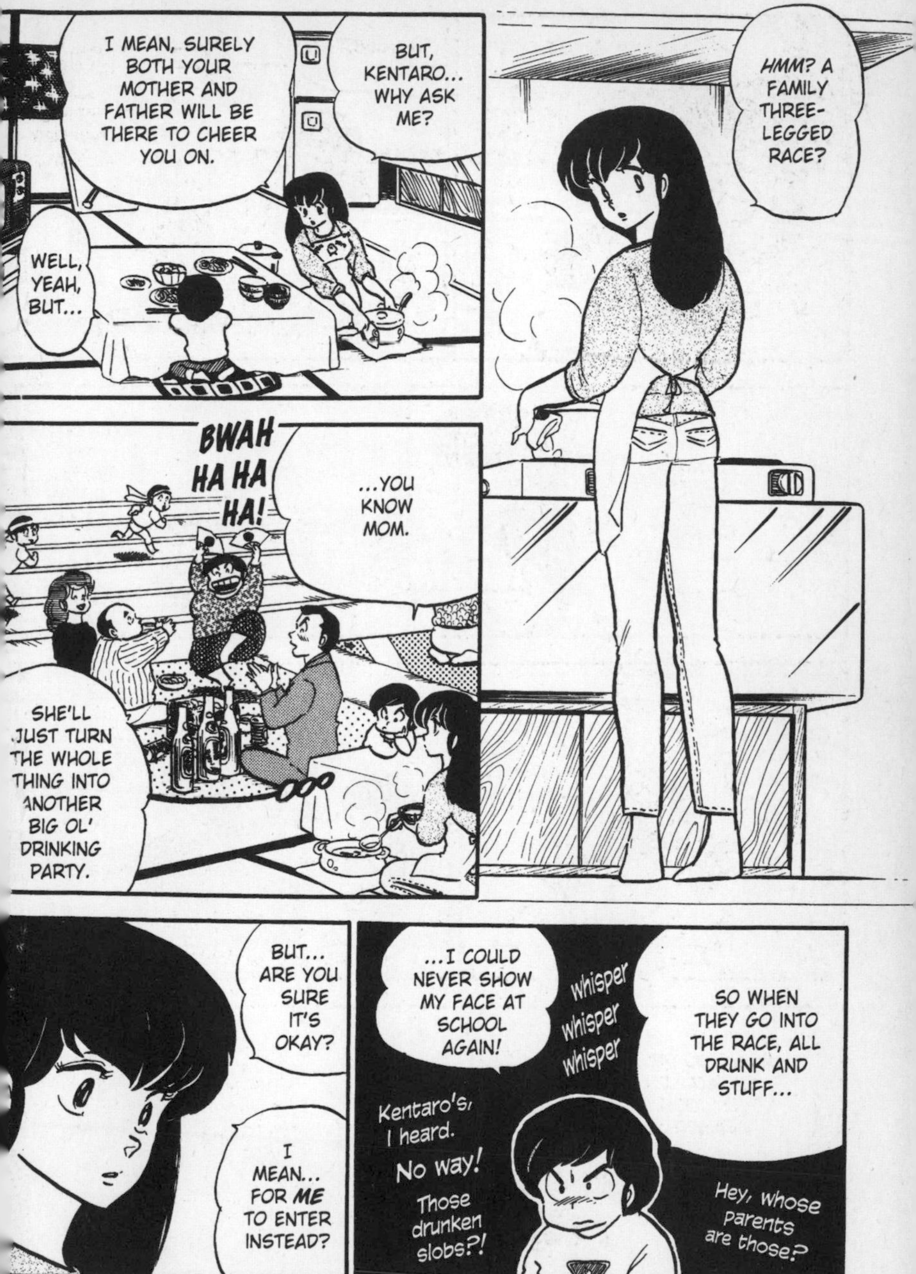
HMM? A FAMILY THREE-LEGGED RACE?
BUT, KENTARO... WHY ASK ME?
I MEAN, SURELY BOTH YOUR MOTHER AND FATHER WILL BE THERE TO CHEER YOU ON.
WELL, YEAH, BUT...
BWAH HA HA HA!
...YOU KNOW MOM.
SHE'LL JUST TURN THE WHOLE THING INTO ANOTHER BIG OL' DRINKING PARTY.
SO WHEN THEY GO INTO THE RACE, ALL DRUNK AND STUFF...
whisper whisper whisper
...I COULD NEVER SHOW MY FACE AT SCHOOL AGAIN!
Hey, whose parents are those?
Kentaro's, I heard.
No way!
Those drunken slobs?!
BUT... ARE YOU SURE IT'S OKAY?
I MEAN... FOR *ME* TO ENTER INSTEAD?

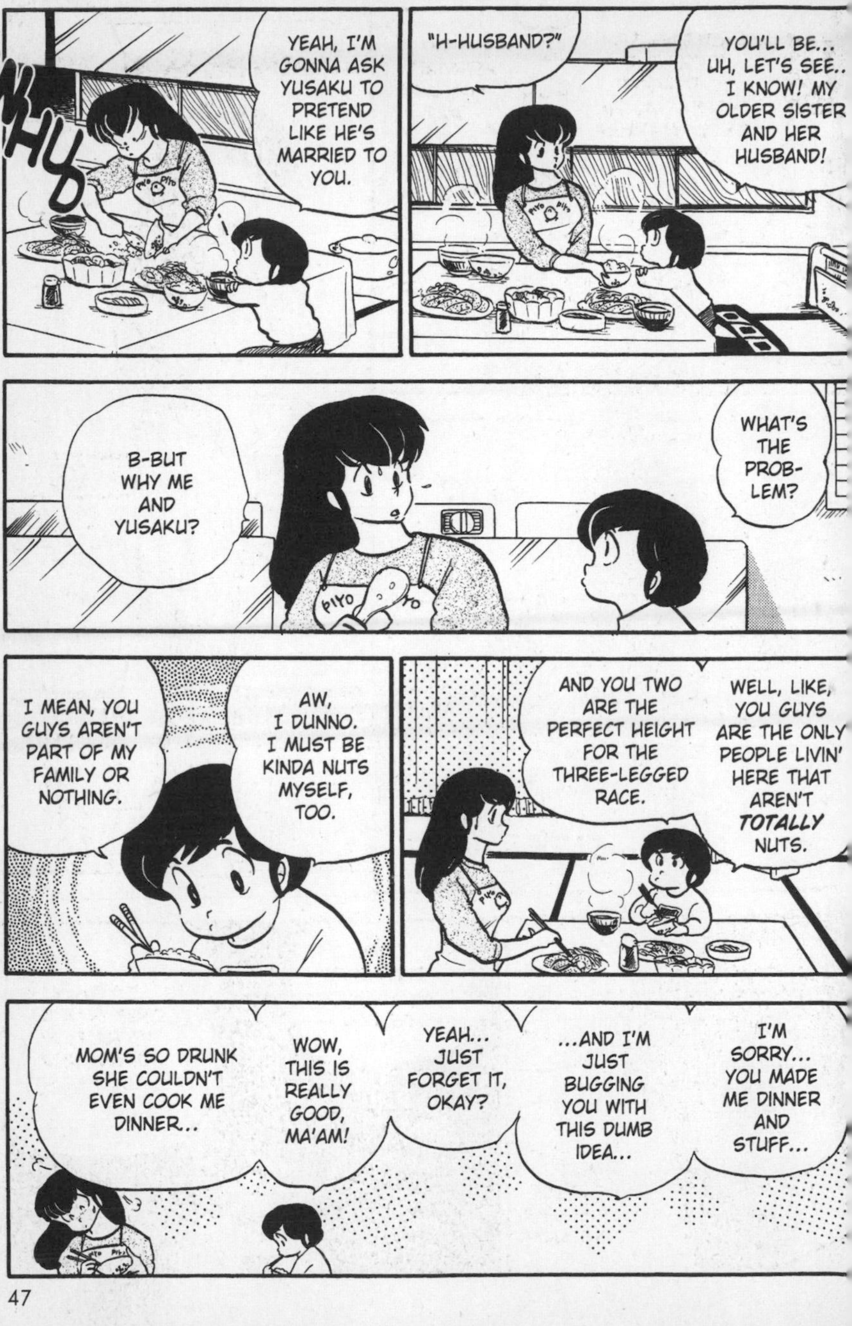
YOU'LL BE... UH, LET'S SEE... I KNOW! MY OLDER SISTER AND HER HUSBAND!
"H-HUSBAND?"
YEAH, I'M GONNA ASK YUSAKU TO PRETEND LIKE HE'S MARRIED TO YOU.
WHUD
WHAT'S THE PROB-LEM?
B-BUT WHY ME AND YUSAKU?
WELL, LIKE, YOU GUYS ARE THE ONLY PEOPLE LIVIN' HERE THAT AREN'T *TOTALLY* NUTS.
AND YOU TWO ARE THE PERFECT HEIGHT FOR THE THREE-LEGGED RACE.
AW, I DUNNO. I MUST BE KINDA NUTS MYSELF, TOO.
I MEAN, YOU GUYS AREN'T PART OF MY FAMILY OR NOTHING.
I'M SORRY... YOU MADE ME DINNER AND STUFF...
...AND I'M JUST BUGGING YOU WITH THIS DUMB IDEA...
YEAH... JUST FORGET IT, OKAY?
WOW, THIS IS REALLY GOOD, MA'AM!
MOM'S SO DRUNK SHE COULDN'T EVEN COOK ME DINNER...

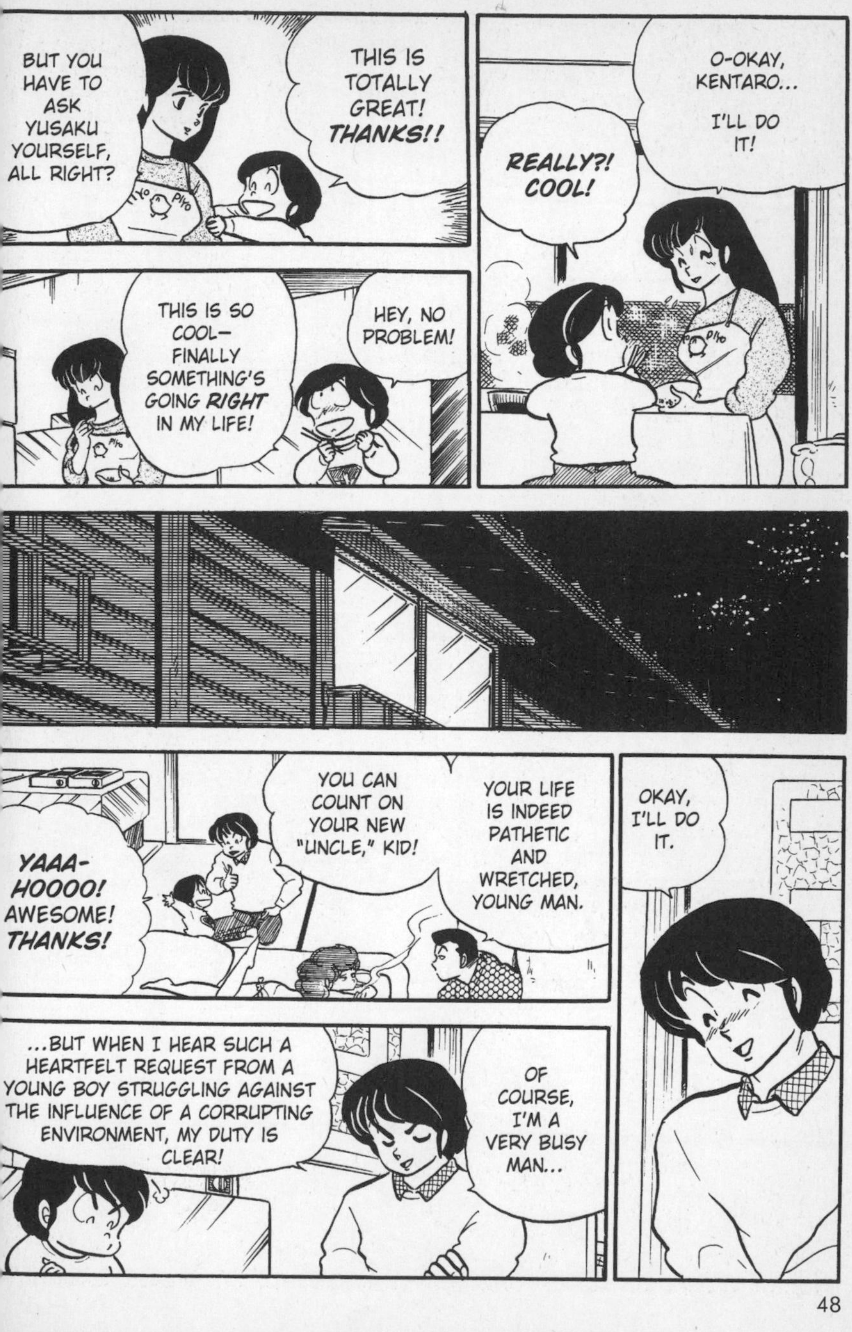
O-OKAY, KENTARO... I'LL DO IT!
REALLY?! COOL!
THIS IS TOTALLY GREAT! THANKS!!
BUT YOU HAVE TO ASK YUSAKU YOURSELF, ALL RIGHT?
HEY, NO PROBLEM!
THIS IS SO COOL— FINALLY SOMETHING'S GOING RIGHT IN MY LIFE!
OKAY, I'LL DO IT.
YOUR LIFE IS INDEED PATHETIC AND WRETCHED, YOUNG MAN.
YOU CAN COUNT ON YOUR NEW "UNCLE," KID!
YAAA-HOOOO! AWESOME! THANKS!
OF COURSE, I'M A VERY BUSY MAN...
...BUT WHEN I HEAR SUCH A HEARTFELT REQUEST FROM A YOUNG BOY STRUGGLING AGAINST THE INFLUENCE OF A CORRUPTING ENVIRONMENT, MY DUTY IS CLEAR!

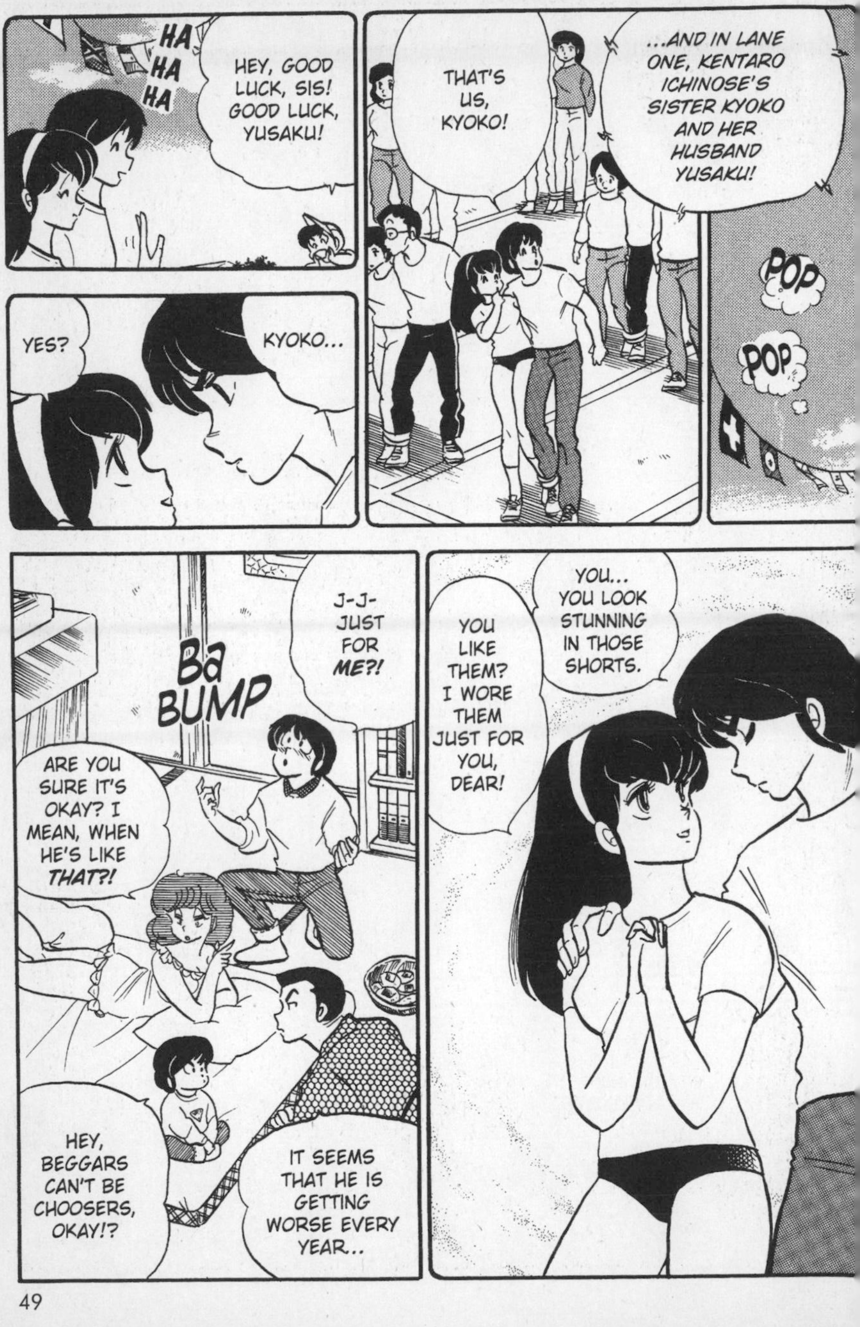
...AND IN LANE ONE, KENTARO ICHINOSE'S SISTER KYOKO AND HER HUSBAND YUSAKU!
POP
POP
THAT'S US, KYOKO!
HA HA HA
HEY, GOOD LUCK, SIS! GOOD LUCK, YUSAKU!
KYOKO...
YES?
YOU... YOU LOOK STUNNING IN THOSE SHORTS.
YOU LIKE THEM? I WORE THEM JUST FOR YOU, DEAR!
J-J-JUST FOR *ME?!*
Ba BUMP
ARE YOU SURE IT'S OKAY? I MEAN, WHEN HE'S LIKE *THAT?!*
IT SEEMS THAT HE IS GETTING WORSE EVERY YEAR...
HEY, BEGGARS CAN'T BE CHOOSERS, OKAY!?

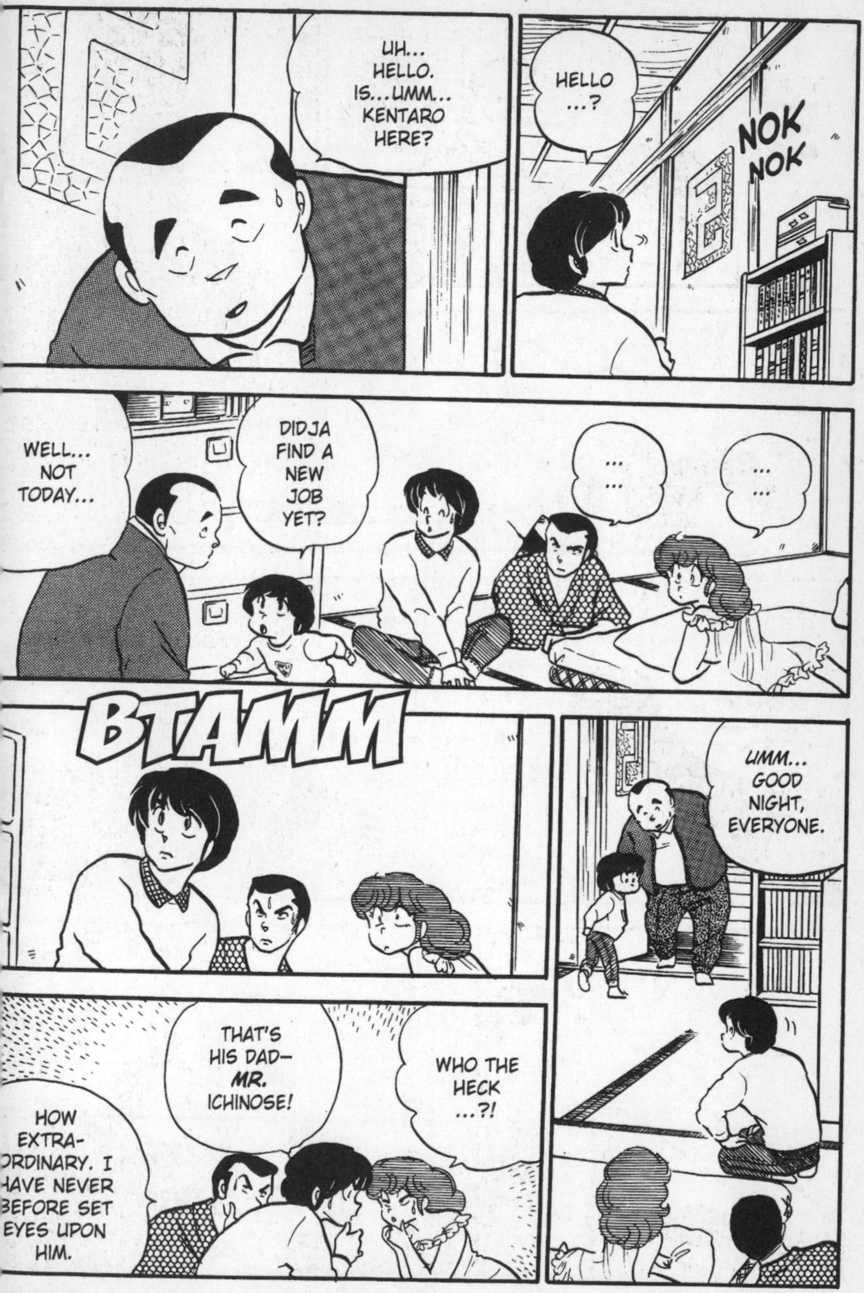
HELLO ...?
NOK NOK
UH... HELLO. IS...UMM... KENTARO HERE?
... ...
... ...
DIDJA FIND A NEW JOB YET?
WELL... NOT TODAY...
UMM... GOOD NIGHT, EVERYONE.
BTAMM
WHO THE HECK ...?!
THAT'S HIS DAD— MR. ICHINOSE!
HOW EXTRA- RDINARY. I AVE NEVER EFORE SET EYES UPON HIM.

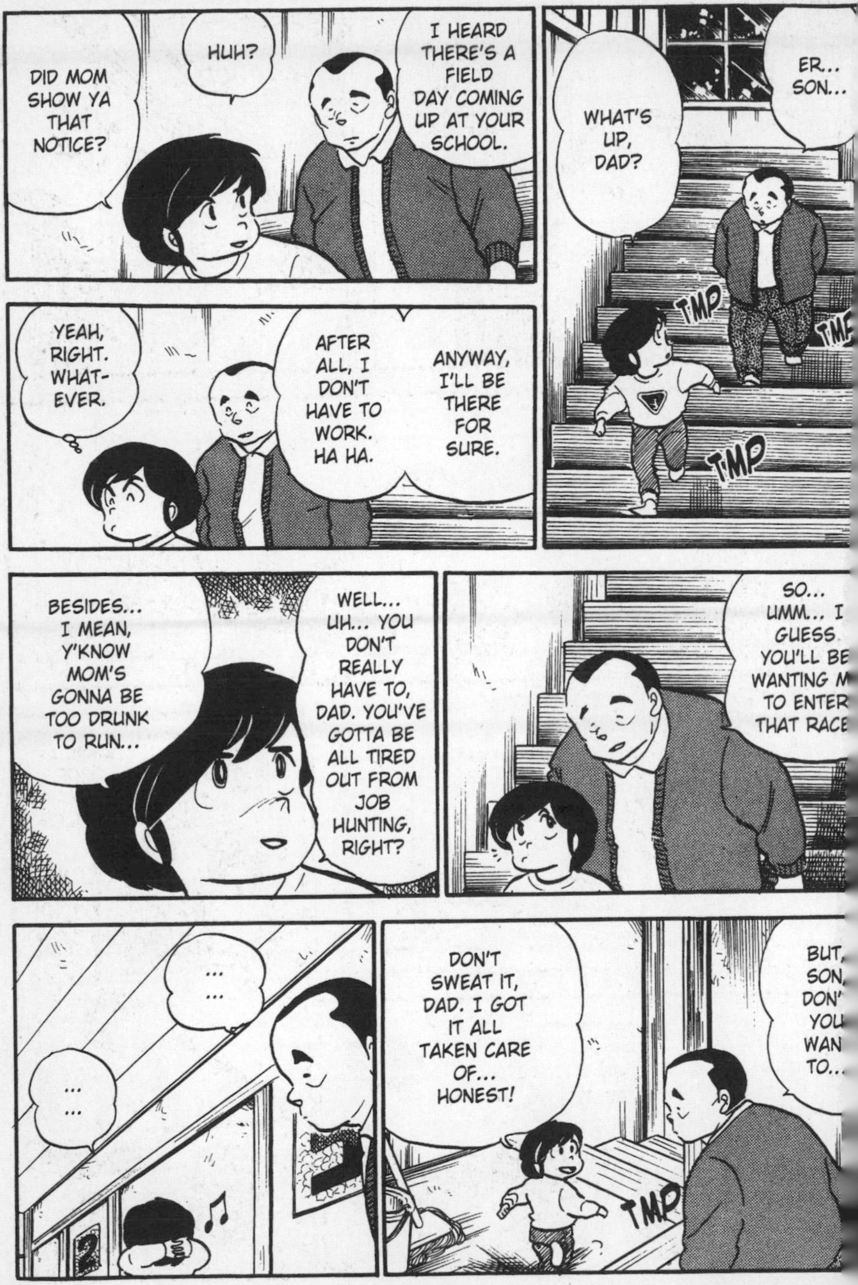
ER... SON...
WHAT'S UP, DAD?
TMP
TMP
TMP
I HEARD THERE'S A FIELD DAY COMING UP AT YOUR SCHOOL.
HUH?
DID MOM SHOW YA THAT NOTICE?
ANYWAY, I'LL BE THERE FOR SURE.
AFTER ALL, I DON'T HAVE TO WORK. HA HA.
YEAH, RIGHT. WHATEVER.
SO... UMM... I GUESS YOU'LL BE WANTING M TO ENTER THAT RACE
WELL... UH... YOU DON'T REALLY HAVE TO, DAD. YOU'VE GOTTA BE ALL TIRED OUT FROM JOB HUNTING, RIGHT?
BESIDES... I MEAN, Y'KNOW MOM'S GONNA BE TOO DRUNK TO RUN...
BUT, SON, DON' YOU WAN TO...
DON'T SWEAT IT, DAD. I GOT IT ALL TAKEN CARE OF... HONEST!
TMP
... ...
... ...

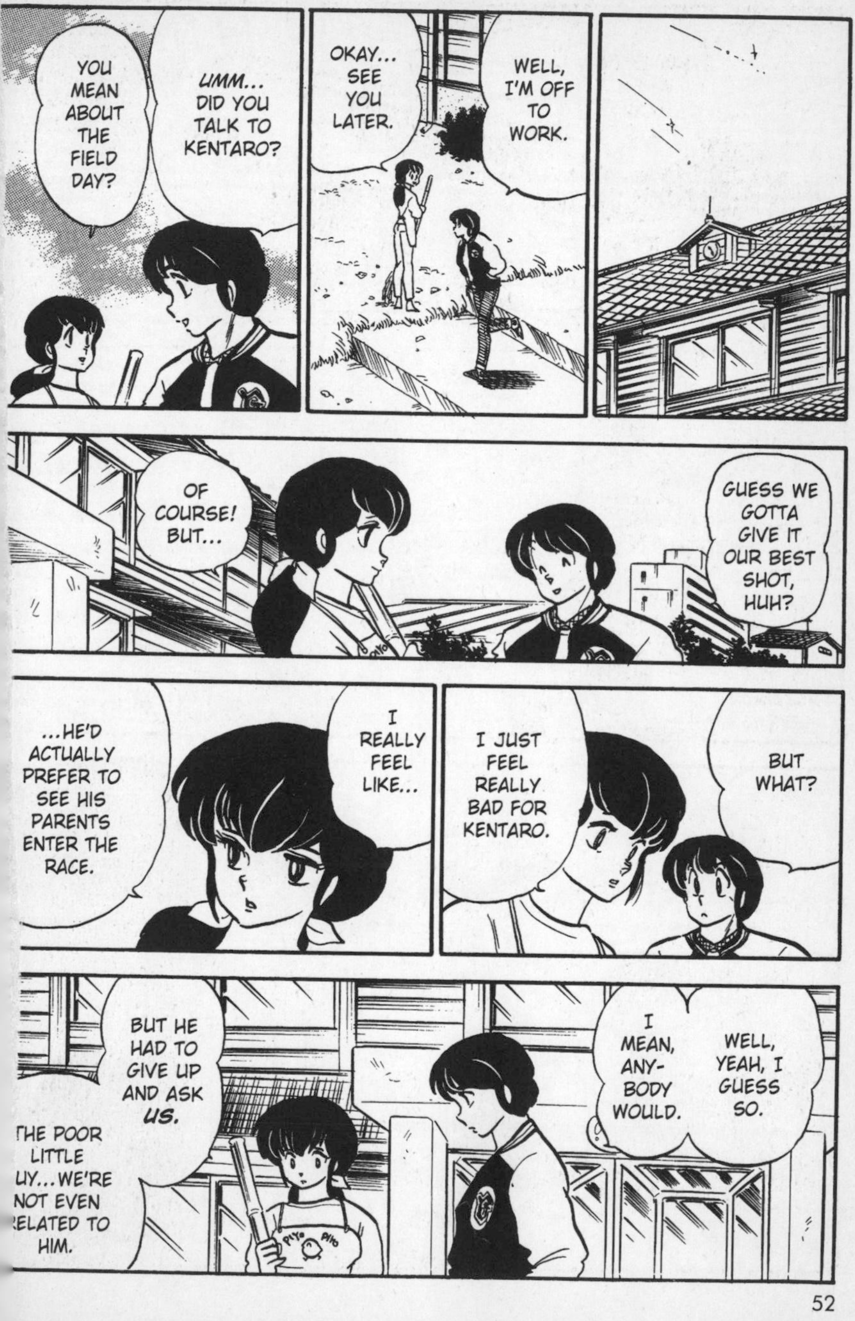
WELL, I'M OFF TO WORK.
OKAY... SEE YOU LATER.
UMM... DID YOU TALK TO KENTARO?
YOU MEAN ABOUT THE FIELD DAY?
GUESS WE GOTTA GIVE IT OUR BEST SHOT, HUH?
OF COURSE! BUT...
BUT WHAT?
I JUST FEEL REALLY BAD FOR KENTARO.
I REALLY FEEL LIKE...
...HE'D ACTUALLY PREFER TO SEE HIS PARENTS ENTER THE RACE.
WELL, YEAH, I GUESS SO.
I MEAN, ANY-BODY WOULD.
BUT HE HAD TO GIVE UP AND ASK *US*.
THE POOR LITTLE GUY... WE'RE NOT EVEN RELATED TO HIM.

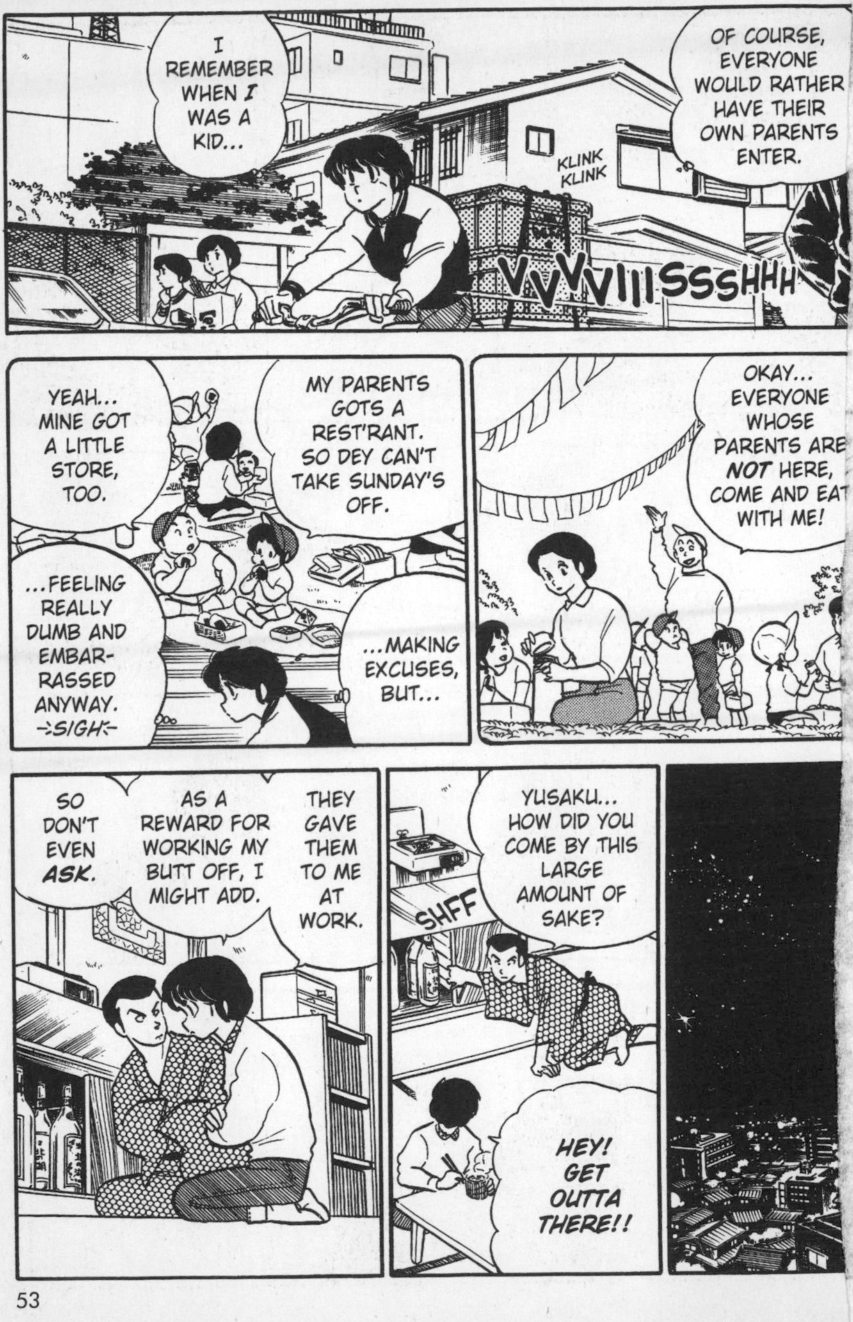
OF COURSE, EVERYONE WOULD RATHER HAVE THEIR OWN PARENTS ENTER.
KLINK KLINK
I REMEMBER WHEN I WAS A KID...
VVVVIIISSSHHH
OKAY... EVERYONE WHOSE PARENTS ARE NOT HERE, COME AND EAT WITH ME!
MY PARENTS GOTS A REST'RANT. SO DEY CAN'T TAKE SUNDAY'S OFF.
YEAH... MINE GOT A LITTLE STORE, TOO.
...MAKING EXCUSES, BUT...
...FEELING REALLY DUMB AND EMBARRASSED ANYWAY.
SIGH
YUSAKU... HOW DID YOU COME BY THIS LARGE AMOUNT OF SAKE?
SHFF
HEY! GET OUTTA THERE!!
THEY GAVE THEM TO ME AT WORK.
AS A REWARD FOR WORKING MY BUTT OFF, I MIGHT ADD.
SO DON'T EVEN ASK.

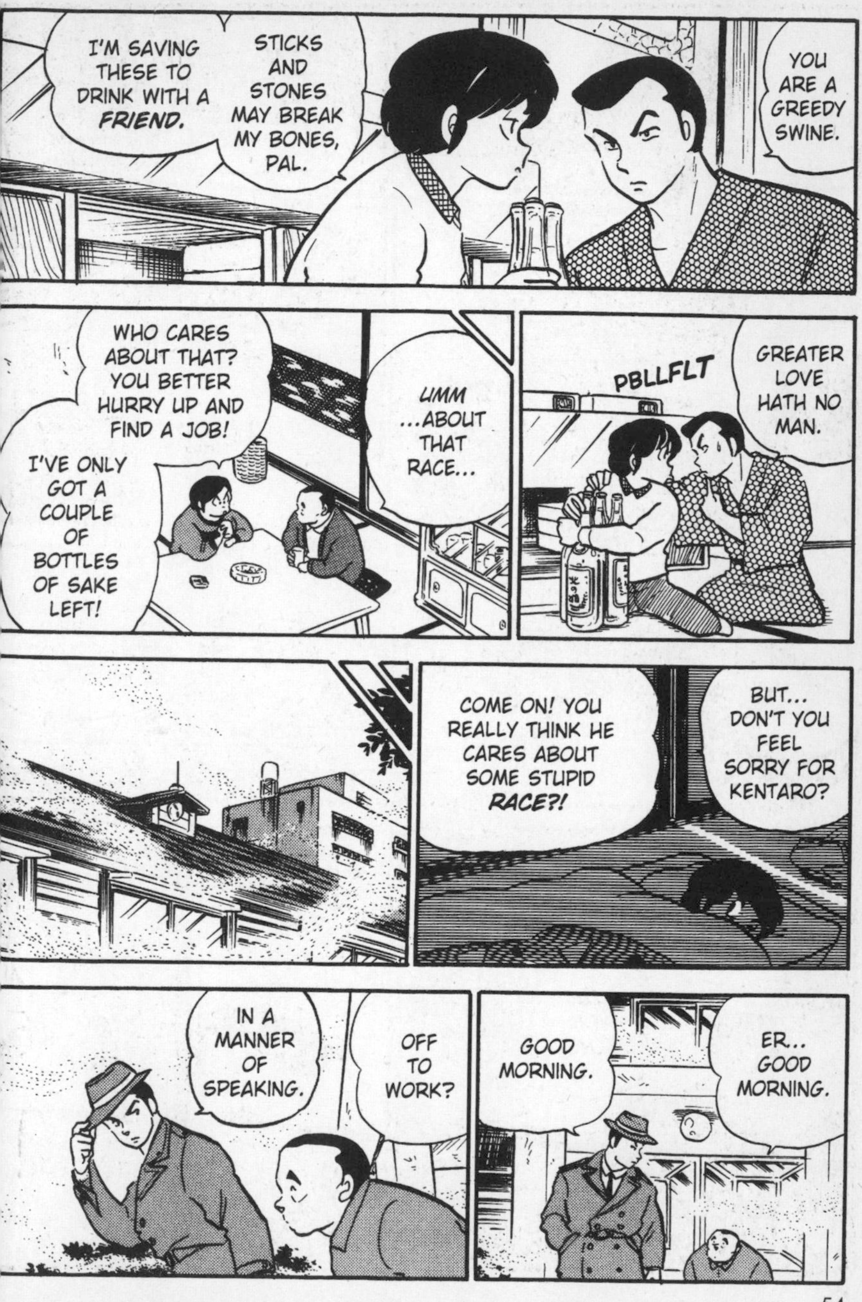
YOU ARE A GREEDY SWINE.
STICKS AND STONES MAY BREAK MY BONES, PAL.
I'M SAVING THESE TO DRINK WITH A *FRIEND.*
GREATER LOVE HATH NO MAN.
PBLLFLT
UMM ...ABOUT THAT RACE...
WHO CARES ABOUT THAT? YOU BETTER HURRY UP AND FIND A JOB!
I'VE ONLY GOT A COUPLE OF BOTTLES OF SAKE LEFT!
BUT... DON'T YOU FEEL SORRY FOR KENTARO?
COME ON! YOU REALLY THINK HE CARES ABOUT SOME STUPID *RACE?!*
ER.. GOOD MORNING.
GOOD MORNING.
OFF TO WORK?
IN A MANNER OF SPEAKING.

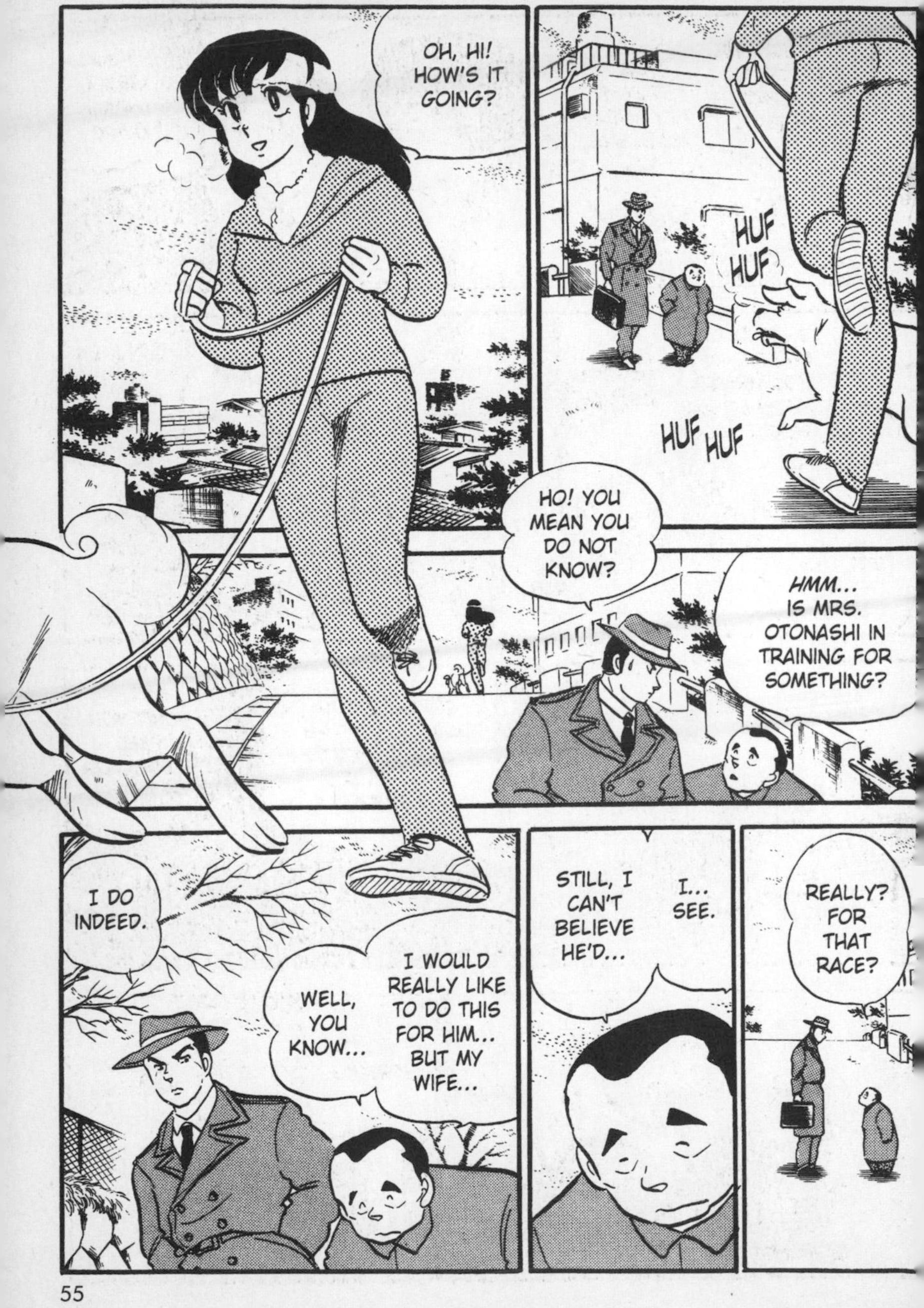
HUF HUF
HUF HUF
OH, HI! HOW'S IT GOING?
HMM... IS MRS. OTONASHI IN TRAINING FOR SOMETHING?
HO! YOU MEAN YOU DO NOT KNOW?
REALLY? FOR THAT RACE?
I... SEE.
STILL, I CAN'T BELIEVE HE'D...
I DO INDEED.
WELL, YOU KNOW...
I WOULD REALLY LIKE TO DO THIS FOR HIM... BUT MY WIFE...

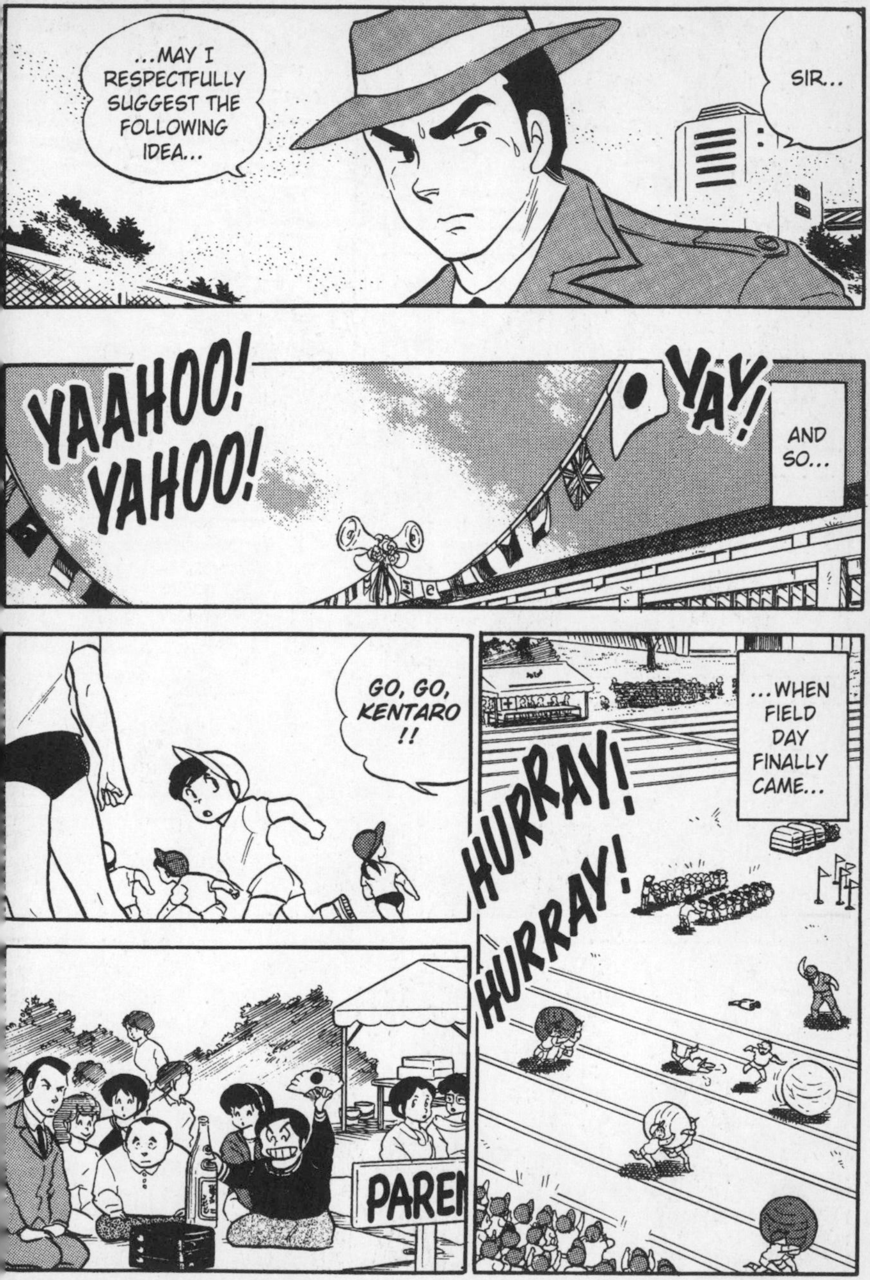
SIR...
...MAY I RESPECTFULLY SUGGEST THE FOLLOWING IDEA...
AND SO...
YAY!
YAAHOO! YAHOO!
...WHEN FIELD DAY FINALLY CAME...
HURRAY! HURRAY!
GO, GO, KENTARO !!
PAREN

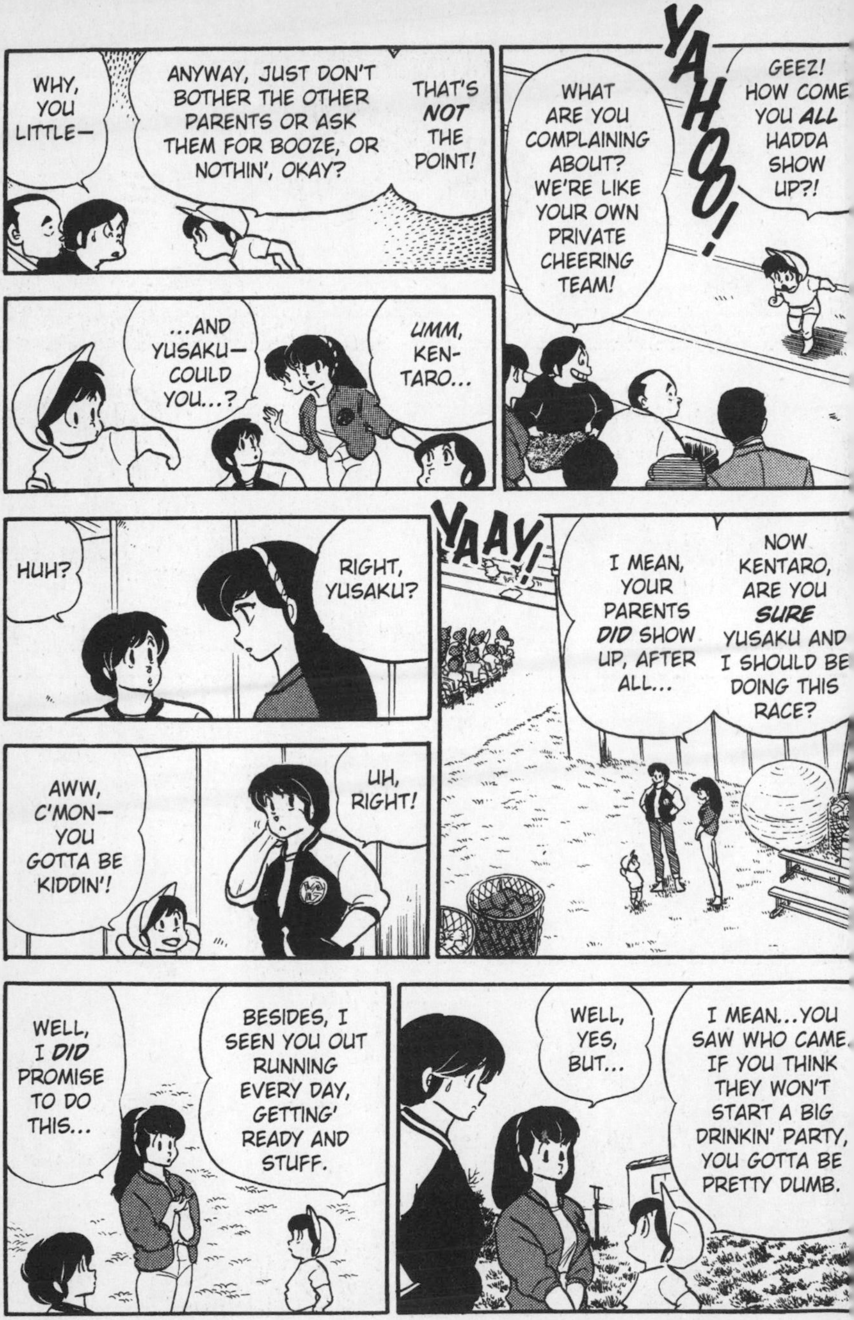
GEEZ! HOW COME YOU **ALL** HADDA SHOW UP?!
YAHOO!
WHAT ARE YOU COMPLAINING ABOUT? WE'RE LIKE YOUR OWN PRIVATE CHEERING TEAM!
THAT'S **NOT** THE POINT!
ANYWAY, JUST DON'T BOTHER THE OTHER PARENTS OR ASK THEM FOR BOOZE, OR NOTHIN', OKAY?
WHY, YOU LITTLE—
UMM, KEN-TARO...
...AND YUSAKU— COULD YOU...?
NOW KENTARO, ARE YOU ***SURE*** YUSAKU AND I SHOULD BE DOING THIS RACE?
I MEAN, YOUR PARENTS ***DID*** SHOW UP, AFTER ALL...
YAAY!
RIGHT, YUSAKU?
HUH?
UH, RIGHT!
AWW, C'MON— YOU GOTTA BE KIDDIN'!
I MEAN...YOU SAW WHO CAME. IF YOU THINK THEY WON'T START A BIG DRINKIN' PARTY, YOU GOTTA BE PRETTY DUMB.
WELL, YES, BUT...
BESIDES, I SEEN YOU OUT RUNNING EVERY DAY, GETTING' READY AND STUFF.
WELL, I ***DID*** PROMISE TO DO THIS...

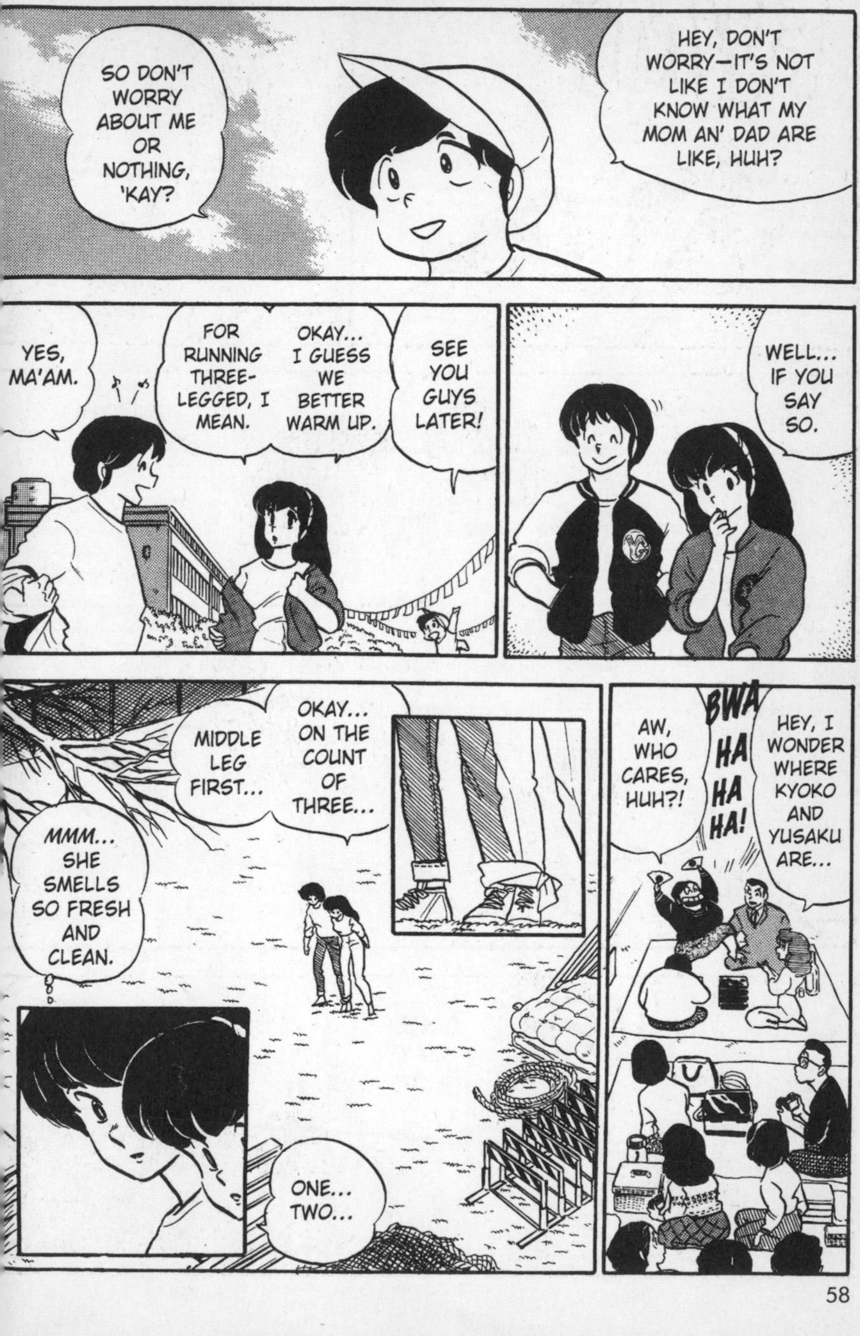
HEY, DON'T WORRY—IT'S NOT LIKE I DON'T KNOW WHAT MY MOM AN' DAD ARE LIKE, HUH?
SO DON'T WORRY ABOUT ME OR NOTHING, 'KAY?
WELL... IF YOU SAY SO.
SEE YOU GUYS LATER!
OKAY... I GUESS WE BETTER WARM UP.
FOR RUNNING THREE-LEGGED, I MEAN.
YES, MA'AM.
HEY, I WONDER WHERE KYOKO AND YUSAKU ARE...
BWA HA HA HA HA!
AW, WHO CARES, HUH?!
OKAY... ON THE COUNT OF THREE...
MIDDLE LEG FIRST...
MMM... SHE SMELLS SO FRESH AND CLEAN.
ONE... TWO...

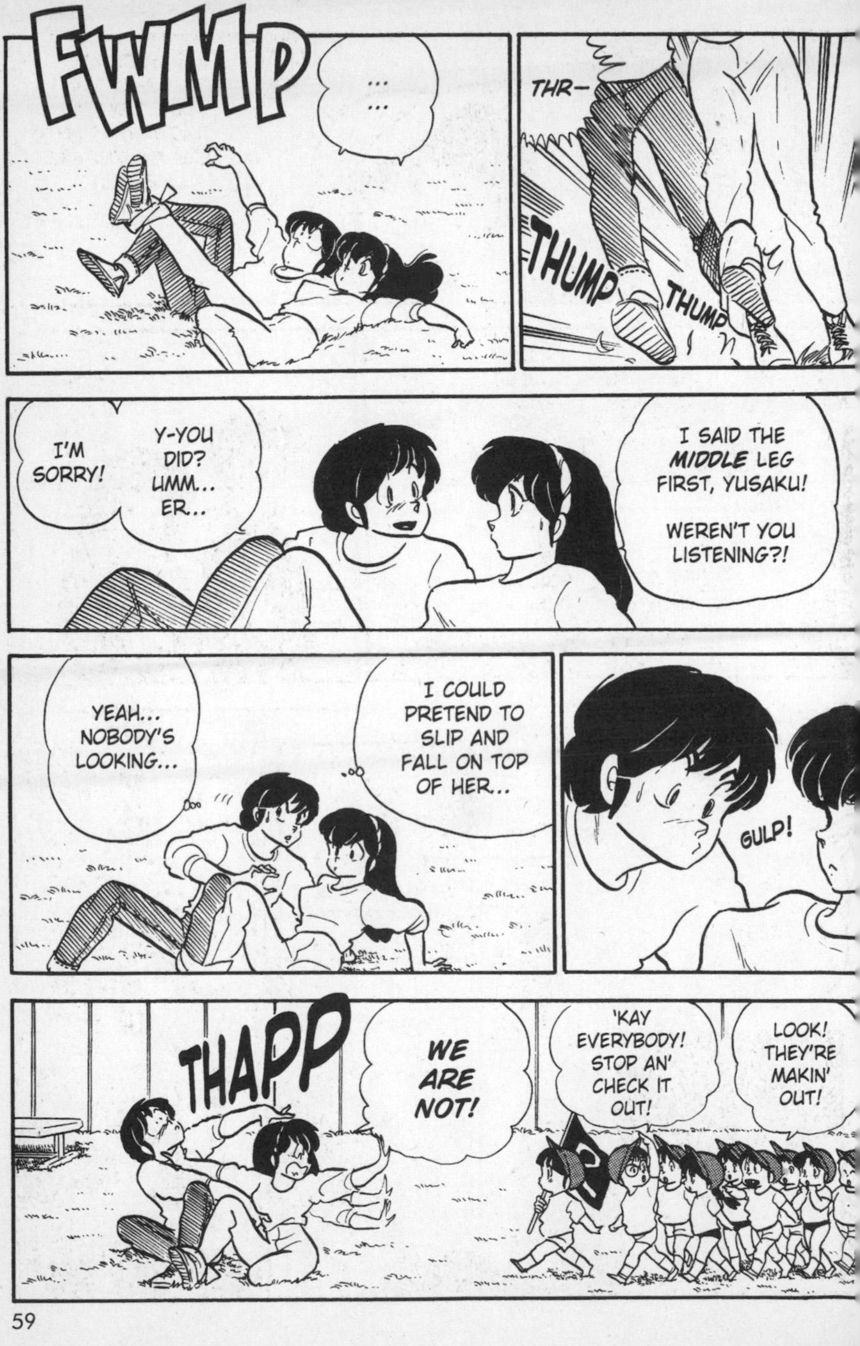
THR—
THUMP
THUMP
FWMP
... ...
I SAID THE *MIDDLE* LEG FIRST, YUSAKU!
WEREN'T YOU LISTENING?!
Y-YOU DID? UMM... ER...
I'M SORRY!
GULP!
I COULD PRETEND TO SLIP AND FALL ON TOP OF HER...
YEAH... NOBODY'S LOOKING...
LOOK! THEY'RE MAKIN' OUT!
'KAY EVERYBODY! STOP AN' CHECK IT OUT!
WE ARE NOT!
THAPP

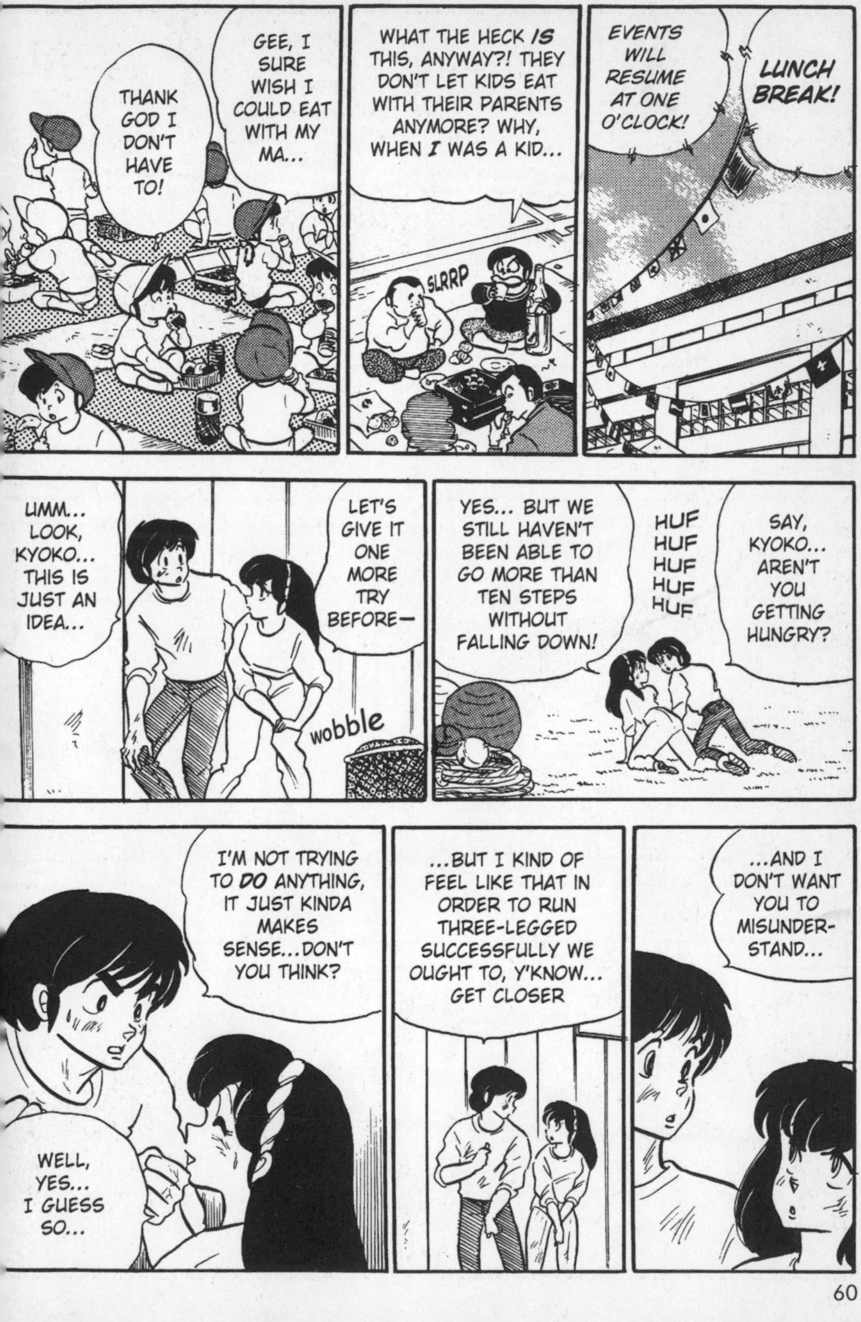
LUNCH BREAK!
EVENTS WILL RESUME AT ONE O'CLOCK!
WHAT THE HECK IS THIS, ANYWAY?! THEY DON'T LET KIDS EAT WITH THEIR PARENTS ANYMORE? WHY, WHEN I WAS A KID...
SLRRP
GEE, I SURE WISH I COULD EAT WITH MY MA...
THANK GOD I DON'T HAVE TO!
SAY, KYOKO... AREN'T YOU GETTING HUNGRY?
HUF HUF HUF HUF HUF
YES... BUT WE STILL HAVEN'T BEEN ABLE TO GO MORE THAN TEN STEPS WITHOUT FALLING DOWN!
LET'S GIVE IT ONE MORE TRY BEFORE—
wobble
UMM... LOOK, KYOKO... THIS IS JUST AN IDEA...
...AND I DON'T WANT YOU TO MISUNDER-STAND...
...BUT I KIND OF FEEL LIKE THAT IN ORDER TO RUN THREE-LEGGED SUCCESSFULLY WE OUGHT TO, Y'KNOW... GET CLOSER
I'M NOT TRYING TO DO ANYTHING, IT JUST KINDA MAKES SENSE...DON'T YOU THINK?
WELL, YES... I GUESS SO...

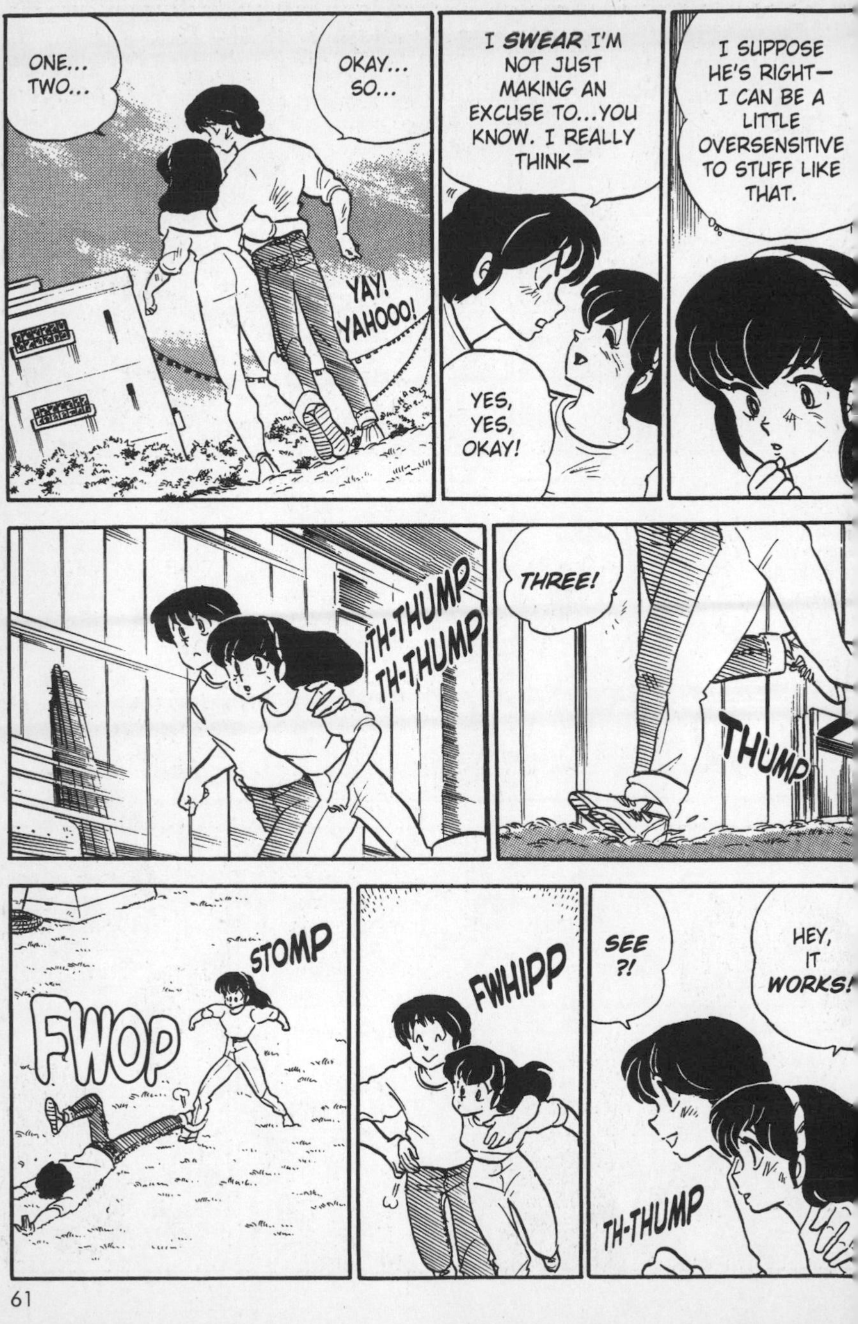
I SUPPOSE HE'S RIGHT— I CAN BE A LITTLE OVERSENSITIVE TO STUFF LIKE THAT.
I SWEAR I'M NOT JUST MAKING AN EXCUSE TO...YOU KNOW. I REALLY THINK—
YES, YES, OKAY!
OKAY... SO...
ONE... TWO...
YAY! YAHOOO!
THREE!
THUMP
TH-THUMP TH-THUMP
HEY, IT WORKS!
SEE ?!
TH-THUMP
FWHIPP
STOMP
FWOP

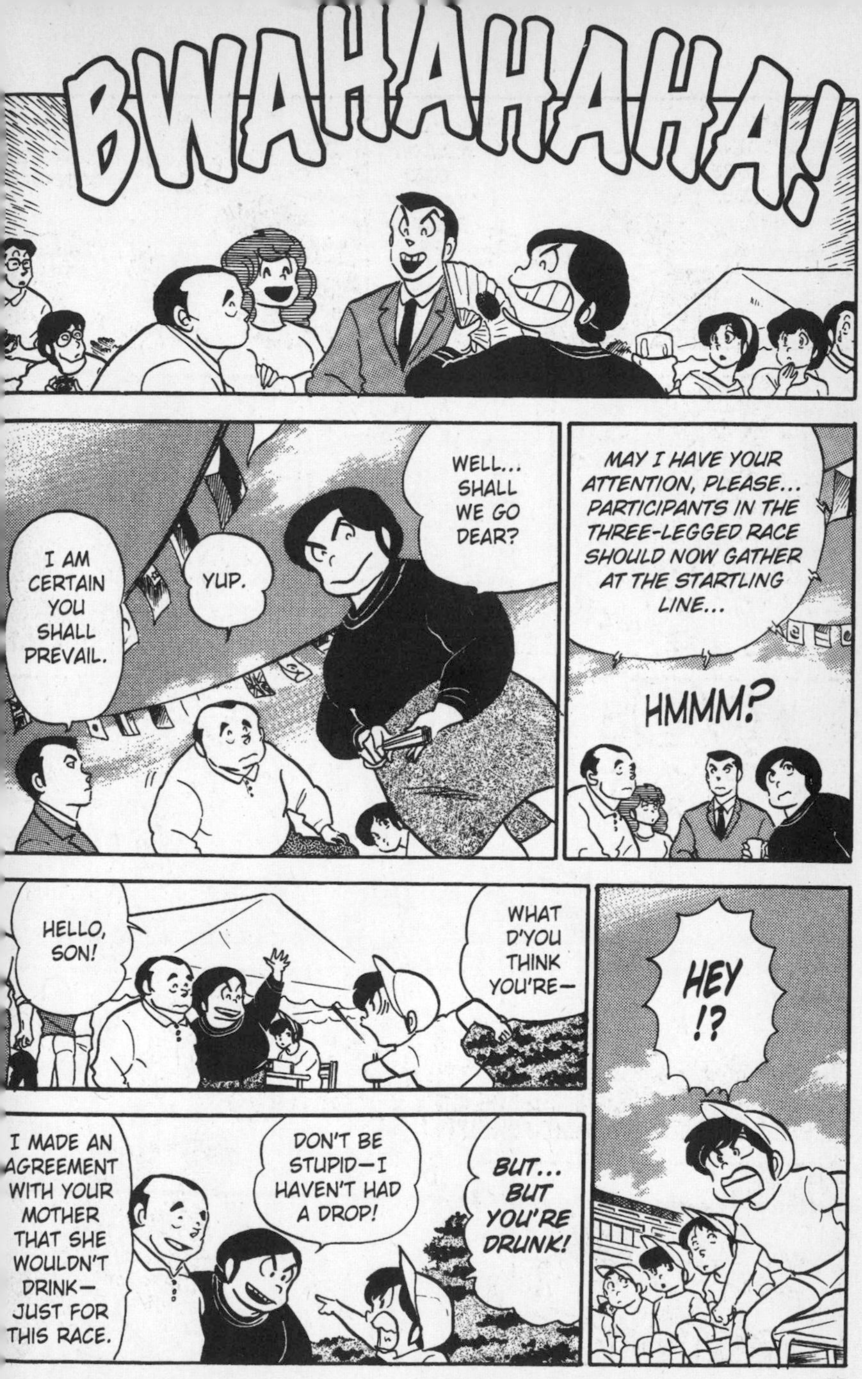
BWAHAHAHA!
MAY I HAVE YOUR ATTENTION, PLEASE... PARTICIPANTS IN THE THREE-LEGGED RACE SHOULD NOW GATHER AT THE STARTLING LINE...
HMMM?
WELL... SHALL WE GO DEAR?
YUP.
I AM CERTAIN YOU SHALL PREVAIL.
HEY !?
WHAT D'YOU THINK YOU'RE—
HELLO, SON!
BUT... BUT YOU'RE DRUNK!
DON'T BE STUPID—I HAVEN'T HAD A DROP!
I MADE AN AGREEMENT WITH YOUR MOTHER THAT SHE WOULDN'T DRINK—JUST FOR THIS RACE.

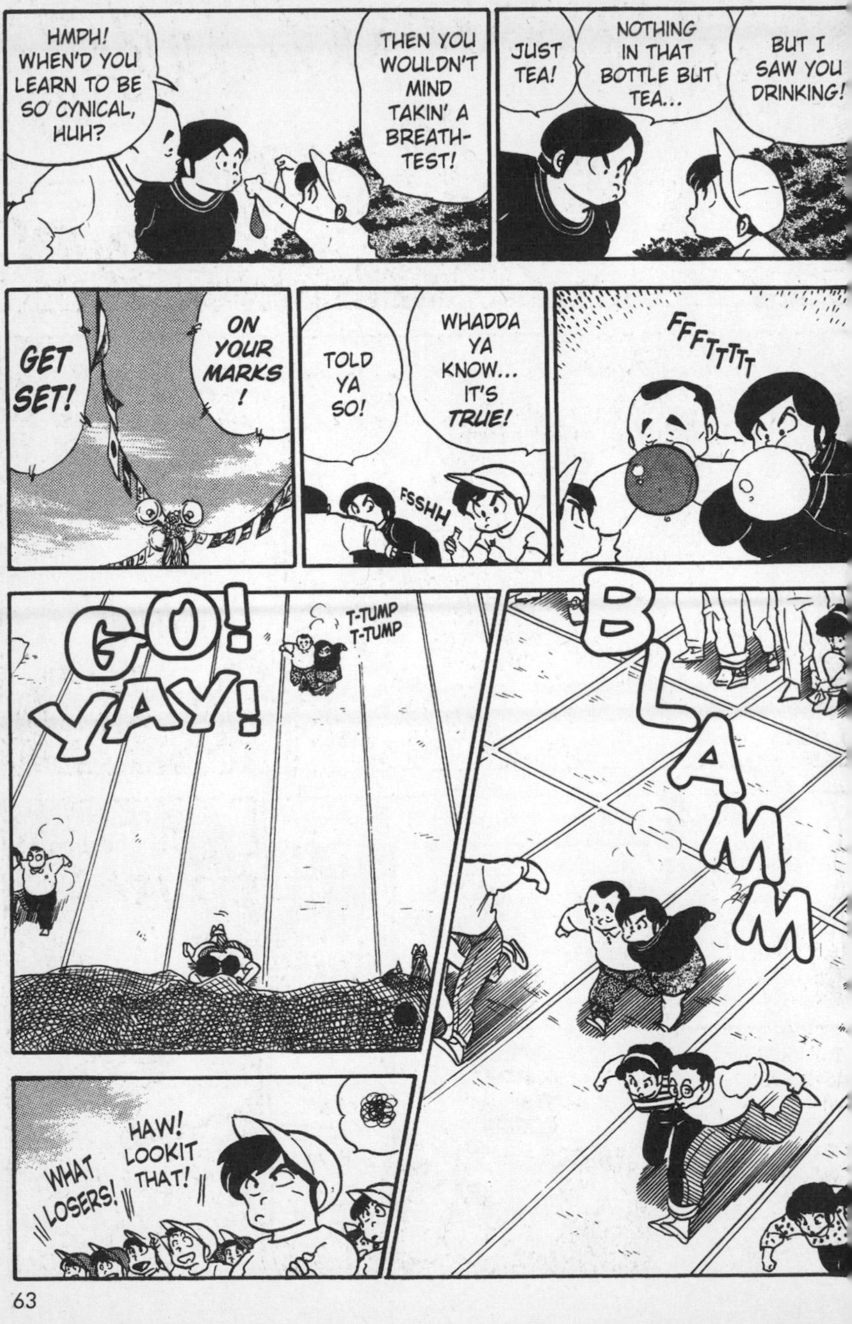
BUT I SAW YOU DRINKING!
NOTHING IN THAT BOTTLE BUT TEA...
JUST TEA!
THEN YOU WOULDN'T MIND TAKIN' A BREATH-TEST!
HMPH! WHEN'D YOU LEARN TO BE SO CYNICAL, HUH?
FFFTTTTTT
WHADDA YA KNOW... IT'S TRUE!
TOLD YA SO!
FSSHH
ON YOUR MARKS!
GET SET!
BLAMM
GO!
YAY!
T-TUMP T-TUMP
HAW! LOOKIT THAT!
WHAT LOSERS!

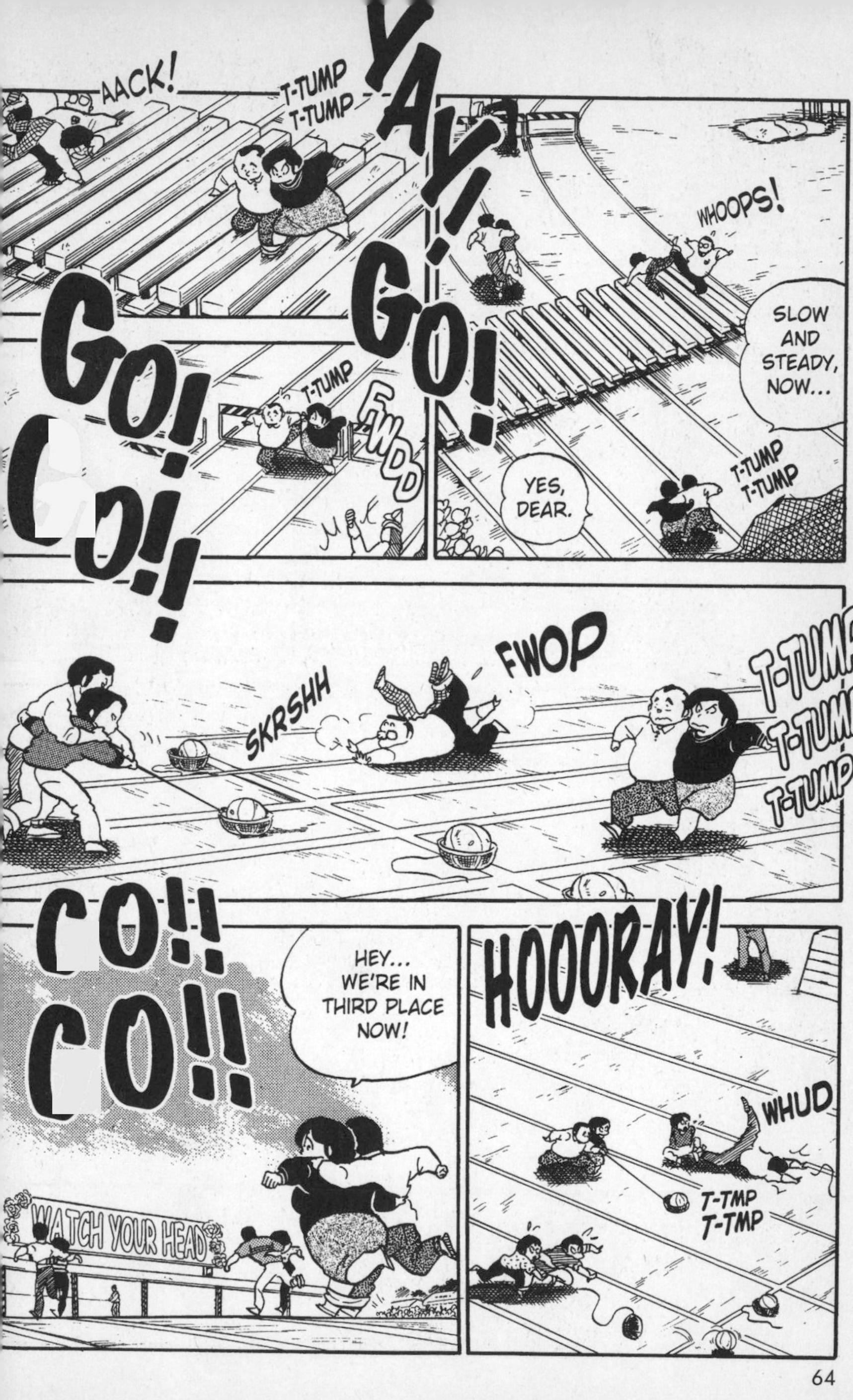
WHOOPS!
SLOW AND STEADY, NOW...
YES, DEAR.
T-TUMP T-TUMP
YAY! GO!
AACK!
T-TUMP T-TUMP
T-TUMP
FWDD
GO!
O!!
T-TUMP T-TUMP T-TUMP
FWOP
SKRSHH
HOOORAY!
WHUD
T-TMP T-TMP
O!!
O!!
HEY... WE'RE IN THIRD PLACE NOW!
WATCH YOUR HEAD

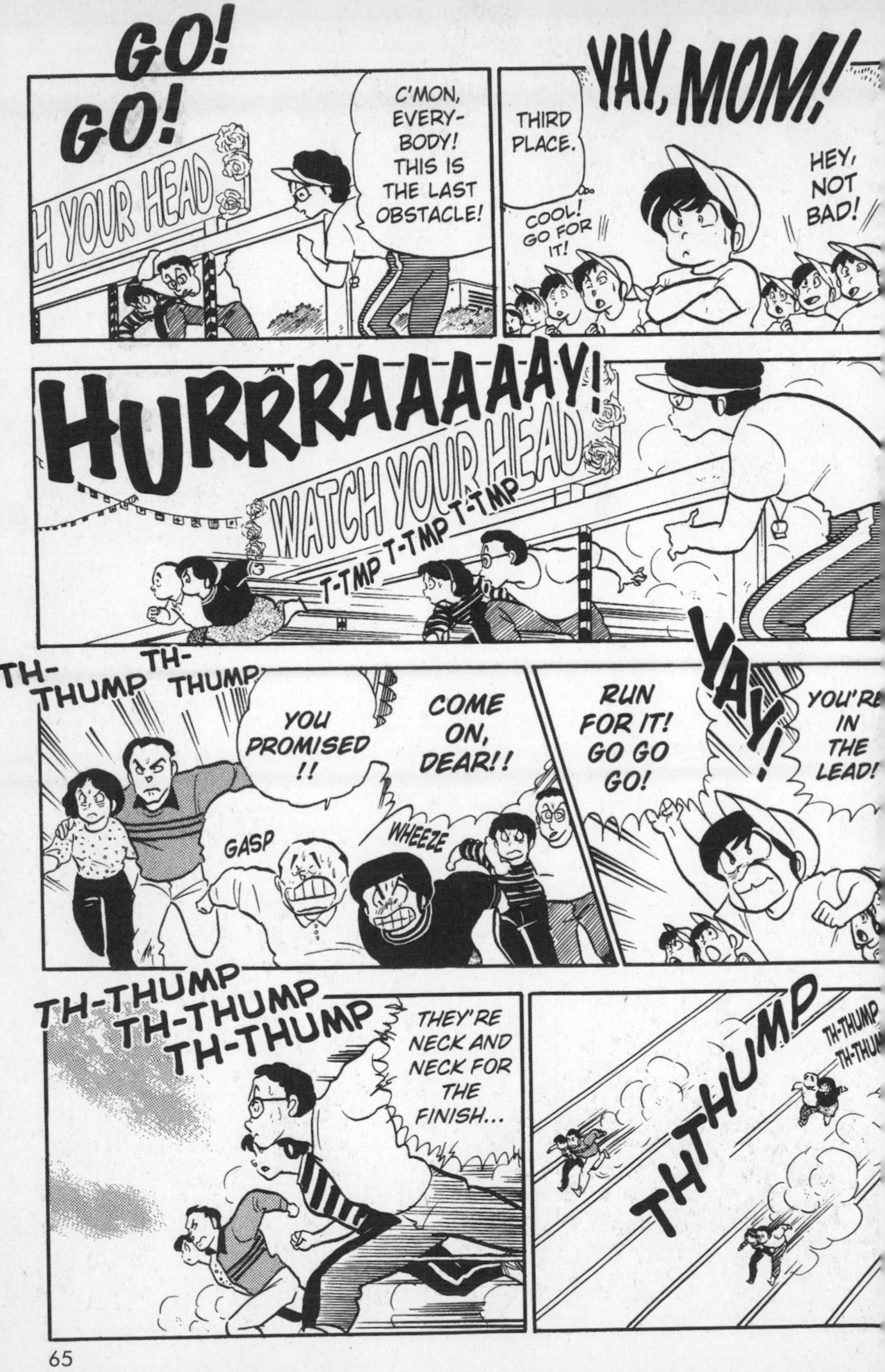
YAY, MOM!
THIRD PLACE.
HEY, NOT BAD!
COOL! GO FOR IT!
GO! GO!
C'MON, EVERY-BODY! THIS IS THE LAST OBSTACLE!
H YOUR HEAD
HURRRAAAAAY!
WATCH YOUR HEAD
T-TMP T-TMP T-TMP T-TMP
YAY!
YOU'R IN THE LEAD!
RUN FOR IT! GO GO GO!
TH-THUMP TH-THUMP
COME ON, DEAR!!
YOU PROMISED!!
GASP
WHEEZE
THTHUMP
TH-THUMP TH-THUM
TH-THUMP TH-THUMP TH-THUMP
THEY'RE NECK AND NECK FOR THE FINISH...

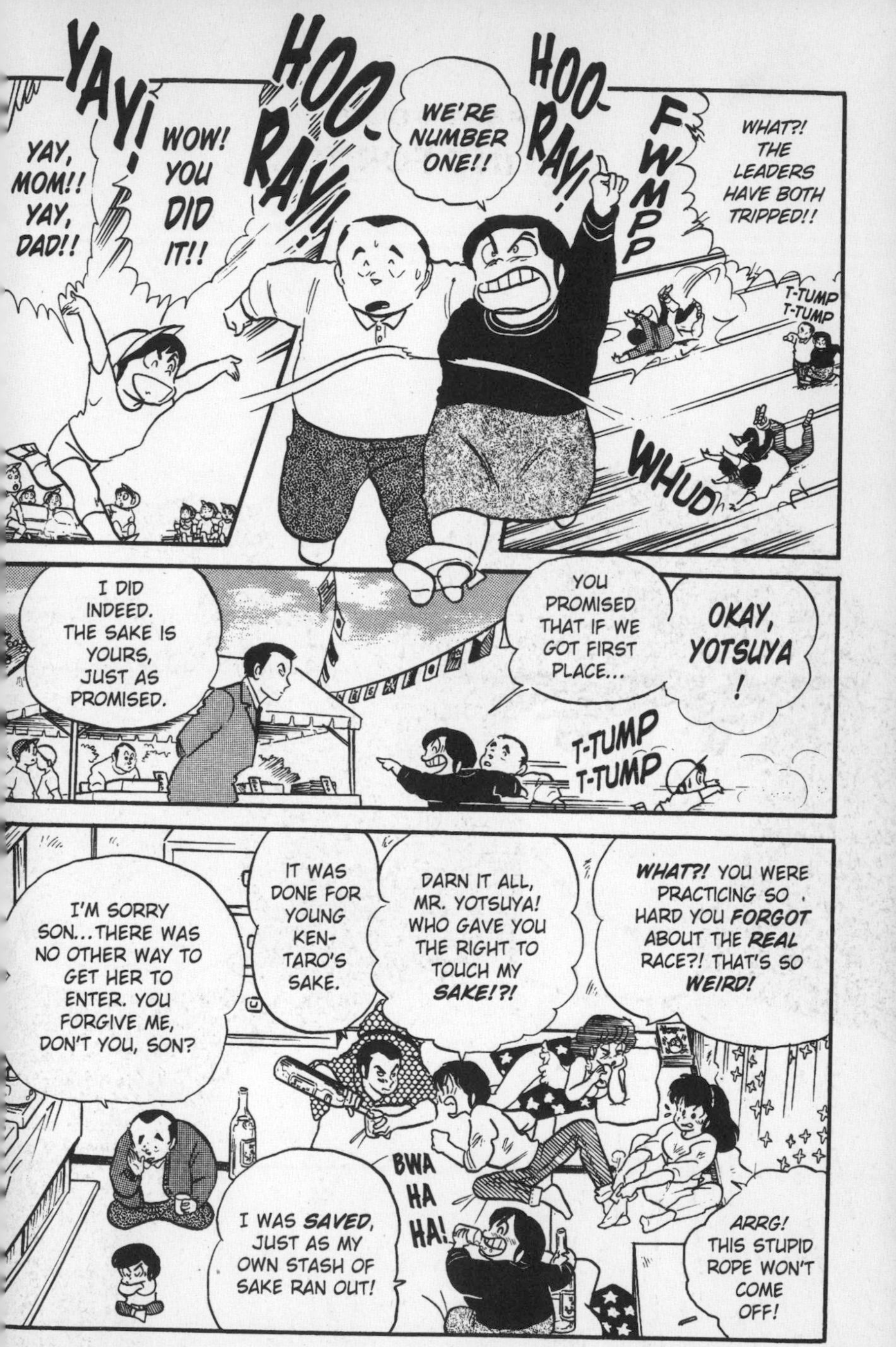
WHAT?! THE LEADERS HAVE BOTH TRIPPED!!
FWMPP
HOO-RAY!
T-TUMP T-TUMP
WHUD
WE'RE NUMBER ONE!!
HOO-RAY!
WOW! YOU DID IT!!
YAY!
YAY, MOM!! YAY, DAD!!
OKAY, YOTSUYA!
YOU PROMISED THAT IF WE GOT FIRST PLACE...
T-TUMP T-TUMP
I DID INDEED. THE SAKE IS YOURS, JUST AS PROMISED.
WHAT?! YOU WERE PRACTICING SO HARD YOU FORGOT ABOUT THE REAL RACE?! THAT'S SO WEIRD!
DARN IT ALL, MR. YOTSUYA! WHO GAVE YOU THE RIGHT TO TOUCH MY SAKE!?!
IT WAS DONE FOR YOUNG KEN-TARO'S SAKE.
I'M SORRY SON...THERE WAS NO OTHER WAY TO GET HER TO ENTER. YOU FORGIVE ME, DON'T YOU, SON?
ARRG! THIS STUPID ROPE WON'T COME OFF!
BWA HA HA!
I WAS SAVED, JUST AS MY OWN STASH OF SAKE RAN OUT!

PART FOUR

FALLING FOR YOU

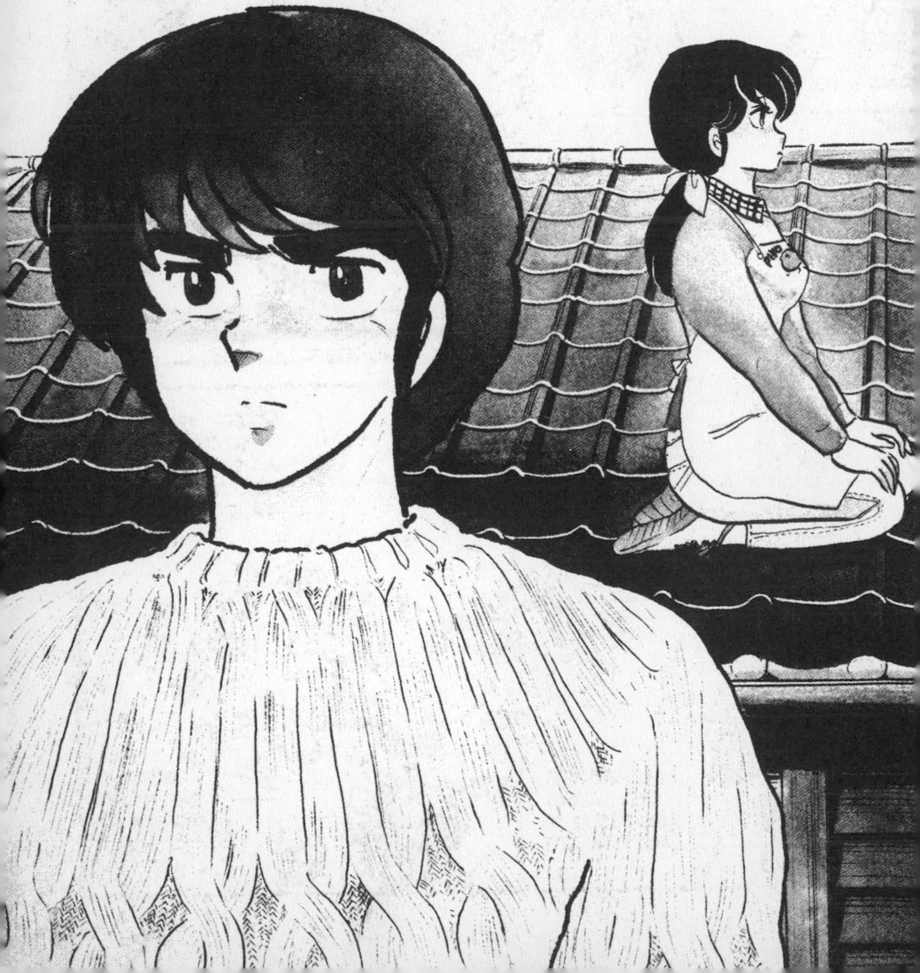

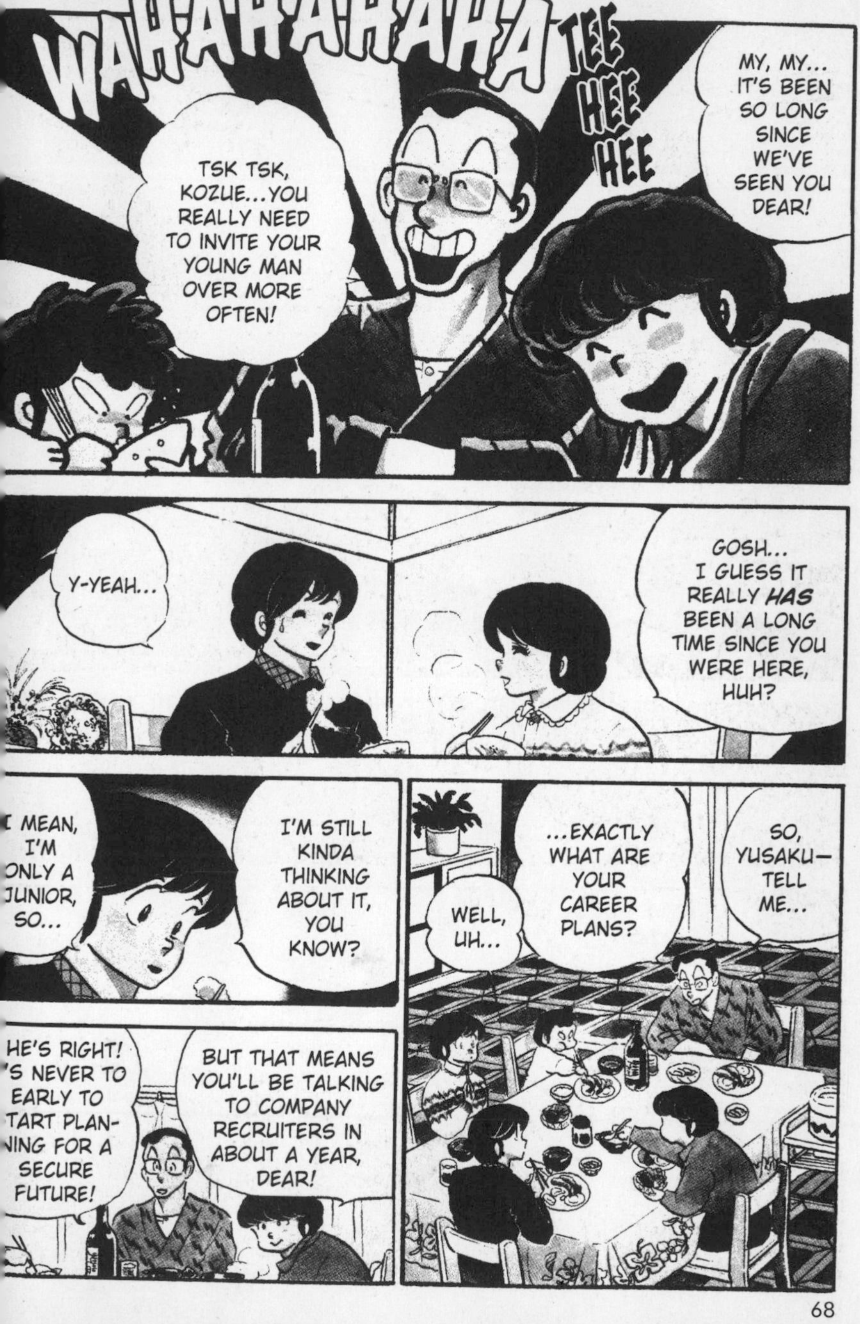
MY, MY... IT'S BEEN SO LONG SINCE WE'VE SEEN YOU DEAR!
TEE HEE HEE
WAHAHAHAHAHA
TSK TSK, KOZUE...YOU REALLY NEED TO INVITE YOUR YOUNG MAN OVER MORE OFTEN!
GOSH... I GUESS IT REALLY HAS BEEN A LONG TIME SINCE YOU WERE HERE, HUH?
Y-YEAH...
SO, YUSAKU— TELL ME...
...EXACTLY WHAT ARE YOUR CAREER PLANS?
WELL, UH...
I'M STILL KINDA THINKING ABOUT IT, YOU KNOW?
I MEAN, I'M ONLY A JUNIOR, SO...
BUT THAT MEANS YOU'LL BE TALKING TO COMPANY RECRUITERS IN ABOUT A YEAR, DEAR!
HE'S RIGHT! 'S NEVER TO EARLY TO TART PLAN-NING FOR A SECURE FUTURE!

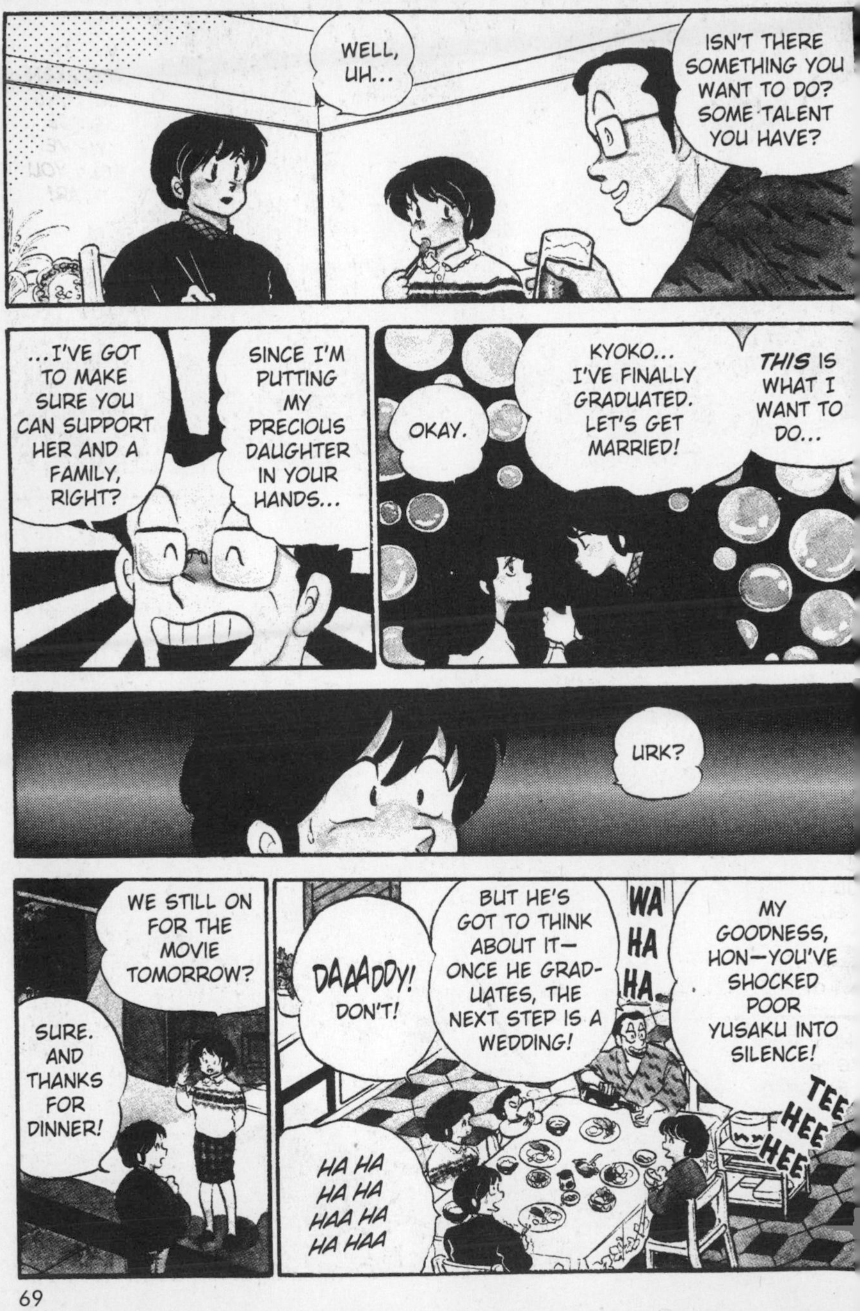
ISN'T THERE SOMETHING YOU WANT TO DO? SOME TALENT YOU HAVE?
WELL, UH...
THIS IS WHAT I WANT TO DO...
KYOKO... I'VE FINALLY GRADUATED. LET'S GET MARRIED!
OKAY.
SINCE I'M PUTTING MY PRECIOUS DAUGHTER IN YOUR HANDS...
...I'VE GOT TO MAKE SURE YOU CAN SUPPORT HER AND A FAMILY, RIGHT?
URK?
MY GOODNESS, HON—YOU'VE SHOCKED POOR YUSAKU INTO SILENCE!
WA HA HA
BUT HE'S GOT TO THINK ABOUT IT—ONCE HE GRAD-UATES, THE NEXT STEP IS A WEDDING!
DAAADDY! DON'T!
TEE HEE HEE
HA HA HA HA HAA HA HA HAA
WE STILL ON FOR THE MOVIE TOMORROW?
SURE. AND THANKS FOR DINNER!

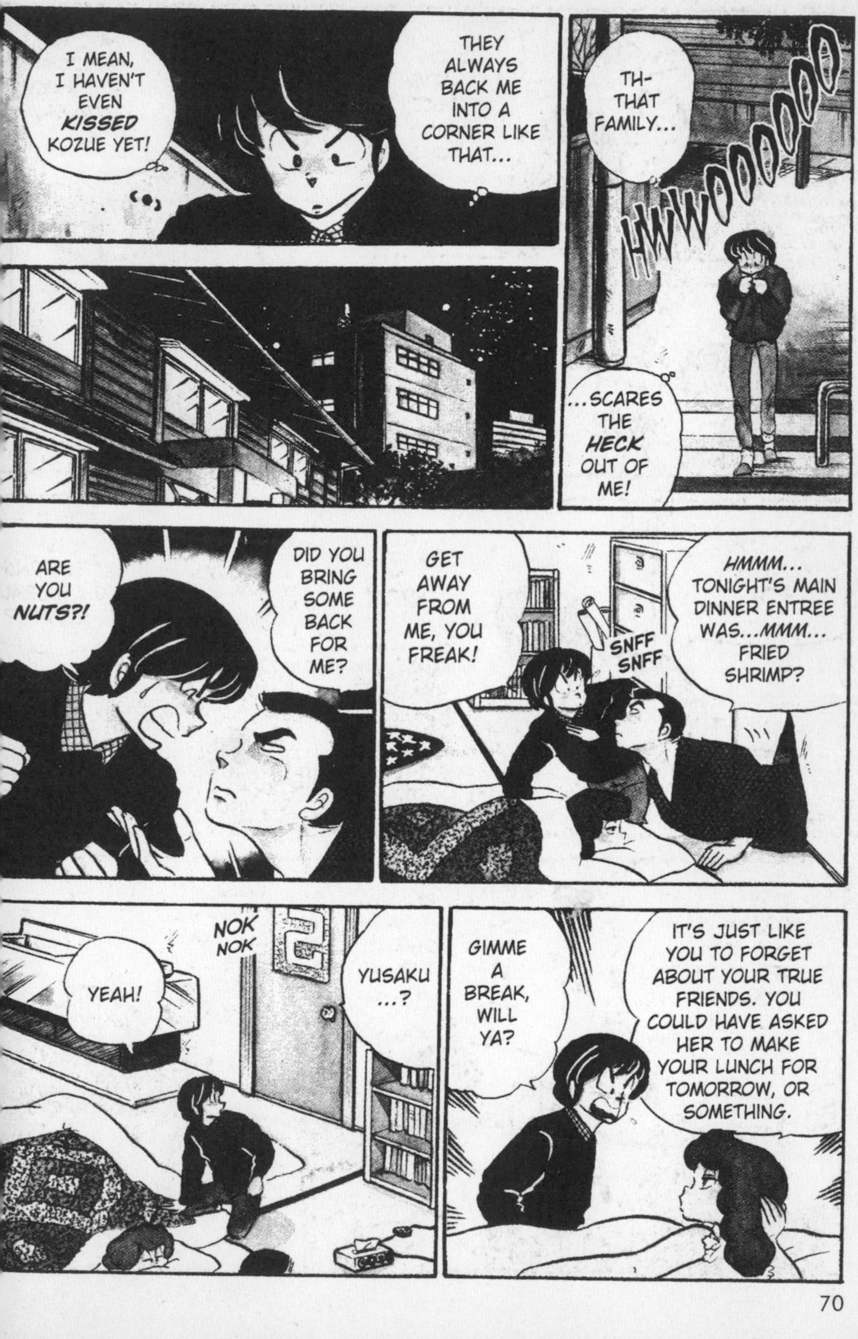
TH-THAT FAMILY...
HWOOOOOO
...SCARES THE *HECK* OUT OF ME!
THEY ALWAYS BACK ME INTO A CORNER LIKE THAT...
I MEAN, I HAVEN'T EVEN *KISSED* KOZUE YET!
HMMM... TONIGHT'S MAIN DINNER ENTREE WAS...MMM... FRIED SHRIMP?
SNFF SNFF
GET AWAY FROM ME, YOU FREAK!
DID YOU BRING SOME BACK FOR ME?
ARE YOU *NUTS?!*
IT'S JUST LIKE YOU TO FORGET ABOUT YOUR TRUE FRIENDS. YOU COULD HAVE ASKED HER TO MAKE YOUR LUNCH FOR TOMORROW, OR SOMETHING.
GIMME A BREAK, WILL YA?
YUSAKU ...?
NOK NOK
YEAH!

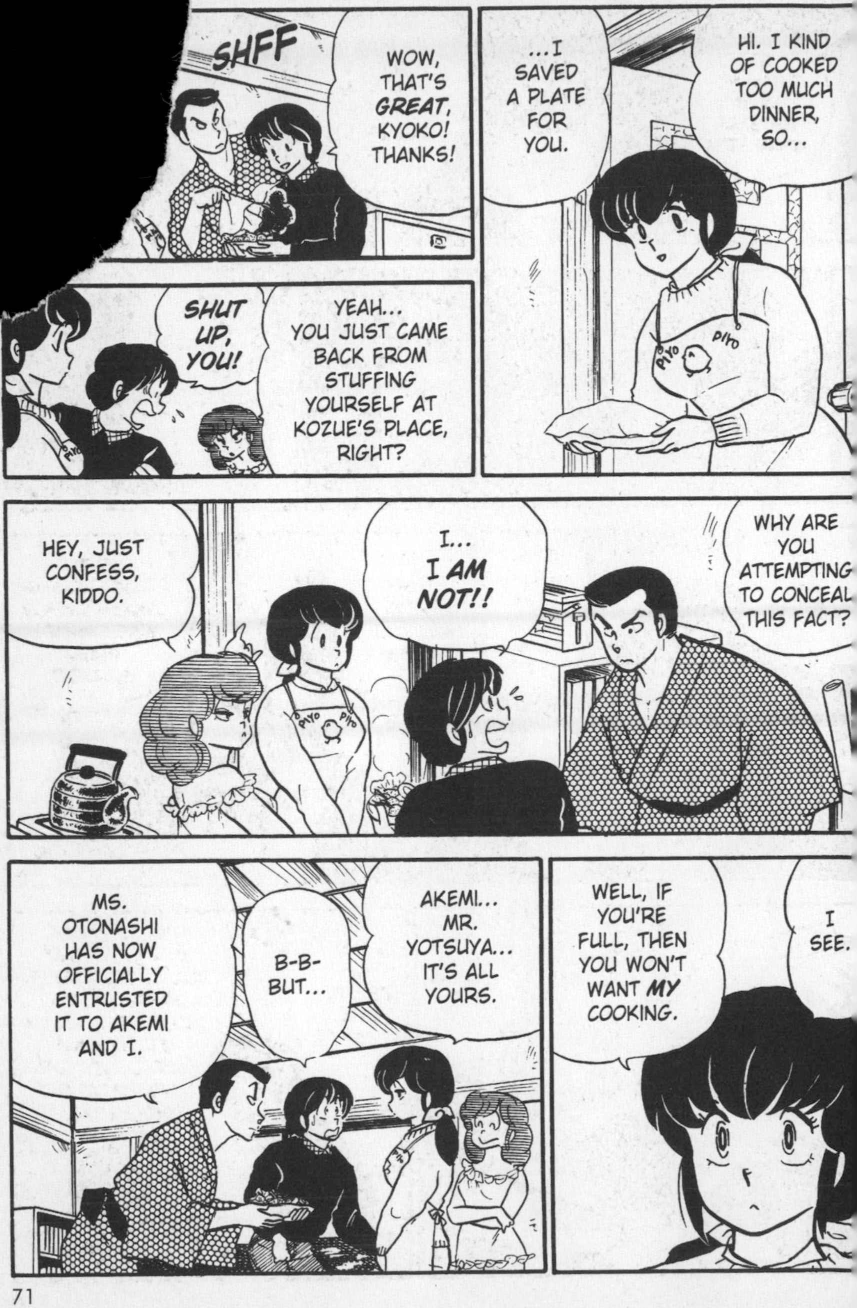
HI. I KIND OF COOKED TOO MUCH DINNER, SO...
...I SAVED A PLATE FOR YOU.
WOW, THAT'S GREAT, KYOKO! THANKS!
SHFF
YEAH... YOU JUST CAME BACK FROM STUFFING YOURSELF AT KOZUE'S PLACE, RIGHT?
SHUT UP, YOU!
WHY ARE YOU ATTEMPTING TO CONCEAL THIS FACT?
I... I AM NOT!!
HEY, JUST CONFESS, KIDDO.
I SEE.
WELL, IF YOU'RE FULL, THEN YOU WON'T WANT MY COOKING.
AKEMI... MR. YOTSUYA... IT'S ALL YOURS.
B-B-BUT...
MS. OTONASHI HAS NOW OFFICIALLY ENTRUSTED IT TO AKEMI AND I.

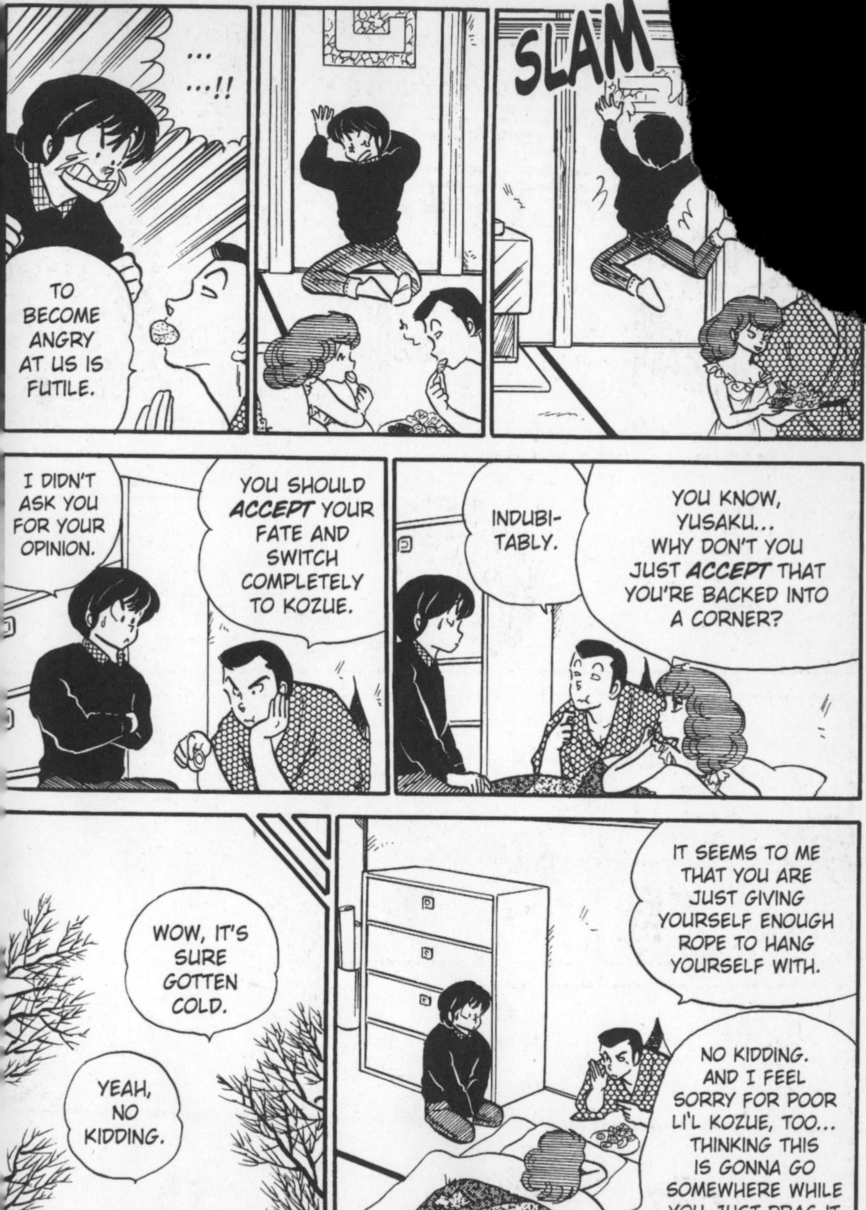
SLAM
...
...!!
TO BECOME ANGRY AT US IS FUTILE.
YOU KNOW, YUSAKU... WHY DON'T YOU JUST ACCEPT THAT YOU'RE BACKED INTO A CORNER?
INDUBITABLY.
YOU SHOULD ACCEPT YOUR FATE AND SWITCH COMPLETELY TO KOZUE.
I DIDN'T ASK YOU FOR YOUR OPINION.
IT SEEMS TO ME THAT YOU ARE JUST GIVING YOURSELF ENOUGH ROPE TO HANG YOURSELF WITH.
NO KIDDING. AND I FEEL SORRY FOR POOR LI'L KOZUE, TOO... THINKING THIS IS GONNA GO SOMEWHERE WHILE YOU JUST DRAG IT ON AND ON AND ON...
WOW, IT'S SURE GOTTEN COLD.
YEAH, NO KIDDING.

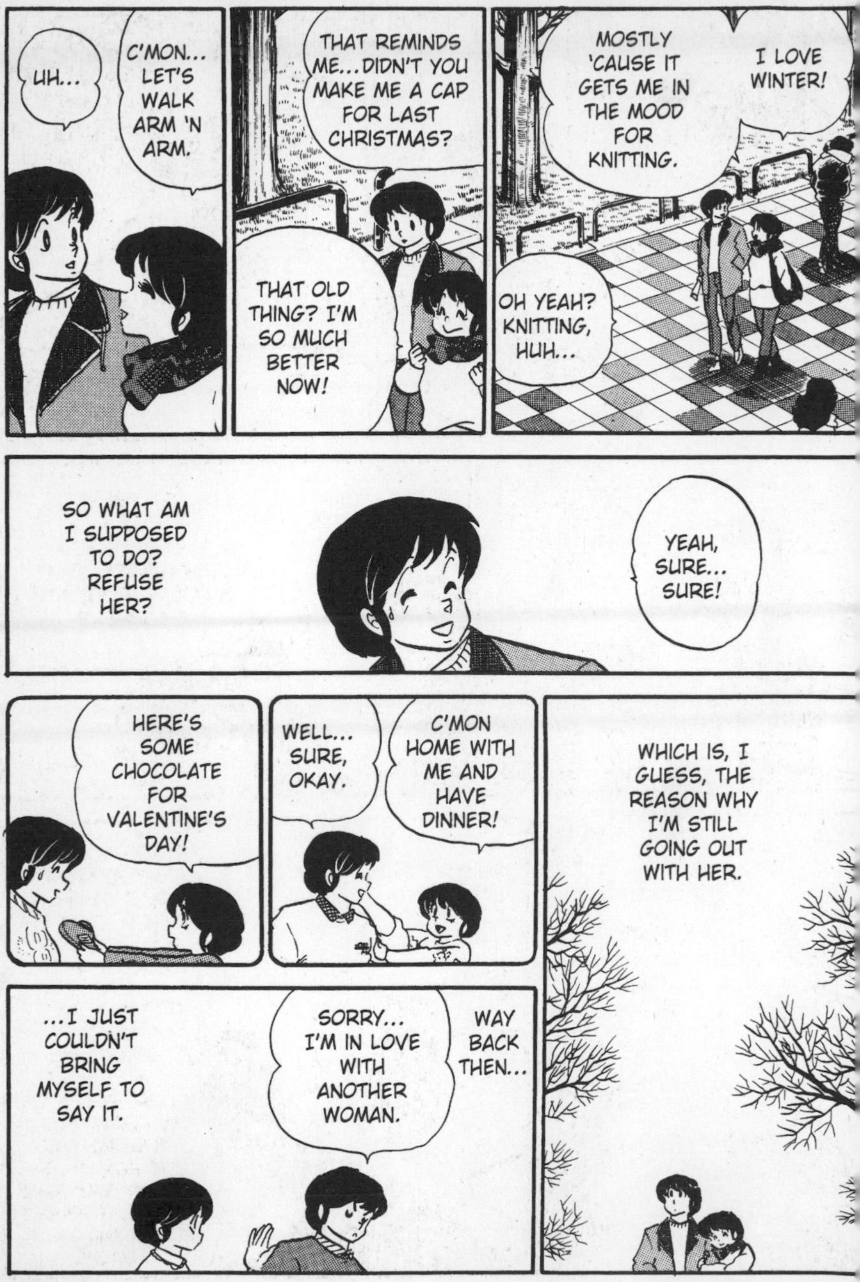
I LOVE WINTER!
MOSTLY 'CAUSE IT GETS ME IN THE MOOD FOR KNITTING.
OH YEAH? KNITTING, HUH...
THAT REMINDS ME...DIDN'T YOU MAKE ME A CAP FOR LAST CHRISTMAS?
THAT OLD THING? I'M SO MUCH BETTER NOW!
C'MON... LET'S WALK ARM 'N ARM.
UH...
YEAH, SURE... SURE!
SO WHAT AM I SUPPOSED TO DO? REFUSE HER?
WHICH IS, I GUESS, THE REASON WHY I'M STILL GOING OUT WITH HER.
C'MON HOME WITH ME AND HAVE DINNER!
WELL... SURE, OKAY.
HERE'S SOME CHOCOLATE FOR VALENTINE'S DAY!
WAY BACK THEN...
SORRY... I'M IN LOVE WITH ANOTHER WOMAN.
...I JUST COULDN'T BRING MYSELF TO SAY IT.

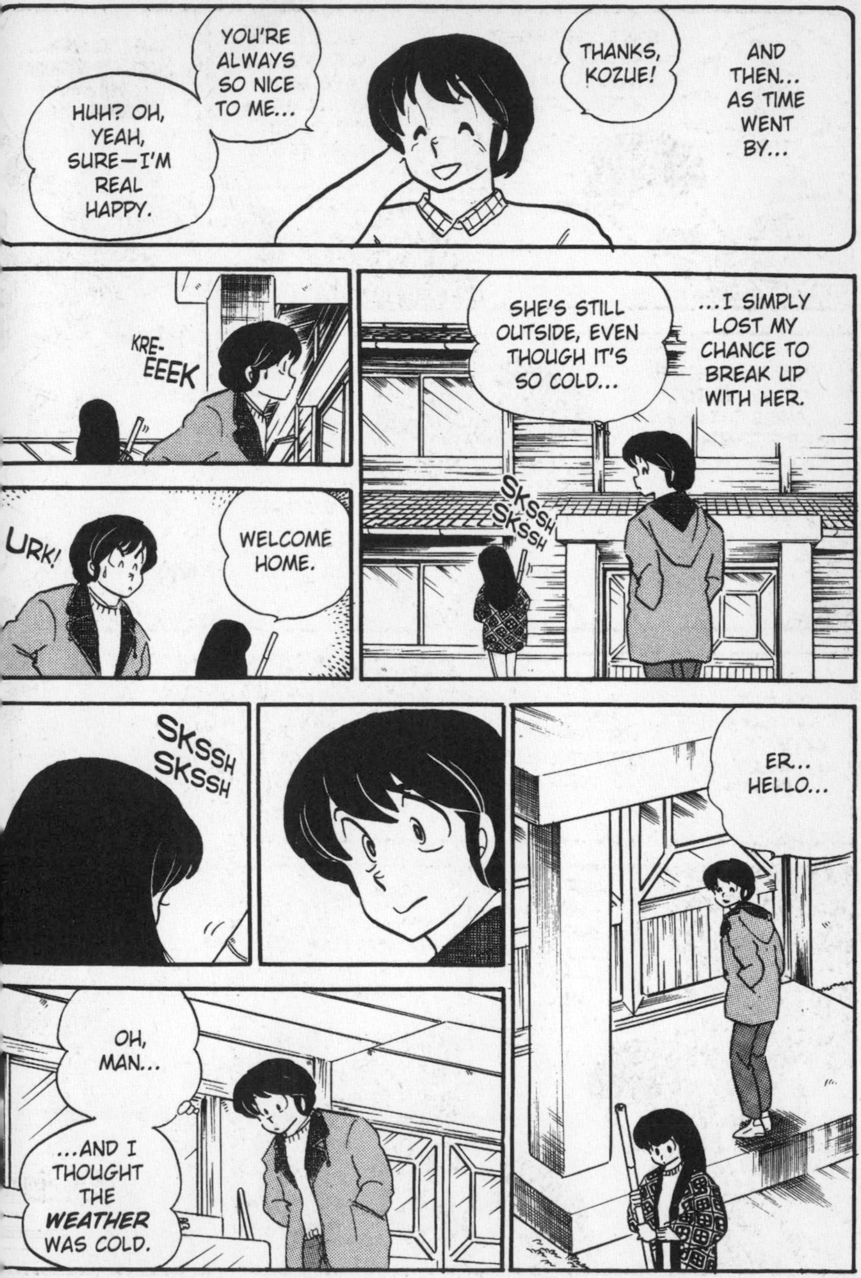
AND THEN... AS TIME WENT BY...
THANKS, KOZUE!
YOU'RE ALWAYS SO NICE TO ME...
HUH? OH, YEAH, SURE—I'M REAL HAPPY.
...I SIMPLY LOST MY CHANCE TO BREAK UP WITH HER.
SHE'S STILL OUTSIDE, EVEN THOUGH IT'S SO COLD...
SKSSH SKSSH
KRE-EEEK
WELCOME HOME.
URK!
ER... HELLO...
SKSSH SKSSH
OH, MAN...
...AND I THOUGHT THE *WEATHER* WAS COLD.

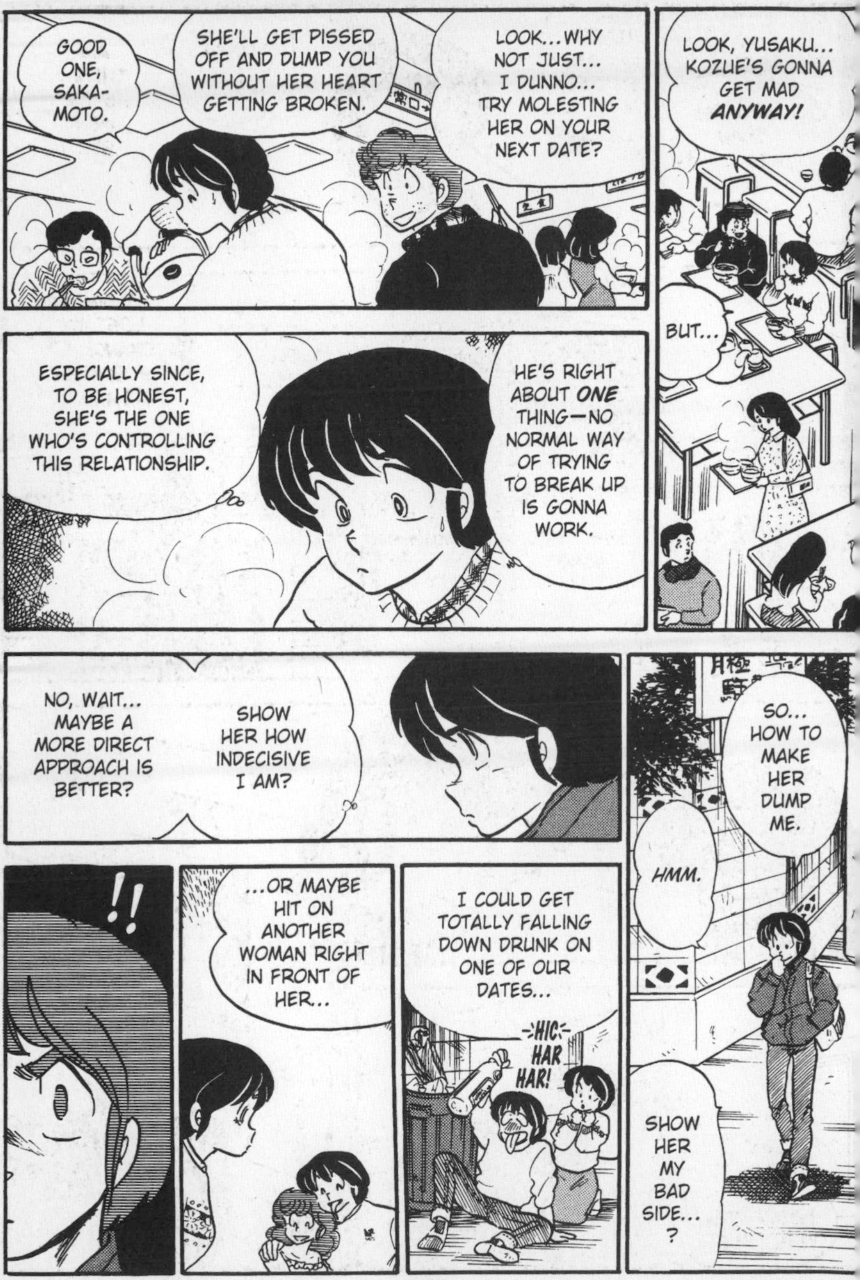
LOOK, YUSAKU... KOZUE'S GONNA GET MAD ANYWAY!
BUT...
LOOK...WHY NOT JUST... I DUNNO... TRY MOLESTING HER ON YOUR NEXT DATE?
SHE'LL GET PISSED OFF AND DUMP YOU WITHOUT HER HEART GETTING BROKEN.
GOOD ONE, SAKA-MOTO.
HE'S RIGHT ABOUT ONE THING—NO NORMAL WAY OF TRYING TO BREAK UP IS GONNA WORK.
ESPECIALLY SINCE, TO BE HONEST, SHE'S THE ONE WHO'S CONTROLLING THIS RELATIONSHIP.
SO... HOW TO MAKE HER DUMP ME.
HMM.
SHOW HER MY BAD SIDE...?
SHOW HER HOW INDECISIVE I AM?
NO, WAIT... MAYBE A MORE DIRECT APPROACH IS BETTER?
I COULD GET TOTALLY FALLING DOWN DRUNK ON ONE OF OUR DATES...
-HIC-
HAR HAR!
...OR MAYBE HIT ON ANOTHER WOMAN RIGHT IN FRONT OF HER...
!!

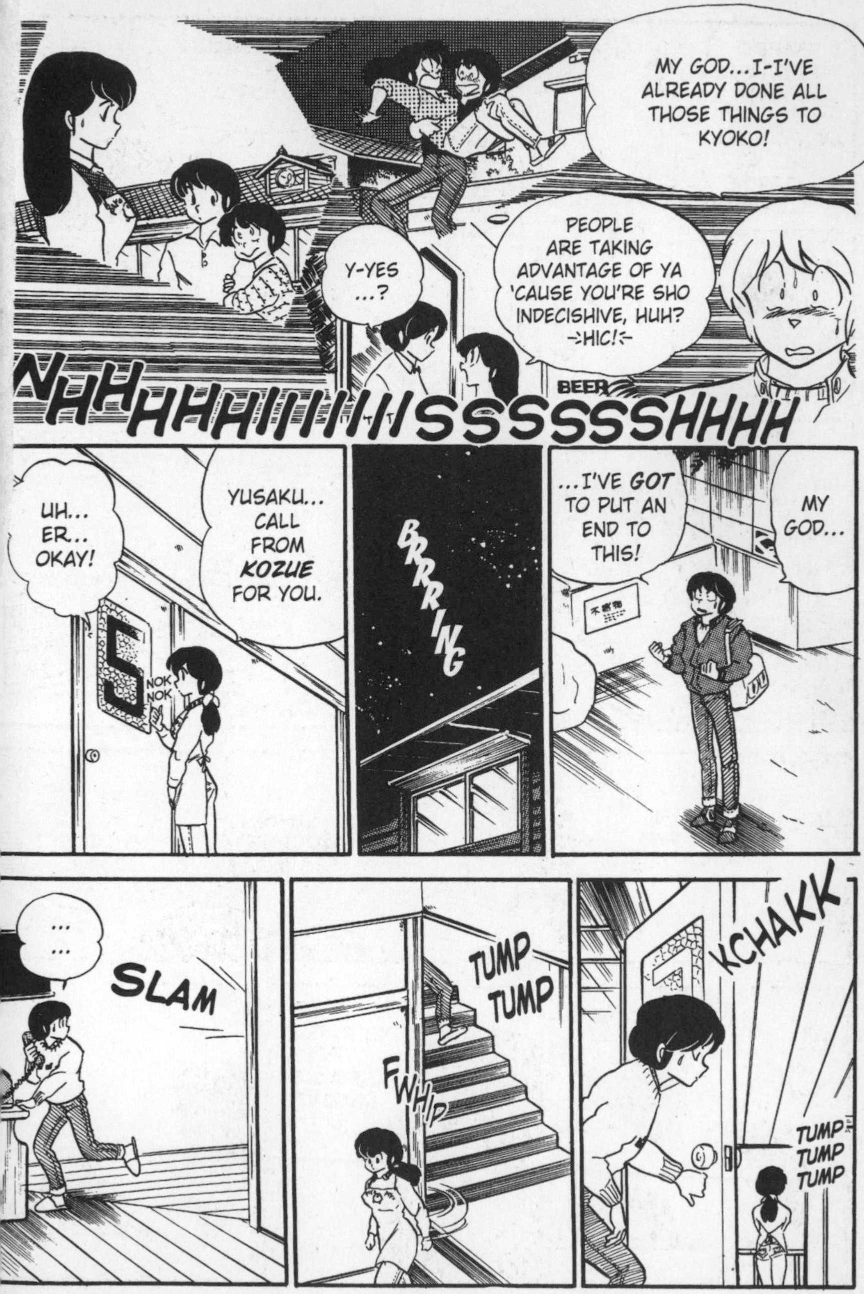
MY GOD...I-I'VE ALREADY DONE ALL THOSE THINGS TO KYOKO!
PEOPLE ARE TAKING ADVANTAGE OF YA 'CAUSE YOU'RE SHO INDECISHIVE, HUH? -HIC!-
Y-YES ...?
BEER
NHHHHIIIIIIISSSSSSSHHHH
MY GOD...
...I'VE GOT TO PUT AN END TO THIS!
BRRRING
YUSAKU... CALL FROM KOZUE FOR YOU.
UH... ER... OKAY!
NOK NOK
KCHAKK
TUMP TUMP TUMP
TUMP TUMP
FWHIP
SLAM
... ...

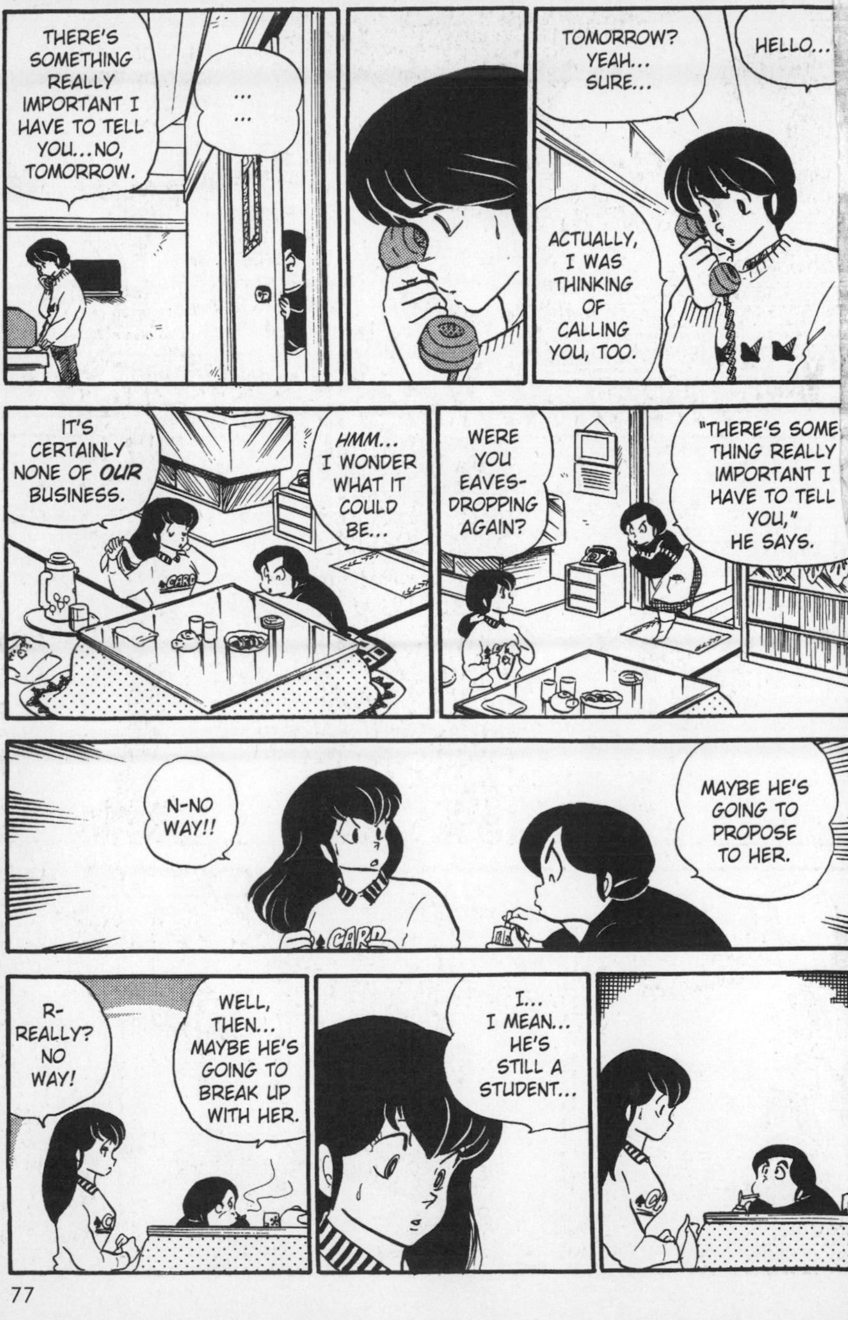
HELLO...
TOMORROW? YEAH... SURE...
ACTUALLY, I WAS THINKING OF CALLING YOU, TOO.
... ...
THERE'S SOMETHING REALLY IMPORTANT I HAVE TO TELL YOU...NO, TOMORROW.
"THERE'S SOME THING REALLY IMPORTANT I HAVE TO TELL YOU," HE SAYS.
WERE YOU EAVES-DROPPING AGAIN?
HMM... I WONDER WHAT IT COULD BE...
IT'S CERTAINLY NONE OF OUR BUSINESS.
MAYBE HE'S GOING TO PROPOSE TO HER.
N-NO WAY!!
I... I MEAN... HE'S STILL A STUDENT...
WELL, THEN... MAYBE HE'S GOING TO BREAK UP WITH HER.
R-REALLY? NO WAY!

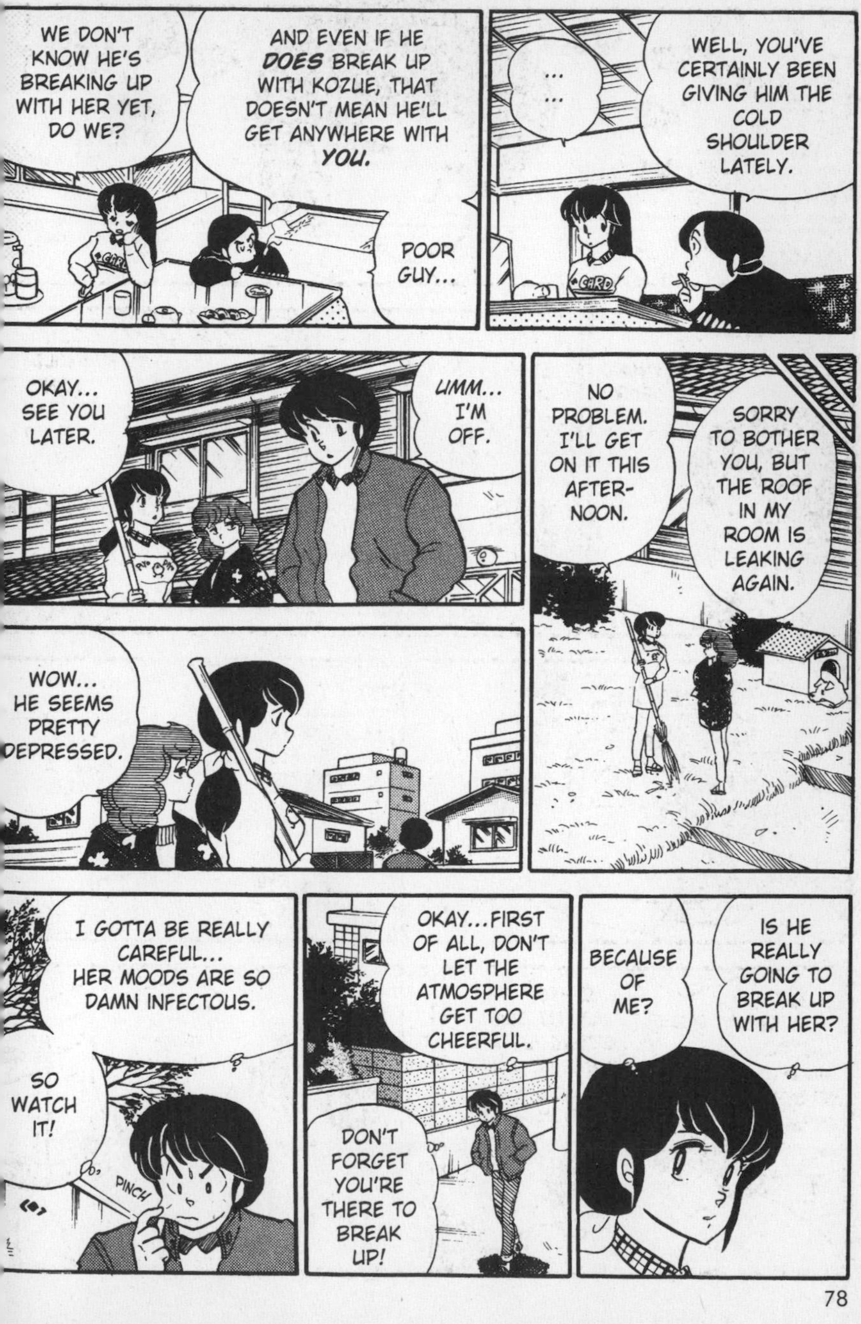
WELL, YOU'VE CERTAINLY BEEN GIVING HIM THE COLD SHOULDER LATELY.
... ...
AND EVEN IF HE DOES BREAK UP WITH KOZUE, THAT DOESN'T MEAN HE'LL GET ANYWHERE WITH YOU.
WE DON'T KNOW HE'S BREAKING UP WITH HER YET, DO WE?
POOR GUY...
SORRY TO BOTHER YOU, BUT THE ROOF IN MY ROOM IS LEAKING AGAIN.
NO PROBLEM. I'LL GET ON IT THIS AFTERNOON.
UMM... I'M OFF.
OKAY... SEE YOU LATER.
WOW... HE SEEMS PRETTY DEPRESSED.
IS HE REALLY GOING TO BREAK UP WITH HER?
BECAUSE OF ME?
OKAY...FIRST OF ALL, DON'T LET THE ATMOSPHERE GET TOO CHEERFUL.
DON'T FORGET YOU'RE THERE TO BREAK UP!
I GOTTA BE REALLY CAREFUL... HER MOODS ARE SO DAMN INFECTOUS.
SO WATCH IT!
PINCH

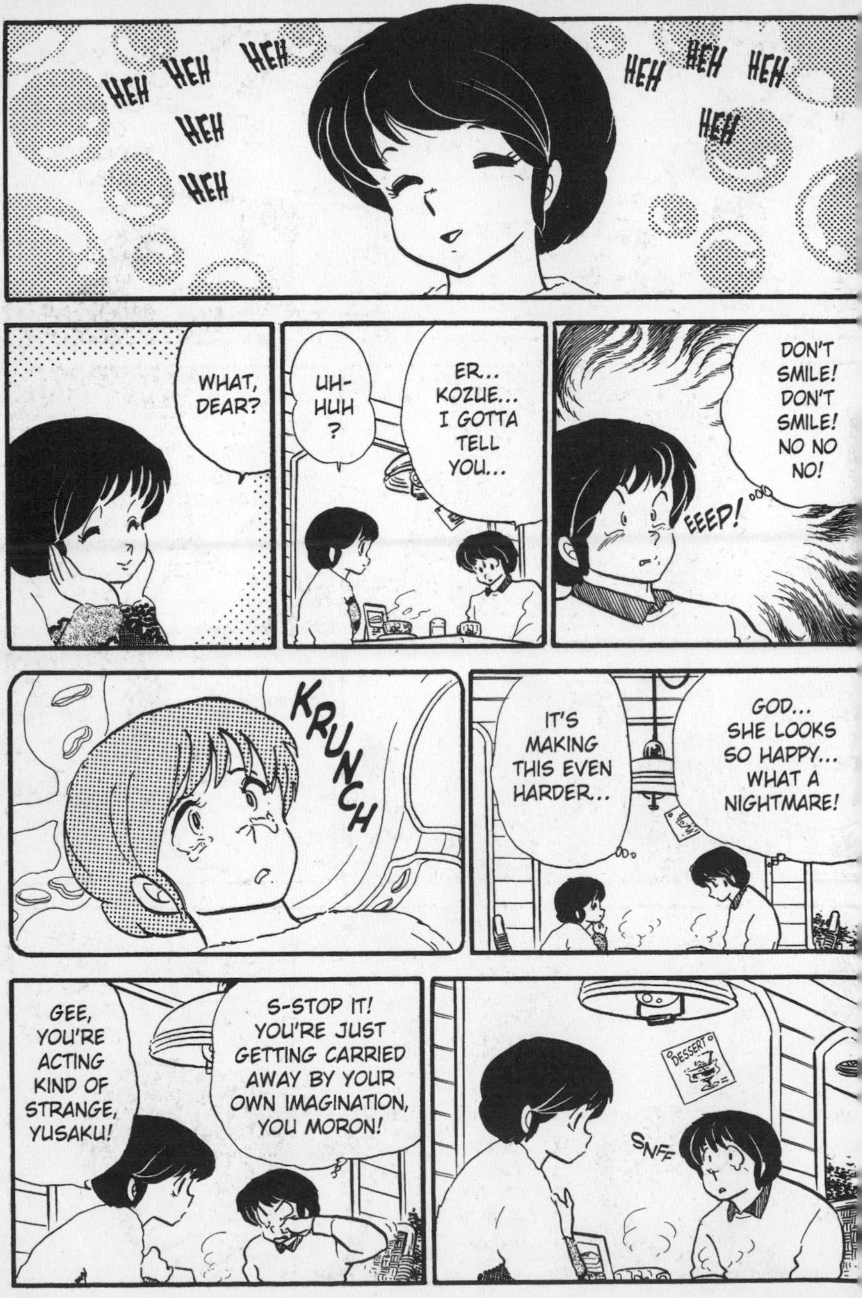
HEH HEH HEH HEH
HEH HEH HEH HEH HEH
DON'T SMILE! DON'T SMILE! NO NO NO!
EEEP!
ER... KOZUE... I GOTTA TELL YOU...
UH-HUH?
WHAT, DEAR?
GOD... SHE LOOKS SO HAPPY... WHAT A NIGHTMARE!
IT'S MAKING THIS EVEN HARDER...
KRUNCH
DESSERT
SNFF
S-STOP IT! YOU'RE JUST GETTING CARRIED AWAY BY YOUR OWN IMAGINATION, YOU MORON!
GEE, YOU'RE ACTING KIND OF STRANGE, YUSAKU!

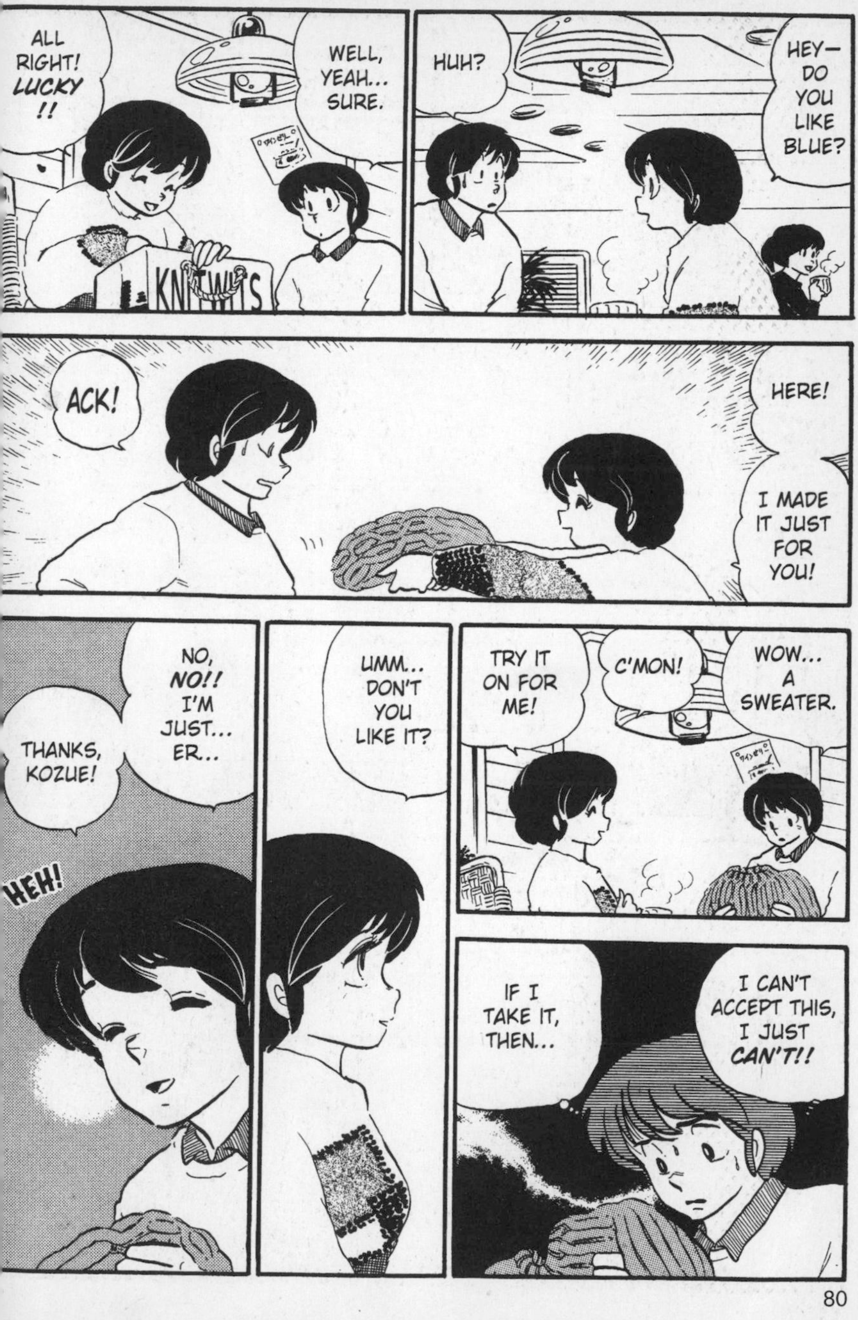
HEY— DO YOU LIKE BLUE?
HUH?
WELL, YEAH... SURE.
ALL RIGHT! *LUCKY* !!
KNITWITS
HERE!
I MADE IT JUST FOR YOU!
ACK!
WOW... A SWEATER.
C'MON!
TRY IT ON FOR ME!
I CAN'T ACCEPT THIS, I JUST *CAN'T!!*
IF I TAKE IT, THEN...
UMM... DON'T YOU LIKE IT?
NO, *NO!!* I'M JUST... ER...
THANKS, KOZUE!
HEH!

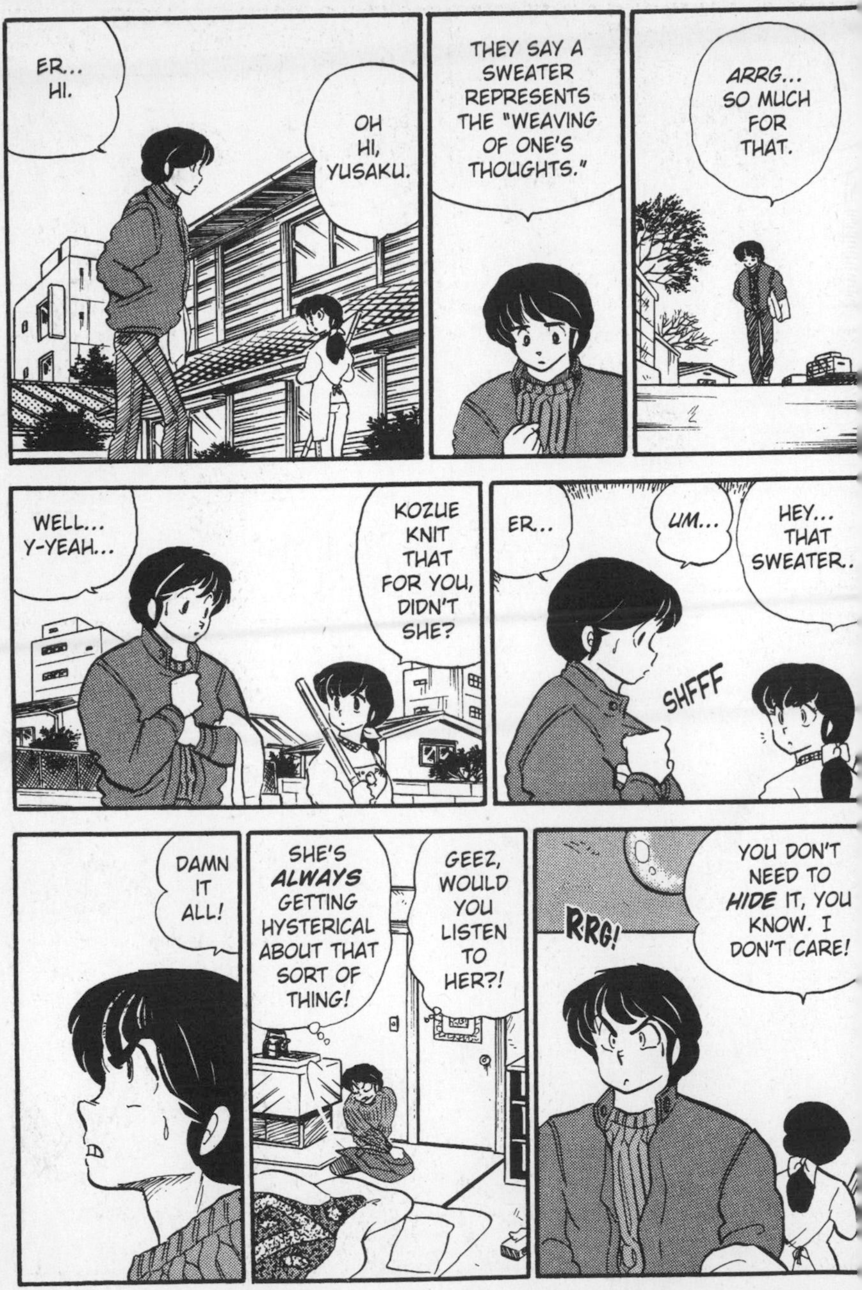
ARRG... SO MUCH FOR THAT.
THEY SAY A SWEATER REPRESENTS THE "WEAVING OF ONE'S THOUGHTS."
OH HI, YUSAKU.
ER... HI.
HEY... THAT SWEATER..
UM...
SHFFF
ER...
KOZUE KNIT THAT FOR YOU, DIDN'T SHE?
WELL... Y-YEAH...
YOU DON'T NEED TO HIDE IT, YOU KNOW. I DON'T CARE!
RRG!
GEEZ, WOULD YOU LISTEN TO HER?!
SHE'S ALWAYS GETTING HYSTERICAL ABOUT THAT SORT OF THING!
DAMN IT ALL!

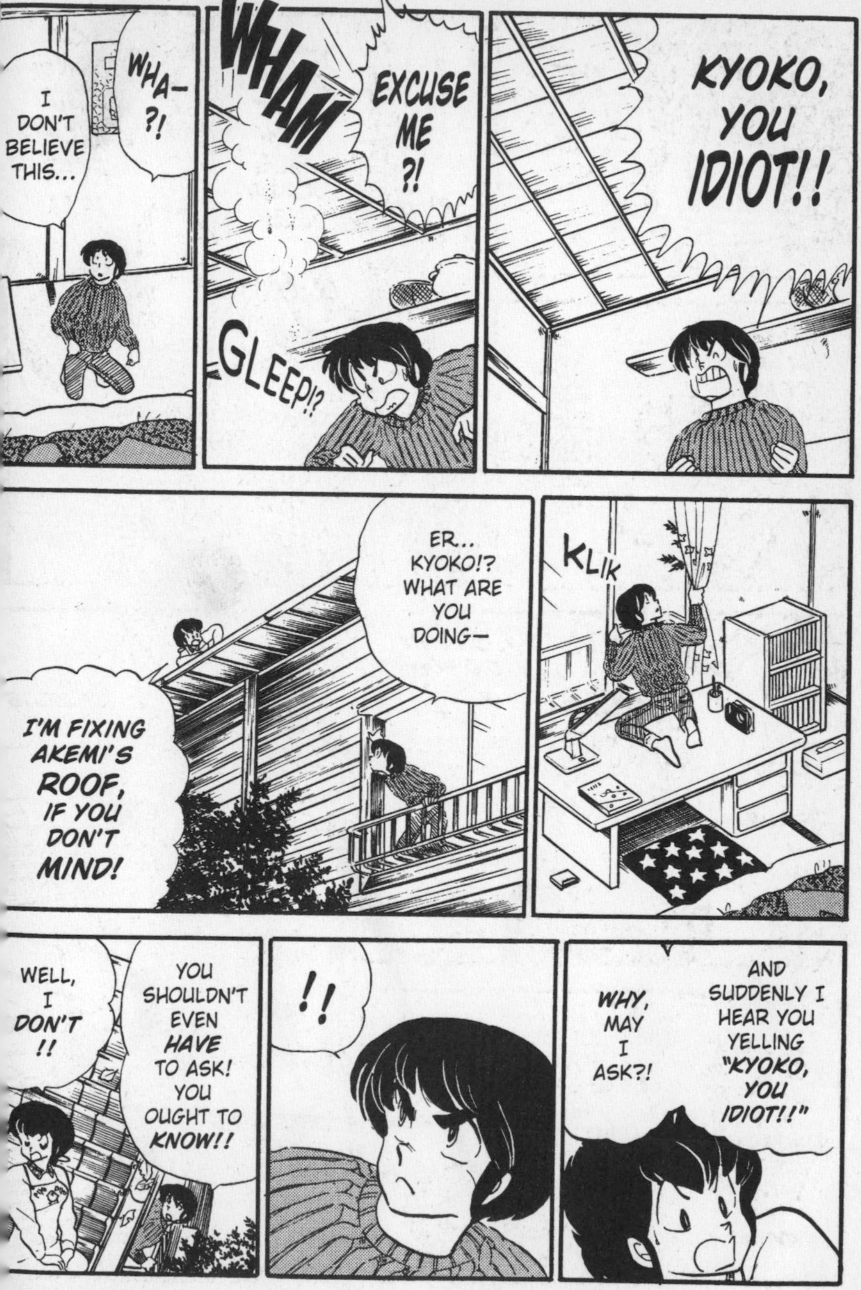

KYOKO, YOU IDIOT!!
EXCUSE ME ?!
WHAM
GLEEP!?
WHA- ?!
I DON'T BELIEVE THIS...
KLIK
ER... KYOKO!? WHAT ARE YOU DOING—
I'M FIXING AKEMI'S ROOF, IF YOU DON'T MIND!
AND SUDDENLY I HEAR YOU YELLING "KYOKO, YOU IDIOT!!"
WHY, MAY I ASK?!
!!
YOU SHOULDN'T EVEN HAVE TO ASK! YOU OUGHT TO KNOW!!
WELL, I DON'T !!

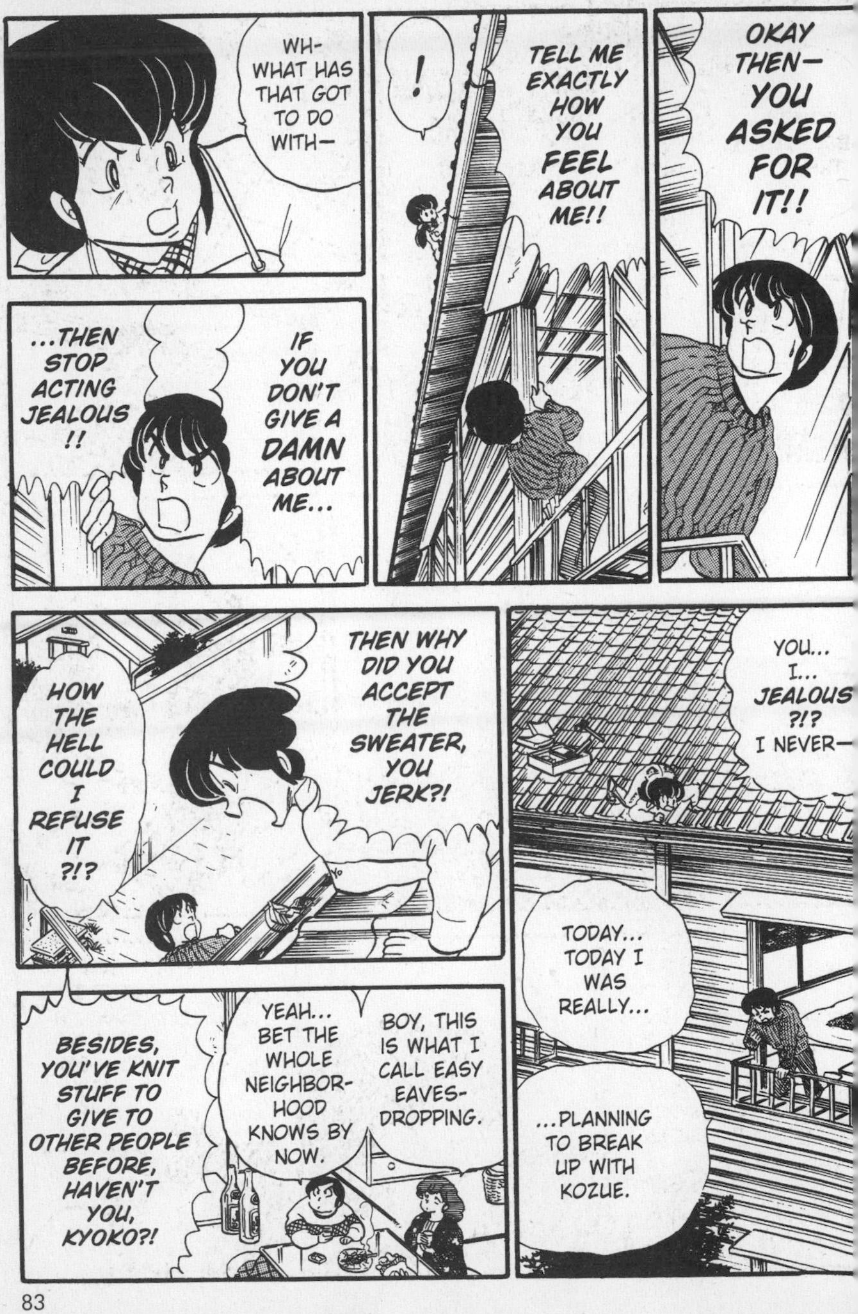
OKAY THEN— YOU ASKED FOR IT!!
TELL ME EXACTLY HOW YOU FEEL ABOUT ME!!
!
WH- WHAT HAS THAT GOT TO DO WITH—
IF YOU DON'T GIVE A DAMN ABOUT ME...
...THEN STOP ACTING JEALOUS!!
YOU... I... JEALOUS?!? I NEVER—
TODAY... TODAY I WAS REALLY...
...PLANNING TO BREAK UP WITH KOZUE.
THEN WHY DID YOU ACCEPT THE SWEATER, YOU JERK?!
HOW THE HELL COULD I REFUSE IT?!?
BOY, THIS IS WHAT I CALL EASY EAVES-DROPPING.
YEAH... BET THE WHOLE NEIGHBOR-HOOD KNOWS BY NOW.
BESIDES, YOU'VE KNIT STUFF TO GIVE TO OTHER PEOPLE BEFORE, HAVEN'T YOU, KYOKO?!

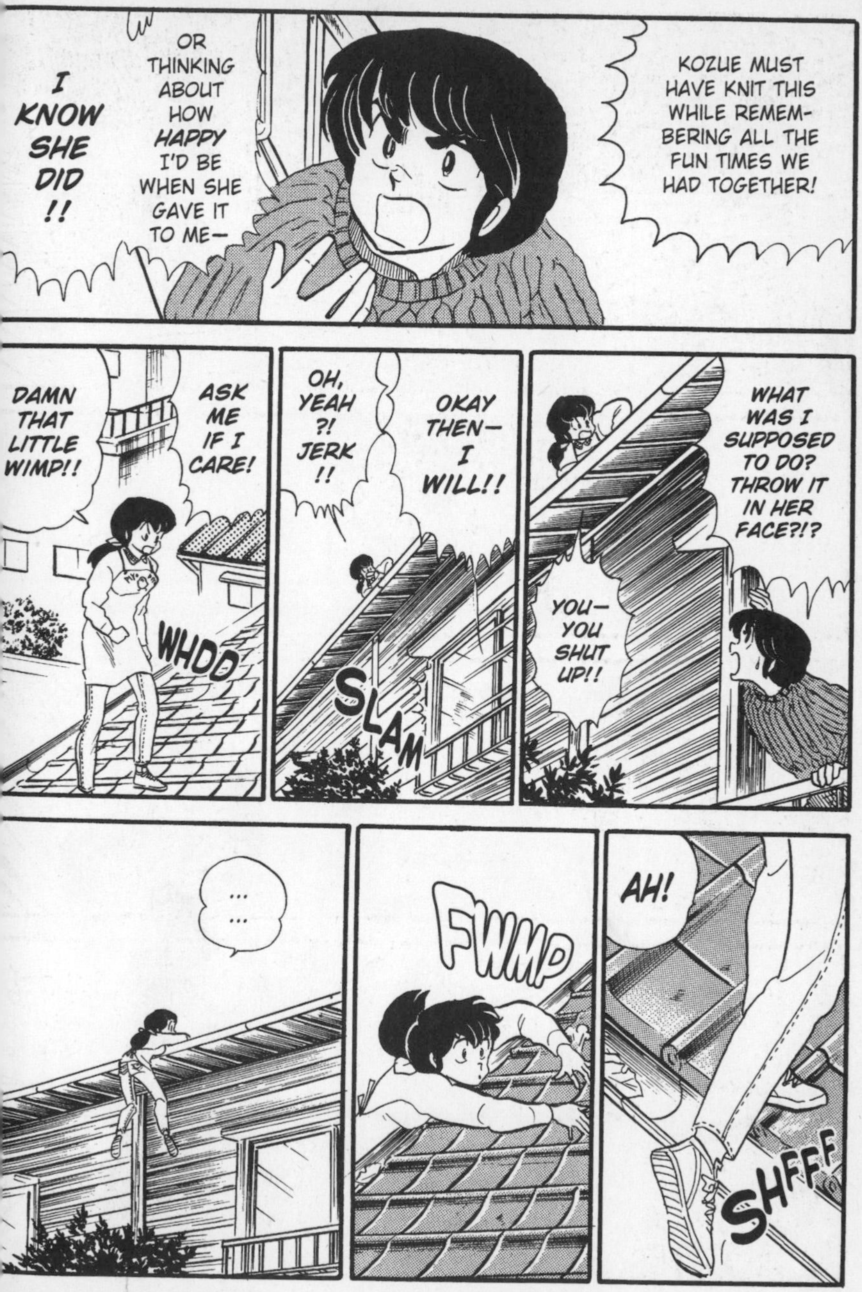
KOZUE MUST HAVE KNIT THIS WHILE REMEMBERING ALL THE FUN TIMES WE HAD TOGETHER!
OR THINKING ABOUT HOW HAPPY I'D BE WHEN SHE GAVE IT TO ME—
I KNOW SHE DID!!
WHAT WAS I SUPPOSED TO DO? THROW IT IN HER FACE?!?
YOU— YOU SHUT UP!!
OKAY THEN— I WILL!!
OH, YEAH?! JERK!!
SLAM
ASK ME IF I CARE!
DAMN THAT LITTLE WIMP!!
WHDD
AH!
SHFFF
FWMP
... ...

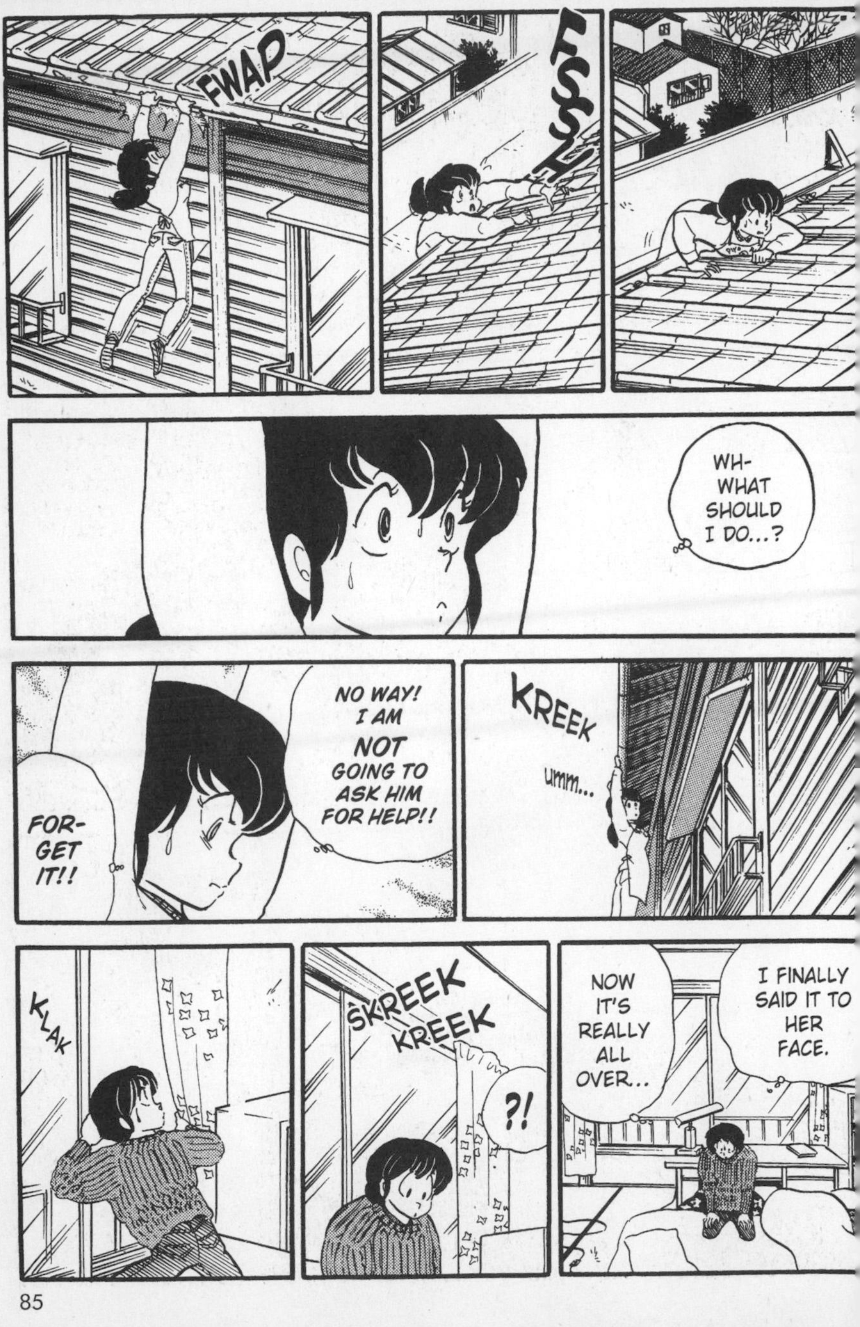
FSSH
FWAP
WH- WHAT SHOULD I DO...?
KREEK
umm...
NO WAY! I AM NOT GOING TO ASK HIM FOR HELP!!
FOR-GET IT!!
I FINALLY SAID IT TO HER FACE.
NOW IT'S REALLY ALL OVER...
SKREEK KREEK
?!
KLAK

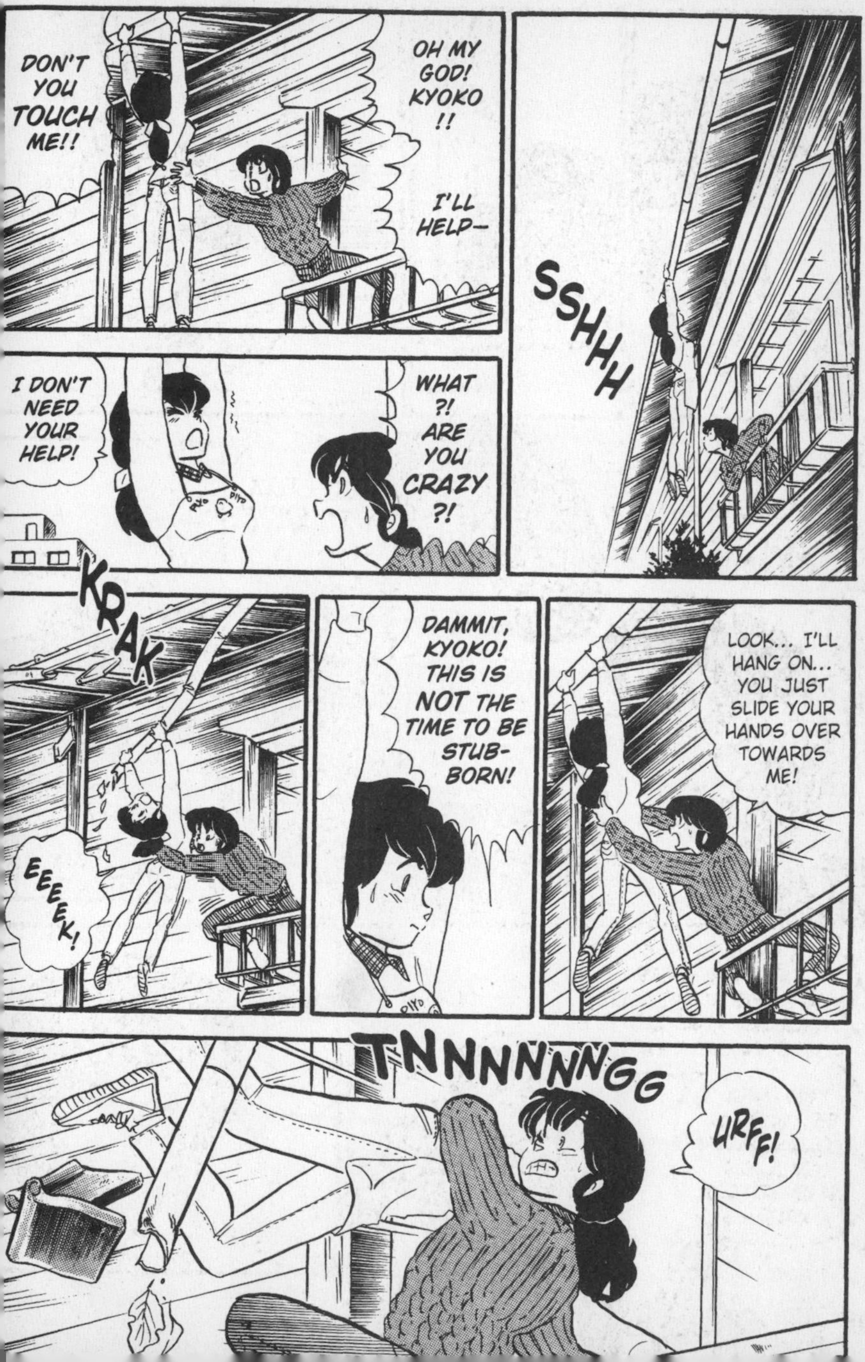
SSHHHH
OH MY GOD! KYOKO!!
DON'T YOU TOUCH ME!!
I'LL HELP—
WHAT?! ARE YOU CRAZY?!
I DON'T NEED YOUR HELP!
LOOK... I'LL HANG ON... YOU JUST SLIDE YOUR HANDS OVER TOWARDS ME!
DAMMIT, KYOKO! THIS IS NOT THE TIME TO BE STUB-BORN!
KRAK
EEEEEK!
TNNNNNNGG
URFF!

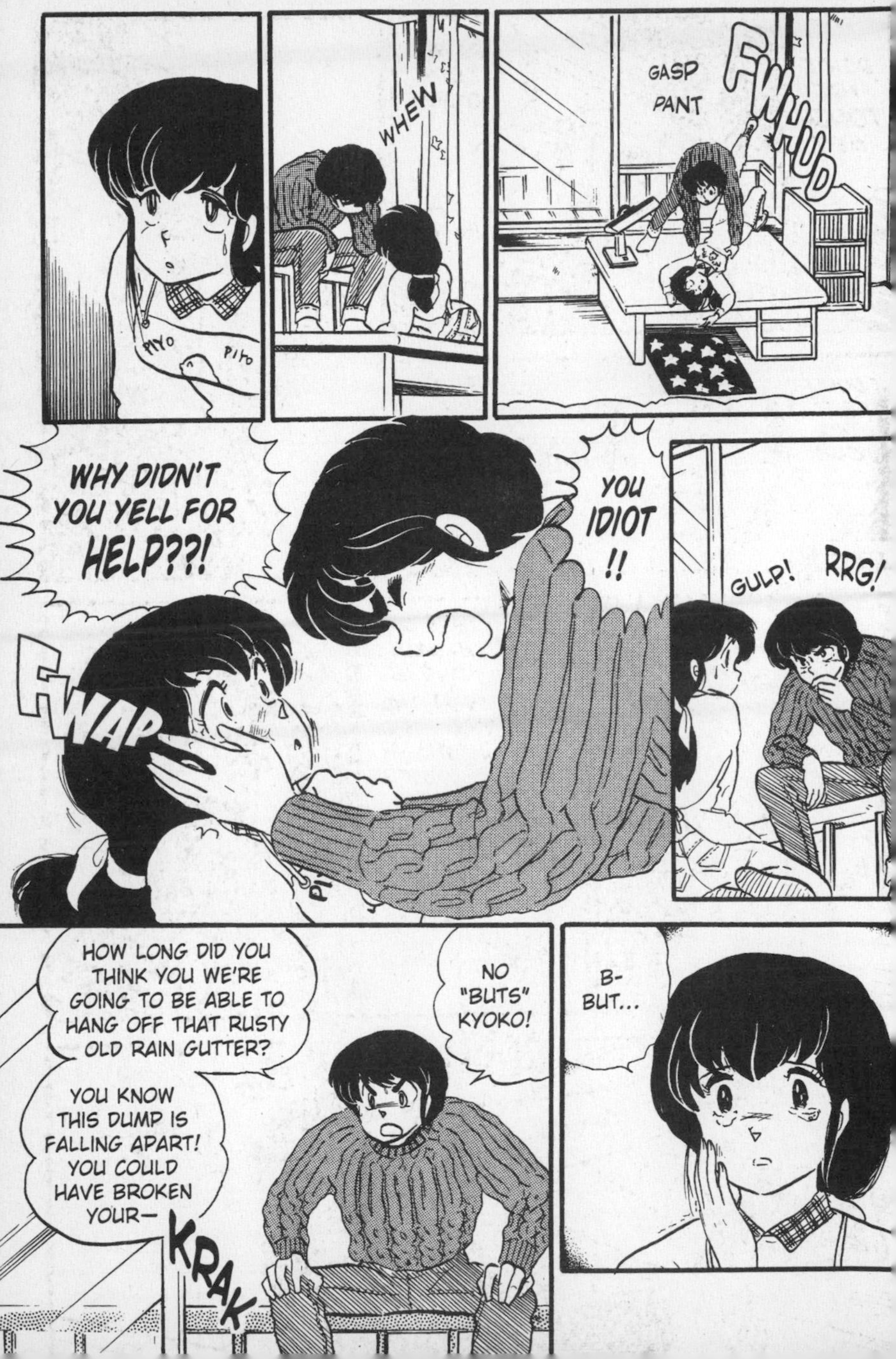
FWHUD
GASP
PANT
WHEW
PIYO PIYO
RRG!
GULP!
YOU IDIOT !!
WHY DIDN'T YOU YELL FOR HELP??!
FWAP
B-BUT...
NO "BUTS" KYOKO!
HOW LONG DID YOU THINK YOU WE'RE GOING TO BE ABLE TO HANG OFF THAT RUSTY OLD RAIN GUTTER?
YOU KNOW THIS DUMP IS FALLING APART! YOU COULD HAVE BROKEN YOUR—
KRAK

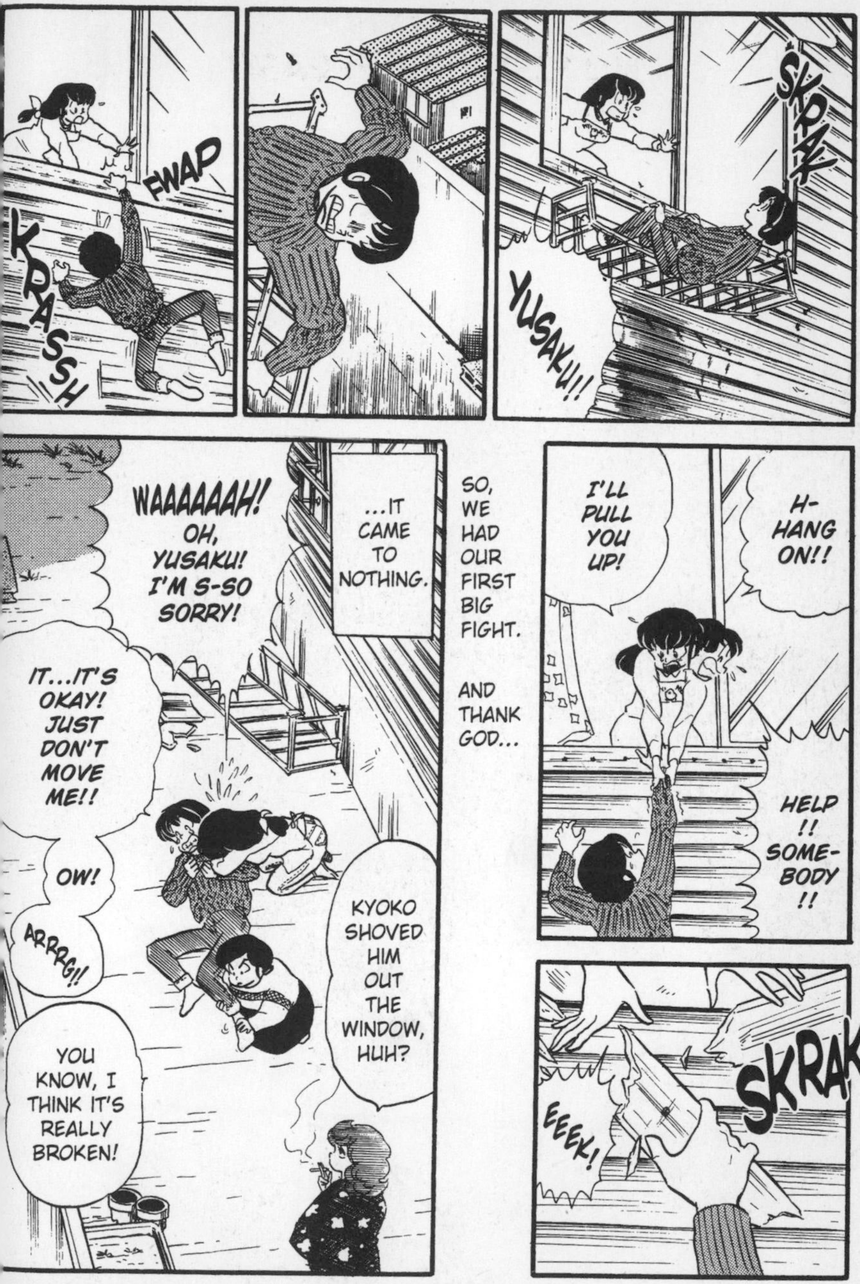
SKRAK
YUSAKU!!
FWAP
KRASSH
H-HANG ON!!
I'LL PULL YOU UP!
HELP!! SOMEBODY!!
SKRAK
EEEK!
SO, WE HAD OUR FIRST BIG FIGHT.
AND THANK GOD...
...IT CAME TO NOTHING.
WAAAAAAH! OH, YUSAKU! I'M S-SO SORRY!
IT...IT'S OKAY! JUST DON'T MOVE ME!!
OW!
ARRRG!!
KYOKO SHOVED HIM OUT THE WINDOW, HUH?
YOU KNOW, I THINK IT'S REALLY BROKEN!

PART FIVE
NO VISITORS, PLEASE!

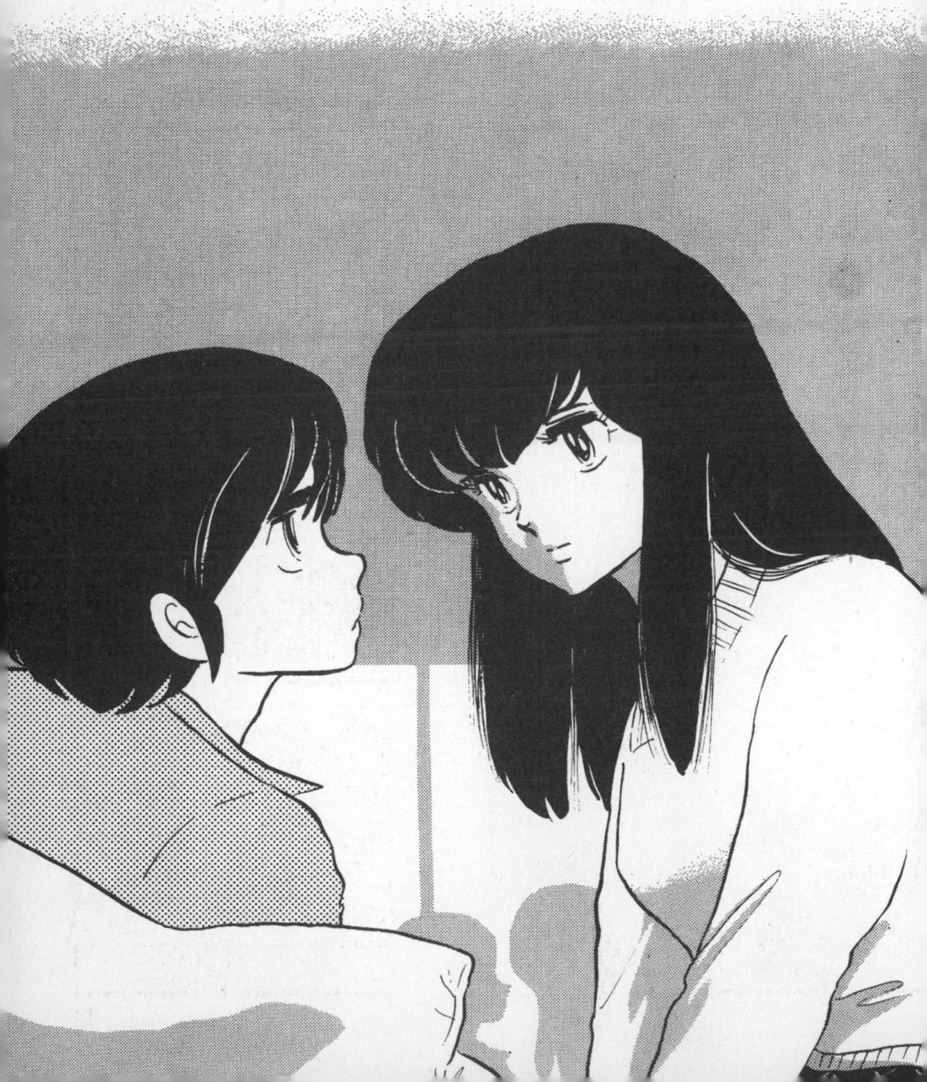

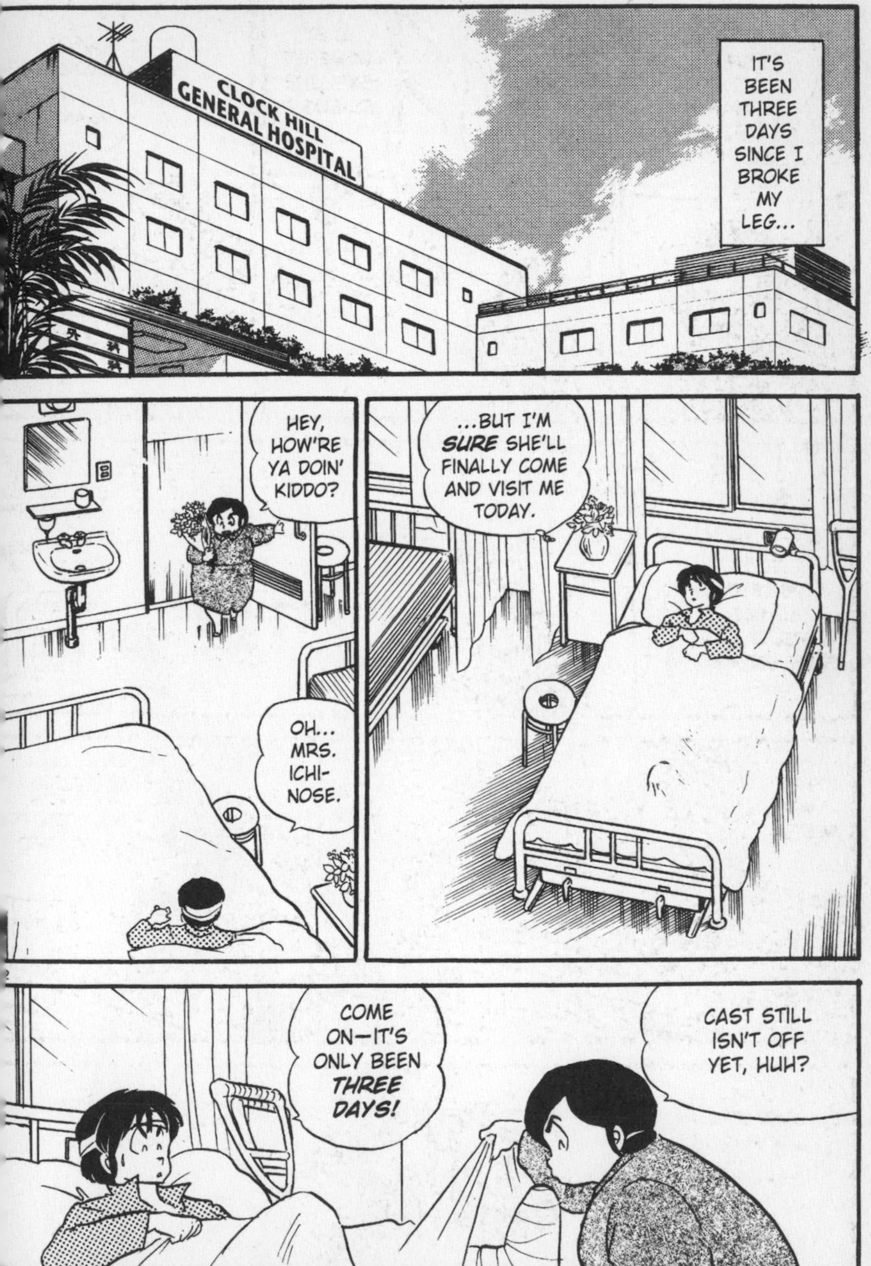
CLOCK HILL GENERAL HOSPITAL
IT'S BEEN THREE DAYS SINCE I BROKE MY LEG...
...BUT I'M *SURE* SHE'LL FINALLY COME AND VISIT ME TODAY.
HEY, HOW'RE YA DOIN' KIDDO?
OH... MRS. ICHI-NOSE.
CAST STILL ISN'T OFF YET, HUH?
COME ON—IT'S ONLY BEEN *THREE DAYS!*

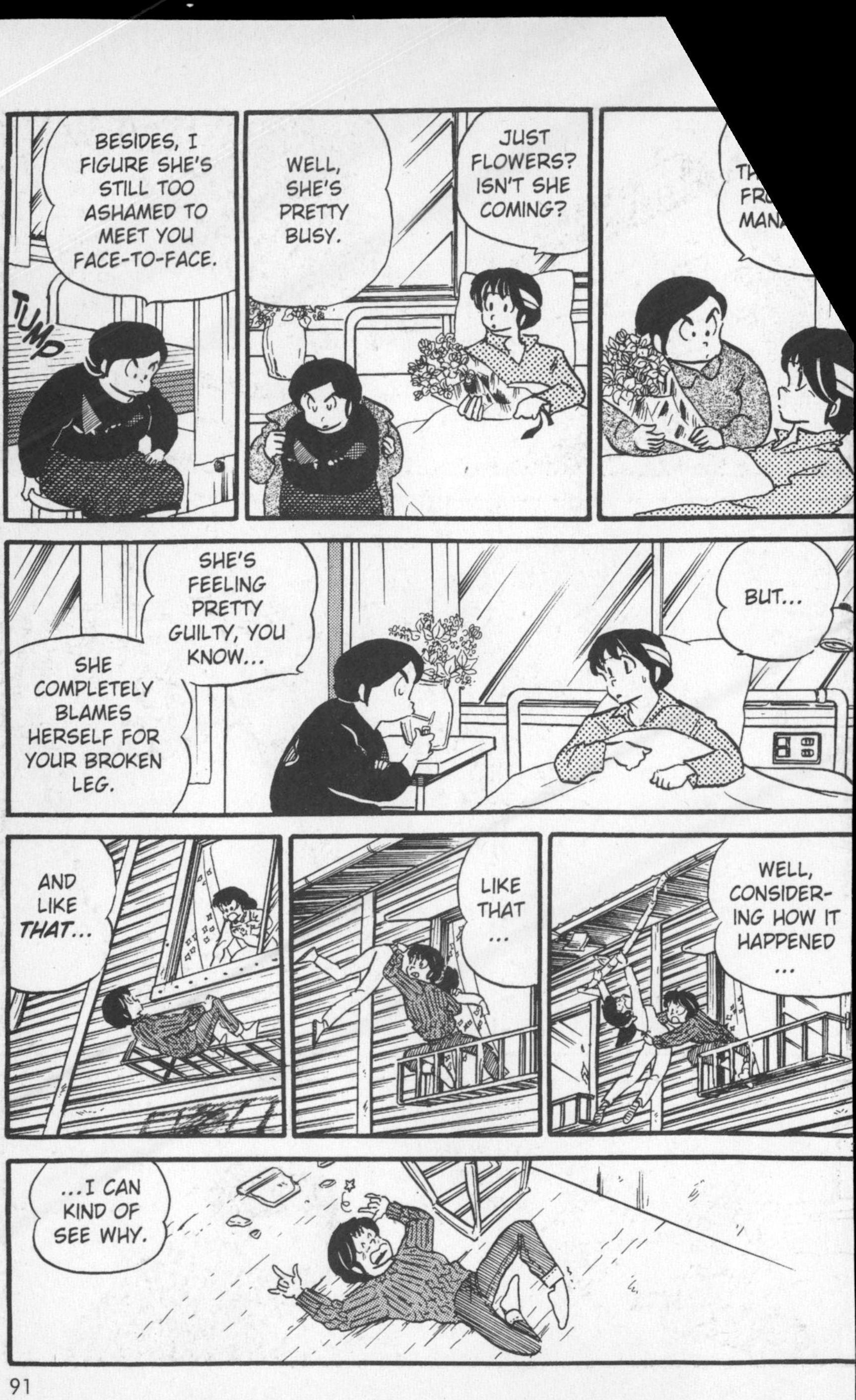
TH
FR
MANA
JUST FLOWERS? ISN'T SHE COMING?
WELL, SHE'S PRETTY BUSY.
BESIDES, I FIGURE SHE'S STILL TOO ASHAMED TO MEET YOU FACE-TO-FACE.
TUMP
BUT...
SHE'S FEELING PRETTY GUILTY, YOU KNOW...
SHE COMPLETELY BLAMES HERSELF FOR YOUR BROKEN LEG.
WELL, CONSIDER-ING HOW IT HAPPENED ...
LIKE THAT ...
AND LIKE *THAT*...
...I CAN KIND OF SEE WHY.

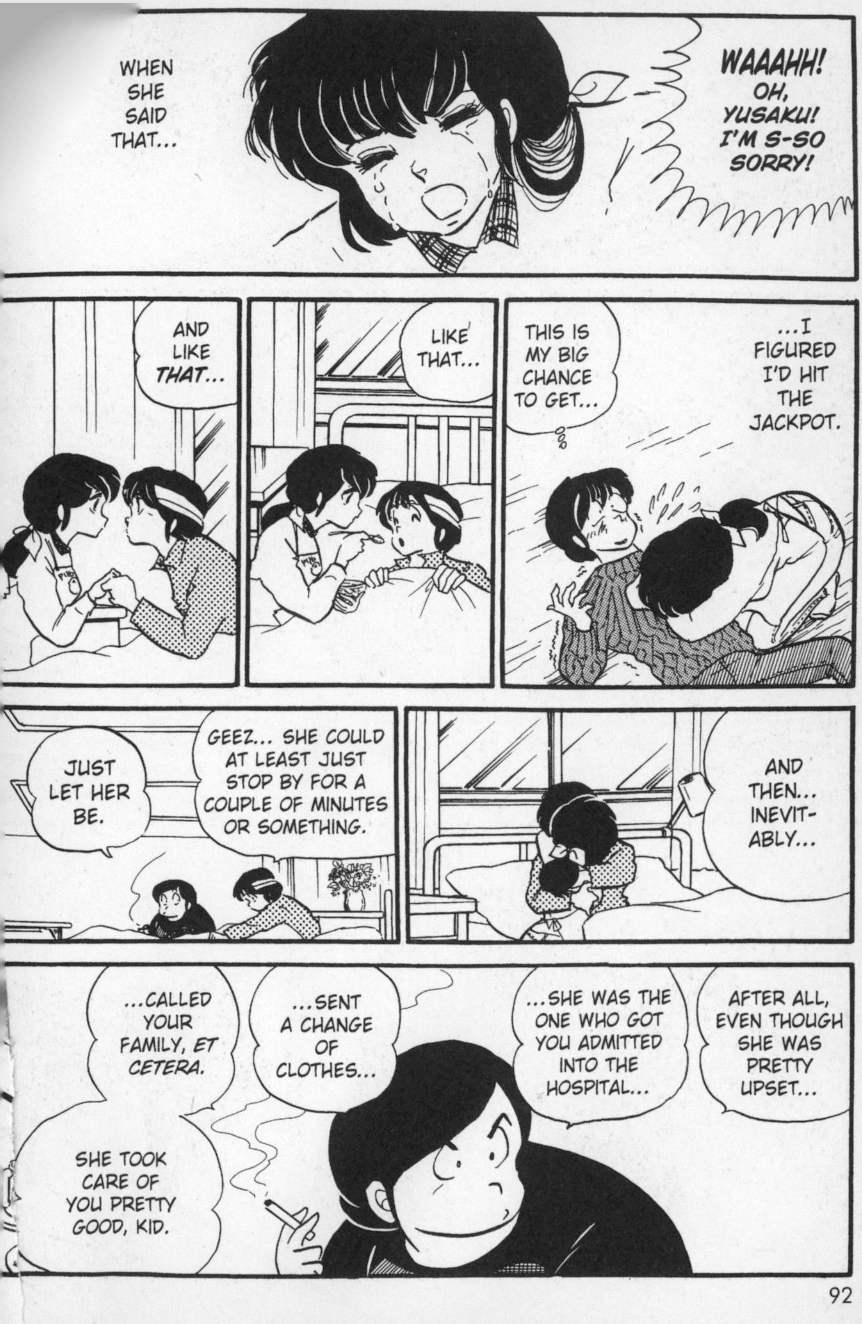
WAAAHH! OH, YUSAKU! I'M S-SO SORRY!
WHEN SHE SAID THAT...
...I FIGURED I'D HIT THE JACKPOT.
THIS IS MY BIG CHANCE TO GET...
LIKE THAT...
AND LIKE *THAT*...
AND THEN... INEVIT-ABLY...
GEEZ... SHE COULD AT LEAST JUST STOP BY FOR A COUPLE OF MINUTES OR SOMETHING.
JUST LET HER BE.
AFTER ALL, EVEN THOUGH SHE WAS PRETTY UPSET...
...SHE WAS THE ONE WHO GOT YOU ADMITTED INTO THE HOSPITAL...
...SENT A CHANGE OF CLOTHES...
...CALLED YOUR FAMILY, *ET CETERA.*
SHE TOOK CARE OF YOU PRETTY GOOD, KID.

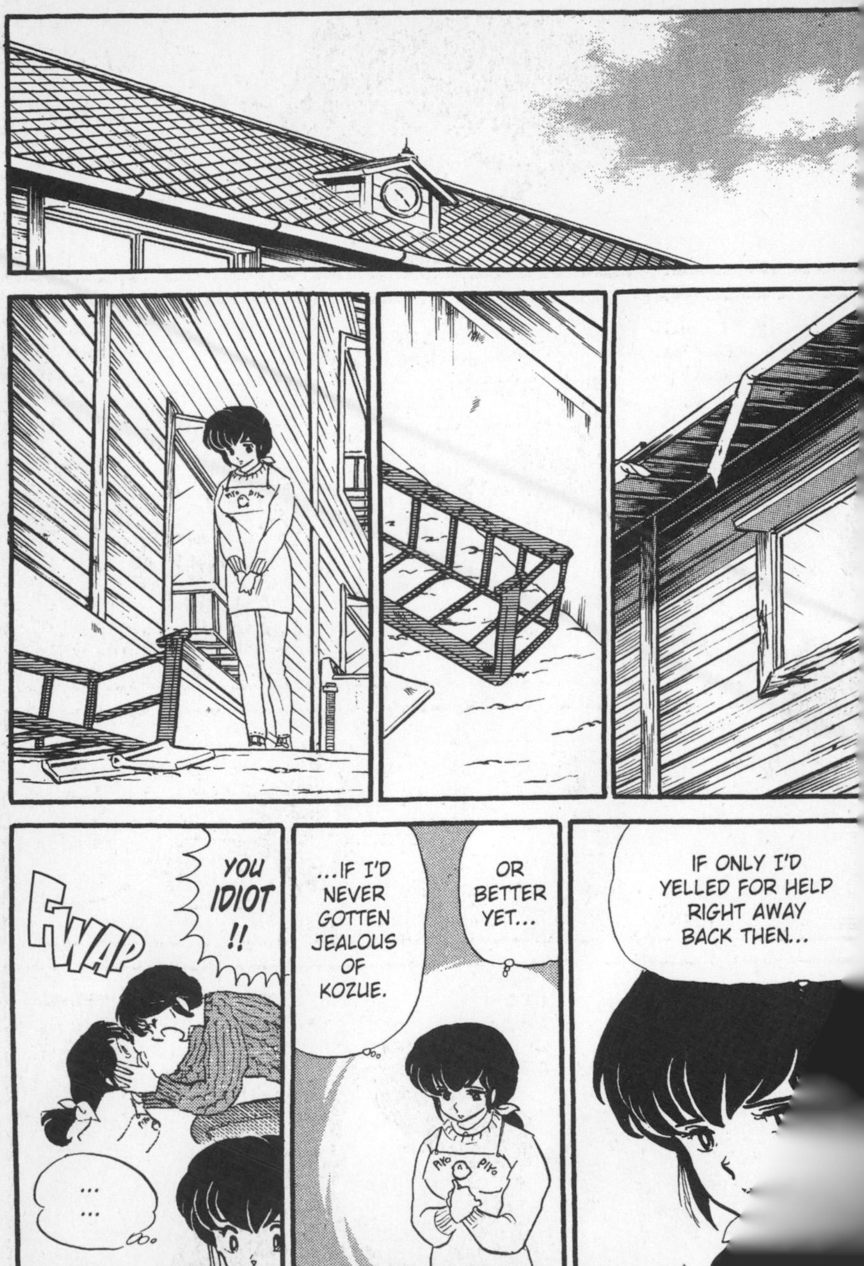
IF ONLY I'D YELLED FOR HELP RIGHT AWAY BACK THEN...
OR BETTER YET...
...IF I'D NEVER GOTTEN JEALOUS OF KOZUE.
YOU IDIOT !!
FWAP
... ...

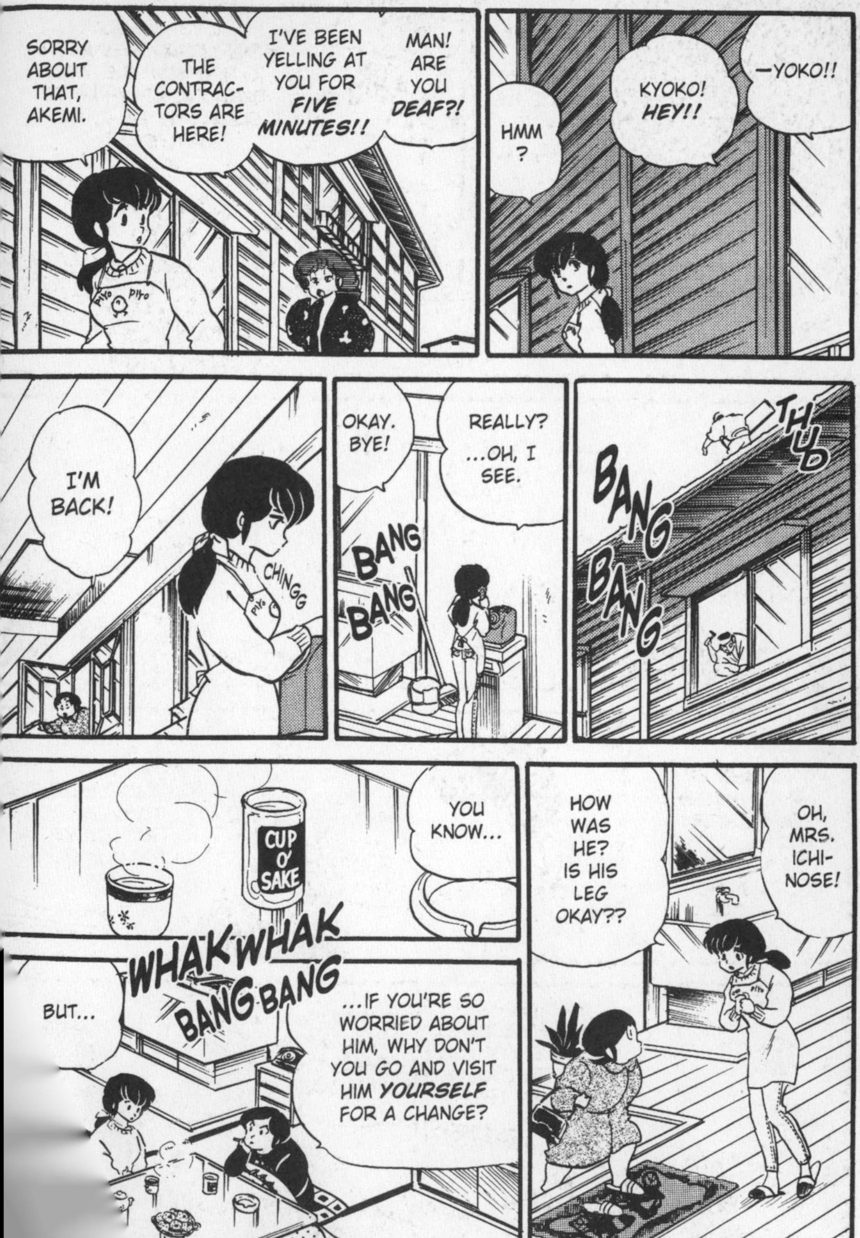
—YOKO!!
KYOKO! HEY!!
HMM ?
MAN! ARE YOU DEAF?!
I'VE BEEN YELLING AT YOU FOR FIVE MINUTES!!
THE CONTRACTORS ARE HERE!
SORRY ABOUT THAT, AKEMI.
THUD
BANG BANG
REALLY? ...OH, I SEE.
OKAY. BYE!
BANG BANG
CHINGG
I'M BACK!
OH, MRS. ICHINOSE!
HOW WAS HE? IS HIS LEG OKAY??
YOU KNOW...
CUP O' SAKE
...IF YOU'RE SO WORRIED ABOUT HIM, WHY DON'T YOU GO AND VISIT HIM YOURSELF FOR A CHANGE?
WHAK WHAK
BANG BANG
BUT...

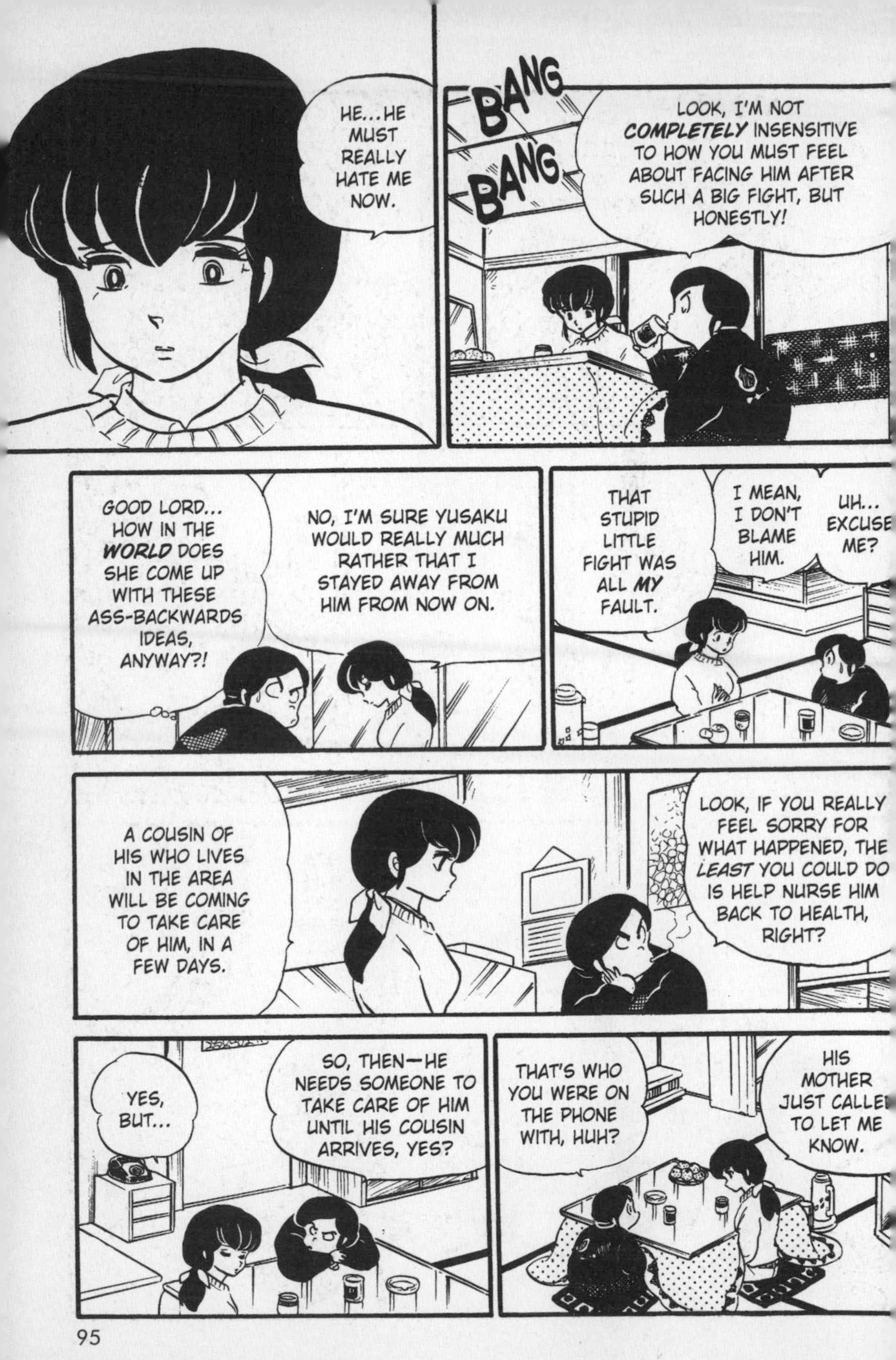
BANG
BANG
LOOK, I'M NOT *COMPLETELY* INSENSITIVE TO HOW YOU MUST FEEL ABOUT FACING HIM AFTER SUCH A BIG FIGHT, BUT HONESTLY!
HE...HE MUST REALLY HATE ME NOW.
UH... EXCUSE ME?
I MEAN, I DON'T BLAME HIM.
THAT STUPID LITTLE FIGHT WAS ALL *MY* FAULT.
NO, I'M SURE YUSAKU WOULD REALLY MUCH RATHER THAT I STAYED AWAY FROM HIM FROM NOW ON.
GOOD LORD... HOW IN THE *WORLD* DOES SHE COME UP WITH THESE ASS-BACKWARDS IDEAS, ANYWAY?!
LOOK, IF YOU REALLY FEEL SORRY FOR WHAT HAPPENED, THE *LEAST* YOU COULD DO IS HELP NURSE HIM BACK TO HEALTH, RIGHT?
A COUSIN OF HIS WHO LIVES IN THE AREA WILL BE COMING TO TAKE CARE OF HIM, IN A FEW DAYS.
HIS MOTHER JUST CALLE TO LET ME KNOW.
THAT'S WHO YOU WERE ON THE PHONE WITH, HUH?
SO, THEN—HE NEEDS SOMEONE TO TAKE CARE OF HIM UNTIL HIS COUSIN ARRIVES, YES?
YES, BUT...

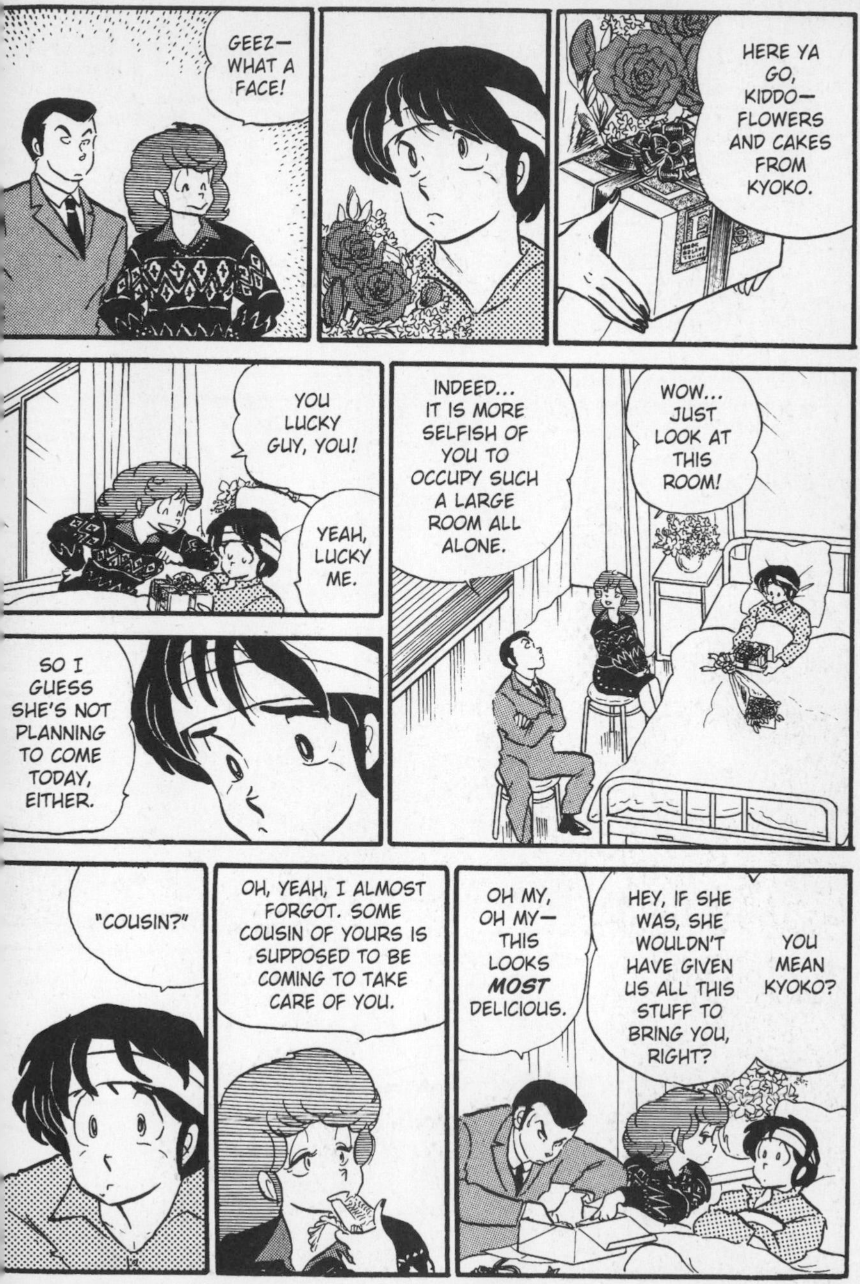
HERE YA GO, KIDDO— FLOWERS AND CAKES FROM KYOKO.
GEEZ— WHAT A FACE!
WOW... JUST LOOK AT THIS ROOM!
INDEED... IT IS MORE SELFISH OF YOU TO OCCUPY SUCH A LARGE ROOM ALL ALONE.
YOU LUCKY GUY, YOU!
YEAH, LUCKY ME.
SO I GUESS SHE'S NOT PLANNING TO COME TODAY, EITHER.
YOU MEAN KYOKO?
HEY, IF SHE WAS, SHE WOULDN'T HAVE GIVEN US ALL THIS STUFF TO BRING YOU, RIGHT?
OH MY, OH MY— THIS LOOKS **MOST** DELICIOUS.
OH, YEAH, I ALMOST FORGOT. SOME COUSIN OF YOURS IS SUPPOSED TO BE COMING TO TAKE CARE OF YOU.
"COUSIN?"

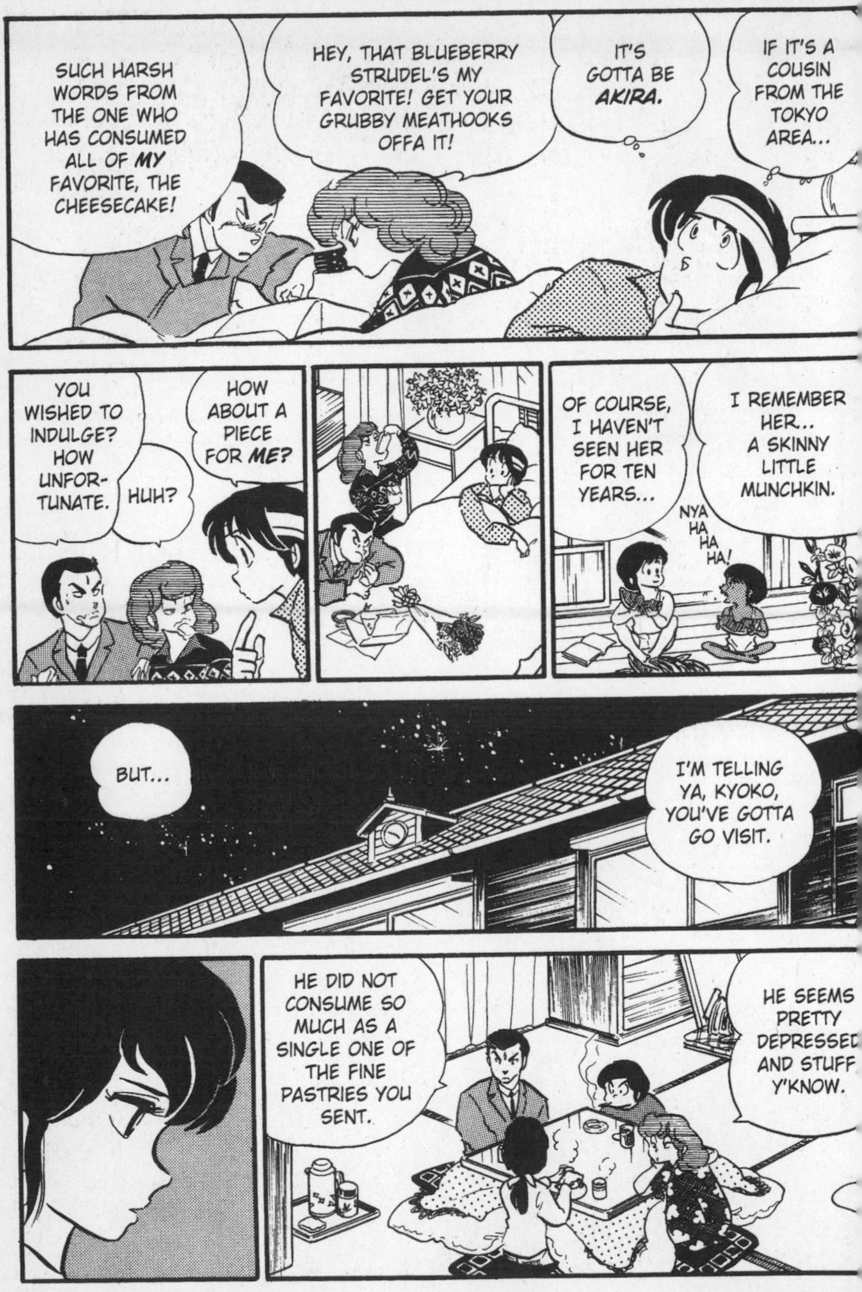
IF IT'S A COUSIN FROM THE TOKYO AREA...
IT'S GOTTA BE *AKIRA.*
HEY, THAT BLUEBERRY STRUDEL'S MY FAVORITE! GET YOUR GRUBBY MEATHOOKS OFFA IT!
SUCH HARSH WORDS FROM THE ONE WHO HAS CONSUMED ALL OF *MY* FAVORITE, THE CHEESECAKE!
I REMEMBER HER... A SKINNY LITTLE MUNCHKIN.
OF COURSE, I HAVEN'T SEEN HER FOR TEN YEARS...
NYA HA HA HA!
HOW ABOUT A PIECE FOR *ME?*
HUH?
YOU WISHED TO INDULGE? HOW UNFORTUNATE.
I'M TELLING YA, KYOKO, YOU'VE GOTTA GO VISIT.
BUT...
HE SEEMS PRETTY DEPRESSED AND STUFF Y'KNOW.
HE DID NOT CONSUME SO MUCH AS A SINGLE ONE OF THE FINE PASTRIES YOU SENT.

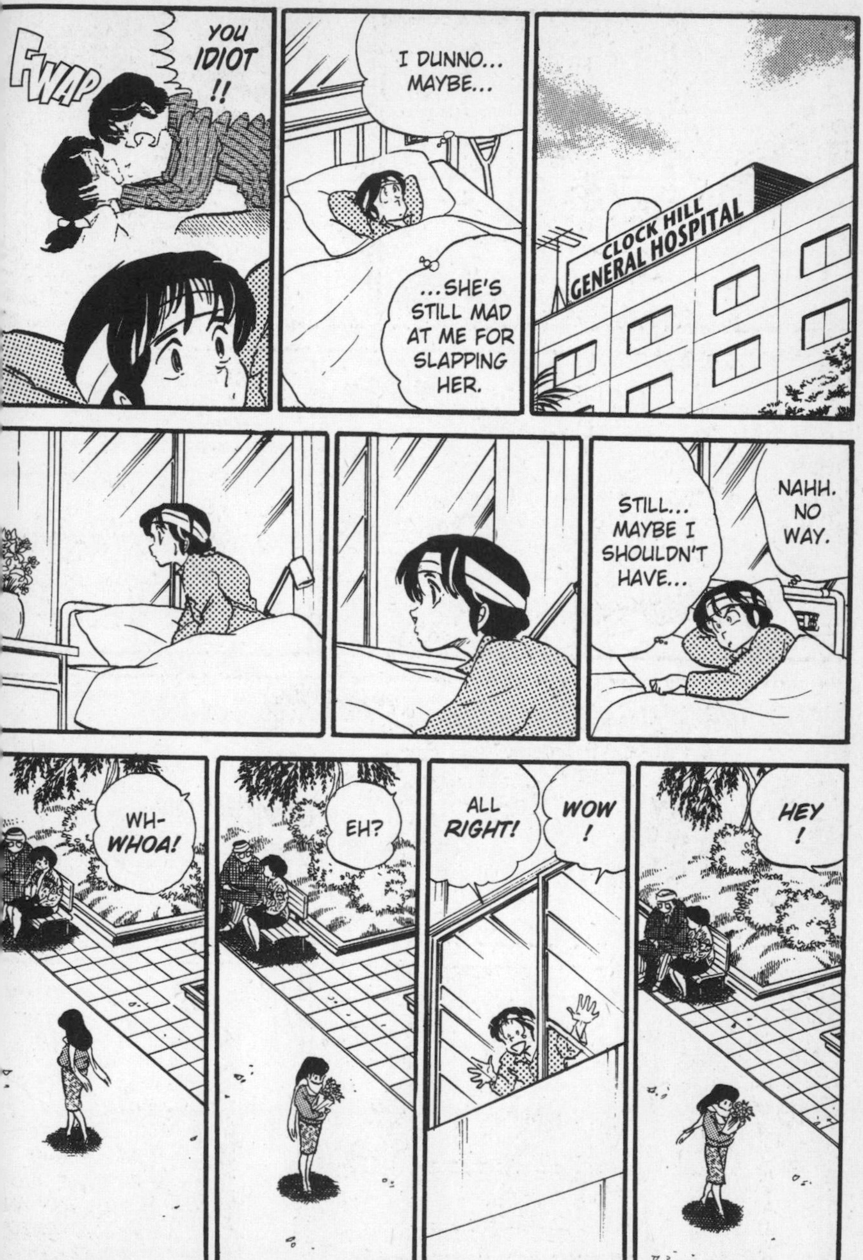
CLOCK HILL GENERAL HOSPITAL
I DUNNO... MAYBE...
...SHE'S STILL MAD AT ME FOR SLAPPING HER.
FWAP
YOU IDIOT !!
STILL... MAYBE I SHOULDN'T HAVE...
NAHH. NO WAY.
HEY !
WOW !
ALL RIGHT!
EH?
WH-WHOA!

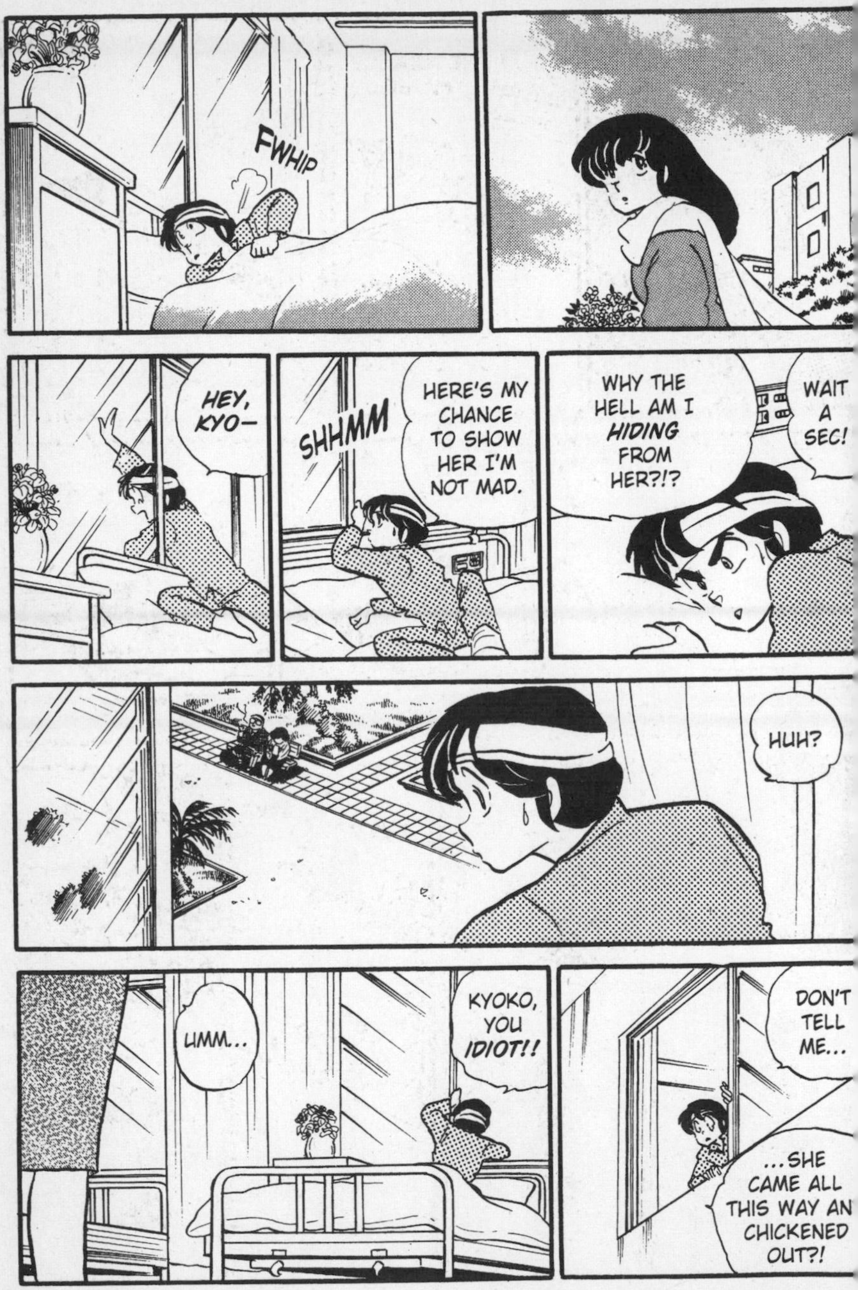
FWHIP
WAIT A SEC!
WHY THE HELL AM I HIDING FROM HER?!?
HERE'S MY CHANCE TO SHOW HER I'M NOT MAD.
SHHMM
HEY, KYO—
HUH?
DON'T TELL ME...
...SHE CAME ALL THIS WAY AN CHICKENED OUT?!
KYOKO, YOU IDIOT!!
UMM...

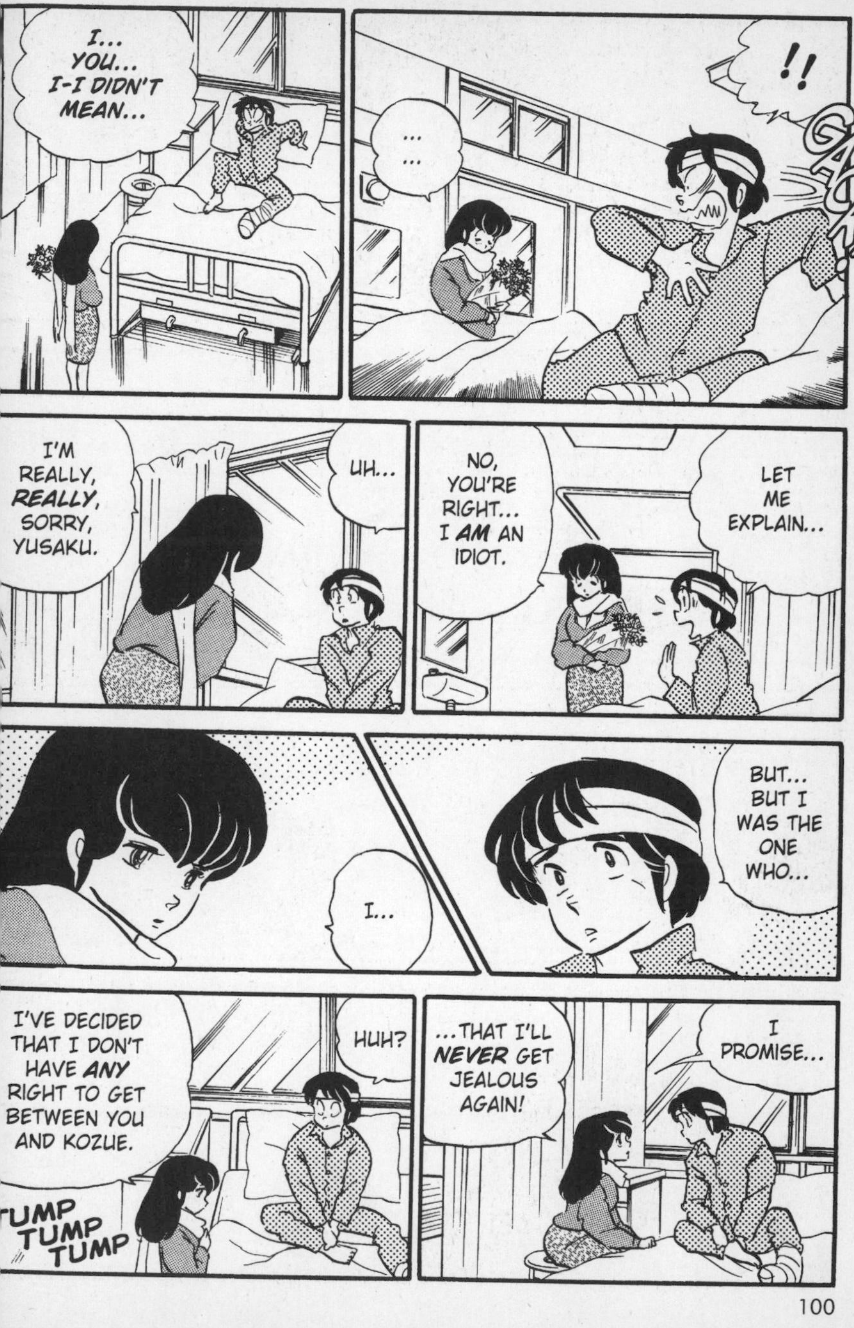
!!
GACK!
... ...
I... YOU... I-I DIDN'T MEAN...
LET ME EXPLAIN...
NO, YOU'RE RIGHT... I **AM** AN IDIOT.
UH...
I'M REALLY, **REALLY**, SORRY, YUSAKU.
BUT... BUT I WAS THE ONE WHO...
I...
I PROMISE...
...THAT I'LL **NEVER** GET JEALOUS AGAIN!
HUH?
I'VE DECIDED THAT I DON'T HAVE **ANY** RIGHT TO GET BETWEEN YOU AND KOZUE.
TUMP TUMP TUMP

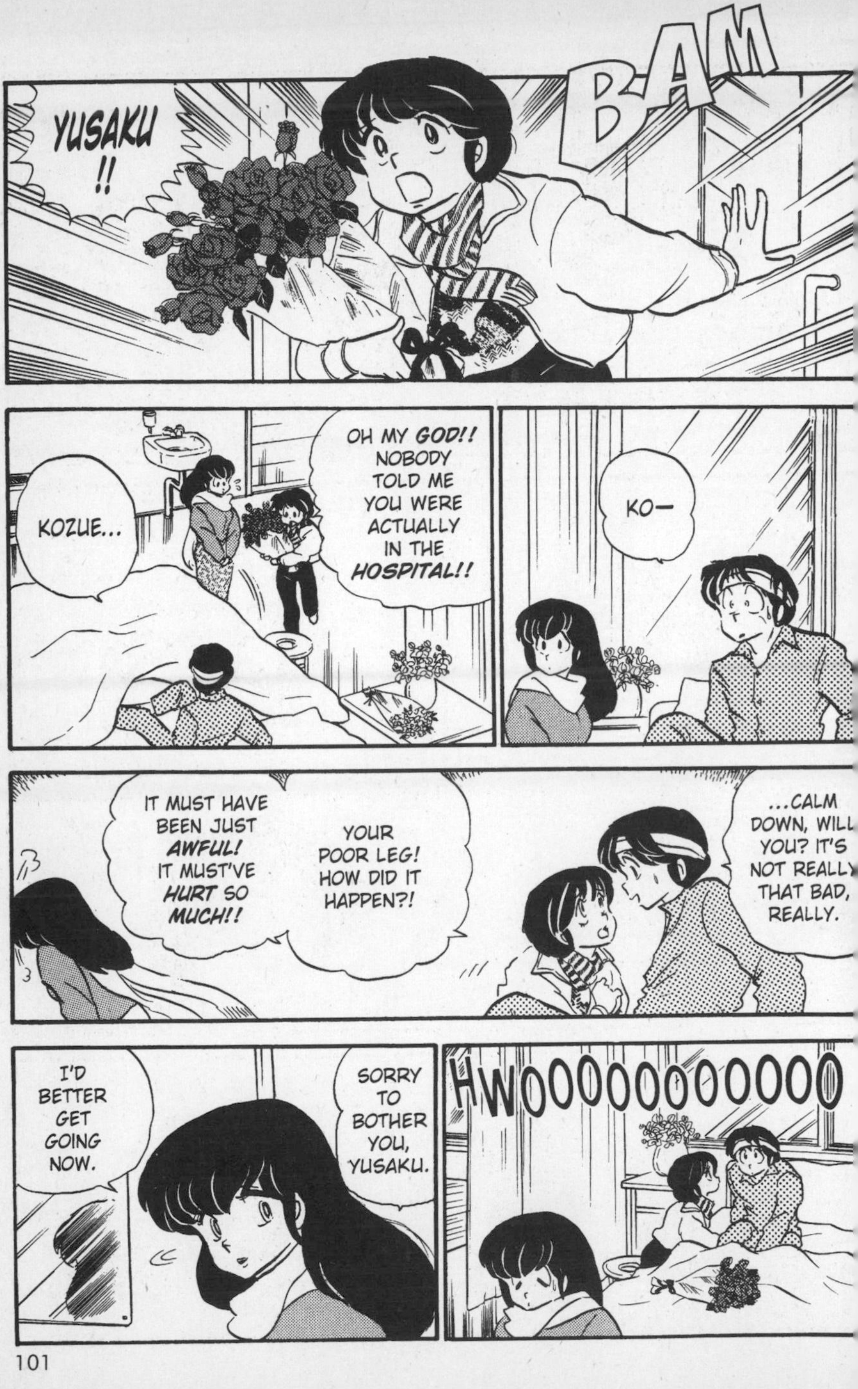
BAM
YUSAKU !!
KO—
OH MY GOD!! NOBODY TOLD ME YOU WERE ACTUALLY IN THE HOSPITAL!!
KOZUE...
...CALM DOWN, WILL YOU? IT'S NOT REALLY THAT BAD, REALLY.
YOUR POOR LEG! HOW DID IT HAPPEN?!
IT MUST HAVE BEEN JUST AWFUL! IT MUST'VE HURT SO MUCH!!
HWOOOOOOOOOOO
SORRY TO BOTHER YOU, YUSAKU.
I'D BETTER GET GOING NOW.

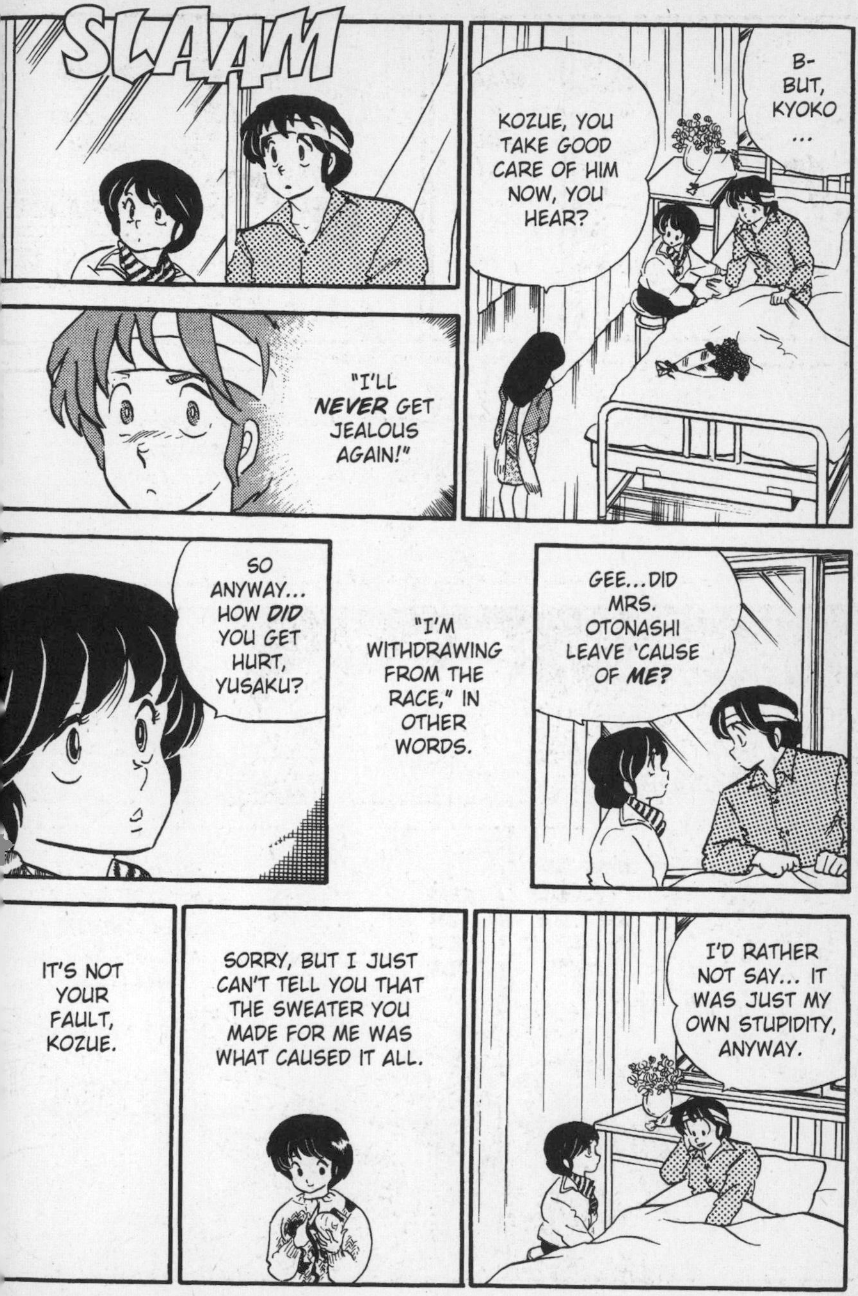
B-BUT, KYOKO ...
KOZUE, YOU TAKE GOOD CARE OF HIM NOW, YOU HEAR?
SLAAM
"I'LL ***NEVER*** GET JEALOUS AGAIN!"
GEE...DID MRS. OTONASHI LEAVE 'CAUSE OF ***ME?***
"I'M WITHDRAWING FROM THE RACE," IN OTHER WORDS.
SO ANYWAY... HOW ***DID*** YOU GET HURT, YUSAKU?
I'D RATHER NOT SAY... IT WAS JUST MY OWN STUPIDITY, ANYWAY.
SORRY, BUT I JUST CAN'T TELL YOU THAT THE SWEATER YOU MADE FOR ME WAS WHAT CAUSED IT ALL.
IT'S NOT YOUR FAULT, KOZUE.

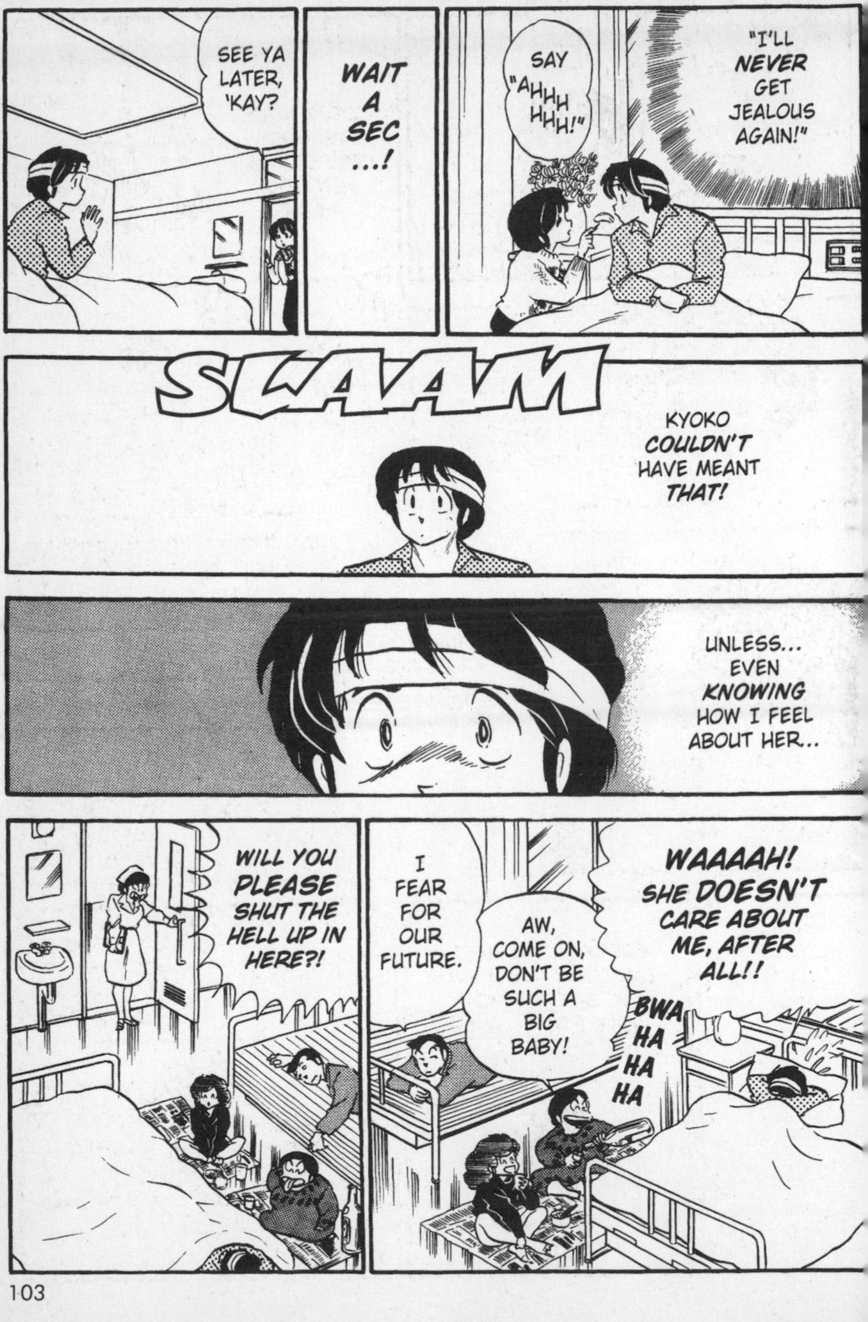
"I'LL NEVER GET JEALOUS AGAIN!"
SAY "AHHHHHH!"
WAIT A SEC...!
SEE YA LATER, 'KAY?
SLAAM
KYOKO COULDN'T HAVE MEANT THAT!
UNLESS... EVEN KNOWING HOW I FEEL ABOUT HER...
WAAAAH! SHE DOESN'T CARE ABOUT ME, AFTER ALL!!
I FEAR FOR OUR FUTURE.
AW, COME ON, DON'T BE SUCH A BIG BABY!
BWA HA HA HA
WILL YOU PLEASE SHUT THE HELL UP IN HERE?!

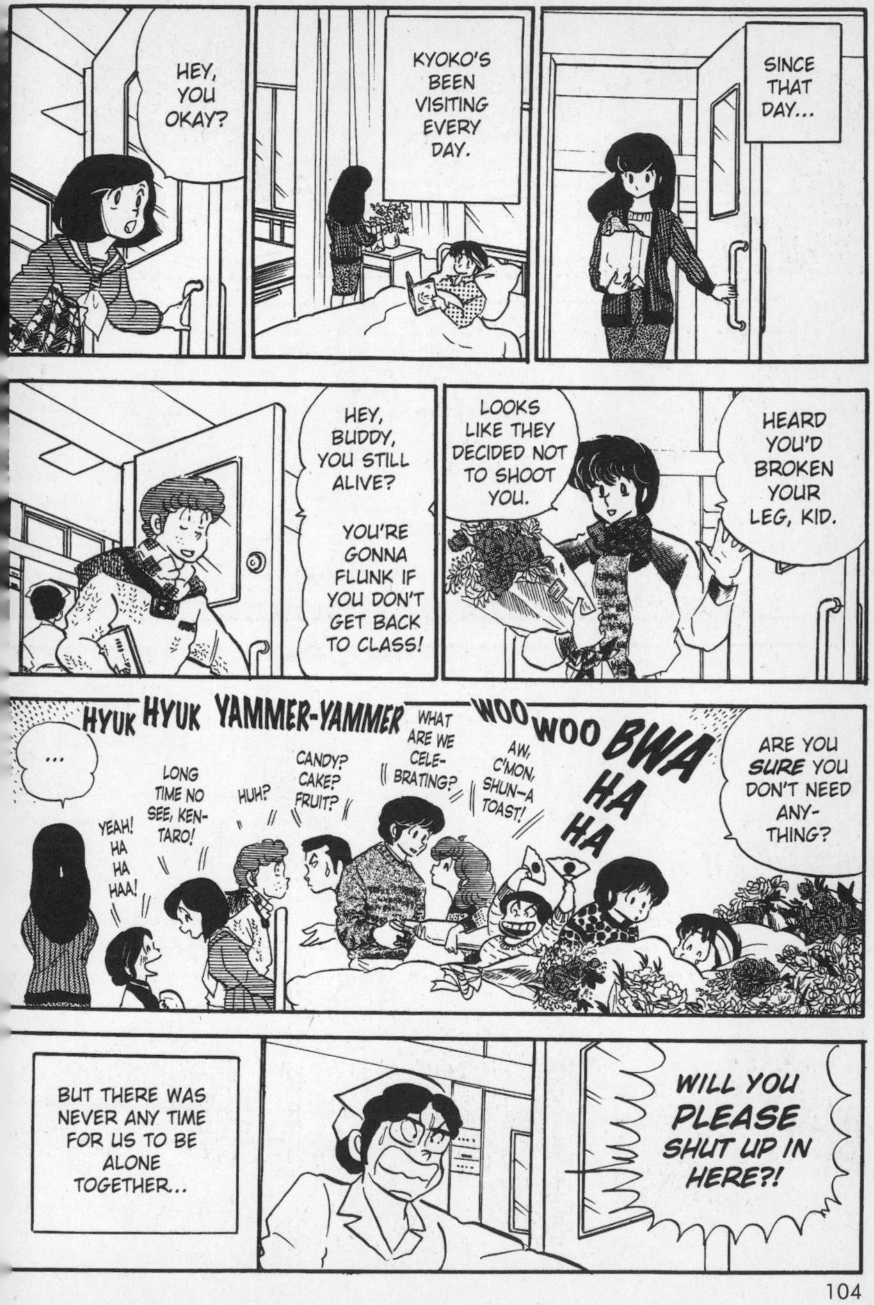
SINCE THAT DAY...
KYOKO'S BEEN VISITING EVERY DAY.
HEY, YOU OKAY?
HEARD YOU'D BROKEN YOUR LEG, KID.
LOOKS LIKE THEY DECIDED NOT TO SHOOT YOU.
HEY, BUDDY, YOU STILL ALIVE?
YOU'RE GONNA FLUNK IF YOU DON'T GET BACK TO CLASS!
ARE YOU SURE YOU DON'T NEED ANYTHING?
BWA HA HA HA
WOO WOO
AW, C'MON, SHUN—A TOAST!
WHAT ARE WE CELEBRATING?
YAMMER-YAMMER
CANDY? CAKE? FRUIT?
HUH?
HYUK HYUK
LONG TIME NO SEE, KENTARO!
YEAH! HA HA HAA!
...
WILL YOU PLEASE SHUT UP IN HERE?!
BUT THERE WAS NEVER ANY TIME FOR US TO BE ALONE TOGETHER...

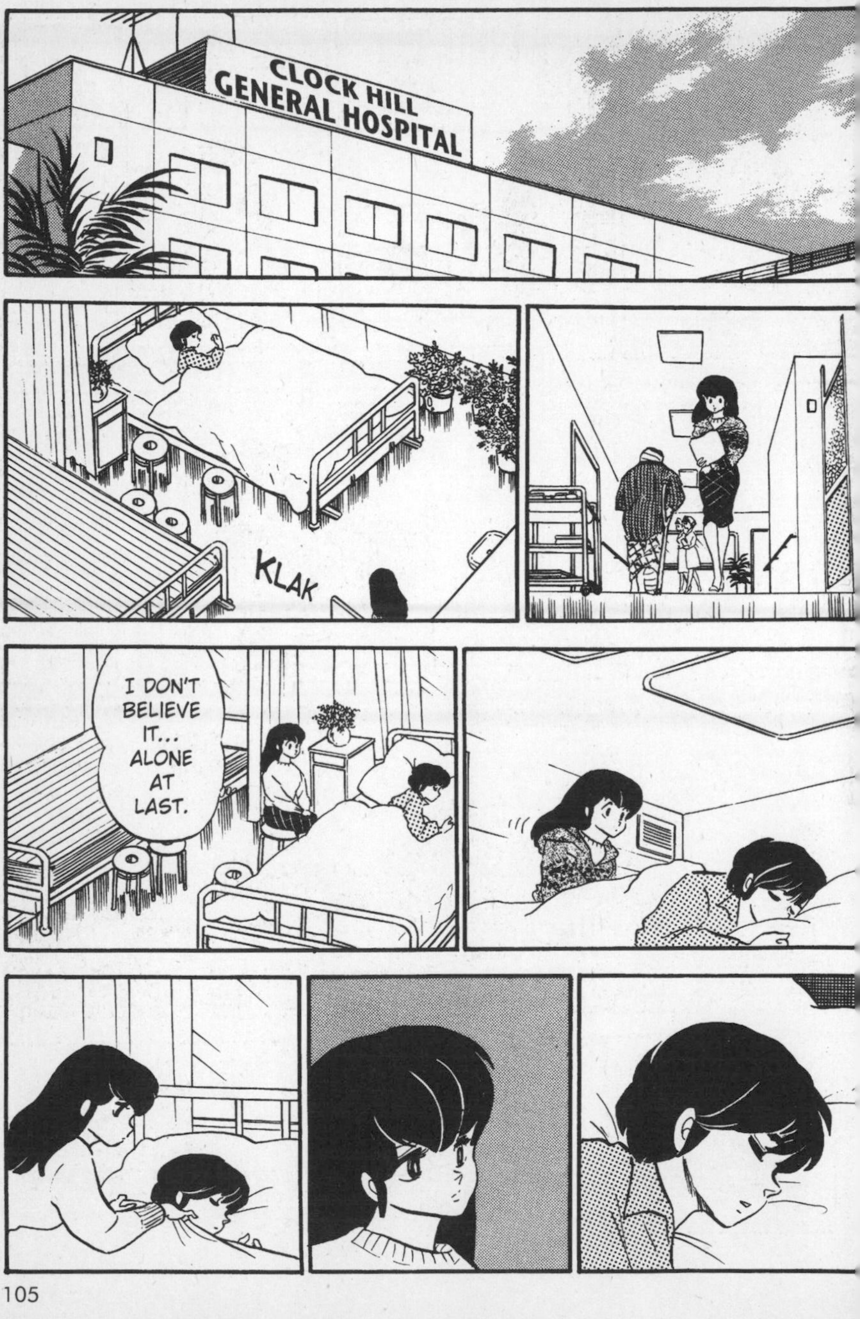
CLOCK HILL
GENERAL HOSPITAL
KLAK
I DON'T BELIEVE IT... ALONE AT LAST.

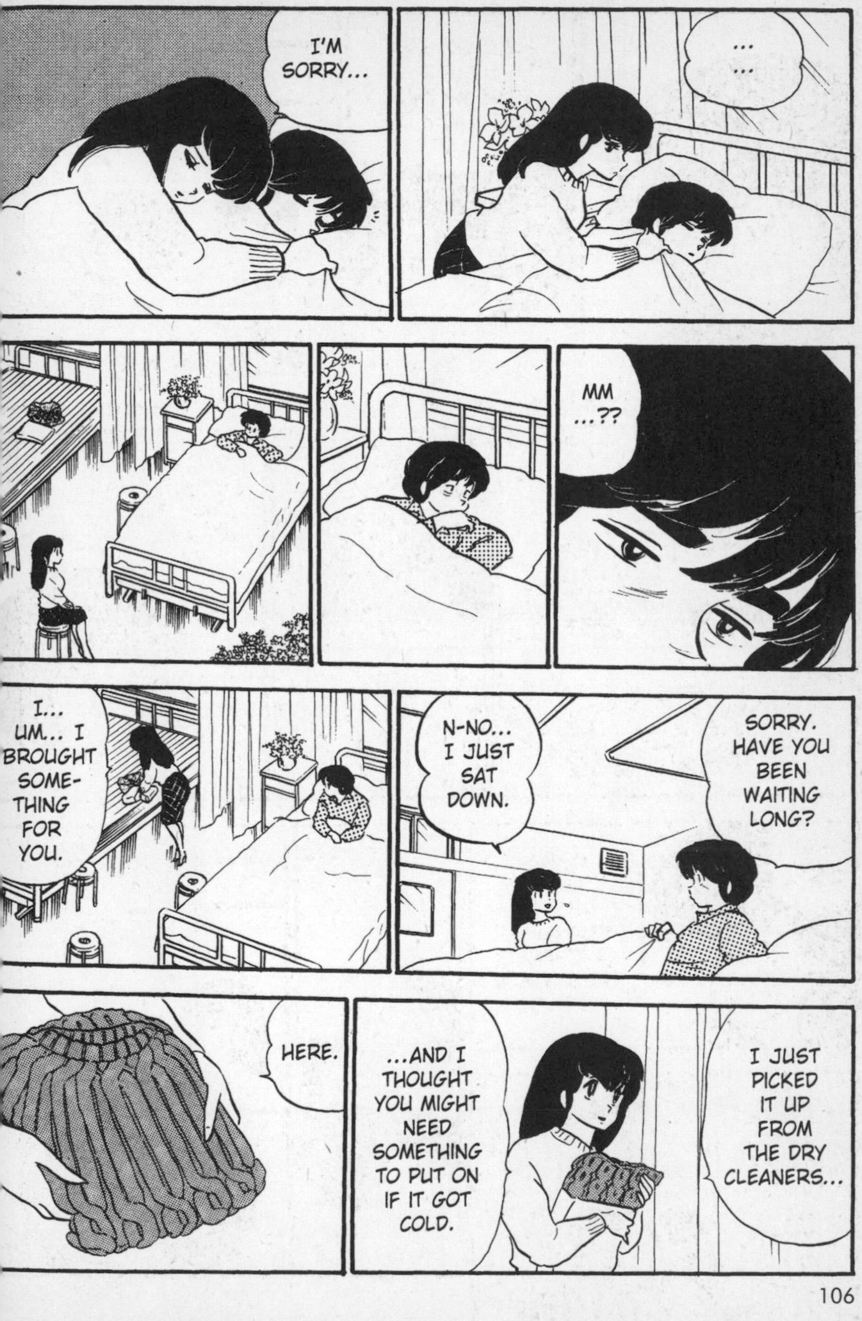
... ...
I'M SORRY...
MM ...??
SORRY. HAVE YOU BEEN WAITING LONG?
N-NO... I JUST SAT DOWN.
I... UM... I BROUGHT SOMETHING FOR YOU.
I JUST PICKED IT UP FROM THE DRY CLEANERS...
...AND I THOUGHT YOU MIGHT NEED SOMETHING TO PUT ON IF IT GOT COLD.
HERE.

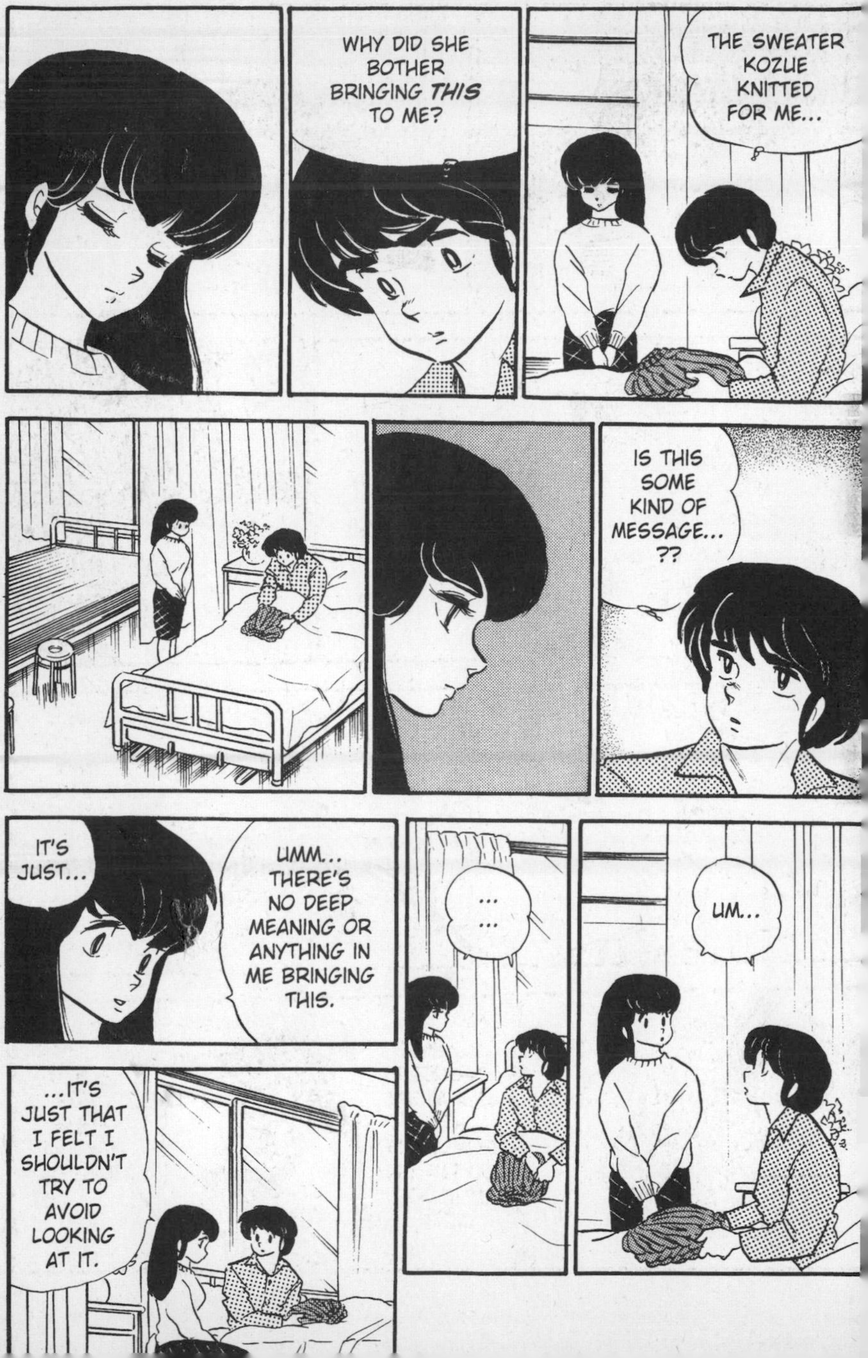
THE SWEATER KOZUE KNITTED FOR ME...
WHY DID SHE BOTHER BRINGING *THIS* TO ME?
IS THIS SOME KIND OF MESSAGE... ??
UM...
... ...
UMM... THERE'S NO DEEP MEANING OR ANYTHING IN ME BRINGING THIS.
IT'S JUST...
...IT'S JUST THAT I FELT I SHOULDN'T TRY TO AVOID LOOKING AT IT.

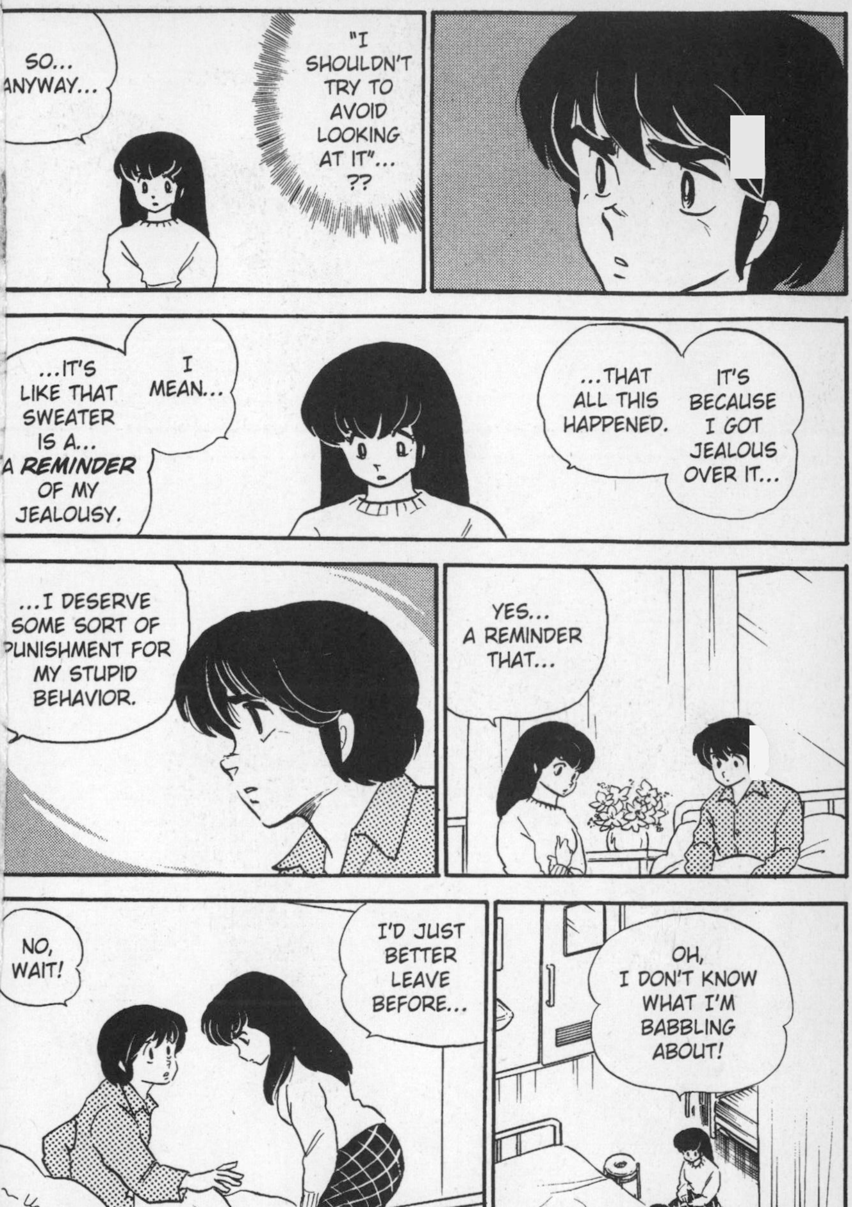
"I SHOULDN'T TRY TO AVOID LOOKING AT IT"... ??
SO... ANYWAY...
IT'S BECAUSE I GOT JEALOUS OVER IT...
...THAT ALL THIS HAPPENED.
I MEAN...
...IT'S LIKE THAT SWEATER IS A... A **REMINDER** OF MY JEALOUSY.
YES... A REMINDER THAT...
...I DESERVE SOME SORT OF PUNISHMENT FOR MY STUPID BEHAVIOR.
OH, I DON'T KNOW WHAT I'M BABBLING ABOUT!
I'D JUST BETTER LEAVE BEFORE...
NO, WAIT!

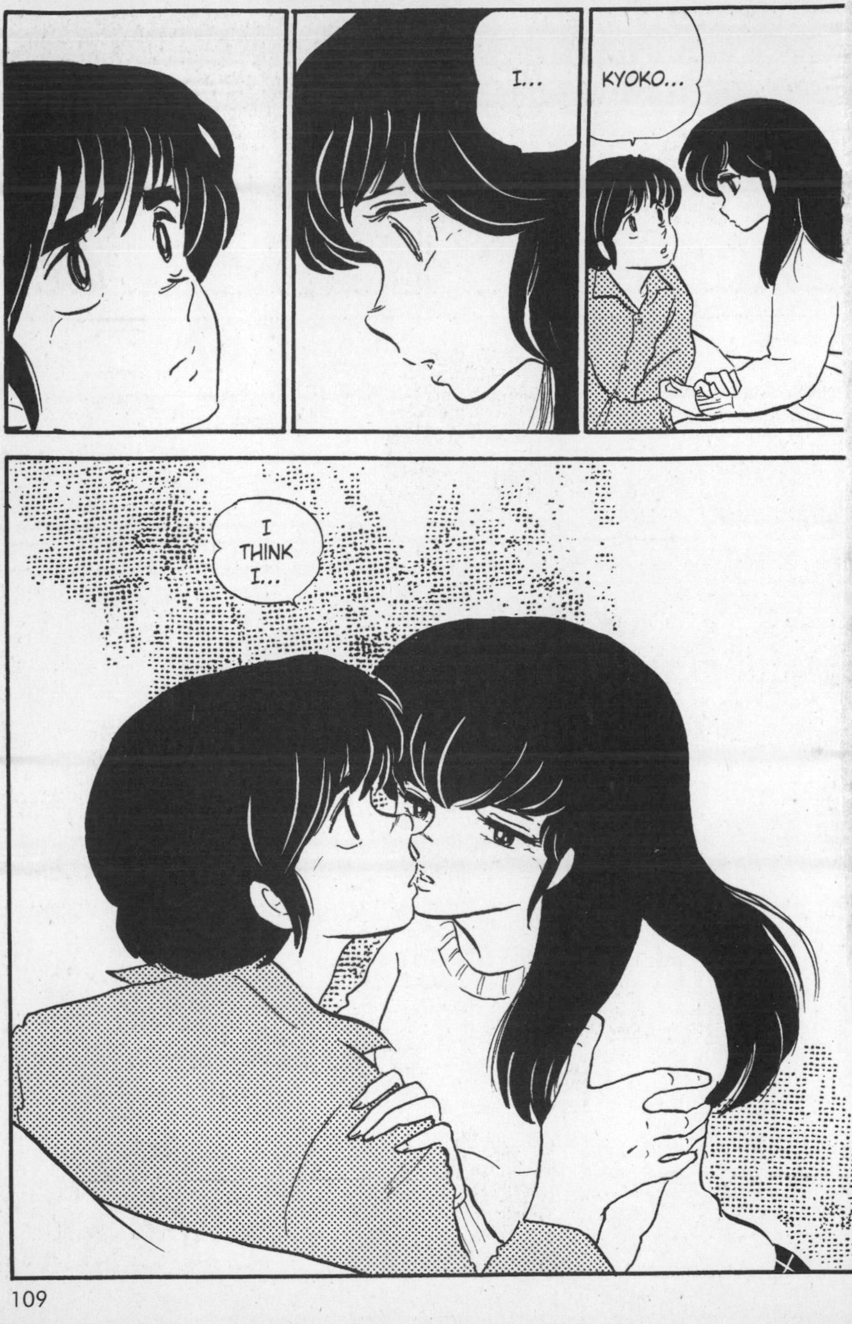
KYOKO...
I...
I THINK I...

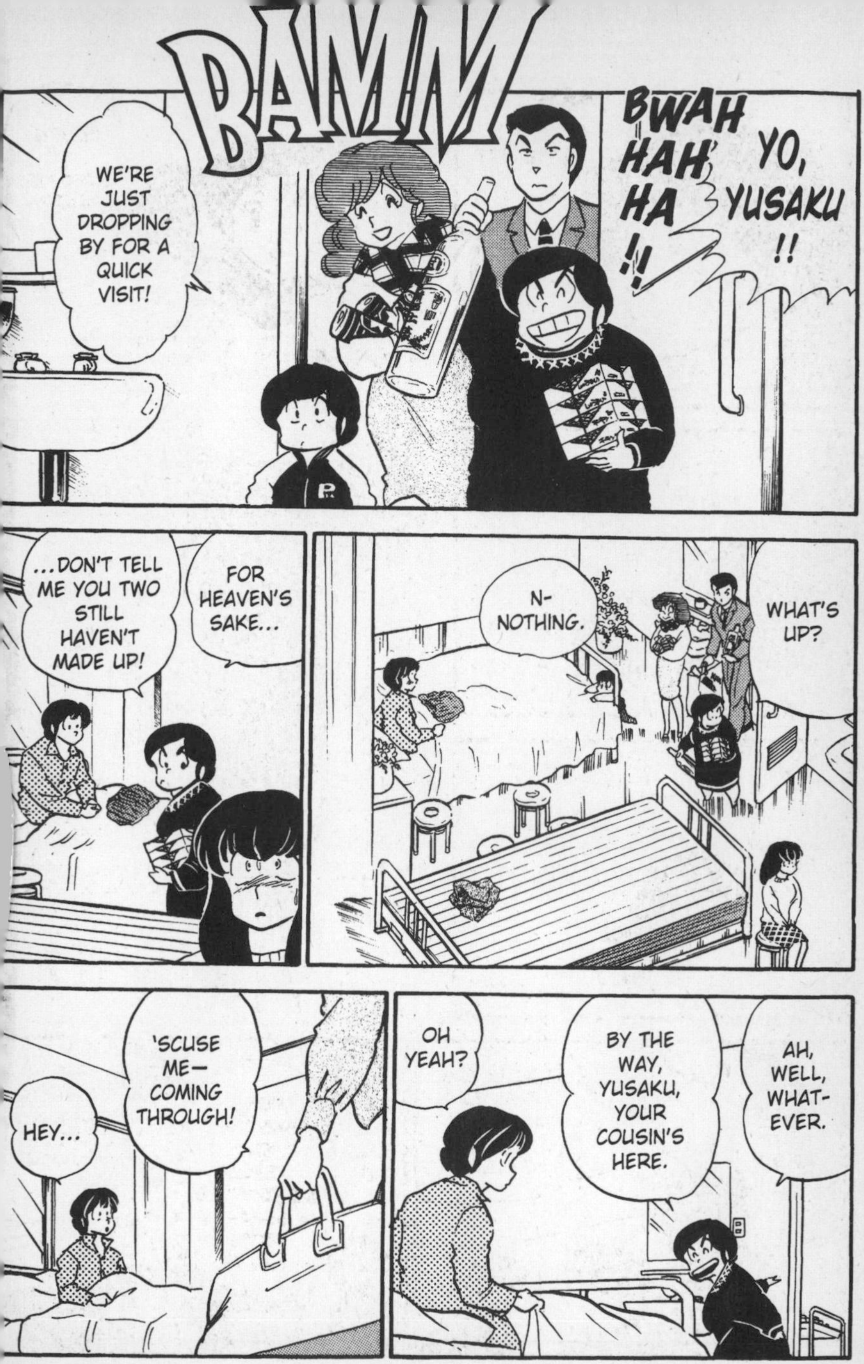
YO, YUSAKU!!
BWAH HAH HA!!
BAMM
WE'RE JUST DROPPING BY FOR A QUICK VISIT!
WHAT'S UP?
N-NOTHING.
FOR HEAVEN'S SAKE...
...DON'T TELL ME YOU TWO STILL HAVEN'T MADE UP!
AH, WELL, WHAT-EVER.
BY THE WAY, YUSAKU, YOUR COUSIN'S HERE.
OH YEAH?
'SCUSE ME—COMING THROUGH!
HEY...

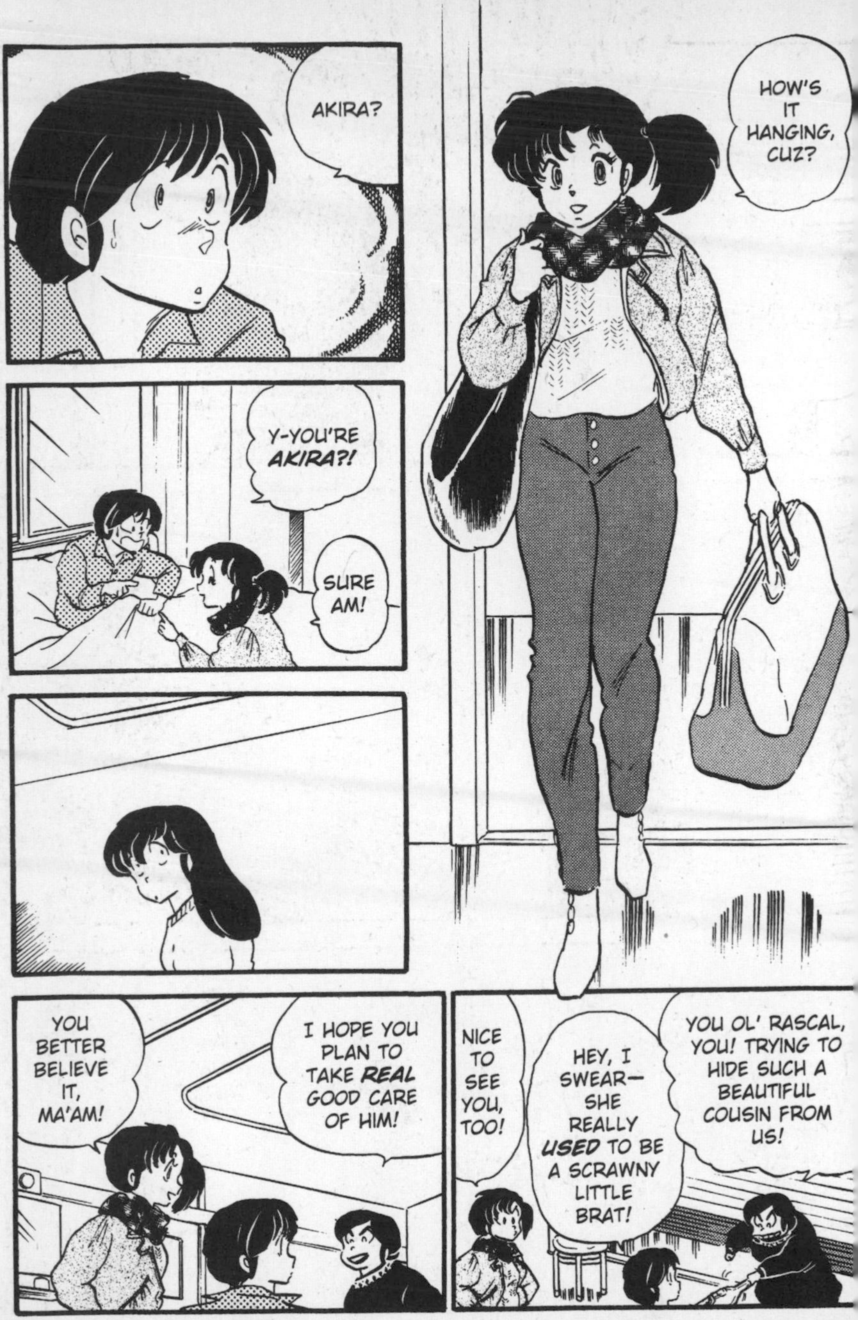
HOW'S IT HANGING, CUZ?
AKIRA?
Y-YOU'RE AKIRA?!
SURE AM!
YOU OL' RASCAL, YOU! TRYING TO HIDE SUCH A BEAUTIFUL COUSIN FROM US!
HEY, I SWEAR— SHE REALLY USED TO BE A SCRAWNY LITTLE BRAT!
NICE TO SEE YOU, TOO!
I HOPE YOU PLAN TO TAKE REAL GOOD CARE OF HIM!
YOU BETTER BELIEVE IT, MA'AM!

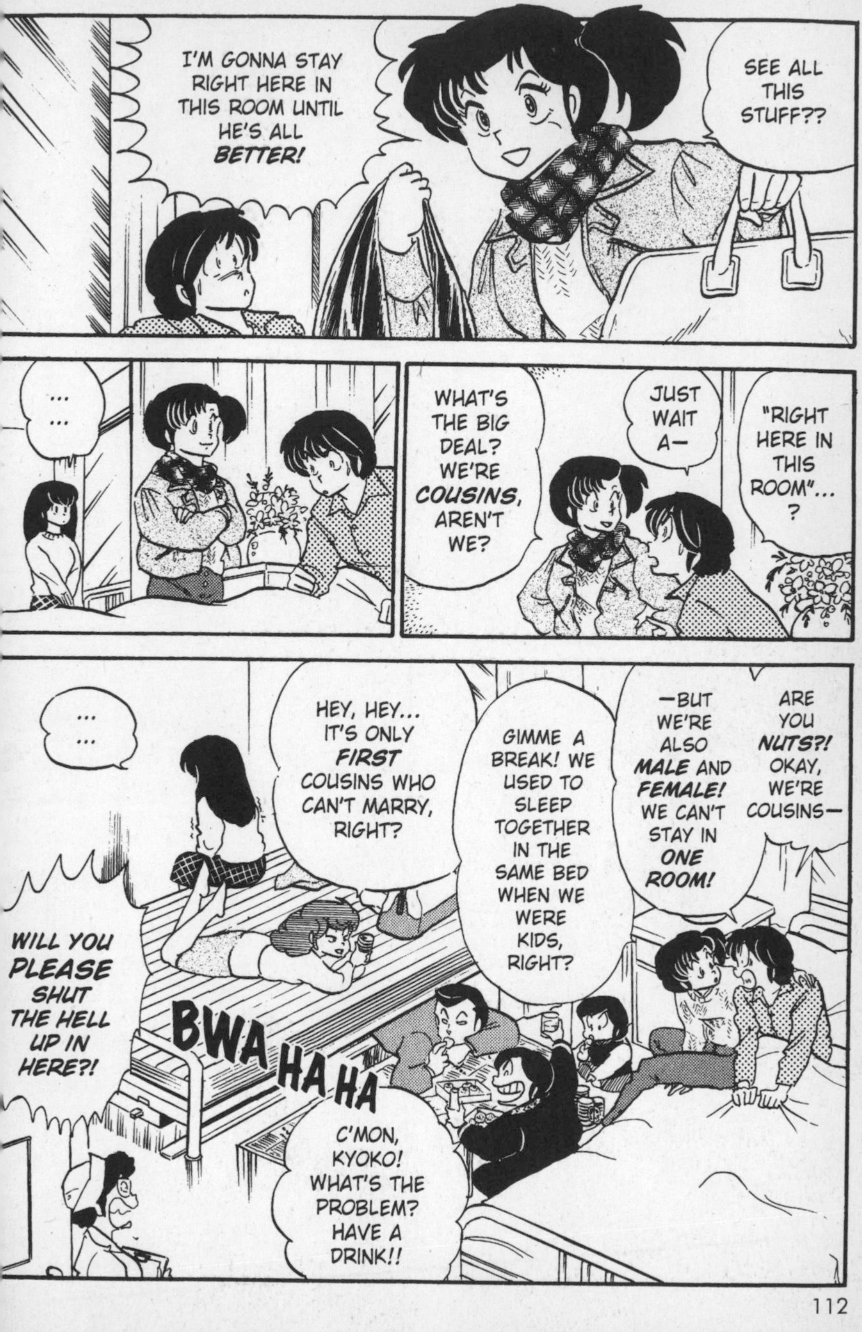
SEE ALL THIS STUFF??
I'M GONNA STAY RIGHT HERE IN THIS ROOM UNTIL HE'S ALL **BETTER!**
"RIGHT HERE IN THIS ROOM"...?
JUST WAIT A—
WHAT'S THE BIG DEAL? WE'RE **COUSINS**, AREN'T WE?
... ...
ARE YOU **NUTS?!** OKAY, WE'RE COUSINS—
—BUT WE'RE ALSO **MALE** AND **FEMALE!** WE CAN'T STAY IN **ONE ROOM!**
GIMME A BREAK! WE USED TO SLEEP TOGETHER IN THE SAME BED WHEN WE WERE KIDS, RIGHT?
HEY, HEY... IT'S ONLY **FIRST** COUSINS WHO CAN'T MARRY, RIGHT?
... ...
BWA HA HA HA
C'MON, KYOKO! WHAT'S THE PROBLEM? HAVE A DRINK!!
WILL YOU PLEASE SHUT THE HELL UP IN HERE?!

PART SIX

MISSION IMPOSSIBLE: THE PARTY CRACKER CASE

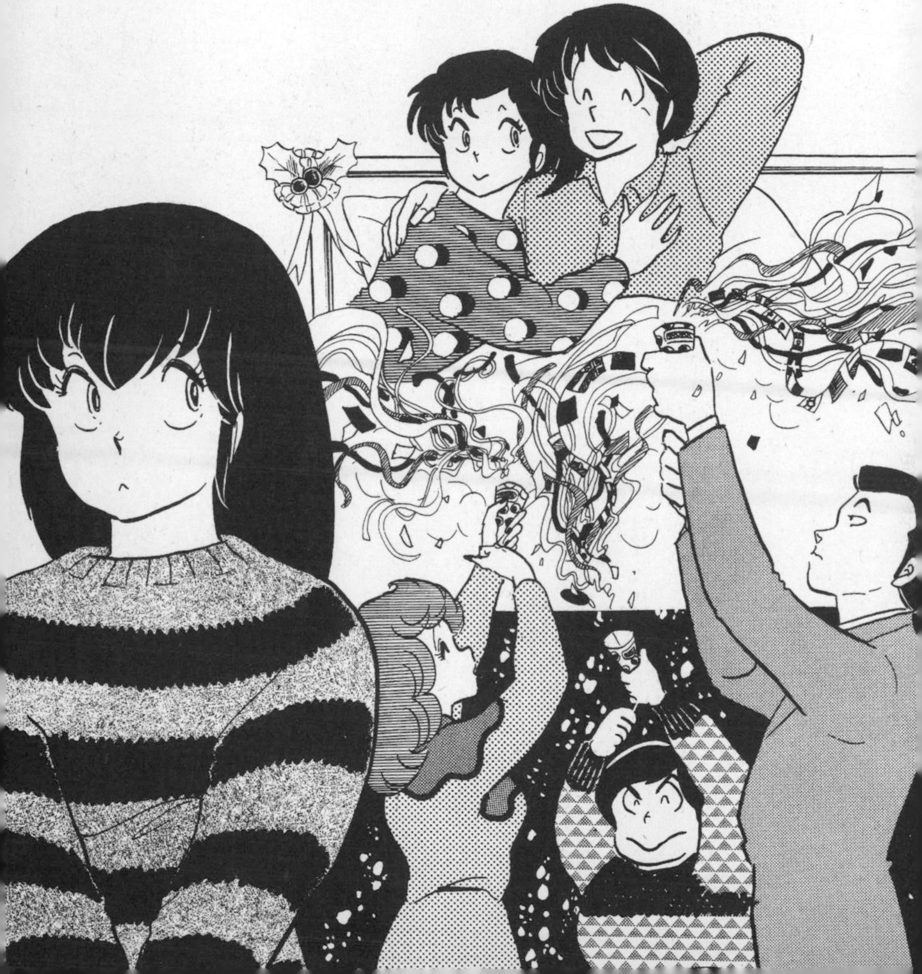

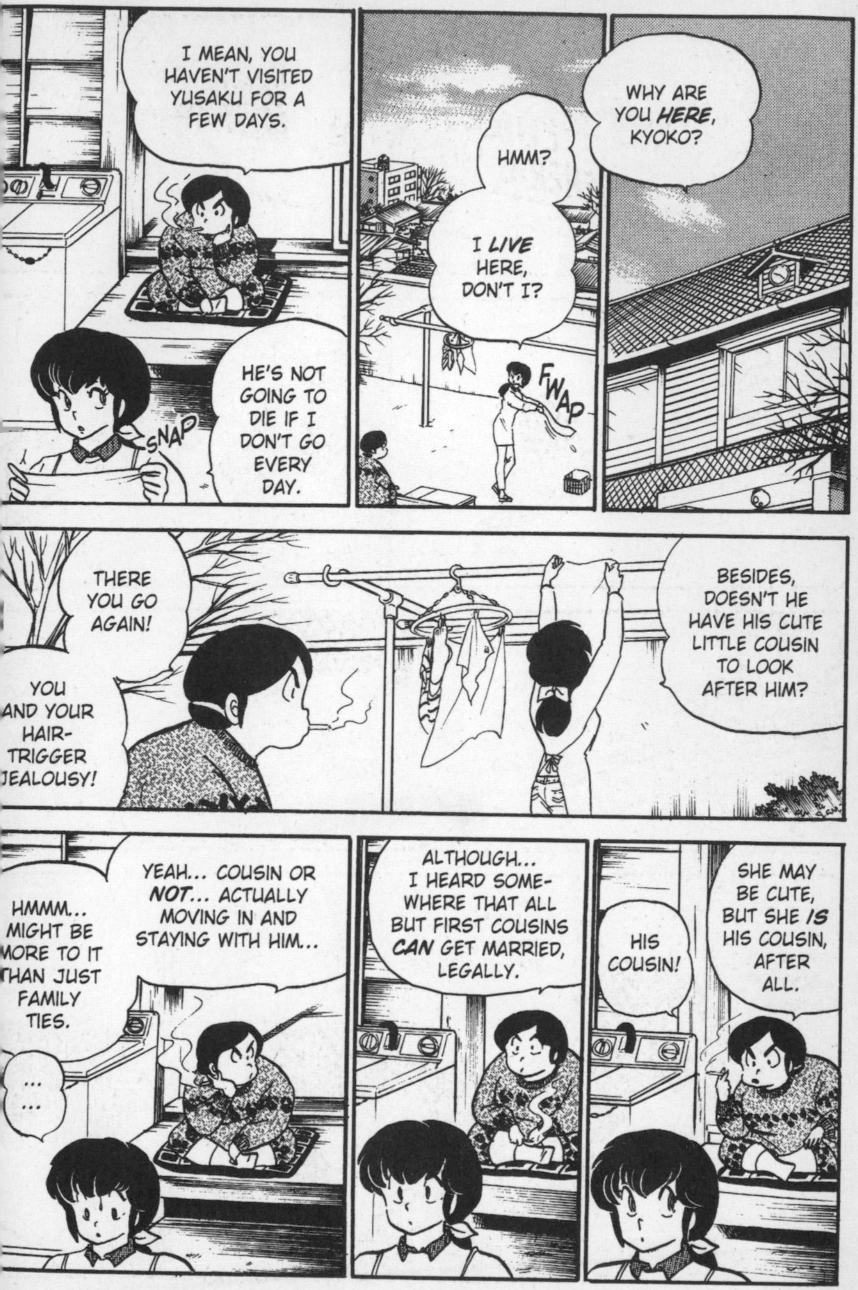
WHY ARE YOU *HERE*, KYOKO?
HMM?
I *LIVE* HERE, DON'T I?
FWAP
I MEAN, YOU HAVEN'T VISITED YUSAKU FOR A FEW DAYS.
HE'S NOT GOING TO DIE IF I DON'T GO EVERY DAY.
SNAP
BESIDES, DOESN'T HE HAVE HIS CUTE LITTLE COUSIN TO LOOK AFTER HIM?
THERE YOU GO AGAIN!
YOU AND YOUR HAIR-TRIGGER JEALOUSY!
SHE MAY BE CUTE, BUT SHE *IS* HIS COUSIN, AFTER ALL.
HIS COUSIN!
ALTHOUGH... I HEARD SOME-WHERE THAT ALL BUT FIRST COUSINS *CAN* GET MARRIED, LEGALLY.
YEAH... COUSIN OR *NOT*... ACTUALLY MOVING IN AND STAYING WITH HIM...
HMMM... MIGHT BE MORE TO IT THAN JUST FAMILY TIES.
... ...

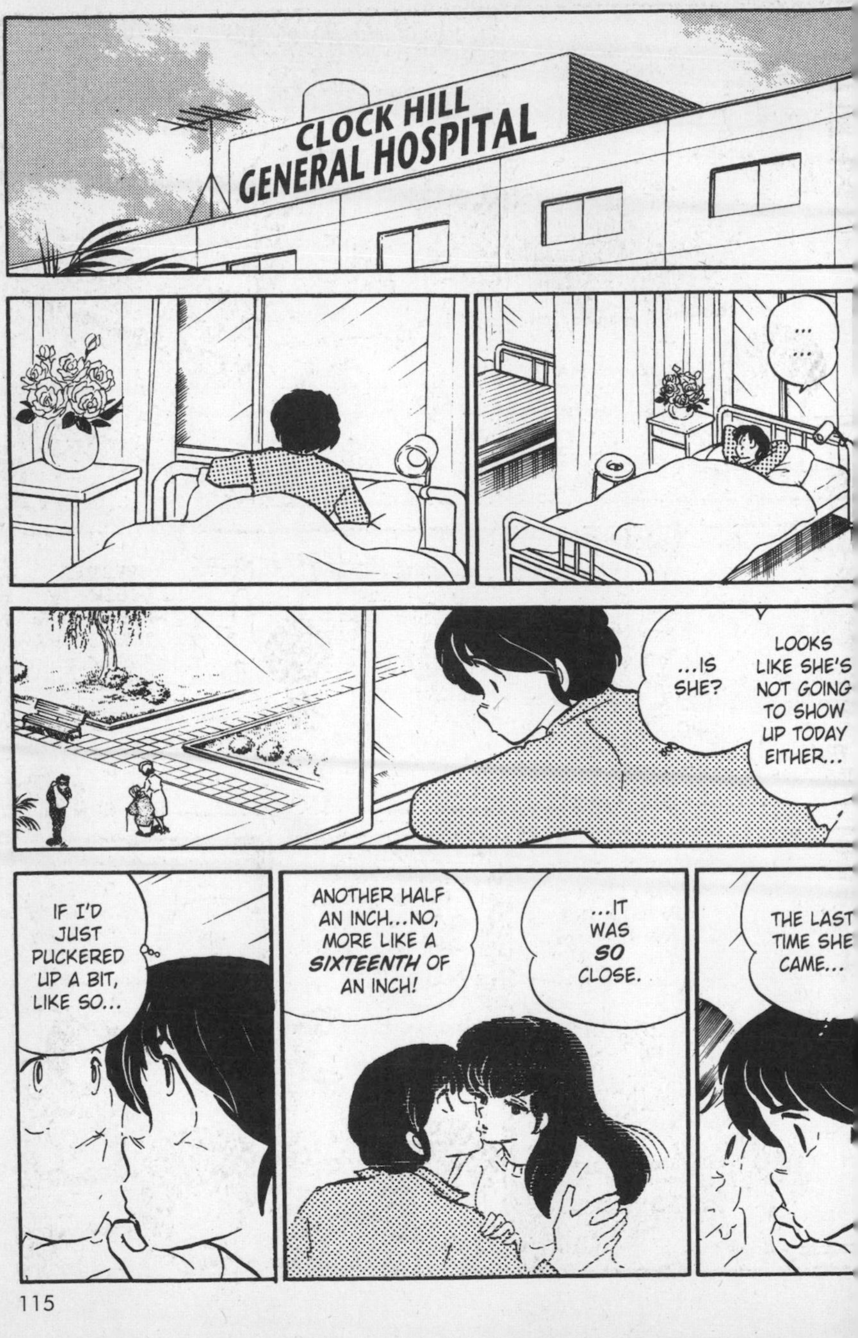
CLOCK HILL GENERAL HOSPITAL
... ...
LOOKS LIKE SHE'S NOT GOING TO SHOW UP TODAY EITHER...
...IS SHE?
THE LAST TIME SHE CAME...
...IT WAS SO CLOSE.
ANOTHER HALF AN INCH...NO, MORE LIKE A SIXTEENTH OF AN INCH!
IF I'D JUST PUCKERED UP A BIT, LIKE SO...

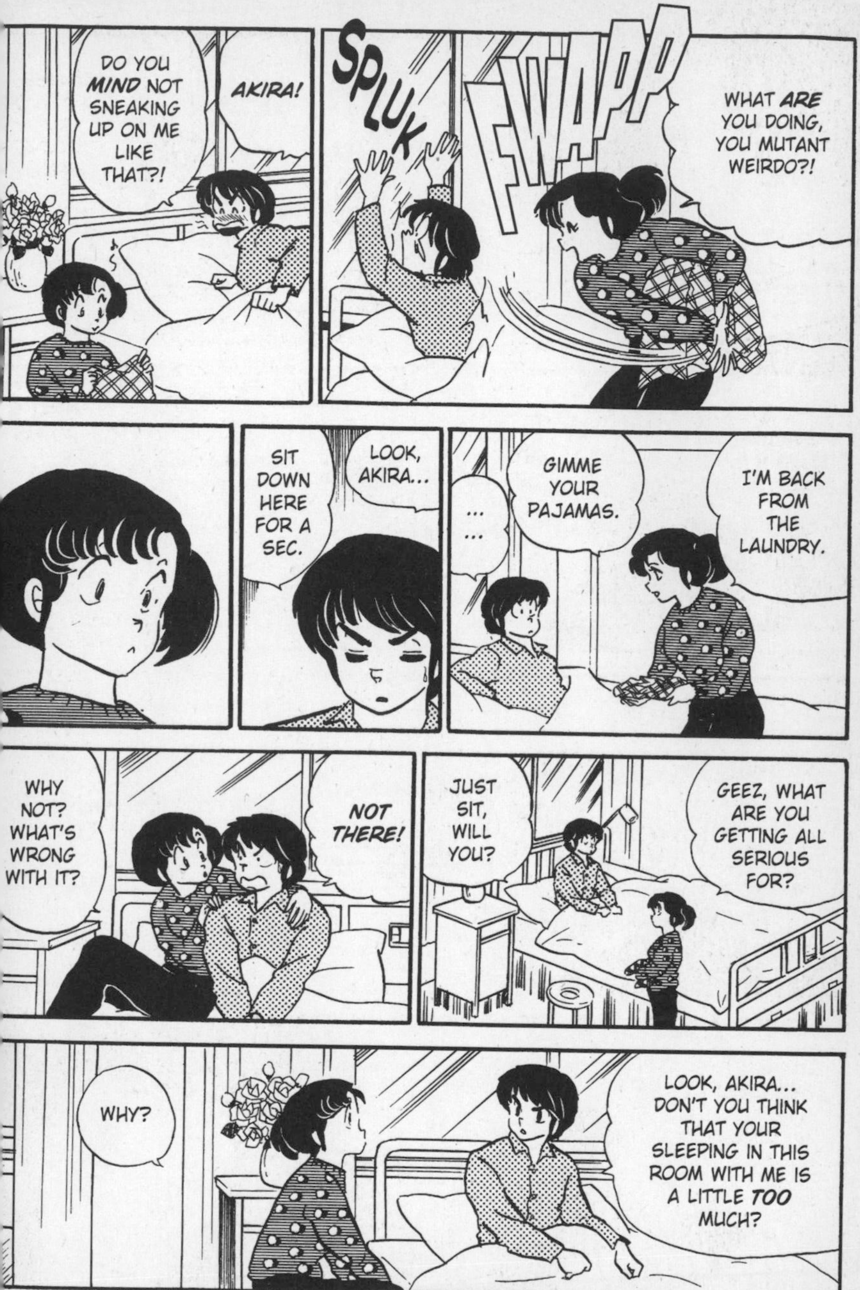
WHAT ARE YOU DOING, YOU MUTANT WEIRDO?!
FWAPP
SPLUK
AKIRA!
DO YOU MIND NOT SNEAKING UP ON ME LIKE THAT?!
I'M BACK FROM THE LAUNDRY.
GIMME YOUR PAJAMAS.
... ...
LOOK, AKIRA...
SIT DOWN HERE FOR A SEC.
GEEZ, WHAT ARE YOU GETTING ALL SERIOUS FOR?
JUST SIT, WILL YOU?
NOT THERE!
WHY NOT? WHAT'S WRONG WITH IT?
LOOK, AKIRA... DON'T YOU THINK THAT YOUR SLEEPING IN THIS ROOM WITH ME IS A LITTLE TOO MUCH?
WHY?

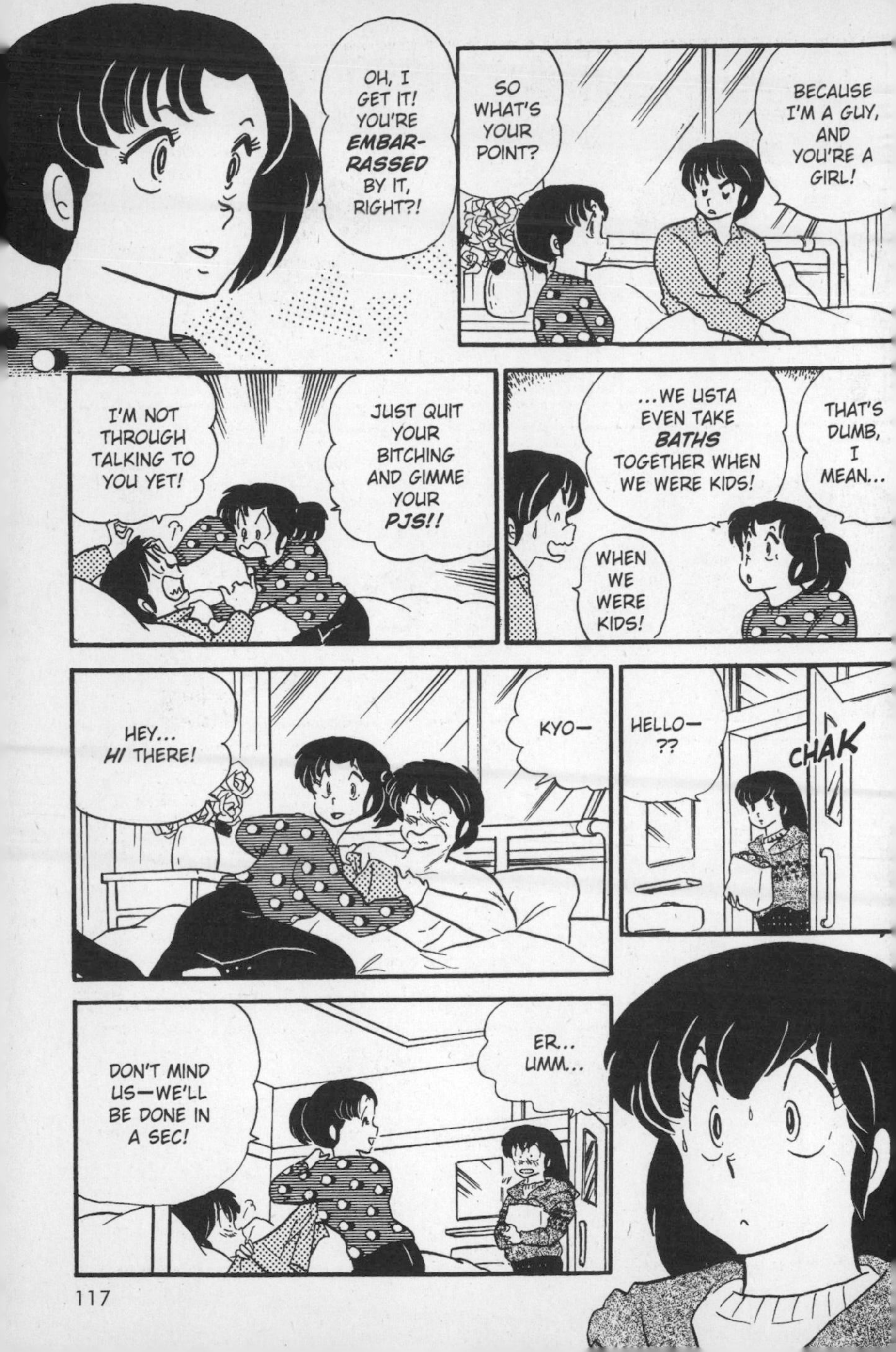
BECAUSE I'M A GUY, AND YOU'RE A GIRL!
SO WHAT'S YOUR POINT?
OH, I GET IT! YOU'RE EMBARRASSED BY IT, RIGHT?!
THAT'S DUMB, I MEAN...
...WE USTA EVEN TAKE BATHS TOGETHER WHEN WE WERE KIDS!
WHEN WE WERE KIDS!
JUST QUIT YOUR BITCHING AND GIMME YOUR PJS!!
I'M NOT THROUGH TALKING TO YOU YET!
CHAK
HELLO— ??
KYO—
HEY... HI THERE!
ER... UMM...
DON'T MIND US—WE'LL BE DONE IN A SEC!

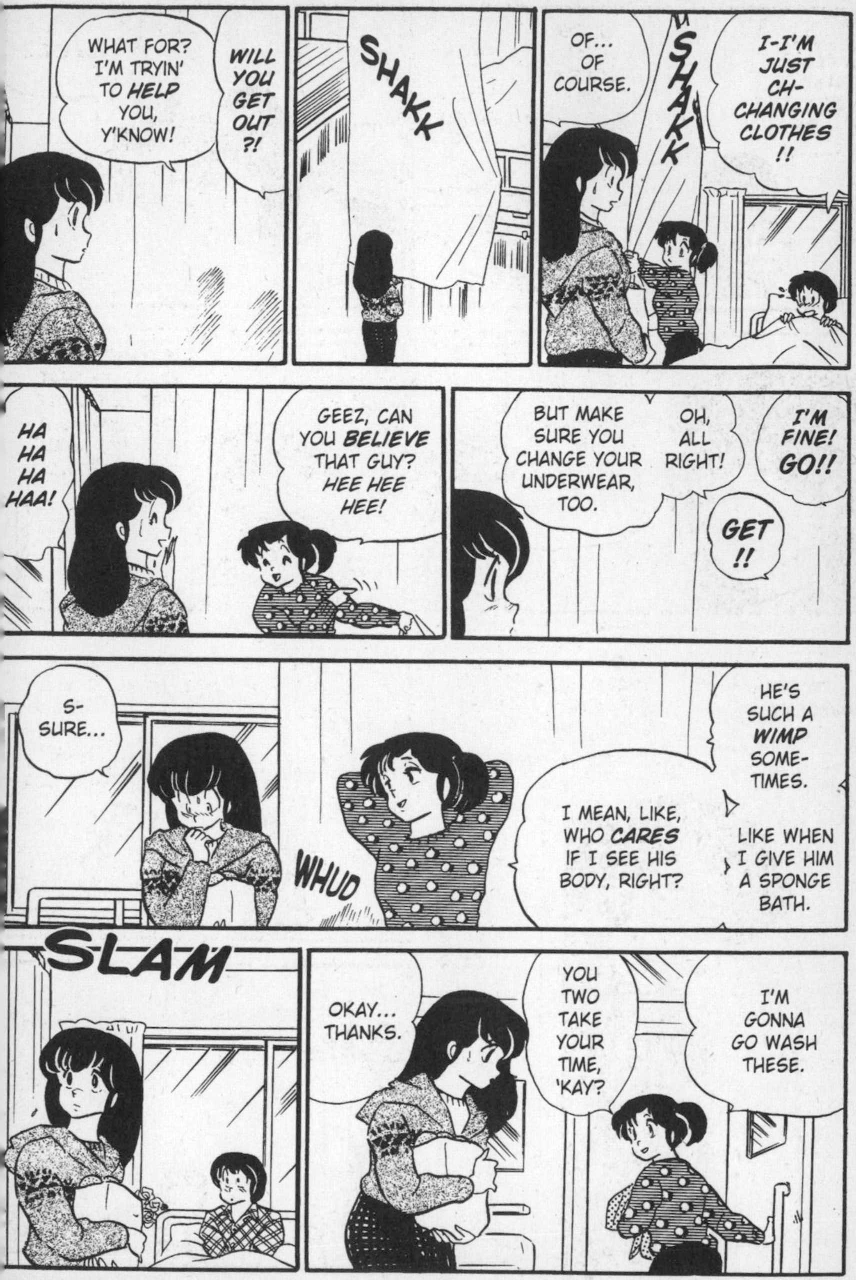
I-I'M JUST CH-CHANGING CLOTHES !!
SHAKK
OF... OF COURSE.
SHAKK
WILL YOU GET OUT ?!
WHAT FOR? I'M TRYIN' TO HELP YOU, Y'KNOW!
I'M FINE! GO!!
GET !!
OH, ALL RIGHT!
BUT MAKE SURE YOU CHANGE YOUR UNDERWEAR, TOO.
GEEZ, CAN YOU BELIEVE THAT GUY? HEE HEE HEE!
HA HA HA HAA!
HE'S SUCH A WIMP SOMETIMES.
LIKE WHEN I GIVE HIM A SPONGE BATH.
I MEAN, LIKE, WHO CARES IF I SEE HIS BODY, RIGHT?
WHUD
S-SURE...
I'M GONNA GO WASH THESE.
YOU TWO TAKE YOUR TIME, 'KAY?
OKAY... THANKS.
SLAM

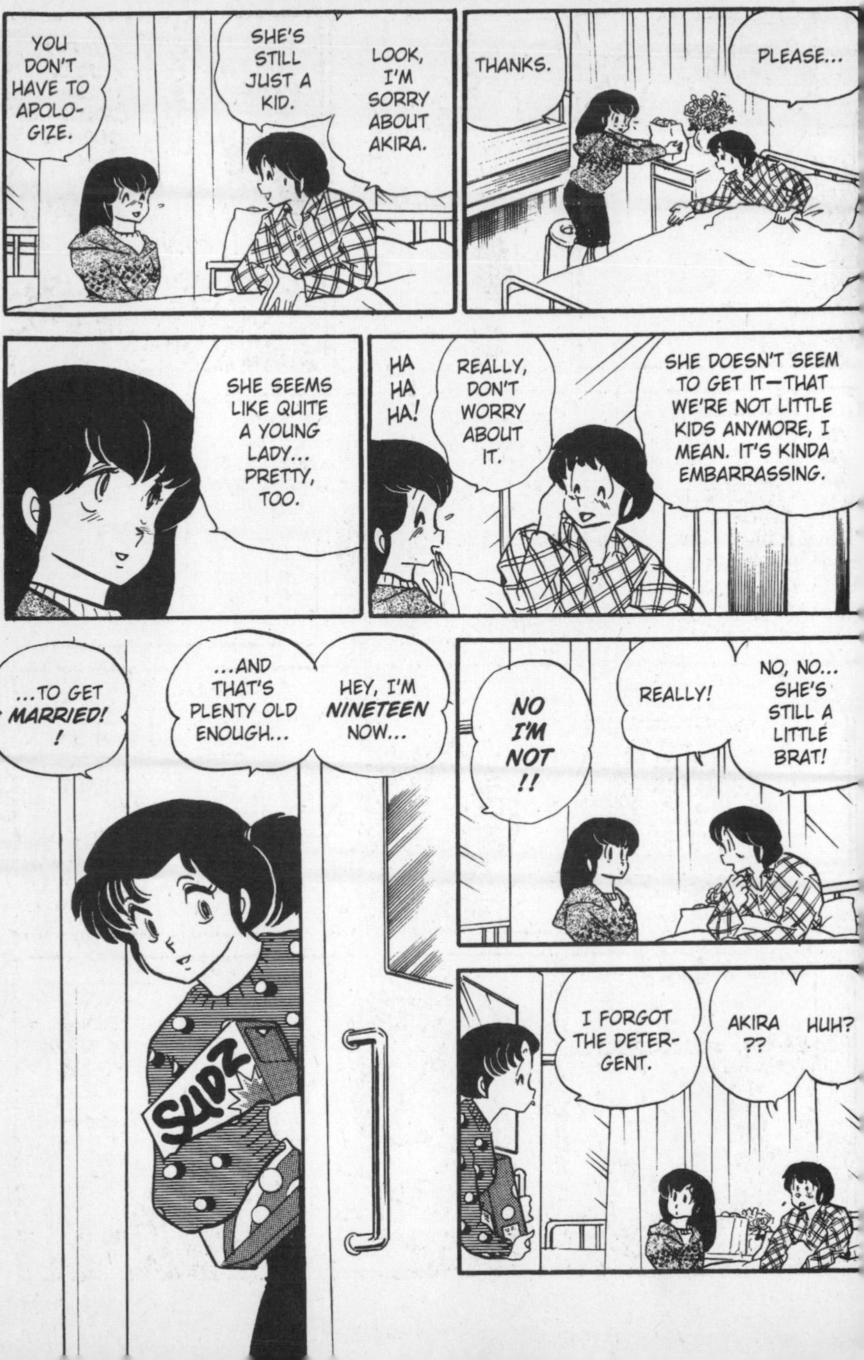
PLEASE...
THANKS.
LOOK, I'M SORRY ABOUT AKIRA.
SHE'S STILL JUST A KID.
YOU DON'T HAVE TO APOLO-GIZE.
SHE DOESN'T SEEM TO GET IT—THAT WE'RE NOT LITTLE KIDS ANYMORE, I MEAN. IT'S KINDA EMBARRASSING.
REALLY, DON'T WORRY ABOUT IT.
HA HA HA!
SHE SEEMS LIKE QUITE A YOUNG LADY... PRETTY, TOO.
NO, NO... SHE'S STILL A LITTLE BRAT!
REALLY!
NO I'M NOT!!
HUH?
AKIRA ??
I FORGOT THE DETER-GENT.
HEY, I'M *NINETEEN* NOW...
...AND THAT'S PLENTY OLD ENOUGH...
...TO GET *MARRIED!!*
SUDZ

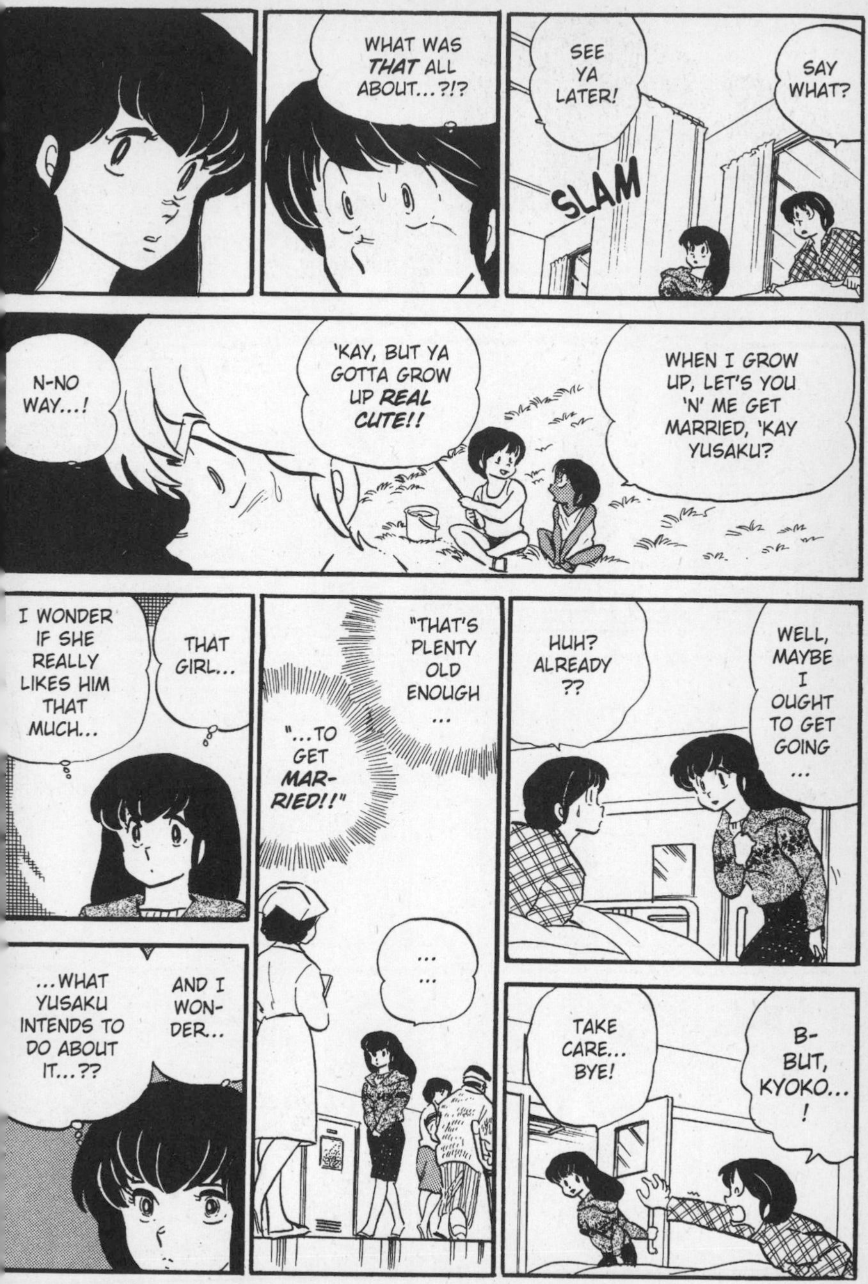
SAY WHAT?
SEE YA LATER!
SLAM
WHAT WAS THAT ALL ABOUT...?!?
WHEN I GROW UP, LET'S YOU 'N' ME GET MARRIED, 'KAY YUSAKU?
'KAY, BUT YA GOTTA GROW UP REAL CUTE!!
N-NO WAY...!
WELL, MAYBE I OUGHT TO GET GOING...
HUH? ALREADY??
B-BUT, KYOKO...!
TAKE CARE... BYE!
"THAT'S PLENTY OLD ENOUGH...
"...TO GET MAR-RIED!!"
......
THAT GIRL...
I WONDER IF SHE REALLY LIKES HIM THAT MUCH...
AND I WON-DER...
...WHAT YUSAKU INTENDS TO DO ABOUT IT...??

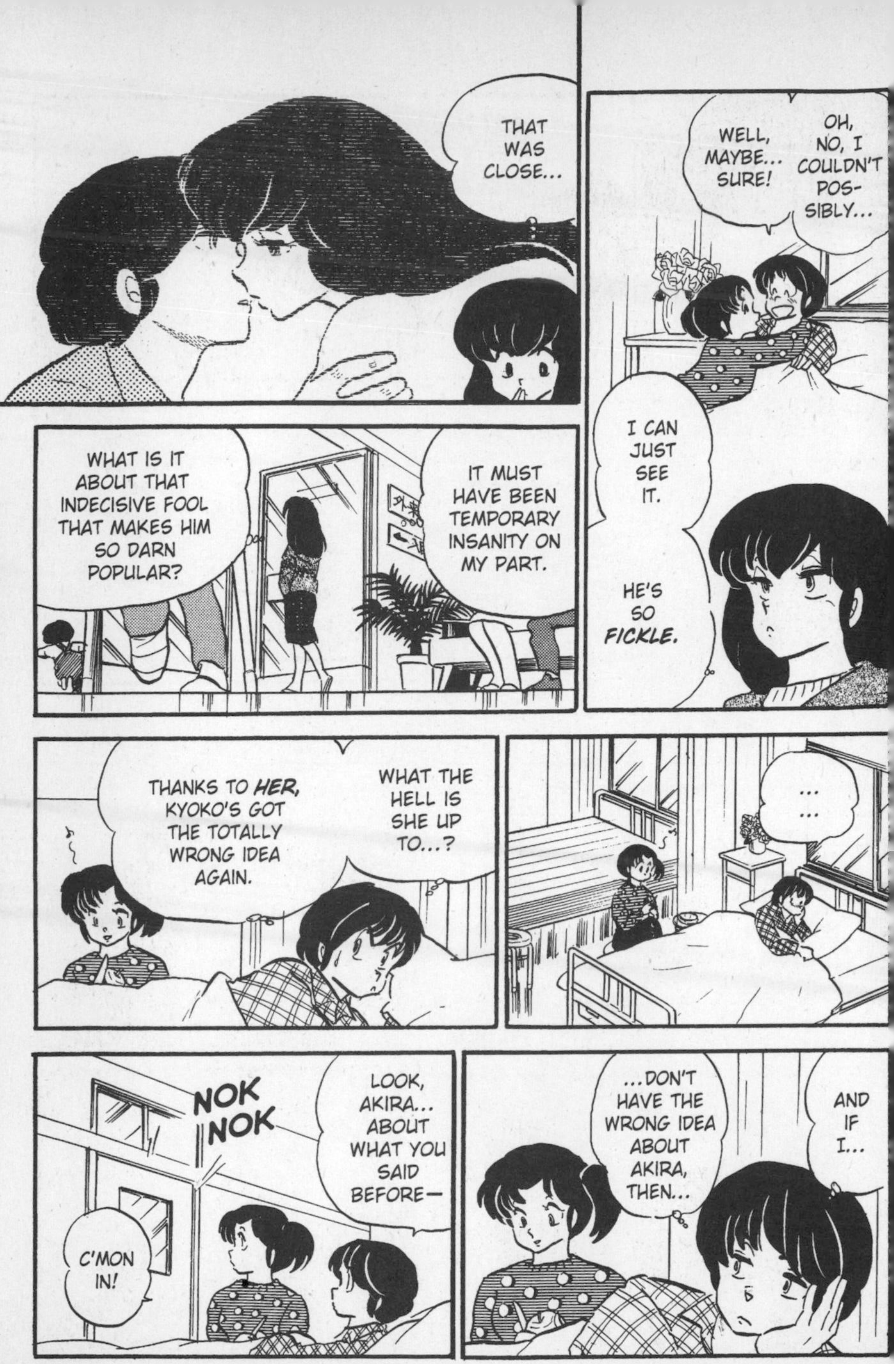
OH, NO, I COULDN'T POS-SIBLY...
WELL, MAYBE... SURE!
I CAN JUST SEE IT.
HE'S SO *FICKLE.*
THAT WAS CLOSE...
IT MUST HAVE BEEN TEMPORARY INSANITY ON MY PART.
WHAT IS IT ABOUT THAT INDECISIVE FOOL THAT MAKES HIM SO DARN POPULAR?
... ...
WHAT THE HELL IS SHE UP TO...?
THANKS TO *HER,* KYOKO'S GOT THE TOTALLY WRONG IDEA AGAIN.
AND IF I...
...DON'T HAVE THE WRONG IDEA ABOUT AKIRA, THEN...
LOOK, AKIRA... ABOUT WHAT YOU SAID BEFORE—
NOK NOK
C'MON IN!

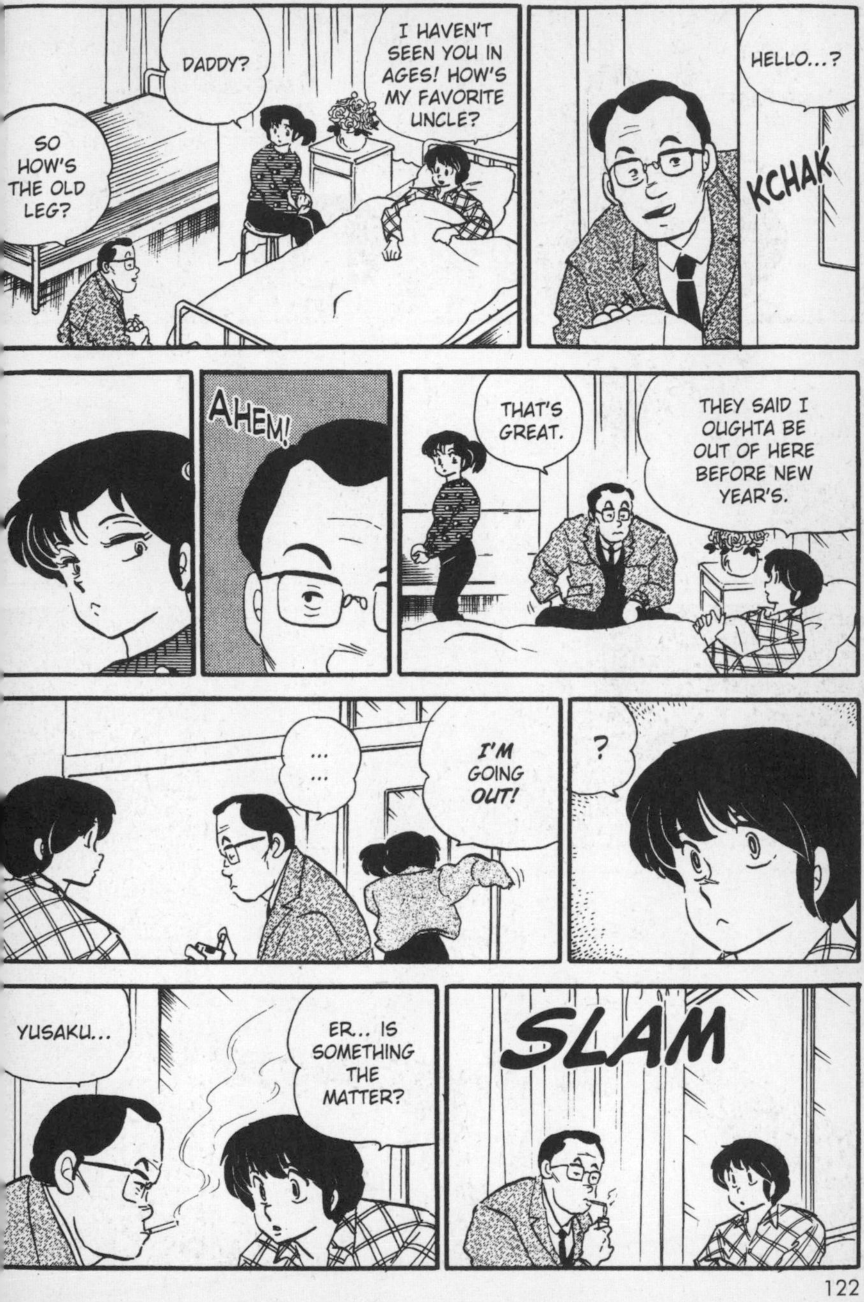
HELLO...?
KCHAK
I HAVEN'T SEEN YOU IN AGES! HOW'S MY FAVORITE UNCLE?
DADDY?
SO HOW'S THE OLD LEG?
THEY SAID I OUGHTA BE OUT OF HERE BEFORE NEW YEAR'S.
THAT'S GREAT.
AHEM!
?
I'M GOING OUT!
... ...
SLAM
ER... IS SOMETHING THE MATTER?
YUSAKU...

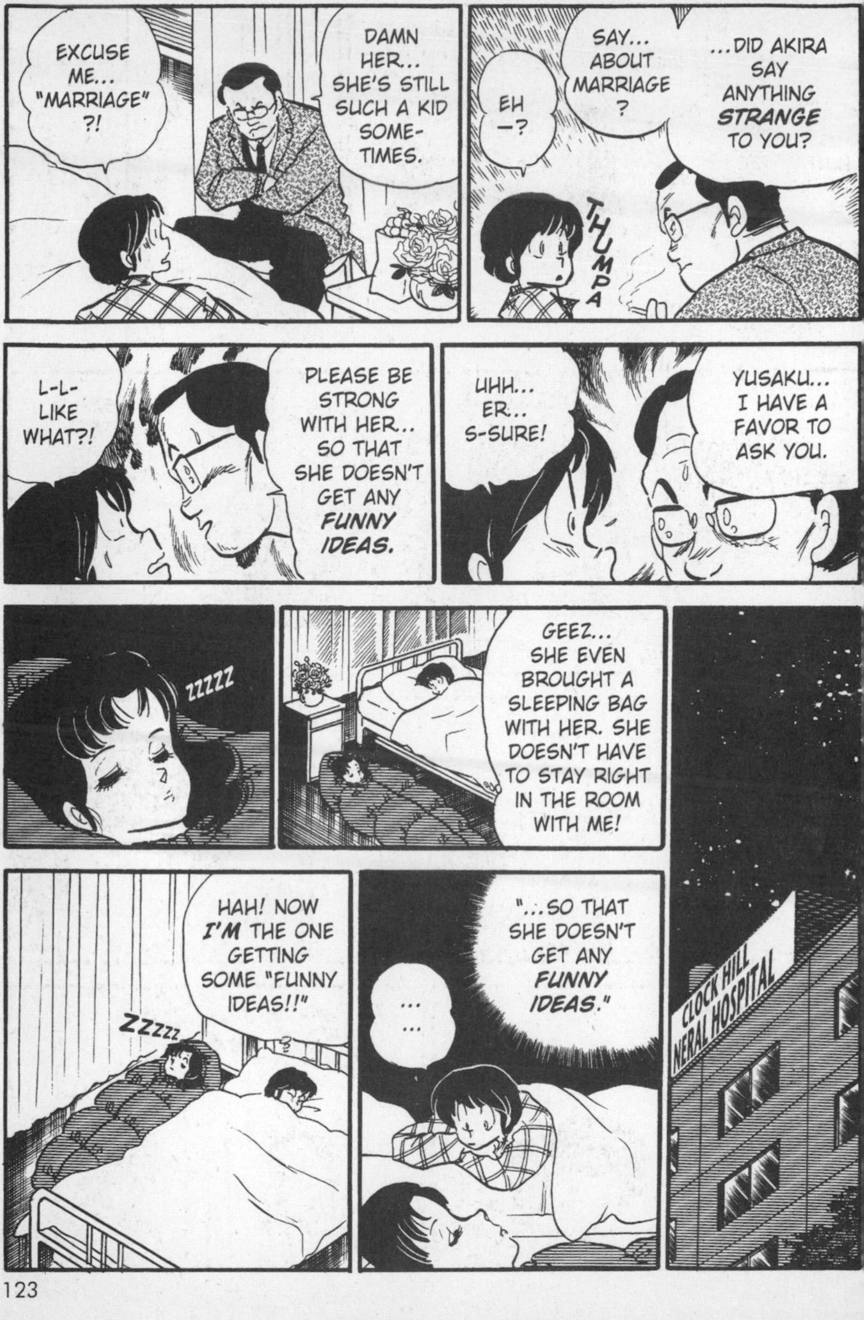
...DID AKIRA SAY ANYTHING STRANGE TO YOU?
SAY... ABOUT MARRIAGE ?
EH —?
THUMPA
DAMN HER... SHE'S STILL SUCH A KID SOME- TIMES.
EXCUSE ME... "MARRIAGE" ?!
YUSAKU... I HAVE A FAVOR TO ASK YOU.
UHH... ER... S-SURE!
PLEASE BE STRONG WITH HER... SO THAT SHE DOESN'T GET ANY FUNNY IDEAS.
L-L- LIKE WHAT?!
CLOCK HILL
NERAL HOSPITAL
GEEZ... SHE EVEN BROUGHT A SLEEPING BAG WITH HER. SHE DOESN'T HAVE TO STAY RIGHT IN THE ROOM WITH ME!
ZZZZZ
"...SO THAT SHE DOESN'T GET ANY FUNNY IDEAS."
... ...
HAH! NOW I'M THE ONE GETTING SOME "FUNNY IDEAS!!"
ZZZZZ

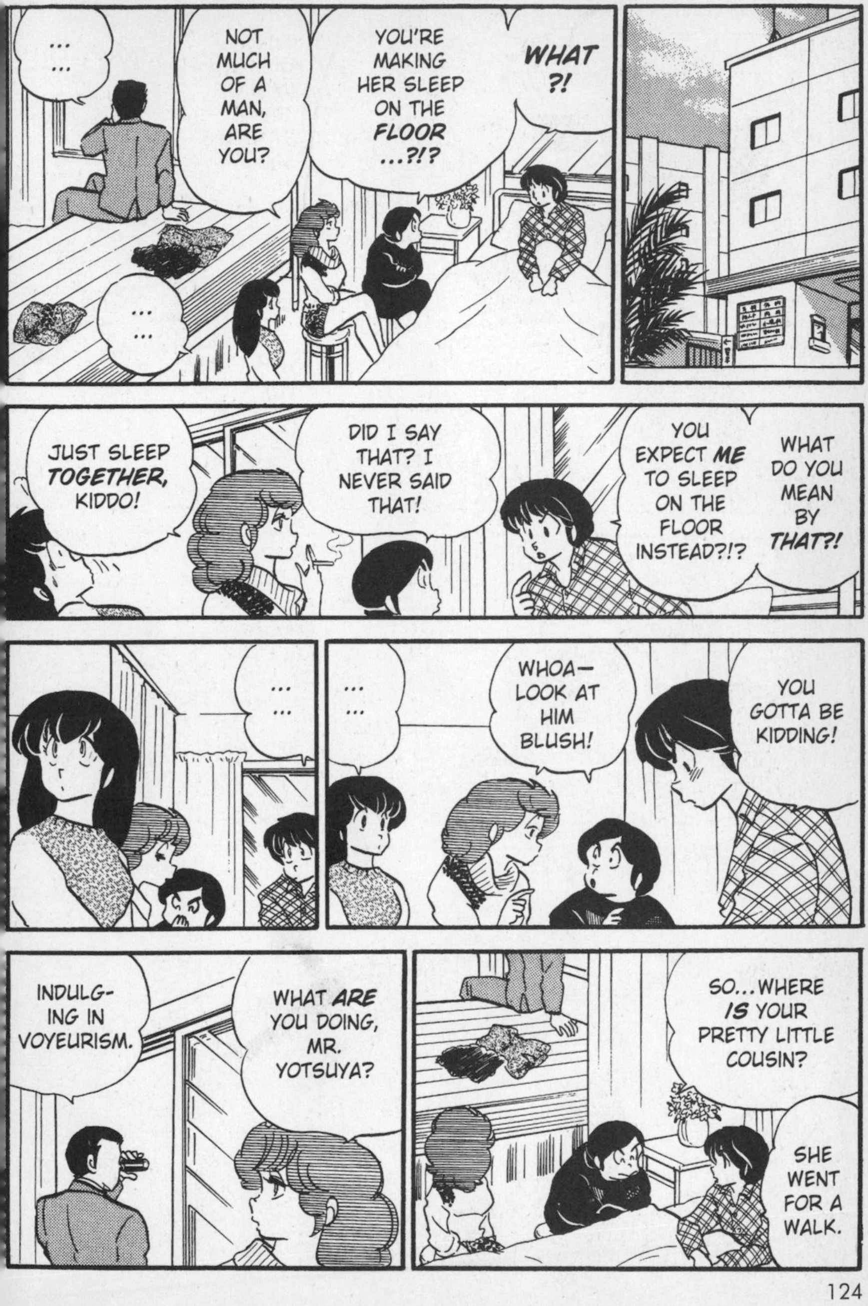
WHAT ?!
YOU'RE MAKING HER SLEEP ON THE FLOOR ...?!?
NOT MUCH OF A MAN, ARE YOU?
... ...
... ...
WHAT DO YOU MEAN BY THAT?!
YOU EXPECT ME TO SLEEP ON THE FLOOR INSTEAD?!?
DID I SAY THAT? I NEVER SAID THAT!
JUST SLEEP TOGETHER, KIDDO!
YOU GOTTA BE KIDDING!
WHOA— LOOK AT HIM BLUSH!
... ...
... ...
SO...WHERE IS YOUR PRETTY LITTLE COUSIN?
SHE WENT FOR A WALK.
WHAT ARE YOU DOING, MR. YOTSUYA?
INDULG-ING IN VOYEURISM.

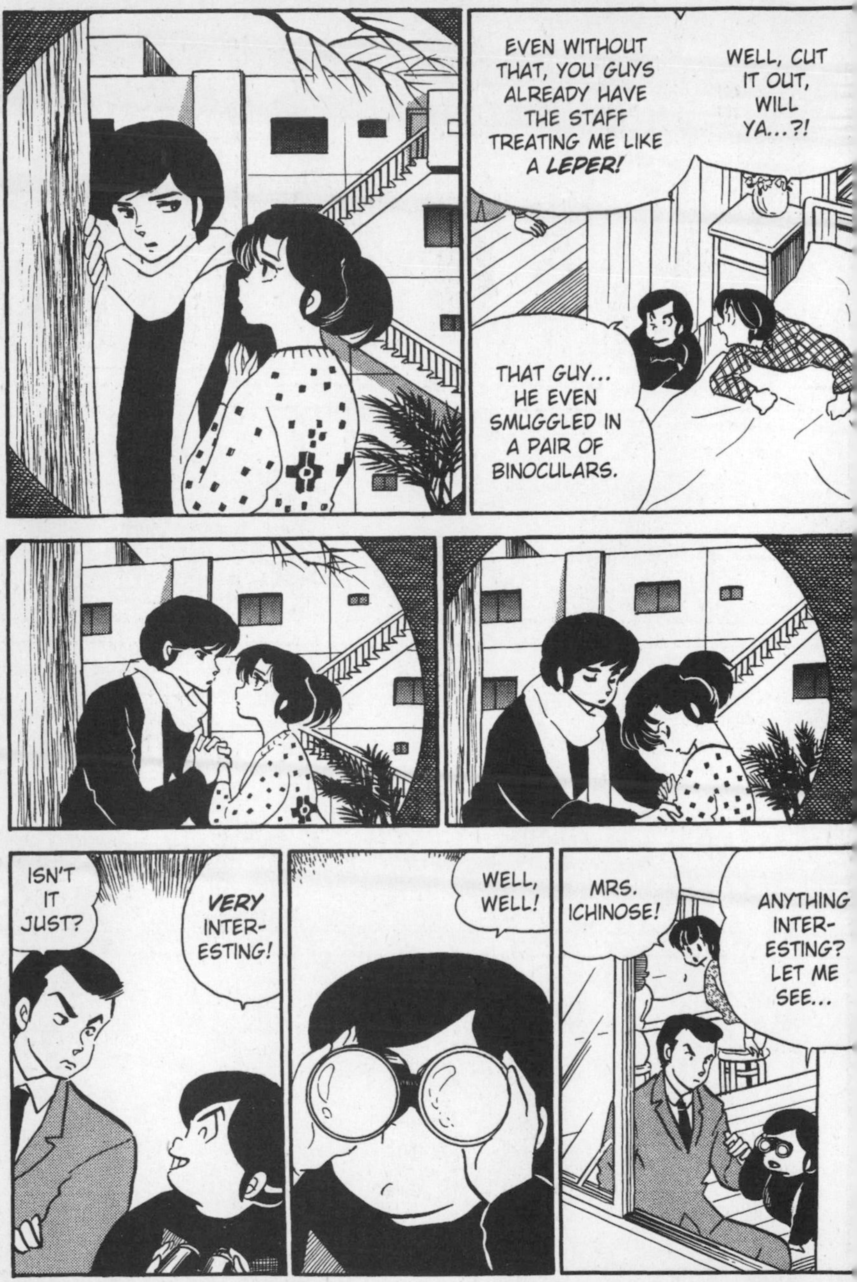
WELL, CUT IT OUT, WILL YA...?!
EVEN WITHOUT THAT, YOU GUYS ALREADY HAVE THE STAFF TREATING ME LIKE A LEPER!
THAT GUY... HE EVEN SMUGGLED IN A PAIR OF BINOCULARS.
ANYTHING INTER-ESTING? LET ME SEE...
MRS. ICHINOSE!
WELL, WELL!
VERY INTER-ESTING!
ISN'T IT JUST?

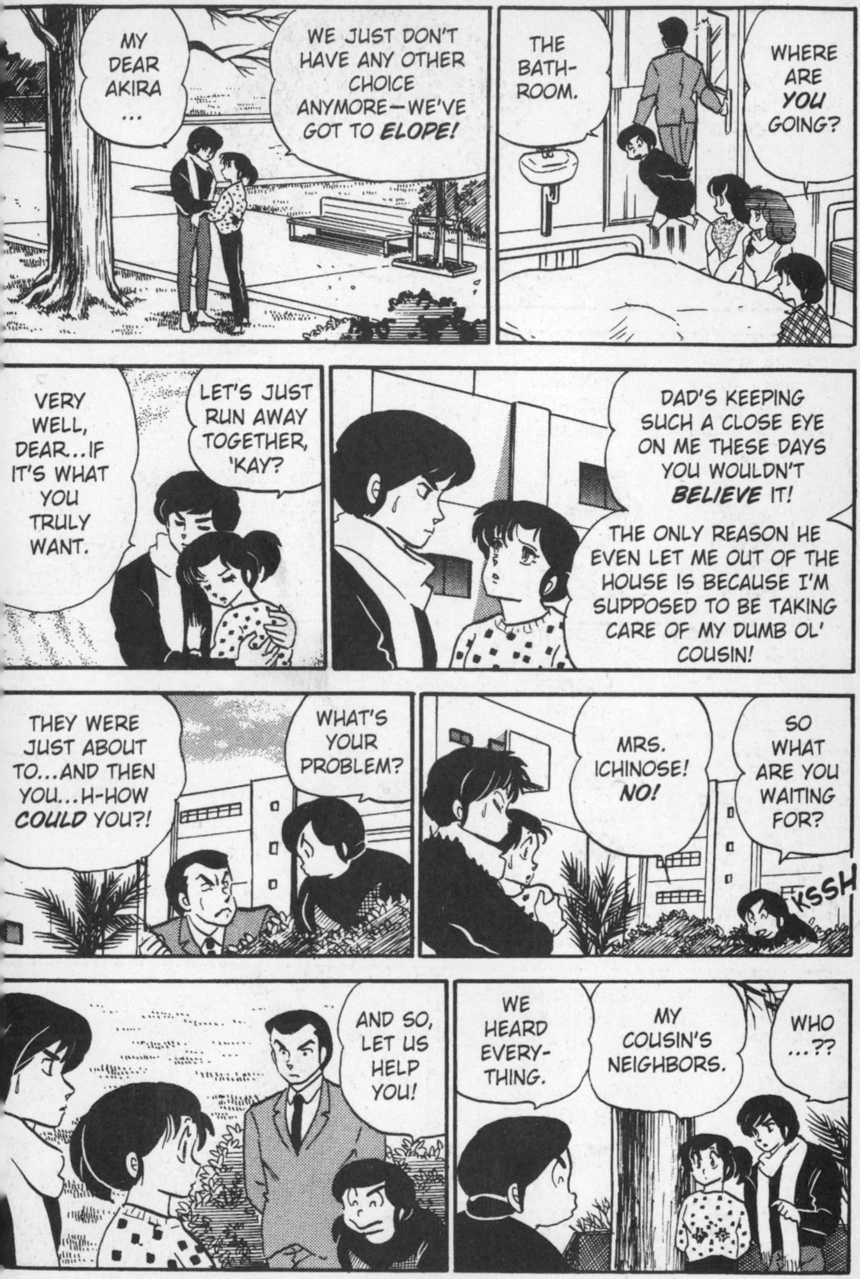
WHERE ARE YOU GOING?
THE BATH-ROOM.
WE JUST DON'T HAVE ANY OTHER CHOICE ANYMORE—WE'VE GOT TO ELOPE!
MY DEAR AKIRA ...
DAD'S KEEPING SUCH A CLOSE EYE ON ME THESE DAYS YOU WOULDN'T BELIEVE IT!
THE ONLY REASON HE EVEN LET ME OUT OF THE HOUSE IS BECAUSE I'M SUPPOSED TO BE TAKING CARE OF MY DUMB OL' COUSIN!
LET'S JUST RUN AWAY TOGETHER, 'KAY?
VERY WELL, DEAR...IF IT'S WHAT YOU TRULY WANT.
SO WHAT ARE YOU WAITING FOR?
KSSH
MRS. ICHINOSE! NO!
WHAT'S YOUR PROBLEM?
THEY WERE JUST ABOUT TO...AND THEN YOU...H-HOW COULD YOU?!
WHO ...??
MY COUSIN'S NEIGHBORS.
WE HEARD EVERY-THING.
AND SO, LET US HELP YOU!

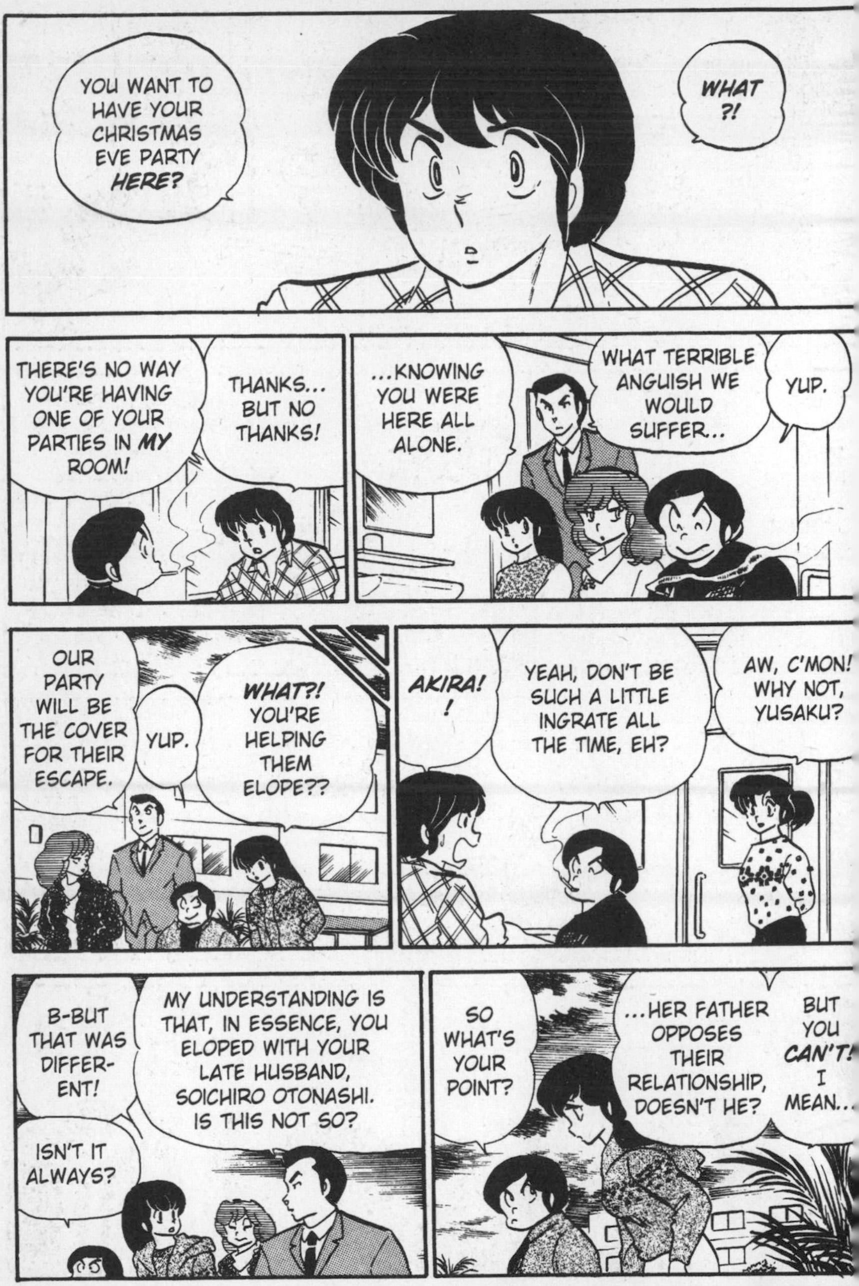
WHAT ?!
YOU WANT TO HAVE YOUR CHRISTMAS EVE PARTY HERE?
YUP.
WHAT TERRIBLE ANGUISH WE WOULD SUFFER...
...KNOWING YOU WERE HERE ALL ALONE.
THANKS... BUT NO THANKS!
THERE'S NO WAY YOU'RE HAVING ONE OF YOUR PARTIES IN MY ROOM!
AW, C'MON! WHY NOT, YUSAKU?
YEAH, DON'T BE SUCH A LITTLE INGRATE ALL THE TIME, EH?
AKIRA!!
WHAT?! YOU'RE HELPING THEM ELOPE??
YUP.
OUR PARTY WILL BE THE COVER FOR THEIR ESCAPE.
BUT YOU CAN'T! I MEAN...
...HER FATHER OPPOSES THEIR RELATIONSHIP, DOESN'T HE?
SO WHAT'S YOUR POINT?
MY UNDERSTANDING IS THAT, IN ESSENCE, YOU ELOPED WITH YOUR LATE HUSBAND, SOICHIRO OTONASHI. IS THIS NOT SO?
B-BUT THAT WAS DIFFER-ENT!
ISN'T IT ALWAYS?

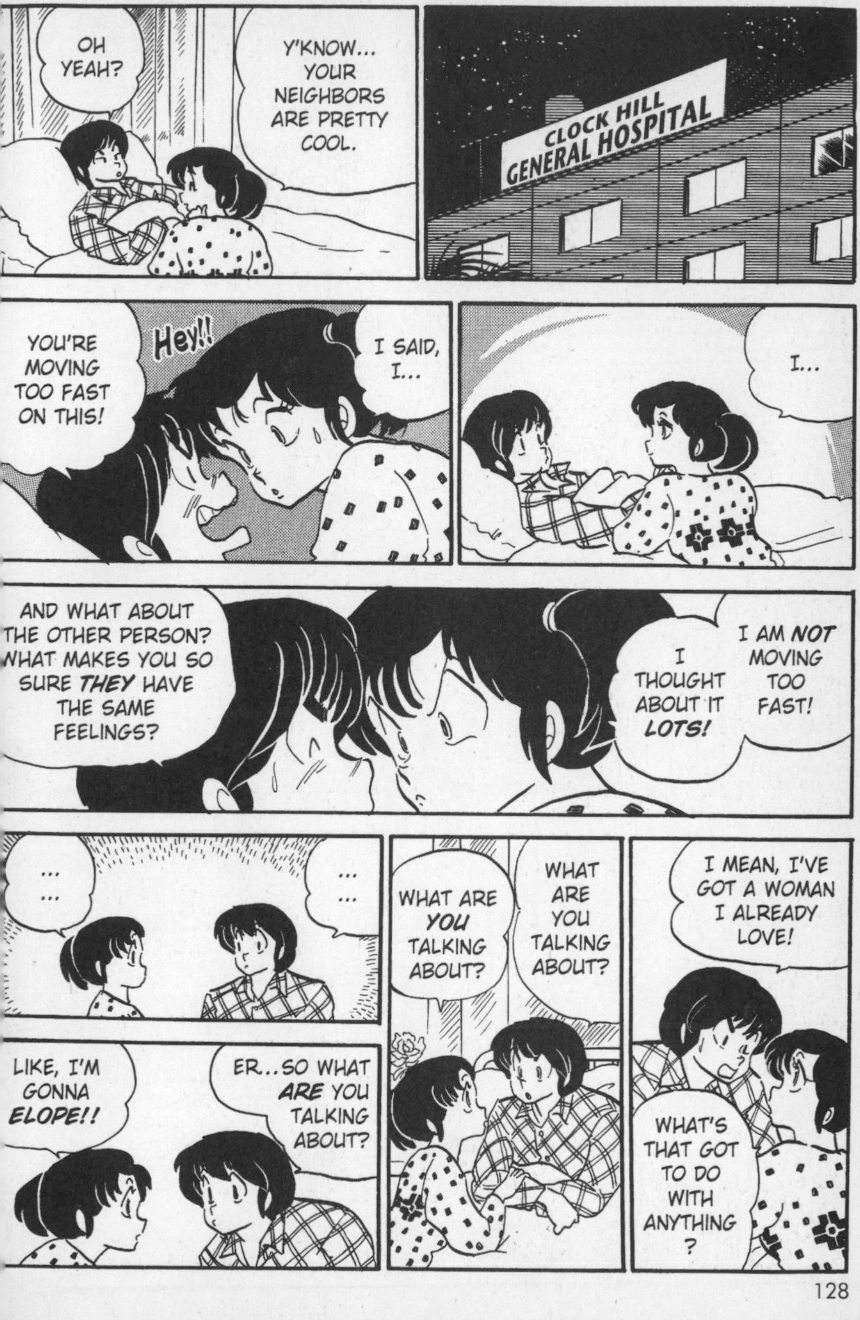
CLOCK HILL GENERAL HOSPITAL
Y'KNOW... YOUR NEIGHBORS ARE PRETTY COOL.
OH YEAH?
I...
I SAID, I...
Hey!!
YOU'RE MOVING TOO FAST ON THIS!
I AM NOT MOVING TOO FAST!
I THOUGHT ABOUT IT LOTS!
AND WHAT ABOUT THE OTHER PERSON? WHAT MAKES YOU SO SURE THEY HAVE THE SAME FEELINGS?
I MEAN, I'VE GOT A WOMAN I ALREADY LOVE!
WHAT'S THAT GOT TO DO WITH ANYTHING?
WHAT ARE YOU TALKING ABOUT?
WHAT ARE YOU TALKING ABOUT?
... ...
... ...
ER...SO WHAT ARE YOU TALKING ABOUT?
LIKE, I'M GONNA ELOPE!!

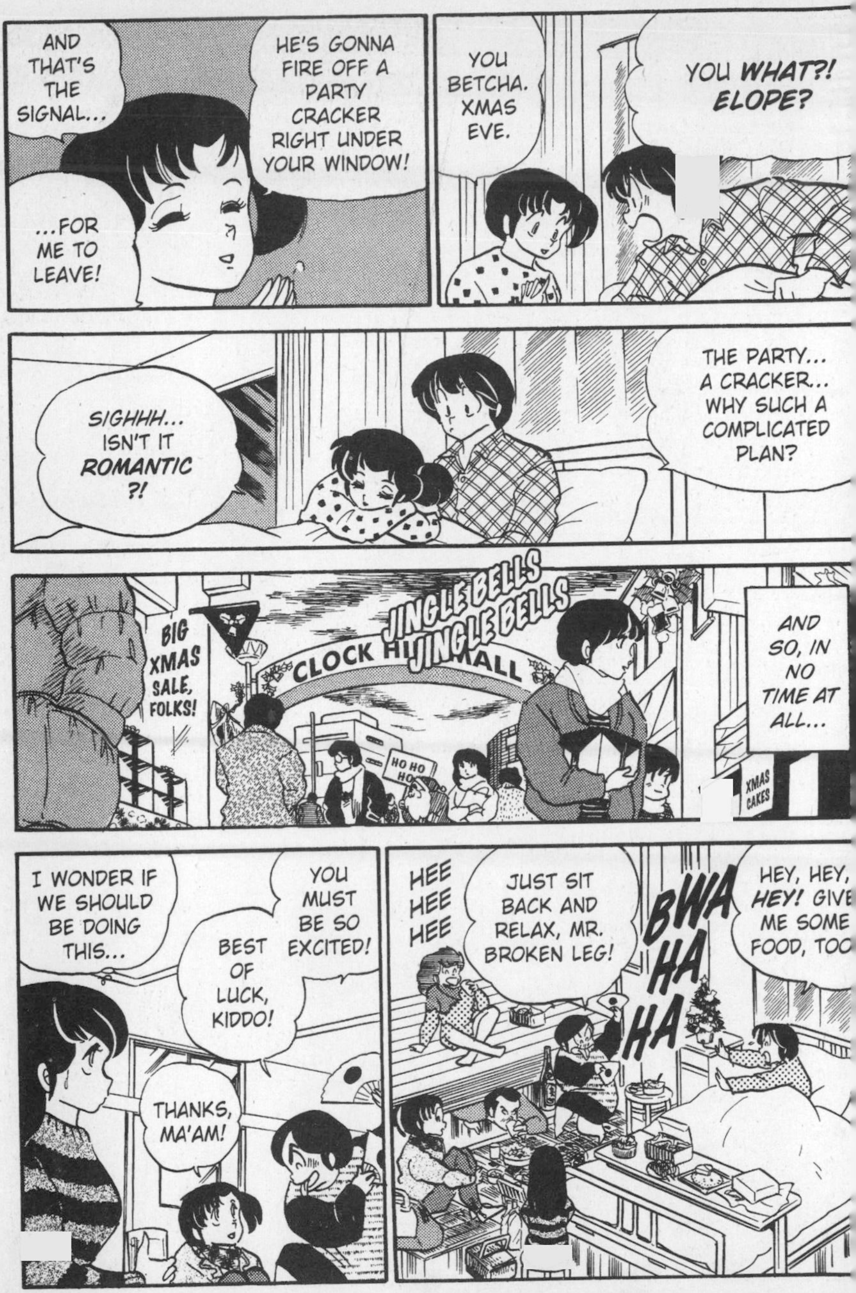
YOU WHAT?! ELOPE?
YOU BETCHA. XMAS EVE.
HE'S GONNA FIRE OFF A PARTY CRACKER RIGHT UNDER YOUR WINDOW!
AND THAT'S THE SIGNAL...
...FOR ME TO LEAVE!
THE PARTY... A CRACKER... WHY SUCH A COMPLICATED PLAN?
SIGHHH... ISN'T IT ROMANTIC ?!
AND SO, IN NO TIME AT ALL...
JINGLE BELLS JINGLE BELLS
CLOCK H MALL
XMAS CAKES
HO HO HO
BIG XMAS SALE, FOLKS!
HEY, HEY, HEY! GIVE ME SOME FOOD, TOO
BWA HA HA HA
JUST SIT BACK AND RELAX, MR. BROKEN LEG!
HEE HEE HEE
YOU MUST BE SO EXCITED!
I WONDER IF WE SHOULD BE DOING THIS...
BEST OF LUCK, KIDDO!
THANKS, MA'AM!

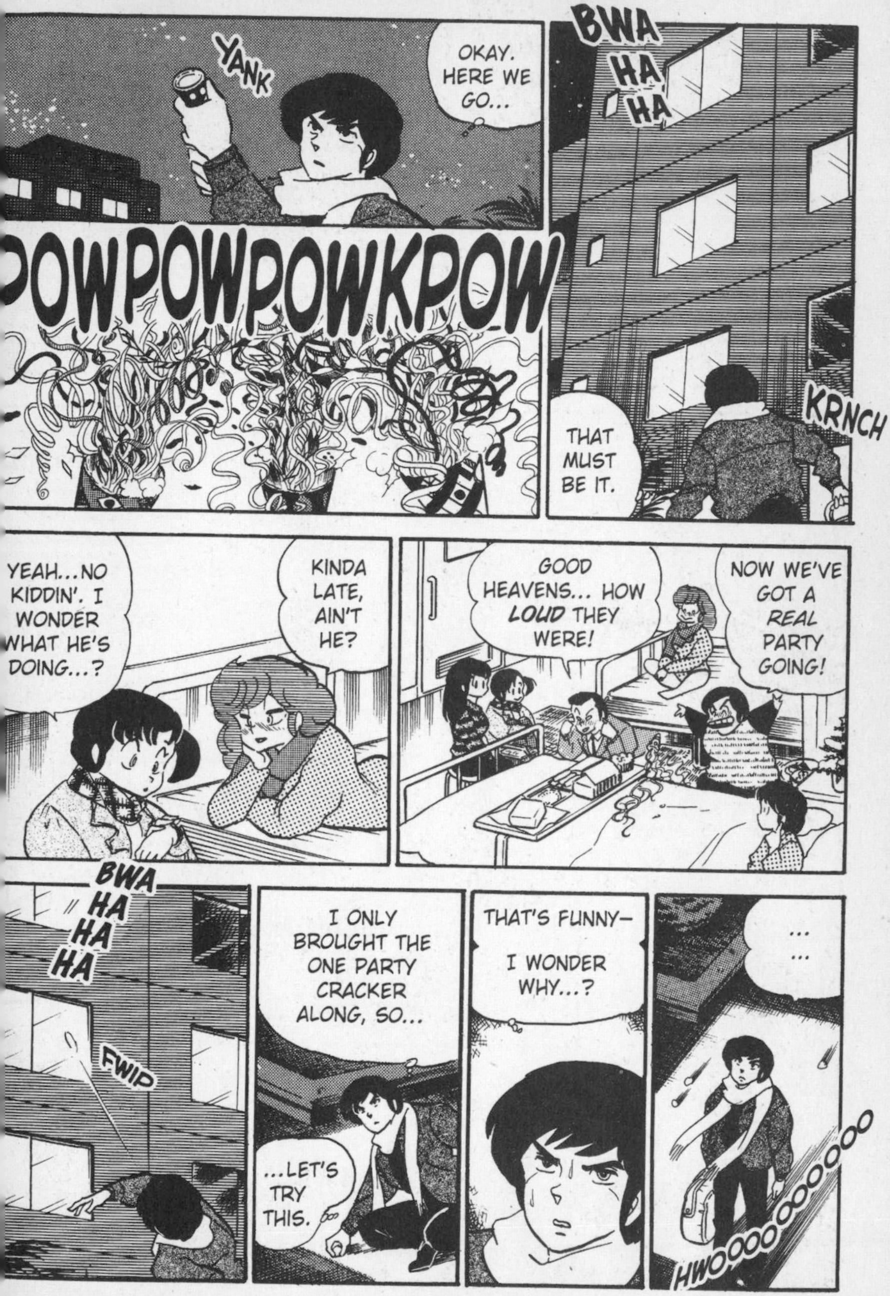
BWA HA HA
KRNCH
THAT MUST BE IT.
YANK
OKAY. HERE WE GO...
POWPOWPOWKPOW
NOW WE'VE GOT A *REAL* PARTY GOING!
GOOD HEAVENS... HOW **LOUD** THEY WERE!
KINDA LATE, AIN'T HE?
YEAH...NO KIDDIN'. I WONDER WHAT HE'S DOING...?
... ...
HWOOOOOOOOOOO
THAT'S FUNNY—
I WONDER WHY...?
I ONLY BROUGHT THE ONE PARTY CRACKER ALONG, SO...
...LET'S TRY THIS.
BWA HA HA HA HA
FWIP

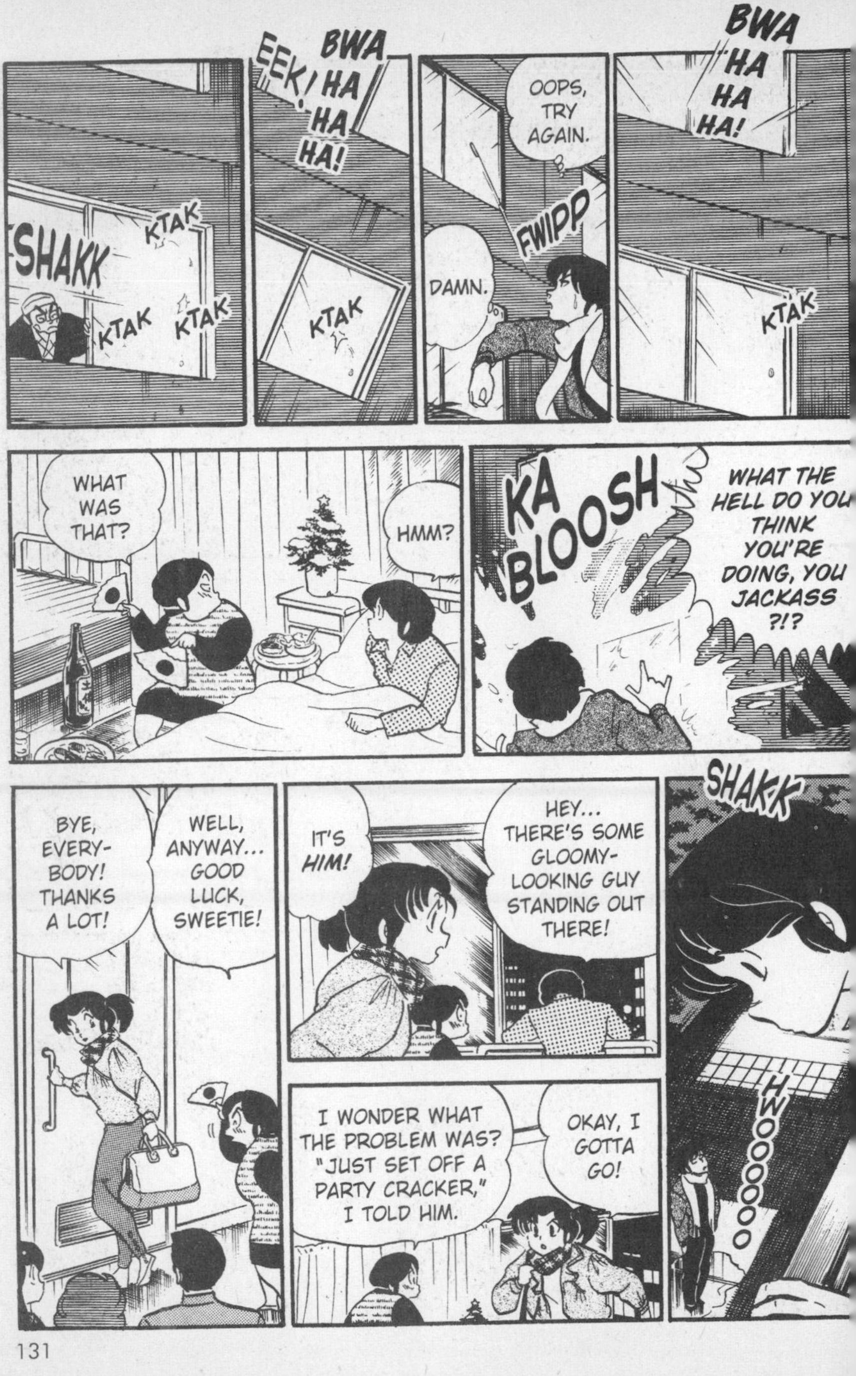
BWA HA HA HA!
KTAK
OOPS, TRY AGAIN.
FWIPP
DAMN.
BWA HA HA HA!
EEK!
KTAK
KTAK
SHAKK
KTAK
KTAK
WHAT THE HELL DO YOU THINK YOU'RE DOING, YOU JACKASS ?!?
KA BLOOSH
HMM?
WHAT WAS THAT?
SHAK-K
HWOOOOOOO
HEY... THERE'S SOME GLOOMY-LOOKING GUY STANDING OUT THERE!
IT'S HIM!
OKAY, I GOTTA GO!
I WONDER WHAT THE PROBLEM WAS? "JUST SET OFF A PARTY CRACKER," I TOLD HIM.
WELL, ANYWAY... GOOD LUCK, SWEETIE!
BYE, EVERY-BODY! THANKS A LOT!

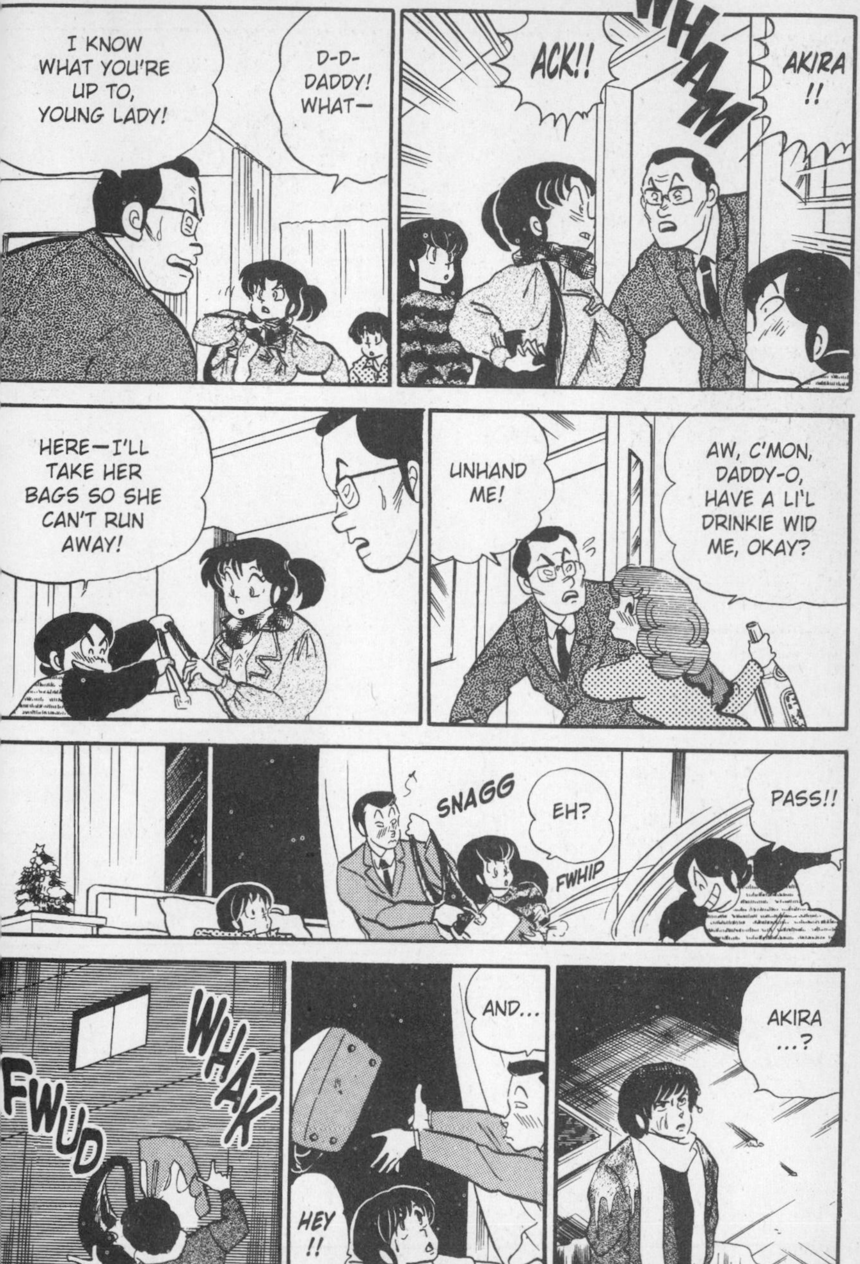
AKIRA !!
WHAM
ACK!!
D-D- DADDY! WHAT—
I KNOW WHAT YOU'RE UP TO, YOUNG LADY!
AW, C'MON, DADDY-O, HAVE A LI'L DRINKIE WID ME, OKAY?
UNHAND ME!
HERE—I'LL TAKE HER BAGS SO SHE CAN'T RUN AWAY!
PASS!!
EH?
SNAGG
FWHIP
AKIRA ...?
AND...
HEY !!
WHAK
FWUD

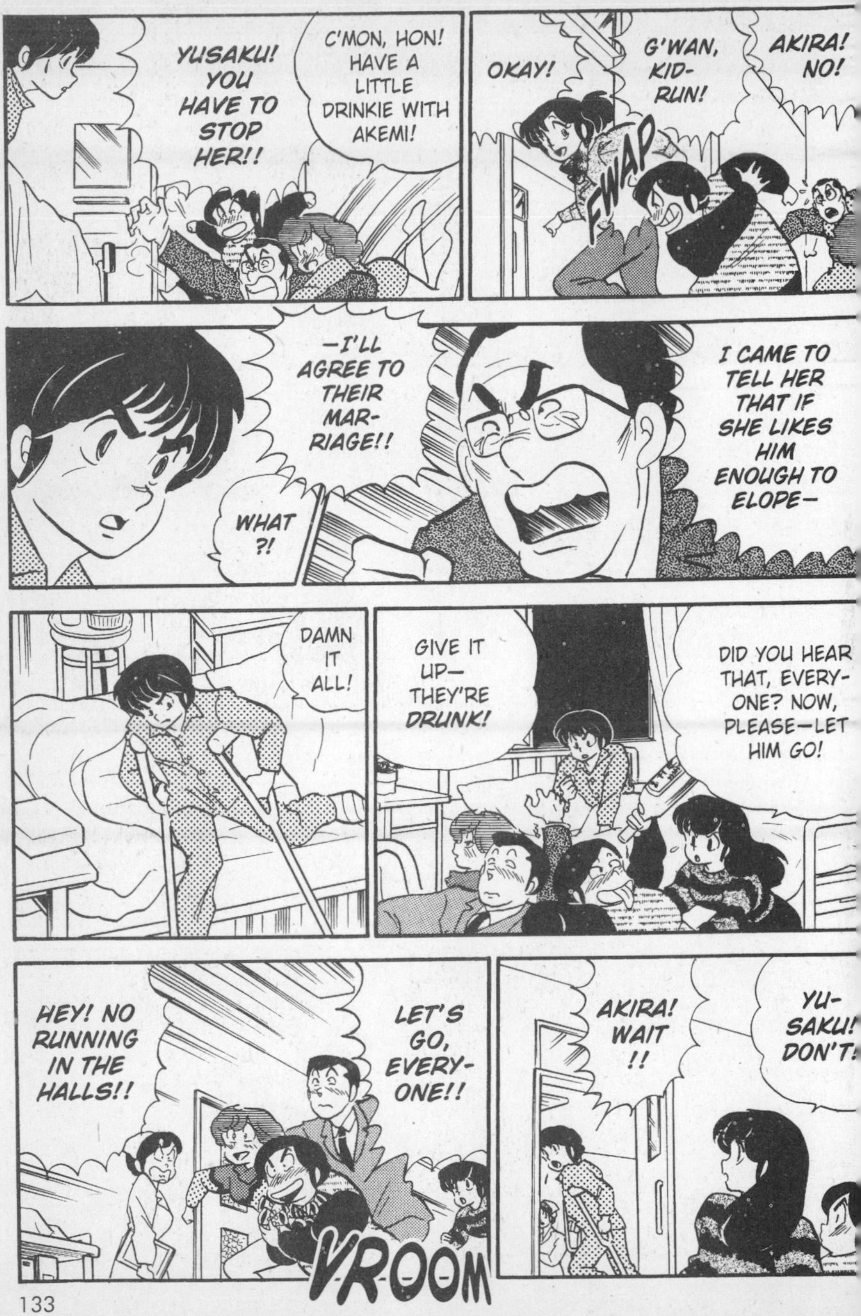
AKIRA! NO!
G'WAN, KID-RUN!
OKAY!
FWAP
C'MON, HON! HAVE A LITTLE DRINKIE WITH AKEMI!
YUSAKU! YOU HAVE TO STOP HER!!
I CAME TO TELL HER THAT IF SHE LIKES HIM ENOUGH TO ELOPE—
—I'LL AGREE TO THEIR MARRIAGE!!
WHAT?!
DID YOU HEAR THAT, EVERYONE? NOW, PLEASE—LET HIM GO!
GIVE IT UP—THEY'RE DRUNK!
DAMN IT ALL!
YUSAKU! DON'T!
AKIRA! WAIT!!
LET'S GO, EVERYONE!!
HEY! NO RUNNING IN THE HALLS!!
VROOM

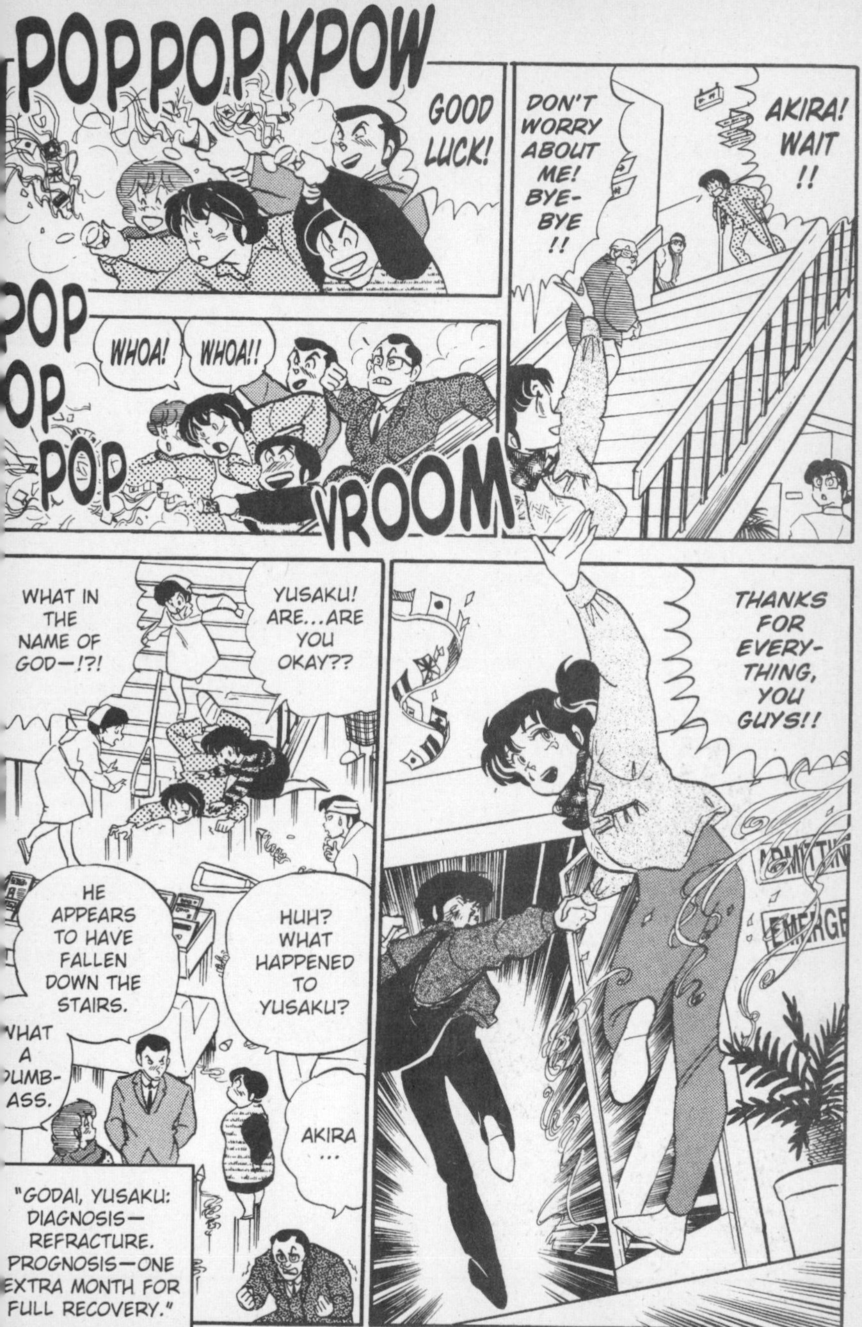
AKIRA! WAIT!!
DON'T WORRY ABOUT ME! BYE-BYE!!
GOOD LUCK!
POPPOP KPOW
WHOA!!
WHOA!
POP
OP
POP
VROOM
THANKS FOR EVERY-THING, YOU GUYS!!
YUSAKU! ARE...ARE YOU OKAY??
WHAT IN THE NAME OF GOD—!?!
HUH? WHAT HAPPENED TO YUSAKU?
HE APPEARS TO HAVE FALLEN DOWN THE STAIRS.
VHAT A UMB-ASS.
AKIRA ...
"GODAI, YUSAKU: DIAGNOSIS—REFRACTURE. PROGNOSIS—ONE EXTRA MONTH FOR FULL RECOVERY."

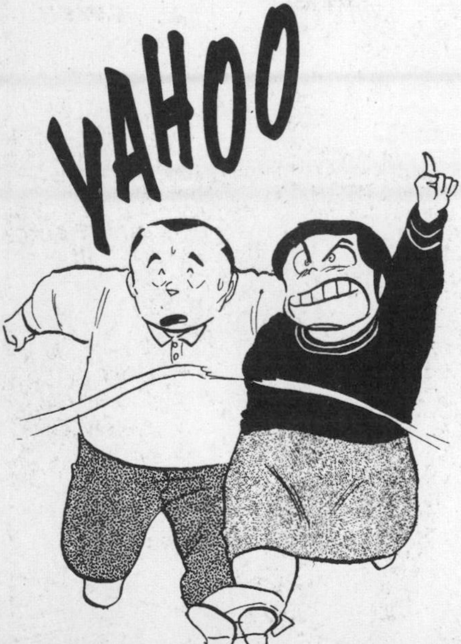
YAHOO

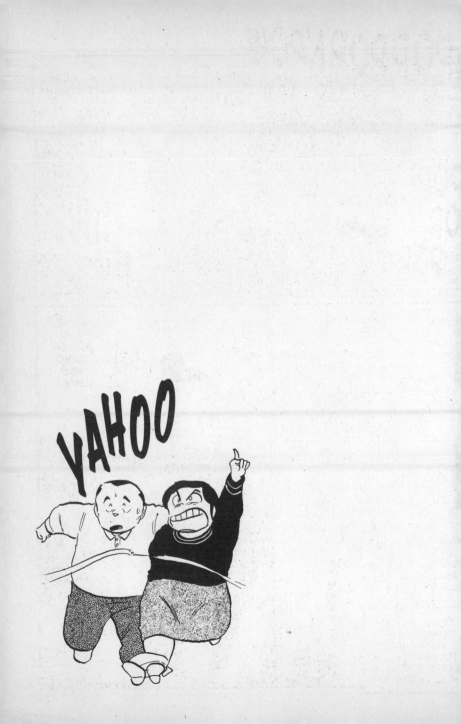

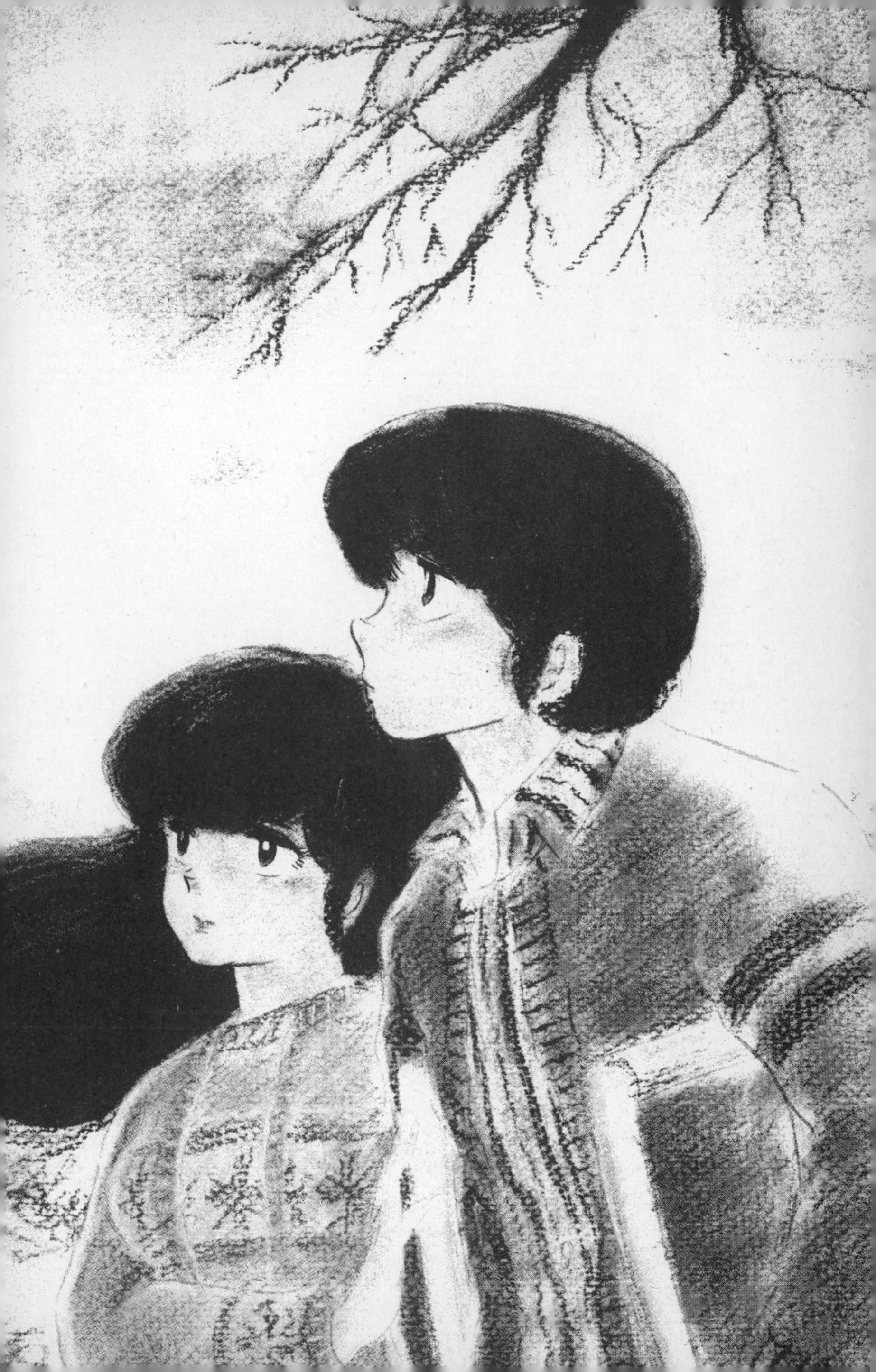

PART SEVEN
BODY OF LOVE

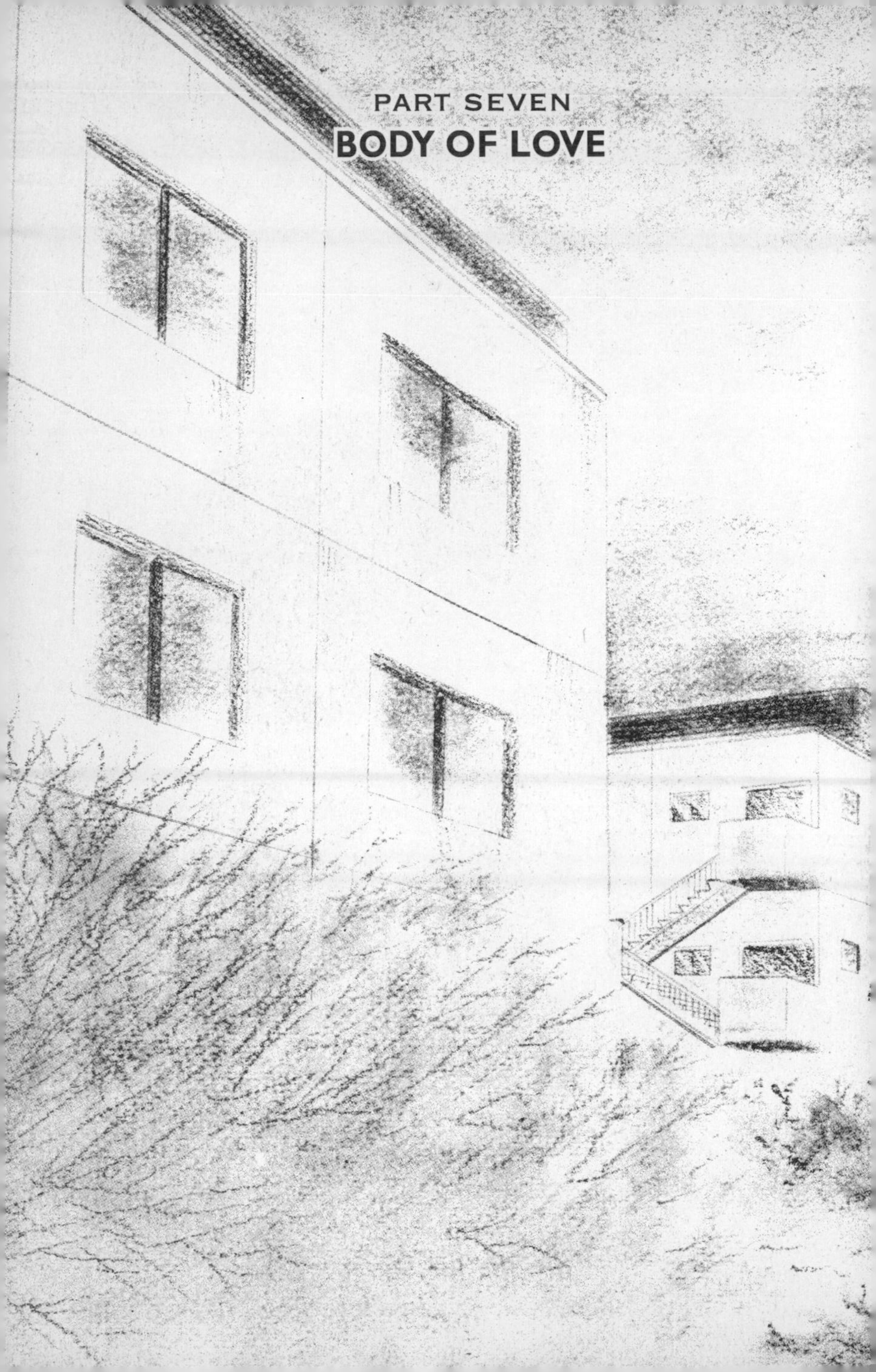

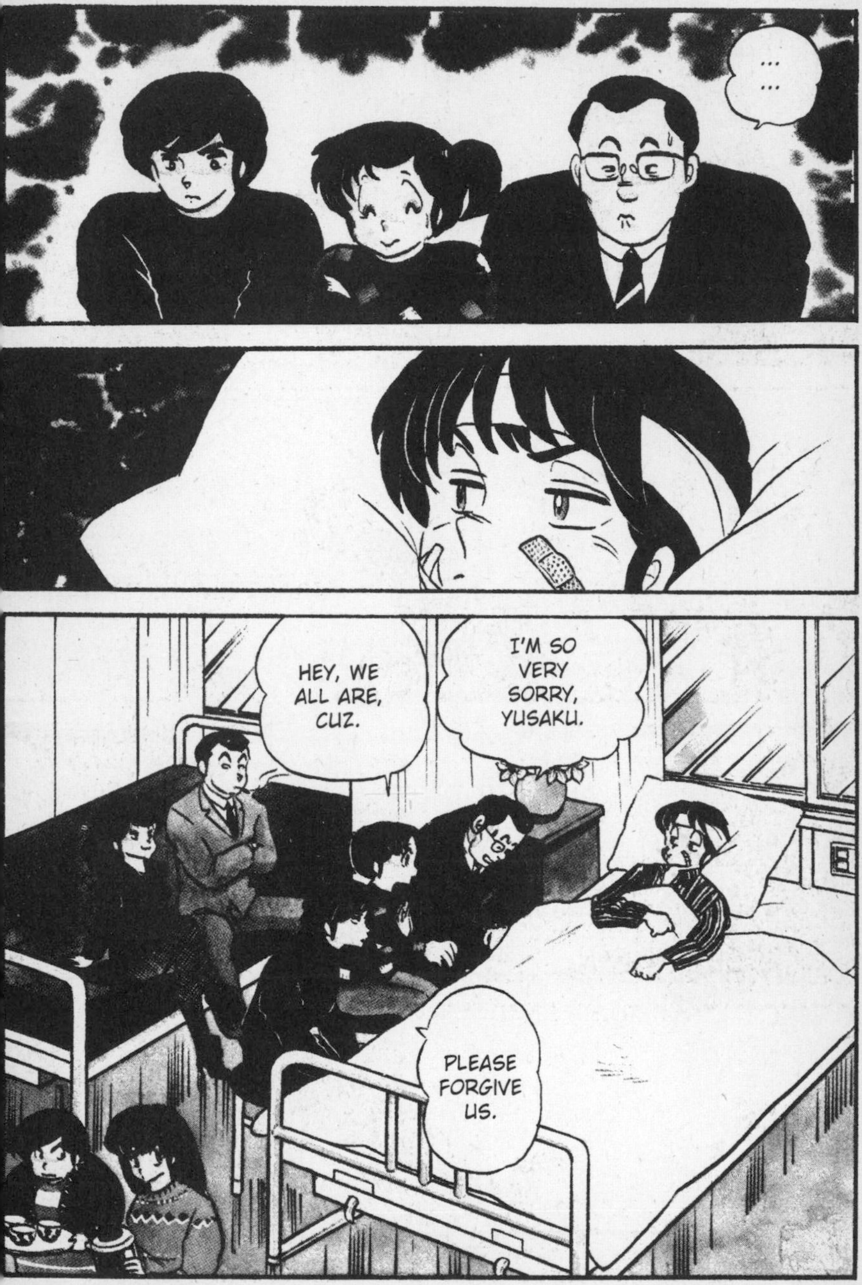
……
I'M SO VERY SORRY, YUSAKU.
HEY, WE ALL ARE, CUZ.
PLEASE FORGIVE US.

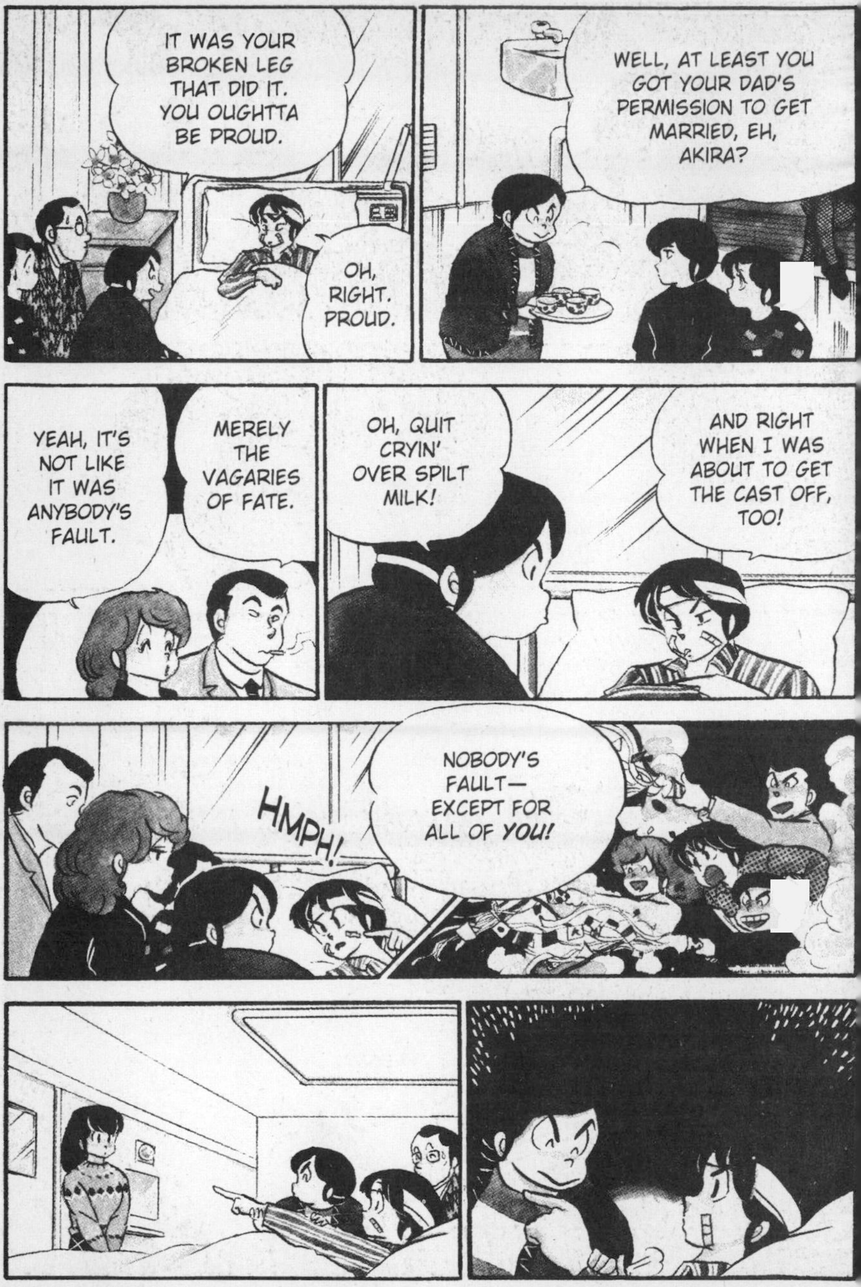
WELL, AT LEAST YOU GOT YOUR DAD'S PERMISSION TO GET MARRIED, EH, AKIRA?
IT WAS YOUR BROKEN LEG THAT DID IT. YOU OUGHTTA BE PROUD.
OH, RIGHT. PROUD.
AND RIGHT WHEN I WAS ABOUT TO GET THE CAST OFF, TOO!
OH, QUIT CRYIN' OVER SPILT MILK!
MERELY THE VAGARIES OF FATE.
YEAH, IT'S NOT LIKE IT WAS ANYBODY'S FAULT.
NOBODY'S FAULT— EXCEPT FOR ALL OF *YOU!*
HMPH!

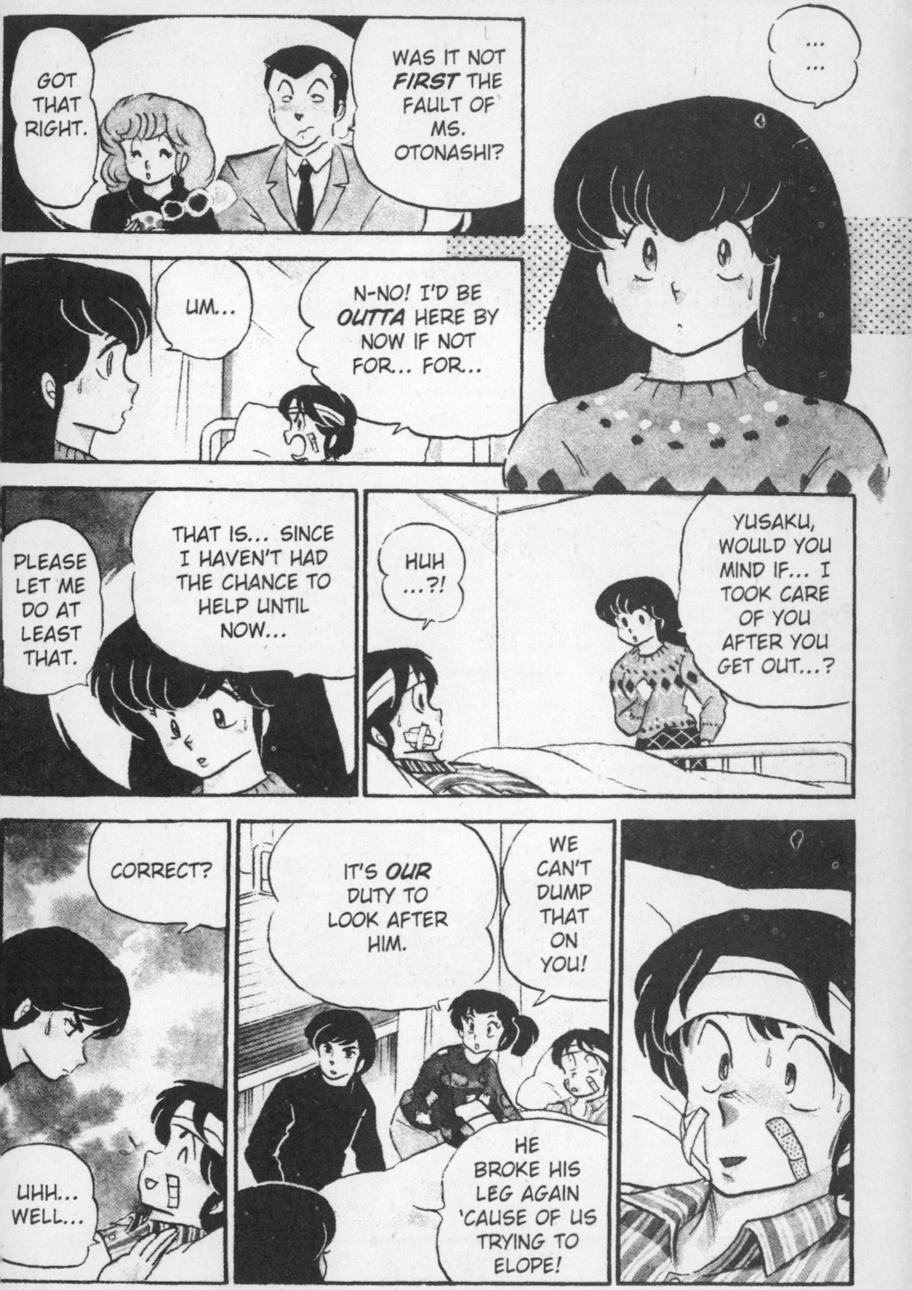
... ...
WAS IT NOT *FIRST* THE FAULT OF MS. OTONASHI?
GOT THAT RIGHT.
N-NO! I'D BE *OUTTA* HERE BY NOW IF NOT FOR... FOR...
UM...
YUSAKU, WOULD YOU MIND IF... I TOOK CARE OF YOU AFTER YOU GET OUT...?
HUH ...?!
THAT IS... SINCE I HAVEN'T HAD THE CHANCE TO HELP UNTIL NOW...
PLEASE LET ME DO AT LEAST THAT.
WE CAN'T DUMP THAT ON YOU!
IT'S *OUR* DUTY TO LOOK AFTER HIM.
HE BROKE HIS LEG AGAIN 'CAUSE OF US TRYING TO ELOPE!
CORRECT?
UHH... WELL...

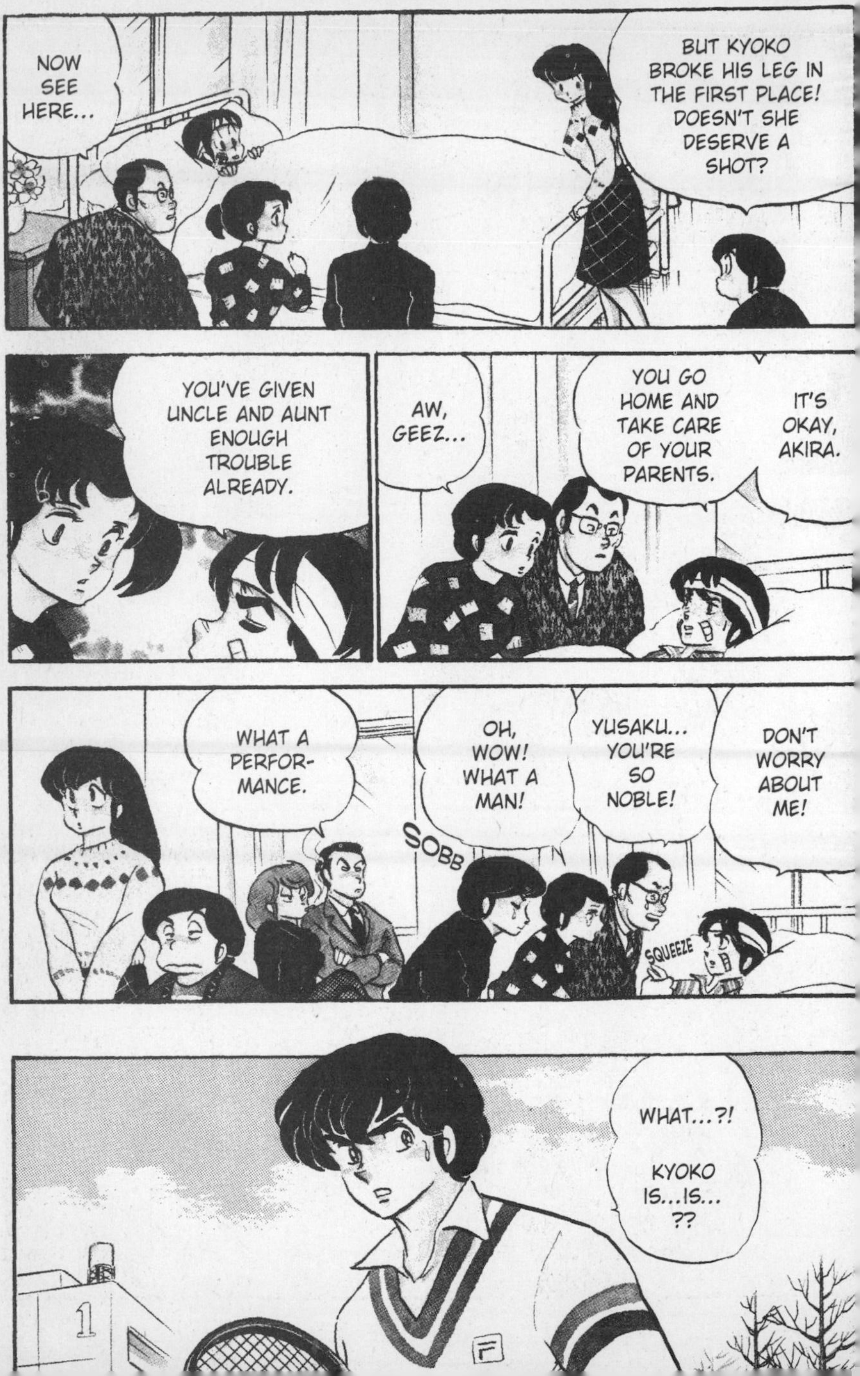
BUT KYOKO BROKE HIS LEG IN THE FIRST PLACE! DOESN'T SHE DESERVE A SHOT?
NOW SEE HERE...
IT'S OKAY, AKIRA.
YOU GO HOME AND TAKE CARE OF YOUR PARENTS.
AW, GEEZ...
YOU'VE GIVEN UNCLE AND AUNT ENOUGH TROUBLE ALREADY.
DON'T WORRY ABOUT ME!
YUSAKU... YOU'RE SO NOBLE!
SQUEEZE
OH, WOW! WHAT A MAN!
SOBB
WHAT A PERFOR-MANCE.
WHAT...?!
KYOKO IS...IS...??

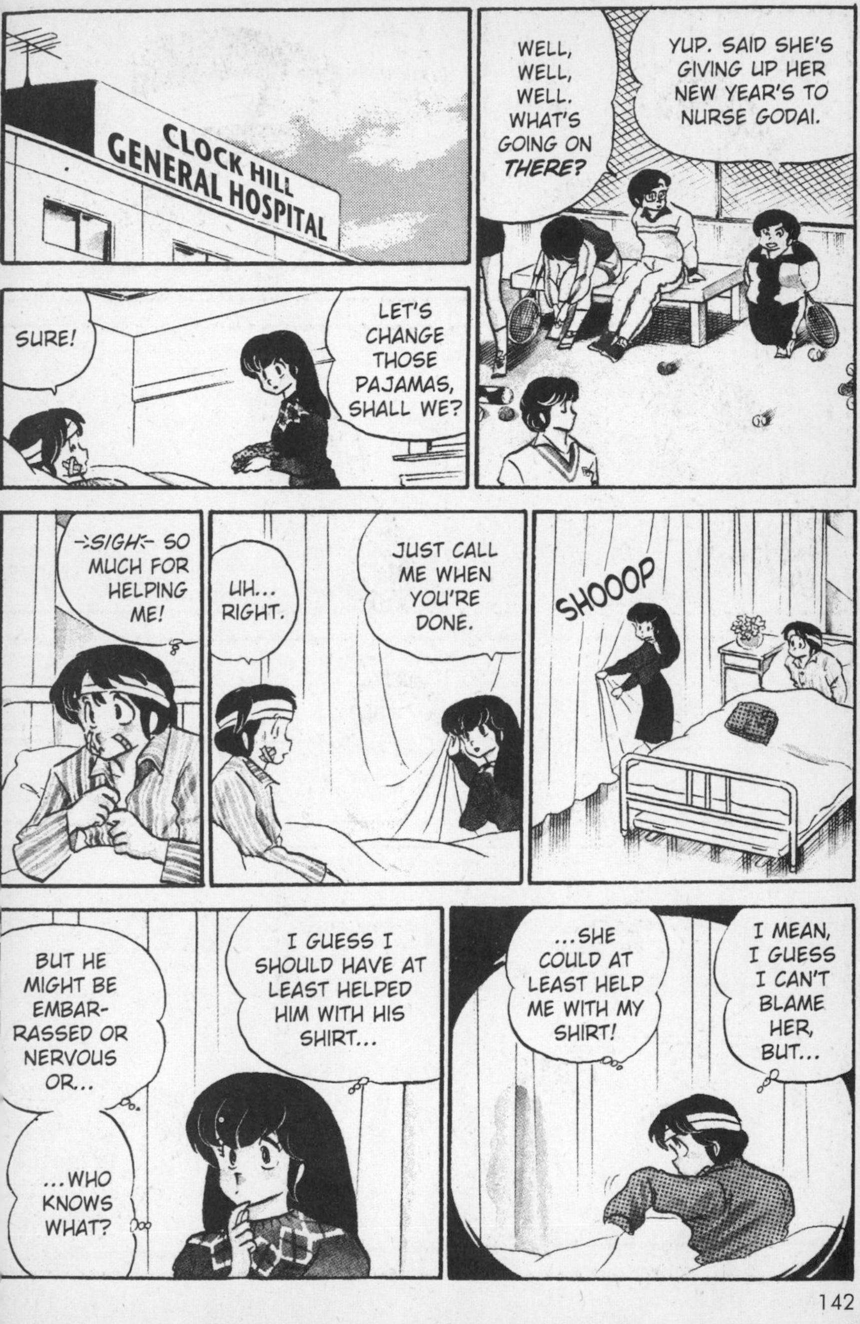
YUP. SAID SHE'S GIVING UP HER NEW YEAR'S TO NURSE GODAI.
WELL, WELL, WELL. WHAT'S GOING ON *THERE?*
CLOCK HILL GENERAL HOSPITAL
LET'S CHANGE THOSE PAJAMAS, SHALL WE?
SURE!
SHOOOP
JUST CALL ME WHEN YOU'RE DONE.
UH... RIGHT.
-SIGH- SO MUCH FOR HELPING ME!
I MEAN, I GUESS I CAN'T BLAME HER, BUT...
...SHE COULD AT LEAST HELP ME WITH MY SHIRT!
I GUESS I SHOULD HAVE AT LEAST HELPED HIM WITH HIS SHIRT...
BUT HE MIGHT BE EMBARRASSED OR NERVOUS OR...
...WHO KNOWS WHAT?

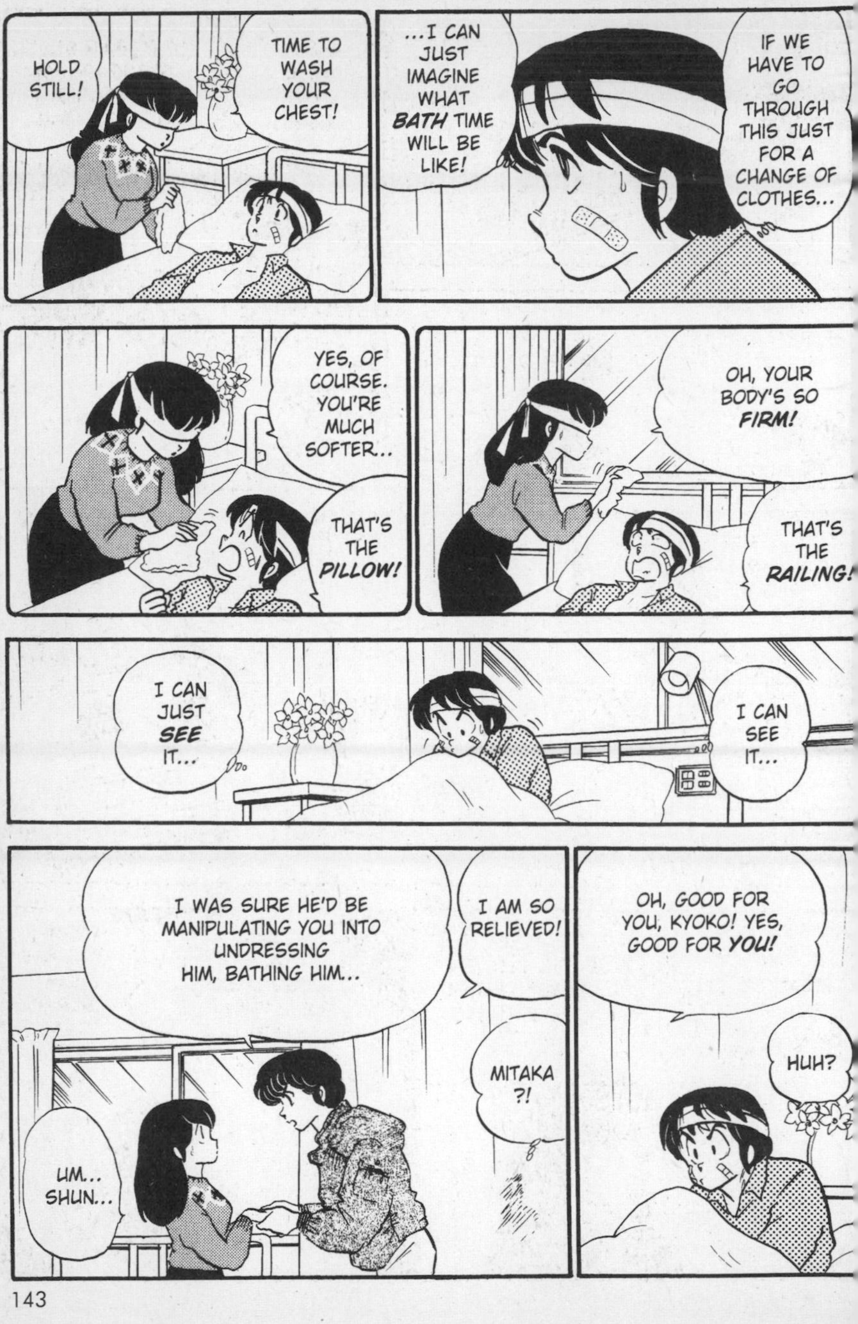
IF WE HAVE TO GO THROUGH THIS JUST FOR A CHANGE OF CLOTHES...
...I CAN JUST IMAGINE WHAT BATH TIME WILL BE LIKE!
TIME TO WASH YOUR CHEST!
HOLD STILL!
OH, YOUR BODY'S SO FIRM!
THAT'S THE RAILING!
YES, OF COURSE. YOU'RE MUCH SOFTER...
THAT'S THE PILLOW!
I CAN SEE IT...
I CAN JUST SEE IT...
OH, GOOD FOR YOU, KYOKO! YES, GOOD FOR YOU!
HUH?
I AM SO RELIEVED!
MITAKA ?!
I WAS SURE HE'D BE MANIPULATING YOU INTO UNDRESSING HIM, BATHING HIM...
UM... SHUN...

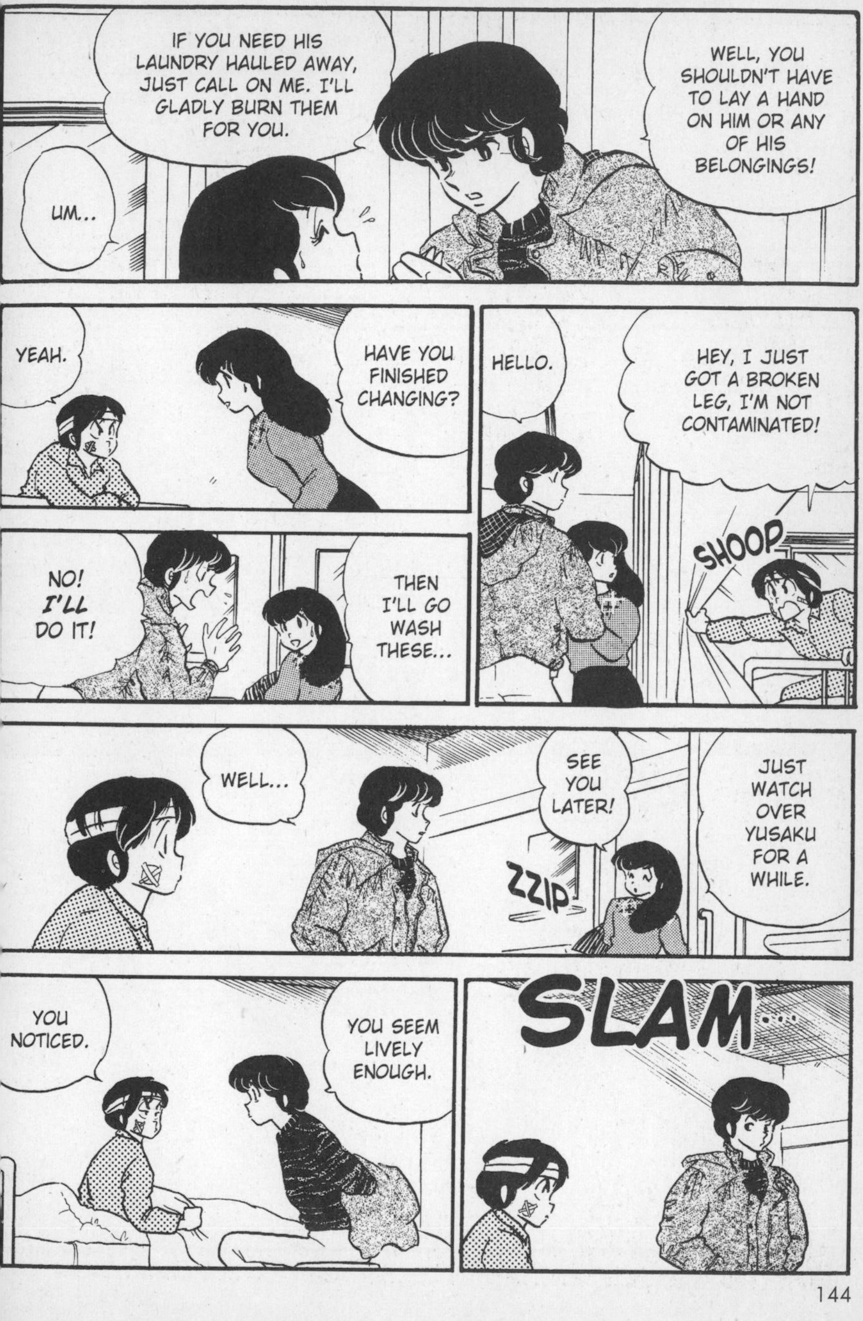
WELL, YOU SHOULDN'T HAVE TO LAY A HAND ON HIM OR ANY OF HIS BELONGINGS!
IF YOU NEED HIS LAUNDRY HAULED AWAY, JUST CALL ON ME. I'LL GLADLY BURN THEM FOR YOU.
UM...
HEY, I JUST GOT A BROKEN LEG, I'M NOT CONTAMINATED!
HELLO.
SHOOP
HAVE YOU FINISHED CHANGING?
YEAH.
THEN I'LL GO WASH THESE...
NO! *I'LL* DO IT!
JUST WATCH OVER YUSAKU FOR A WHILE.
SEE YOU LATER!
ZZIP
WELL...
SLAM...
YOU SEEM LIVELY ENOUGH.
YOU NOTICED.

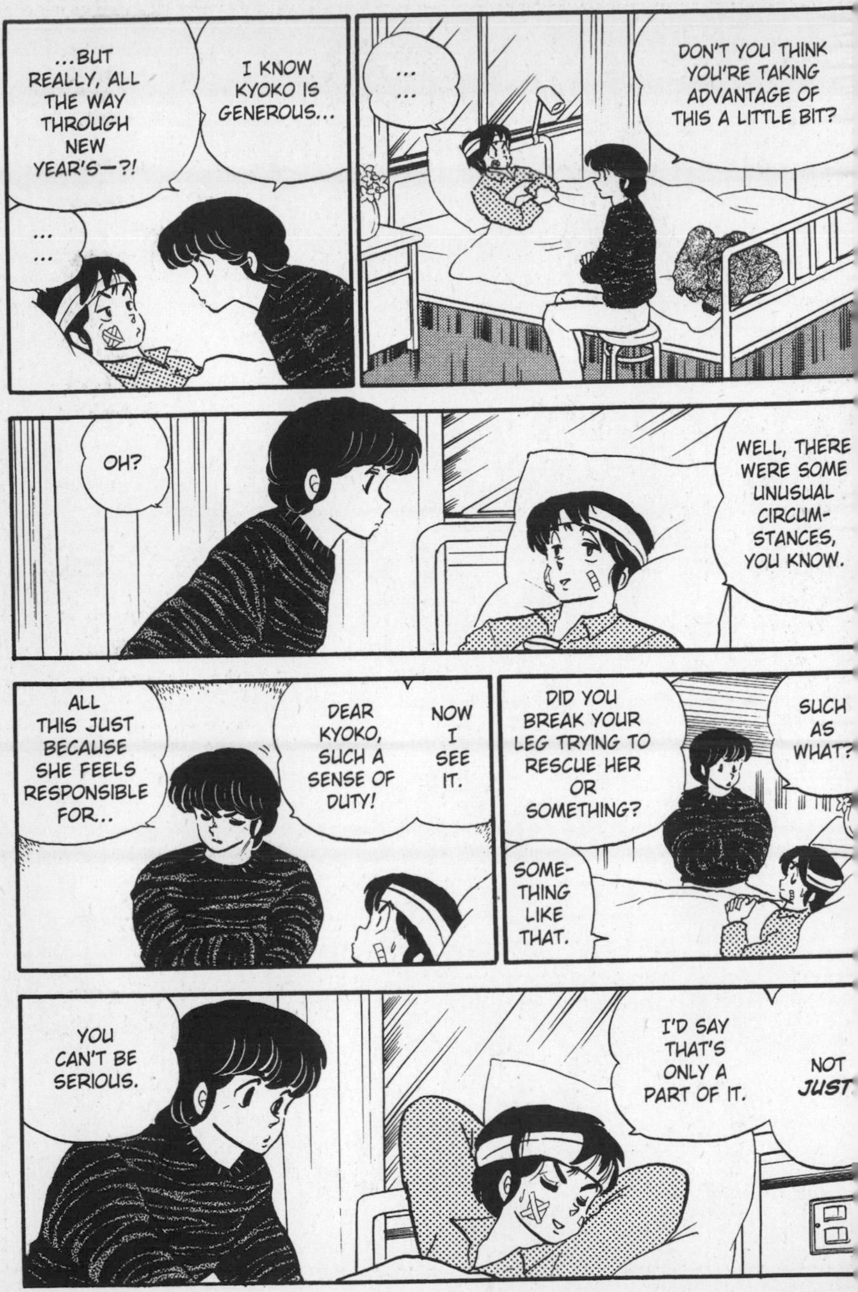
DON'T YOU THINK YOU'RE TAKING ADVANTAGE OF THIS A LITTLE BIT?
... ...
I KNOW KYOKO IS GENEROUS...
...BUT REALLY, ALL THE WAY THROUGH NEW YEAR'S—?!
... ...
WELL, THERE WERE SOME UNUSUAL CIRCUM-STANCES, YOU KNOW.
OH?
SUCH AS WHAT?
DID YOU BREAK YOUR LEG TRYING TO RESCUE HER OR SOMETHING?
SOME-THING LIKE THAT.
NOW I SEE IT.
DEAR KYOKO, SUCH A SENSE OF DUTY!
ALL THIS JUST BECAUSE SHE FEELS RESPONSIBLE FOR...
NOT *JUST*
I'D SAY THAT'S ONLY A PART OF IT.
YOU CAN'T BE SERIOUS.

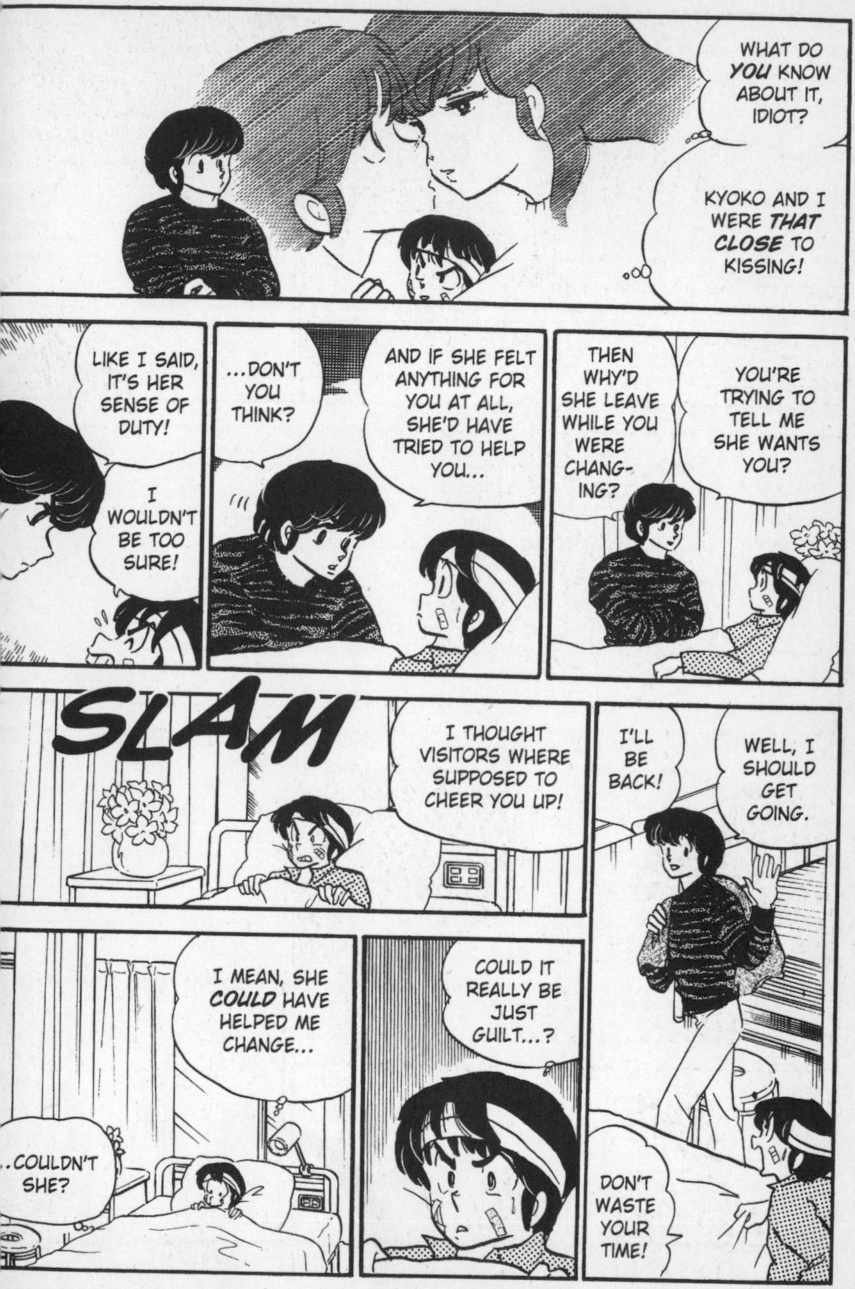
WHAT DO YOU KNOW ABOUT IT, IDIOT?
KYOKO AND I WERE THAT CLOSE TO KISSING!
YOU'RE TRYING TO TELL ME SHE WANTS YOU?
THEN WHY'D SHE LEAVE WHILE YOU WERE CHANG-ING?
AND IF SHE FELT ANYTHING FOR YOU AT ALL, SHE'D HAVE TRIED TO HELP YOU...
...DON'T YOU THINK?
LIKE I SAID, IT'S HER SENSE OF DUTY!
I WOULDN'T BE TOO SURE!
WELL, I SHOULD GET GOING.
I'LL BE BACK!
DON'T WASTE YOUR TIME!
SLAM
I THOUGHT VISITORS WHERE SUPPOSED TO CHEER YOU UP!
COULD IT REALLY BE JUST GUILT...?
I MEAN, SHE COULD HAVE HELPED ME CHANGE...
...COULDN'T SHE?

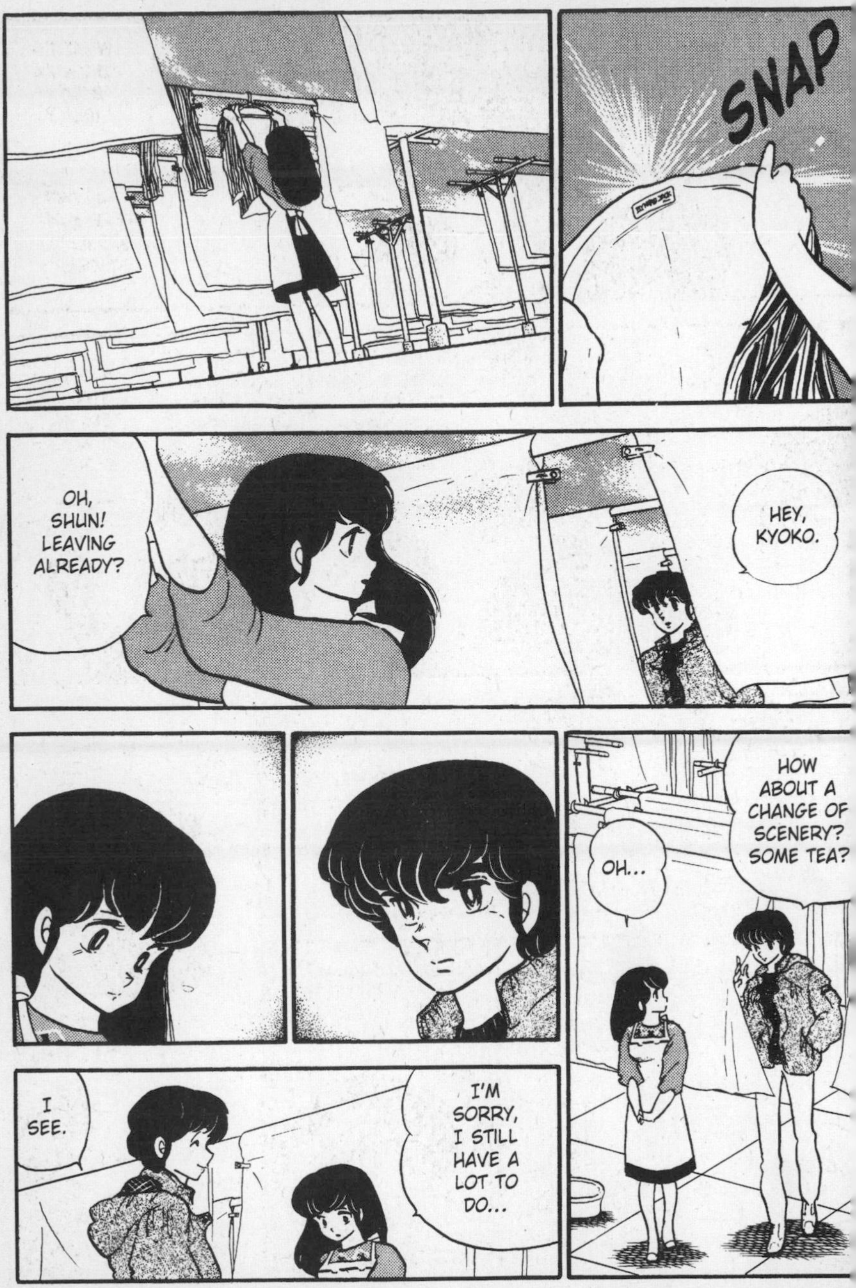
SNAP
HEY, KYOKO.
OH, SHUN! LEAVING ALREADY?
HOW ABOUT A CHANGE OF SCENERY? SOME TEA?
OH...
I'M SORRY, I STILL HAVE A LOT TO DO...
I SEE.

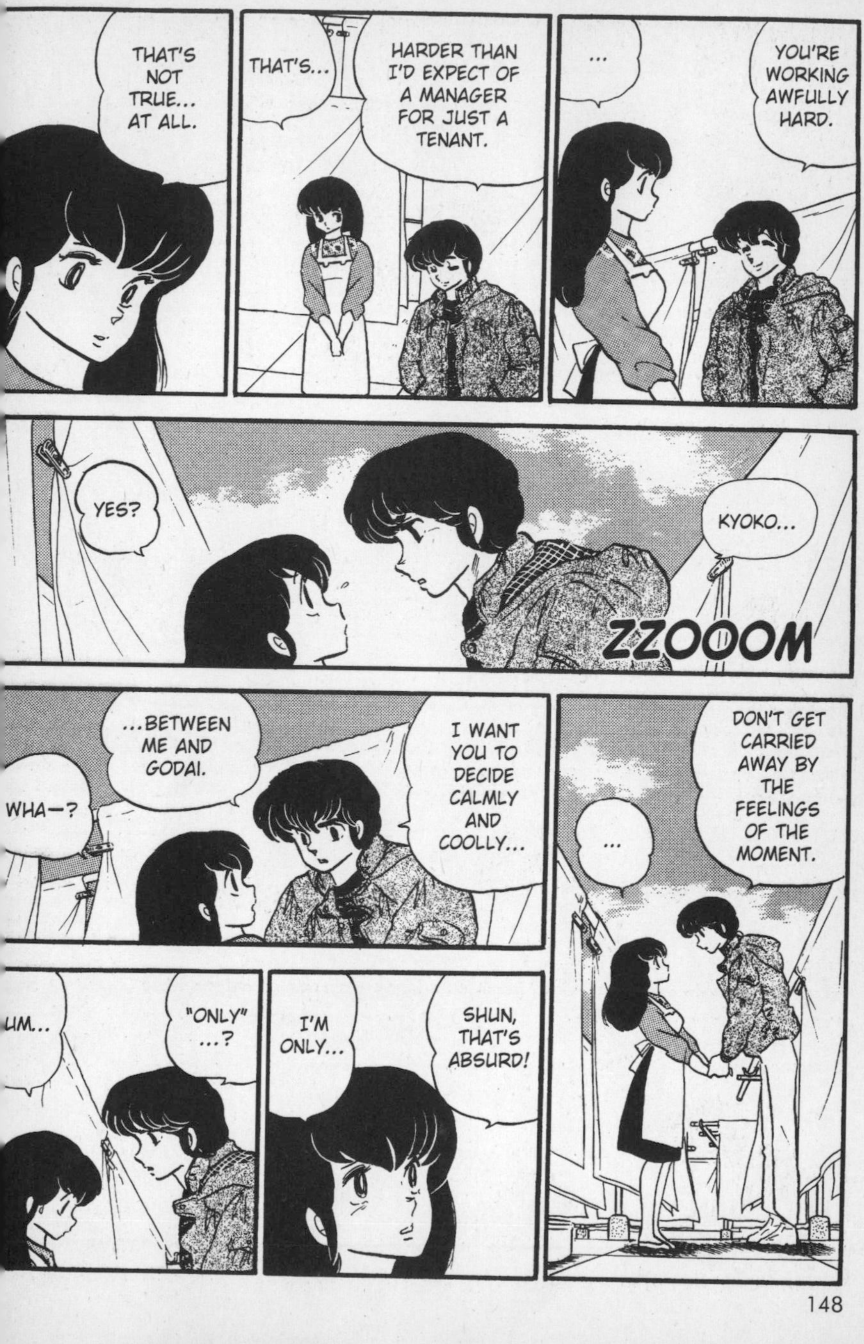
YOU'RE WORKING AWFULLY HARD.
...
HARDER THAN I'D EXPECT OF A MANAGER FOR JUST A TENANT.
THAT'S...
THAT'S NOT TRUE... AT ALL.
KYOKO...
YES?
ZZOOOM
DON'T GET CARRIED AWAY BY THE FEELINGS OF THE MOMENT.
...
I WANT YOU TO DECIDE CALMLY AND COOLLY...
...BETWEEN ME AND GODAI.
WHA—?
SHUN, THAT'S ABSURD!
I'M ONLY...
"ONLY" ...?
UM...

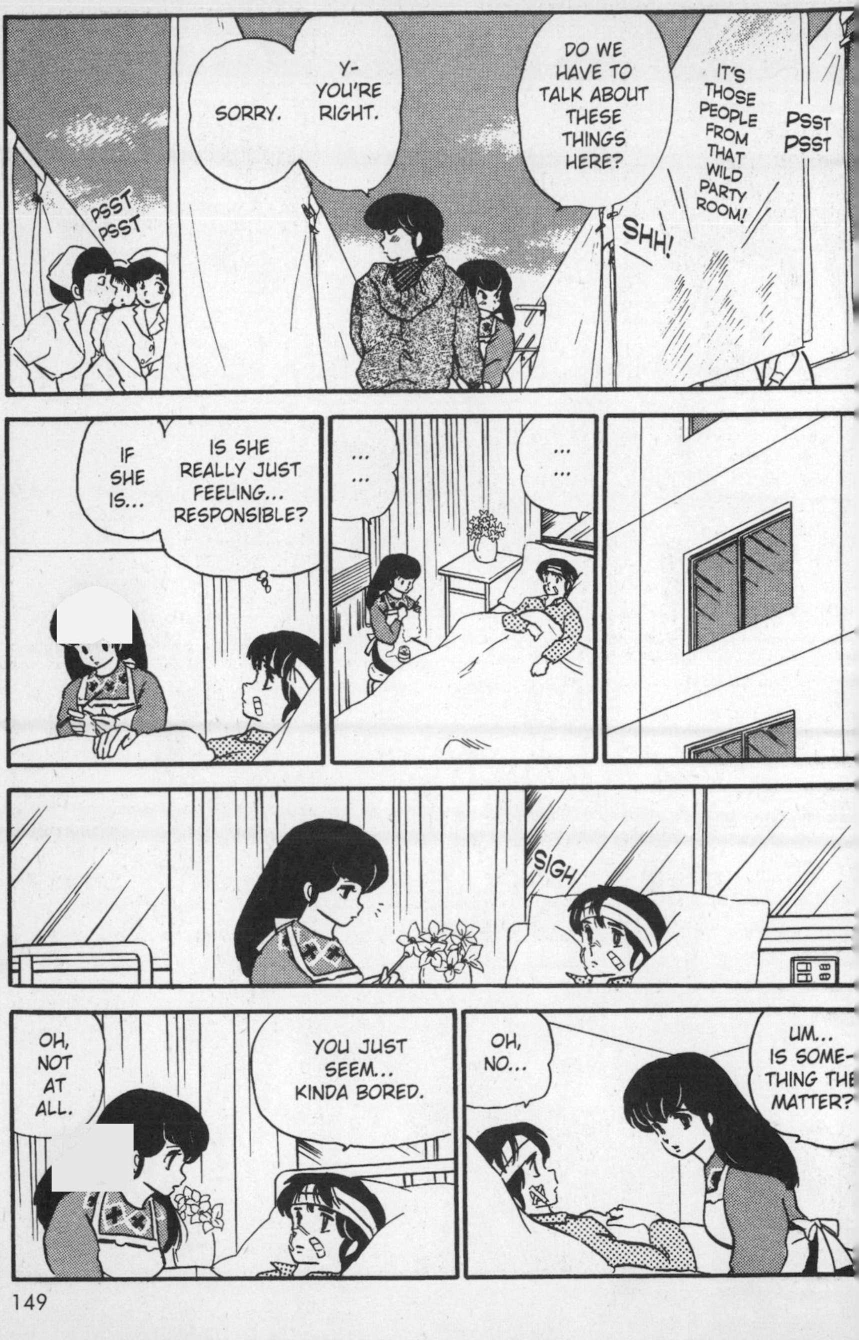
PSST PSST
IT'S THOSE PEOPLE FROM THAT WILD PARTY ROOM!
SHH!
DO WE HAVE TO TALK ABOUT THESE THINGS HERE?
Y- YOU'RE RIGHT.
SORRY.
PSST PSST
... ...
... ...
IS SHE REALLY JUST FEELING... RESPONSIBLE?
IF SHE IS...
SIGH
UM... IS SOME-THING THE MATTER?
OH, NO...
YOU JUST SEEM... KINDA BORED.
OH, NOT AT ALL.

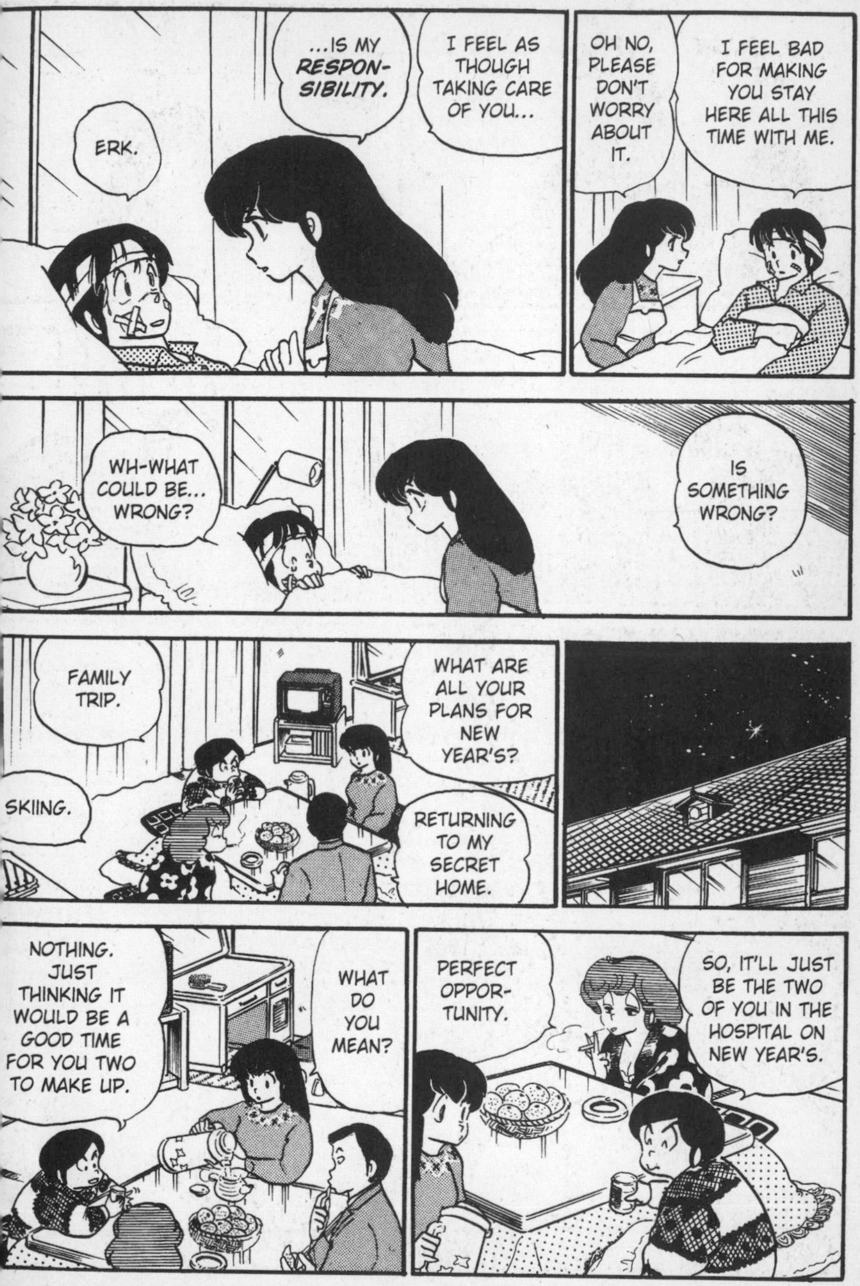

I FEEL BAD FOR MAKING YOU STAY HERE ALL THIS TIME WITH ME.
OH NO, PLEASE DON'T WORRY ABOUT IT.
I FEEL AS THOUGH TAKING CARE OF YOU...
...IS MY ***RESPONSIBILITY.***
ERK.
IS SOMETHING WRONG?
WH-WHAT COULD BE... WRONG?
WHAT ARE ALL YOUR PLANS FOR NEW YEAR'S?
RETURNING TO MY SECRET HOME.
FAMILY TRIP.
SKIING.
SO, IT'LL JUST BE THE TWO OF YOU IN THE HOSPITAL ON NEW YEAR'S.
PERFECT OPPORTUNITY.
WHAT DO YOU MEAN?
NOTHING. JUST THINKING IT WOULD BE A GOOD TIME FOR YOU TWO TO MAKE UP.

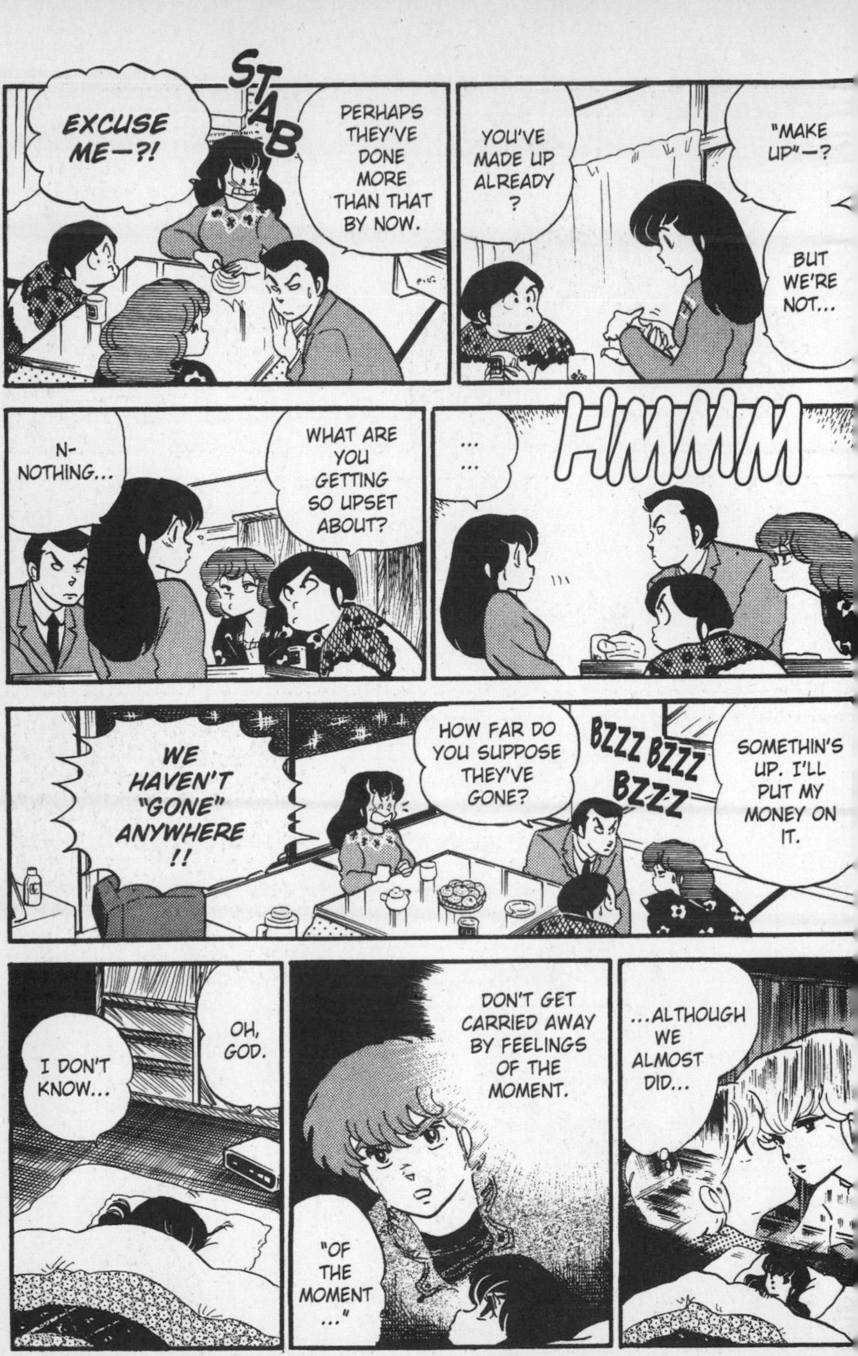

YOU'VE MADE UP ALREADY ?
"MAKE UP"—?
BUT WE'RE NOT...
PERHAPS THEY'VE DONE MORE THAN THAT BY NOW.
STAB
EXCUSE ME—?!
HMMMM
... ...
WHAT ARE YOU GETTING SO UPSET ABOUT?
N-NOTHING...
SOMETHIN'S UP. I'LL PUT MY MONEY ON IT.
BZZZ BZZZ BZ-Z-Z
HOW FAR DO YOU SUPPOSE THEY'VE GONE?
WE HAVEN'T "GONE" ANYWHERE !!
...ALTHOUGH WE ALMOST DID...
DON'T GET CARRIED AWAY BY FEELINGS OF THE MOMENT.
"OF THE MOMENT..."
OH, GOD.
I DON'T KNOW...

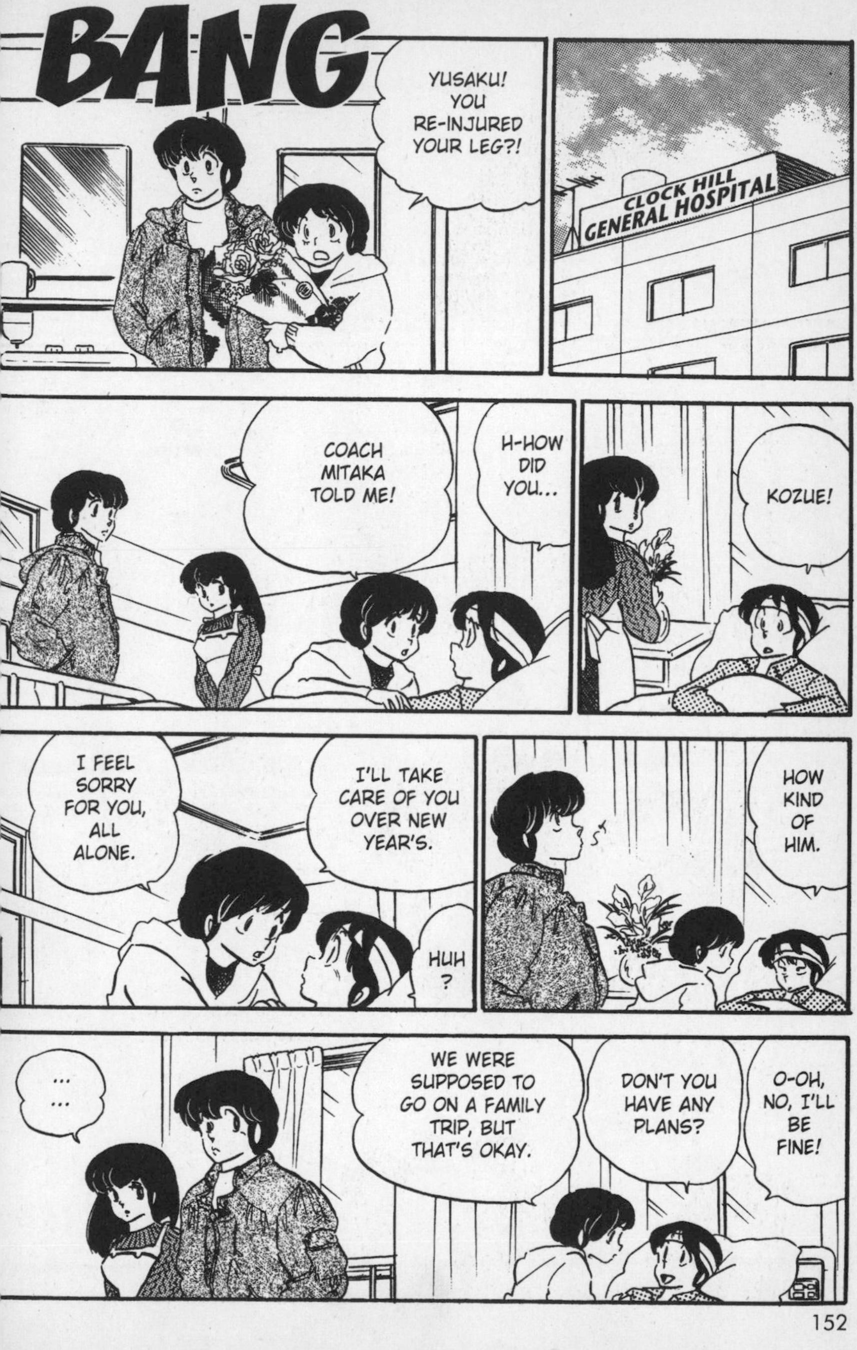
CLOCK HILL GENERAL HOSPITAL
BANG
YUSAKU! YOU RE-INJURED YOUR LEG?!
KOZUE!
H-HOW DID YOU...
COACH MITAKA TOLD ME!
HOW KIND OF HIM.
I'LL TAKE CARE OF YOU OVER NEW YEAR'S.
I FEEL SORRY FOR YOU, ALL ALONE.
HUH?
O-OH, NO, I'LL BE FINE!
DON'T YOU HAVE ANY PLANS?
WE WERE SUPPOSED TO GO ON A FAMILY TRIP, BUT THAT'S OKAY.
... ...

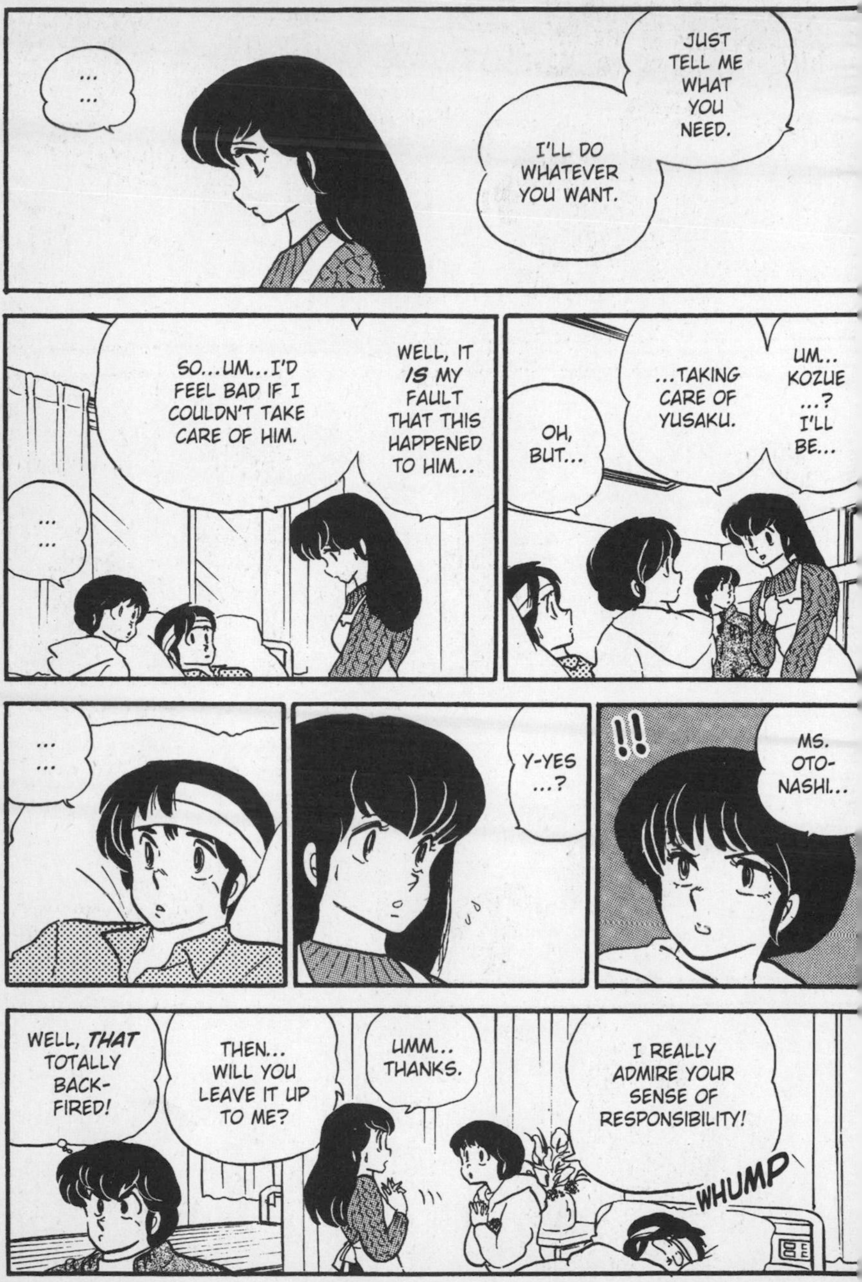
JUST TELL ME WHAT YOU NEED.
I'LL DO WHATEVER YOU WANT.
......
UM... KOZUE...? I'LL BE...
...TAKING CARE OF YUSAKU.
OH, BUT...
WELL, IT *IS* MY FAULT THAT THIS HAPPENED TO HIM...
SO...UM...I'D FEEL BAD IF I COULDN'T TAKE CARE OF HIM.
......
!!
MS. OTO-NASHI...
Y-YES...?
......
I REALLY ADMIRE YOUR SENSE OF RESPONSIBILITY!
WHUMP
UMM... THANKS.
THEN... WILL YOU LEAVE IT UP TO ME?
WELL, *THAT* TOTALLY BACK-FIRED!

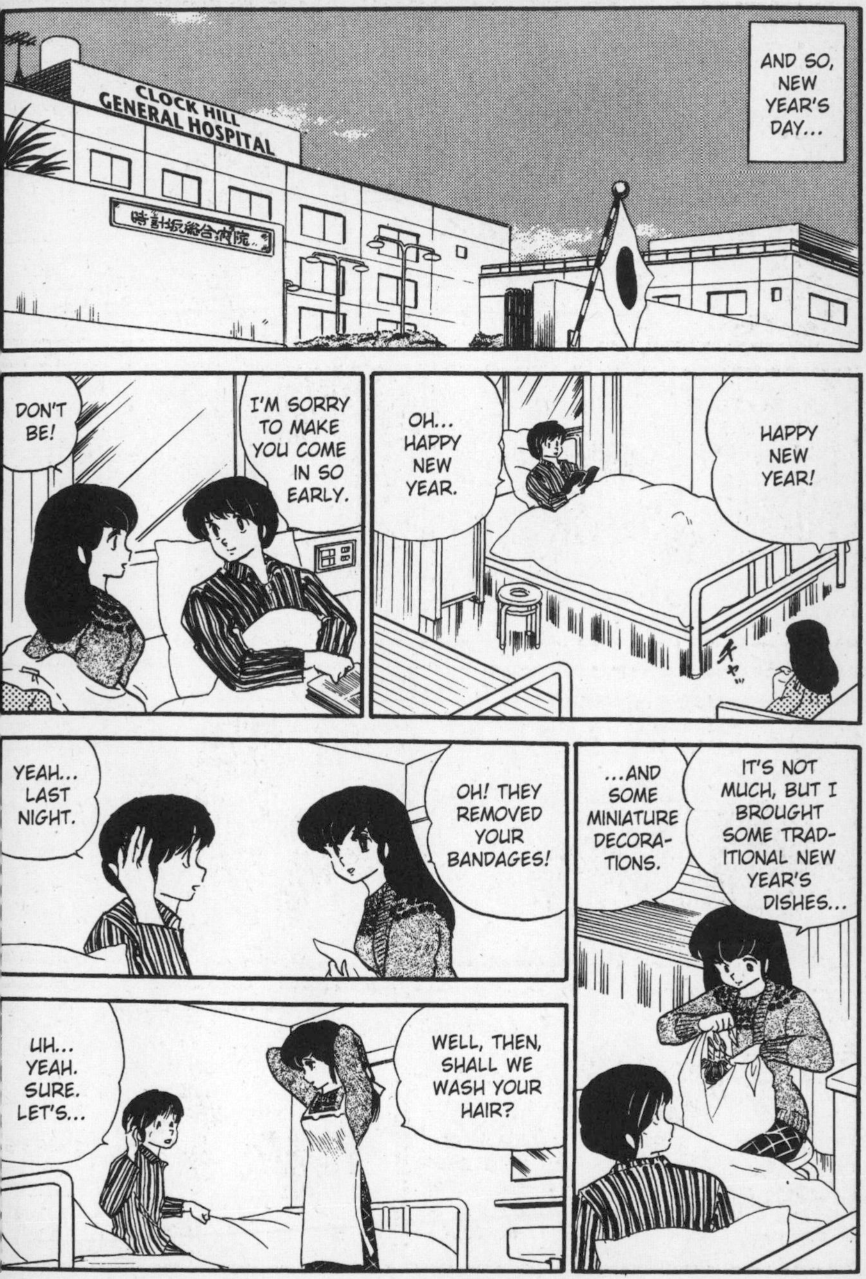
AND SO, NEW YEAR'S DAY...
CLOCK HILL GENERAL HOSPITAL
時計坂総合病院
HAPPY NEW YEAR!
OH... HAPPY NEW YEAR.
チャ
I'M SORRY TO MAKE YOU COME IN SO EARLY.
DON'T BE!
IT'S NOT MUCH, BUT I BROUGHT SOME TRADITIONAL NEW YEAR'S DISHES...
...AND SOME MINIATURE DECORATIONS.
OH! THEY REMOVED YOUR BANDAGES!
YEAH... LAST NIGHT.
WELL, THEN, SHALL WE WASH YOUR HAIR?
UH... YEAH. SURE. LET'S...

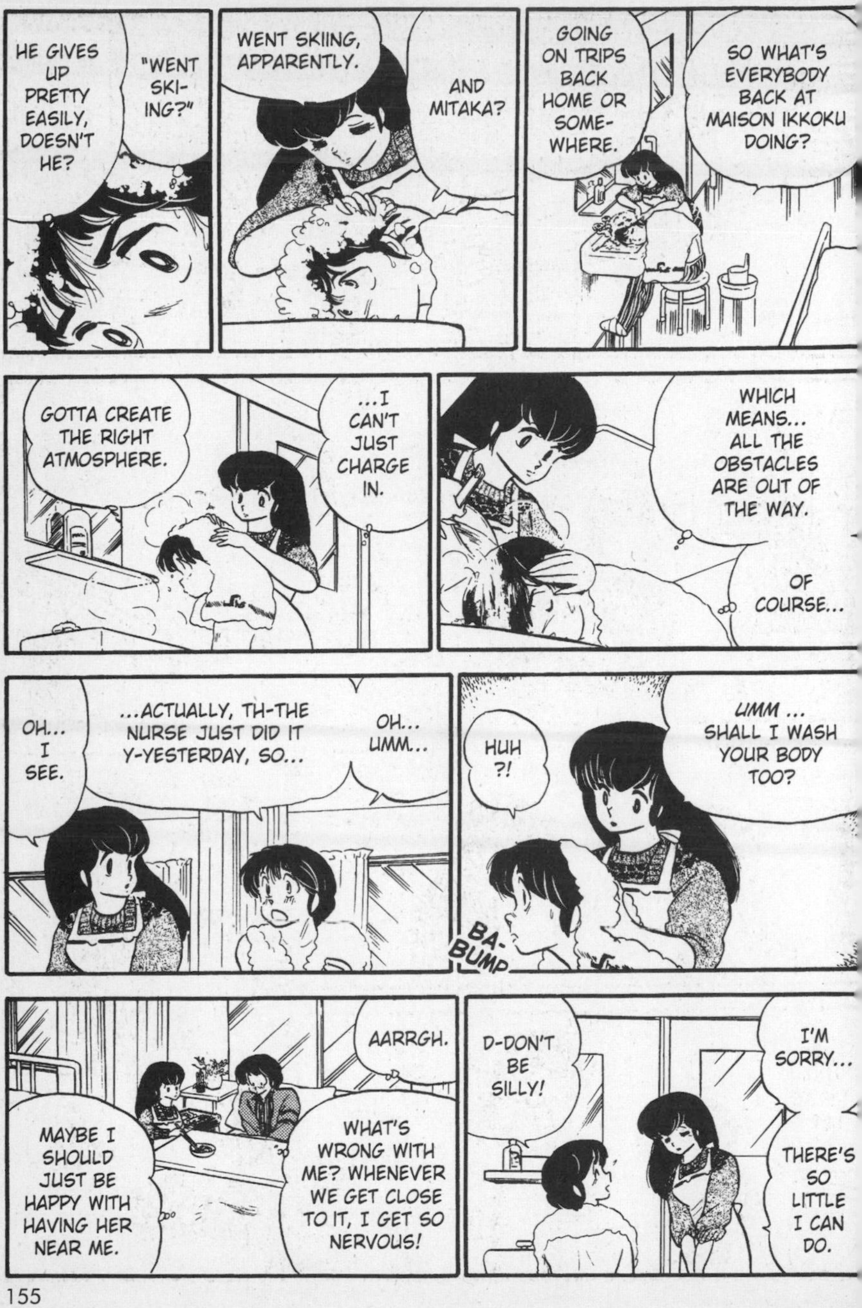
SO WHAT'S EVERYBODY BACK AT MAISON IKKOKU DOING?
GOING ON TRIPS BACK HOME OR SOMEWHERE.
AND MITAKA?
WENT SKIING, APPARENTLY.
"WENT SKI-ING?"
HE GIVES UP PRETTY EASILY, DOESN'T HE?
WHICH MEANS... ALL THE OBSTACLES ARE OUT OF THE WAY.
OF COURSE...
...I CAN'T JUST CHARGE IN.
GOTTA CREATE THE RIGHT ATMOSPHERE.
UMM ... SHALL I WASH YOUR BODY TOO?
HUH ?!
BA-BUMP
OH... UMM...
...ACTUALLY, TH-THE NURSE JUST DID IT Y-YESTERDAY, SO...
OH... I SEE.
I'M SORRY...
THERE'S SO LITTLE I CAN DO.
D-DON'T BE SILLY!
AARRGH.
WHAT'S WRONG WITH ME? WHENEVER WE GET CLOSE TO IT, I GET SO NERVOUS!
MAYBE I SHOULD JUST BE HAPPY WITH HAVING HER NEAR ME.

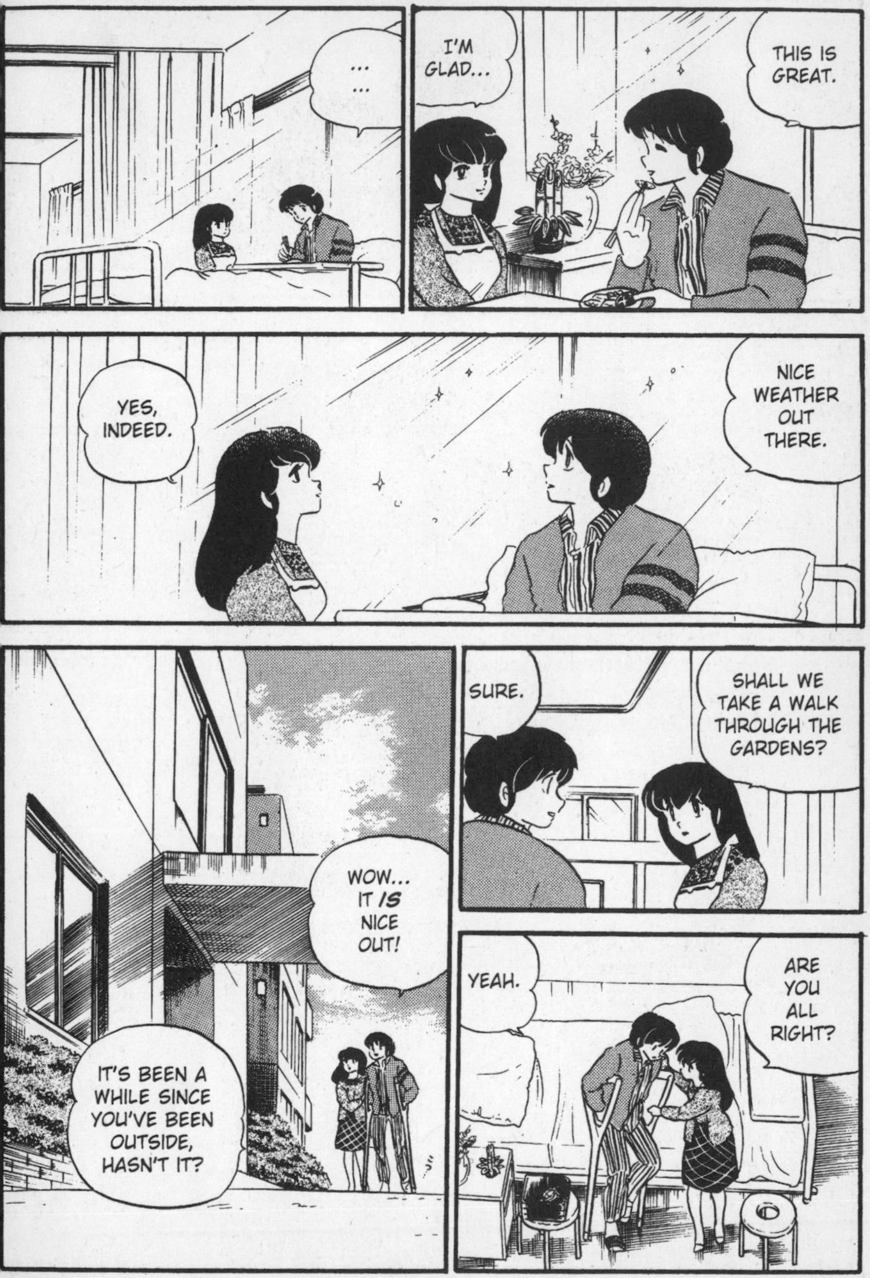
THIS IS GREAT.
I'M GLAD...
... ...
NICE WEATHER OUT THERE.
YES, INDEED.
SHALL WE TAKE A WALK THROUGH THE GARDENS?
SURE.
ARE YOU ALL RIGHT?
YEAH.
WOW... IT *IS* NICE OUT!
IT'S BEEN A WHILE SINCE YOU'VE BEEN OUTSIDE, HASN'T IT?

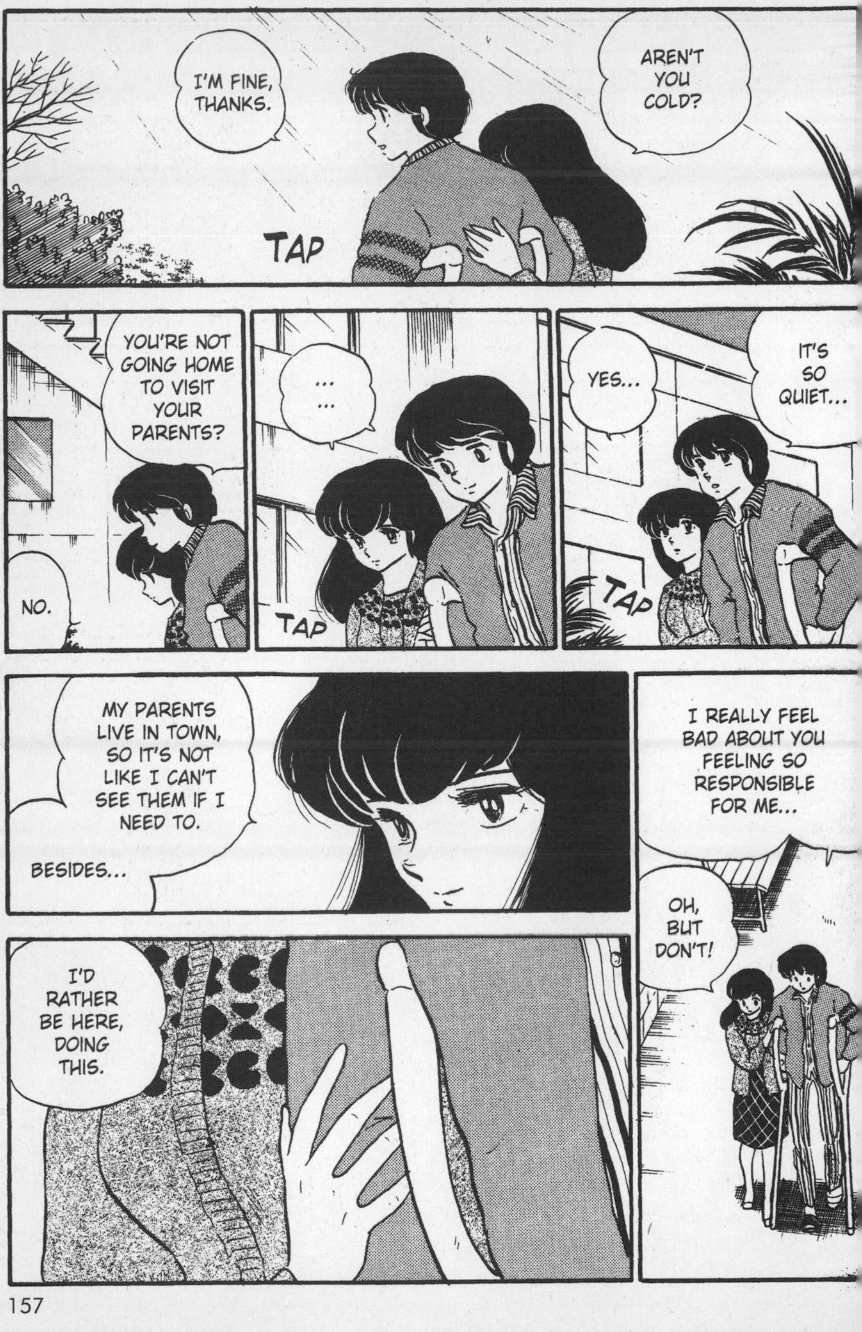
AREN'T YOU COLD?
I'M FINE, THANKS.
TAP
IT'S SO QUIET...
YES...
TAP
... ...
TAP
YOU'RE NOT GOING HOME TO VISIT YOUR PARENTS?
NO.
I REALLY FEEL BAD ABOUT YOU FEELING SO RESPONSIBLE FOR ME...
OH, BUT DON'T!
MY PARENTS LIVE IN TOWN, SO IT'S NOT LIKE I CAN'T SEE THEM IF I NEED TO.
BESIDES...
I'D RATHER BE HERE, DOING THIS.

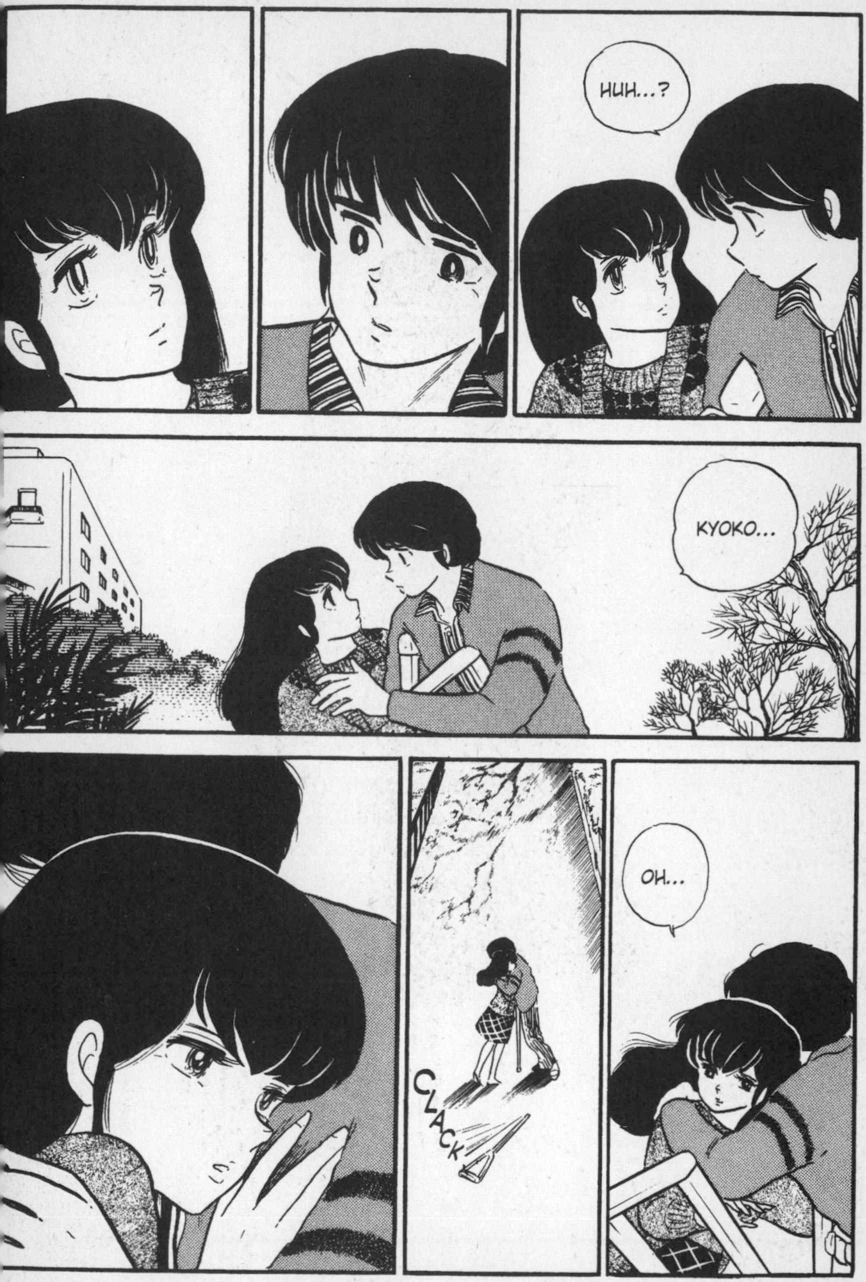
HUH...?
KYOKO...
OH...
CLACK

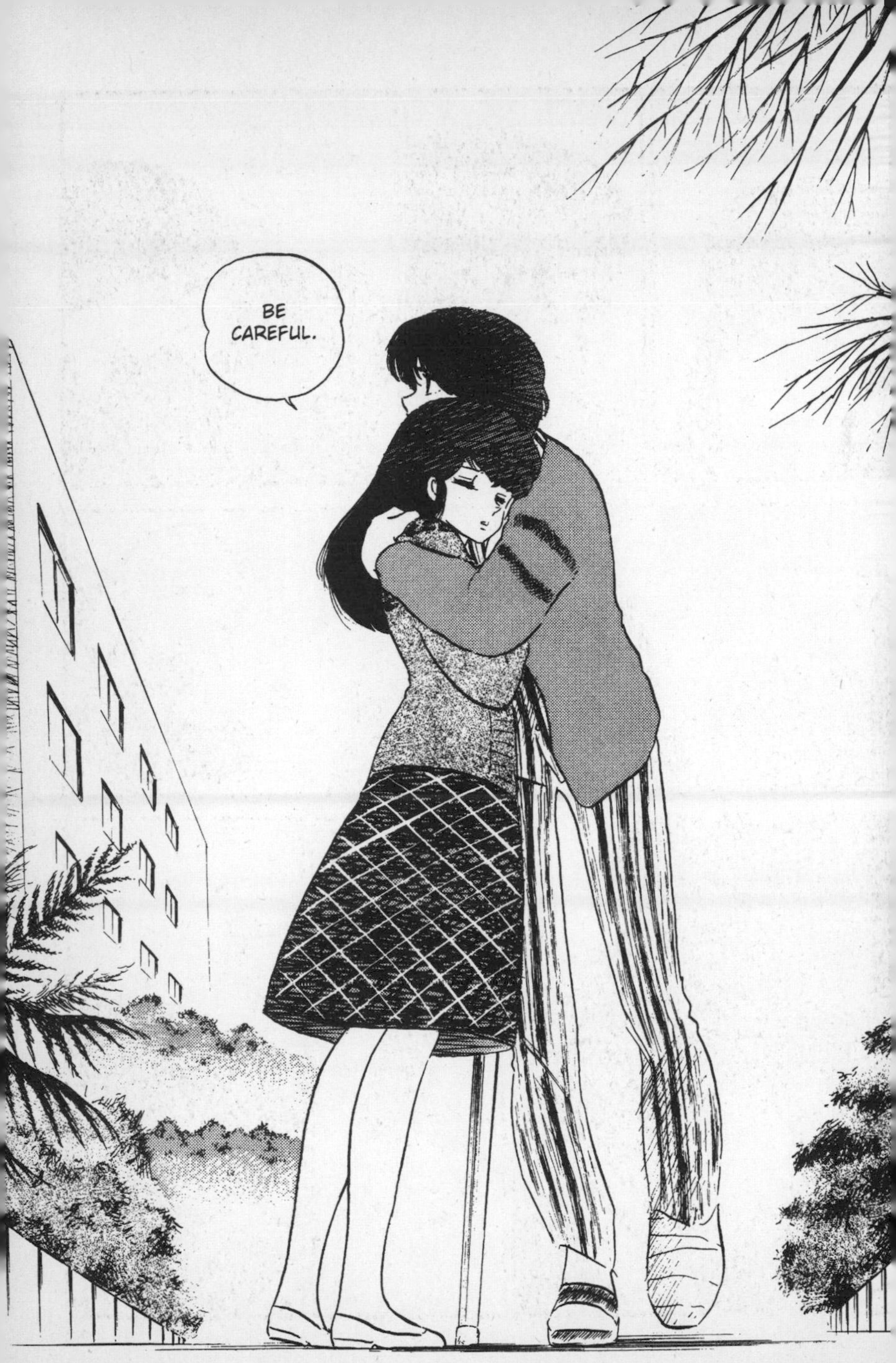
BE CAREFUL.

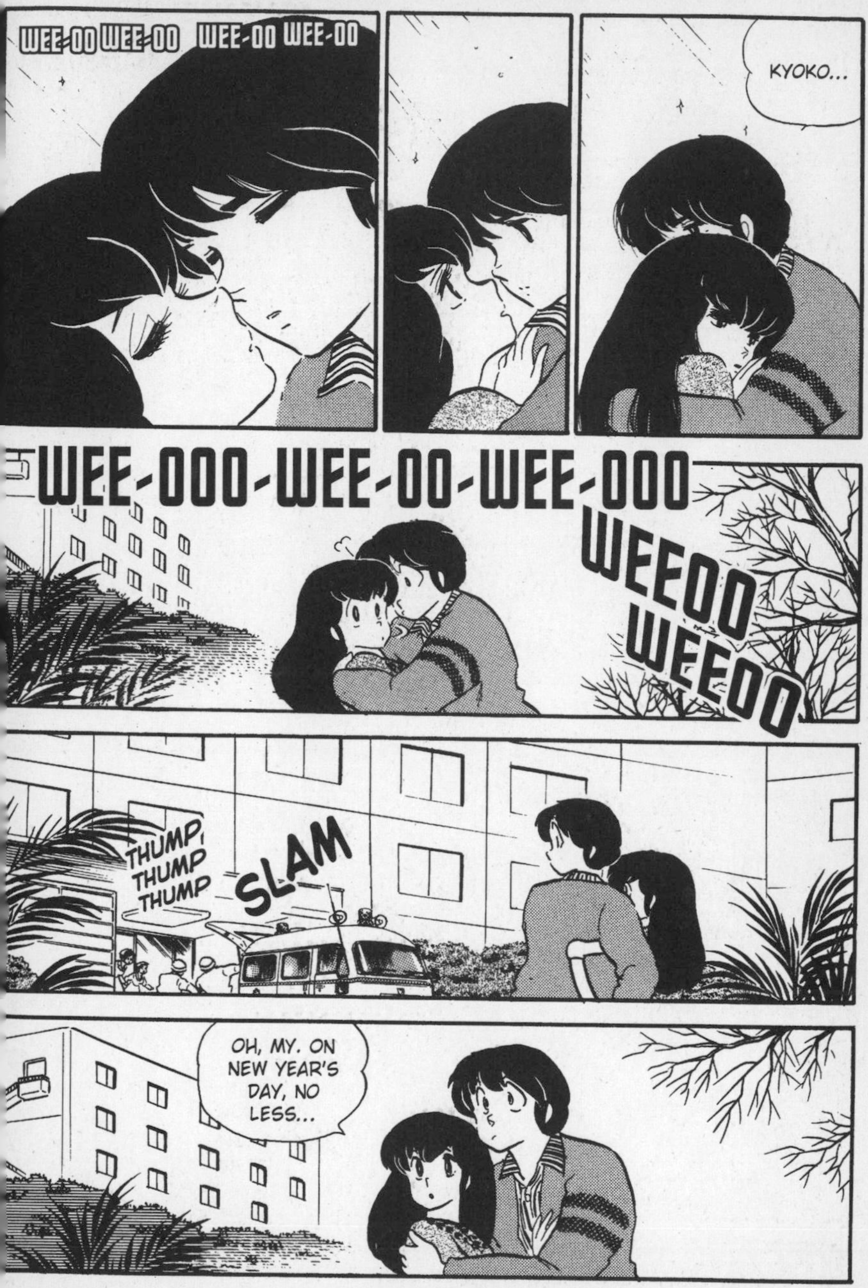
KYOKO...
WEE-OO WEE-OO WEE-OO WEE-OO
WEE-OOO-WEE-OO-WEE-OOO
WEEOO WEEOO
SLAM
THUMP, THUMP THUMP
OH, MY. ON NEW YEAR'S DAY, NO LESS...

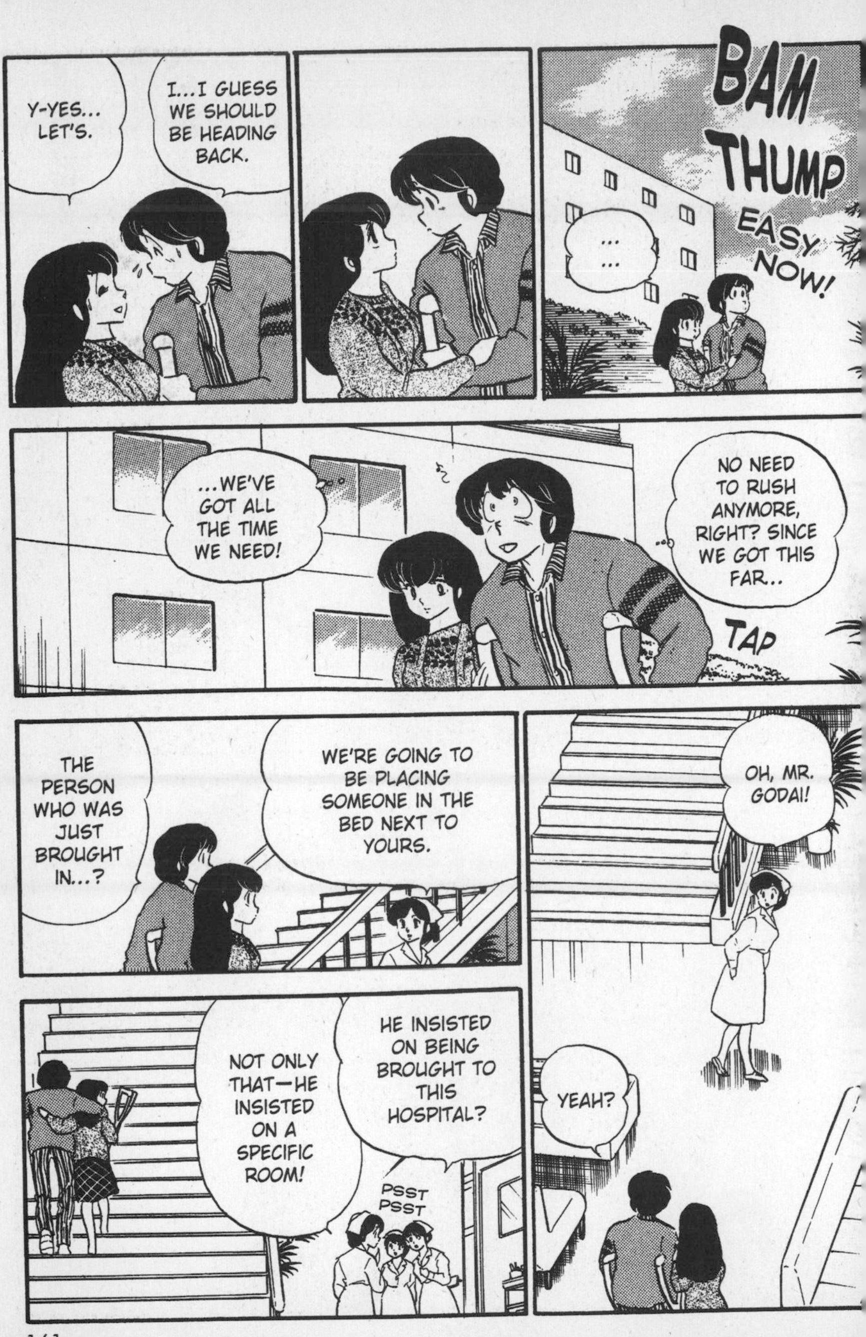
BAM
THUMP
EASY NOW!
... ...
I...I GUESS WE SHOULD BE HEADING BACK.
Y-YES... LET'S.
NO NEED TO RUSH ANYMORE, RIGHT? SINCE WE GOT THIS FAR...
TAP
...WE'VE GOT ALL THE TIME WE NEED!
OH, MR. GODAI!
YEAH?
WE'RE GOING TO BE PLACING SOMEONE IN THE BED NEXT TO YOURS.
THE PERSON WHO WAS JUST BROUGHT IN...?
HE INSISTED ON BEING BROUGHT TO THIS HOSPITAL?
NOT ONLY THAT—HE INSISTED ON A SPECIFIC ROOM!
PSST PSST

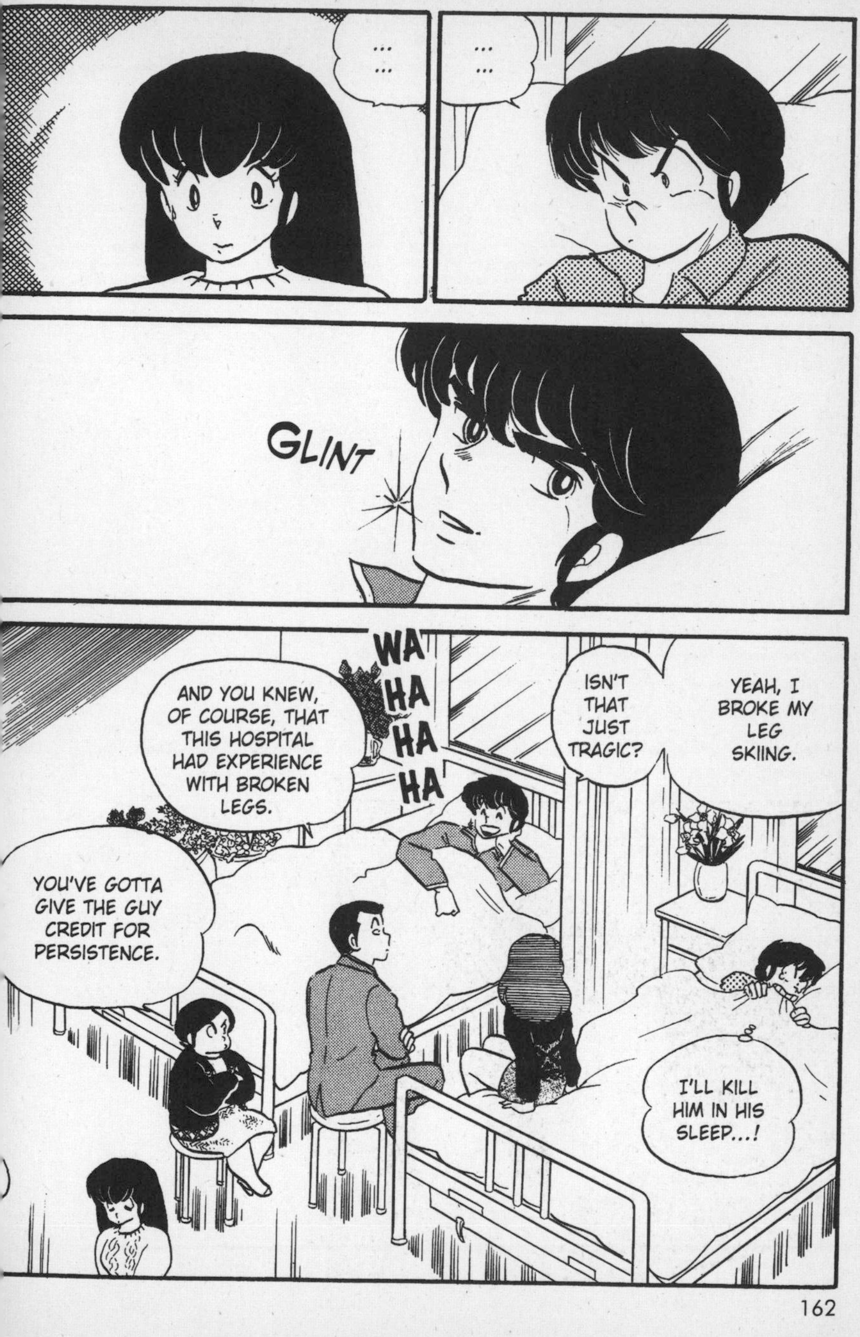
...
...
...
...
GLINT
YEAH, I BROKE MY LEG SKIING.
ISN'T THAT JUST TRAGIC?
WA HA HA HA HA
AND YOU KNEW, OF COURSE, THAT THIS HOSPITAL HAD EXPERIENCE WITH BROKEN LEGS.
YOU'VE GOTTA GIVE THE GUY CREDIT FOR PERSISTENCE.
I'LL KILL HIM IN HIS SLEEP...!

PART EIGHT

MESSAGE IN THE SNOW

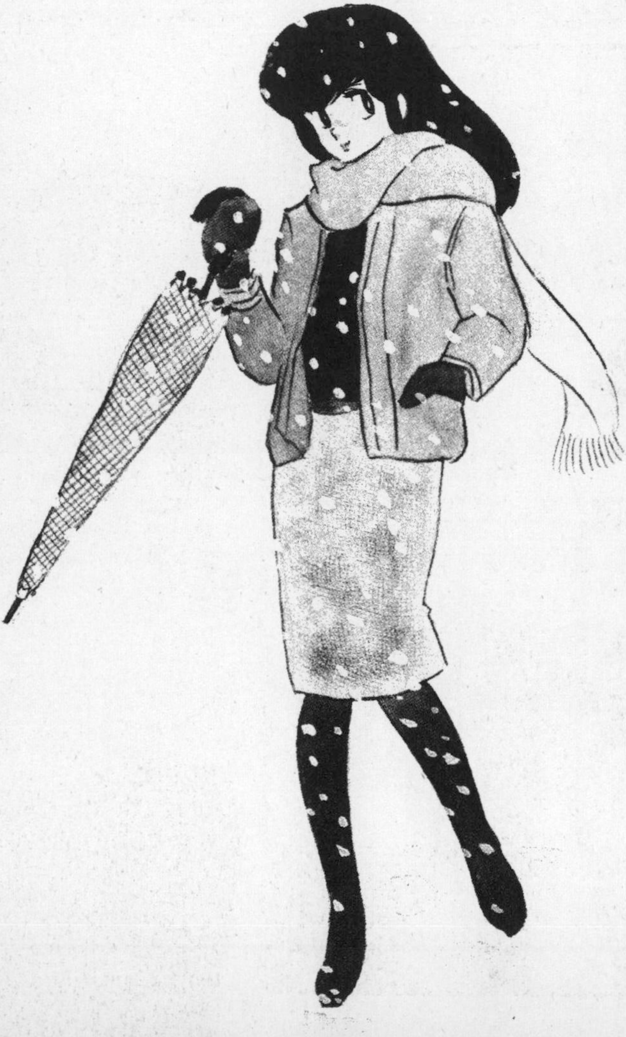

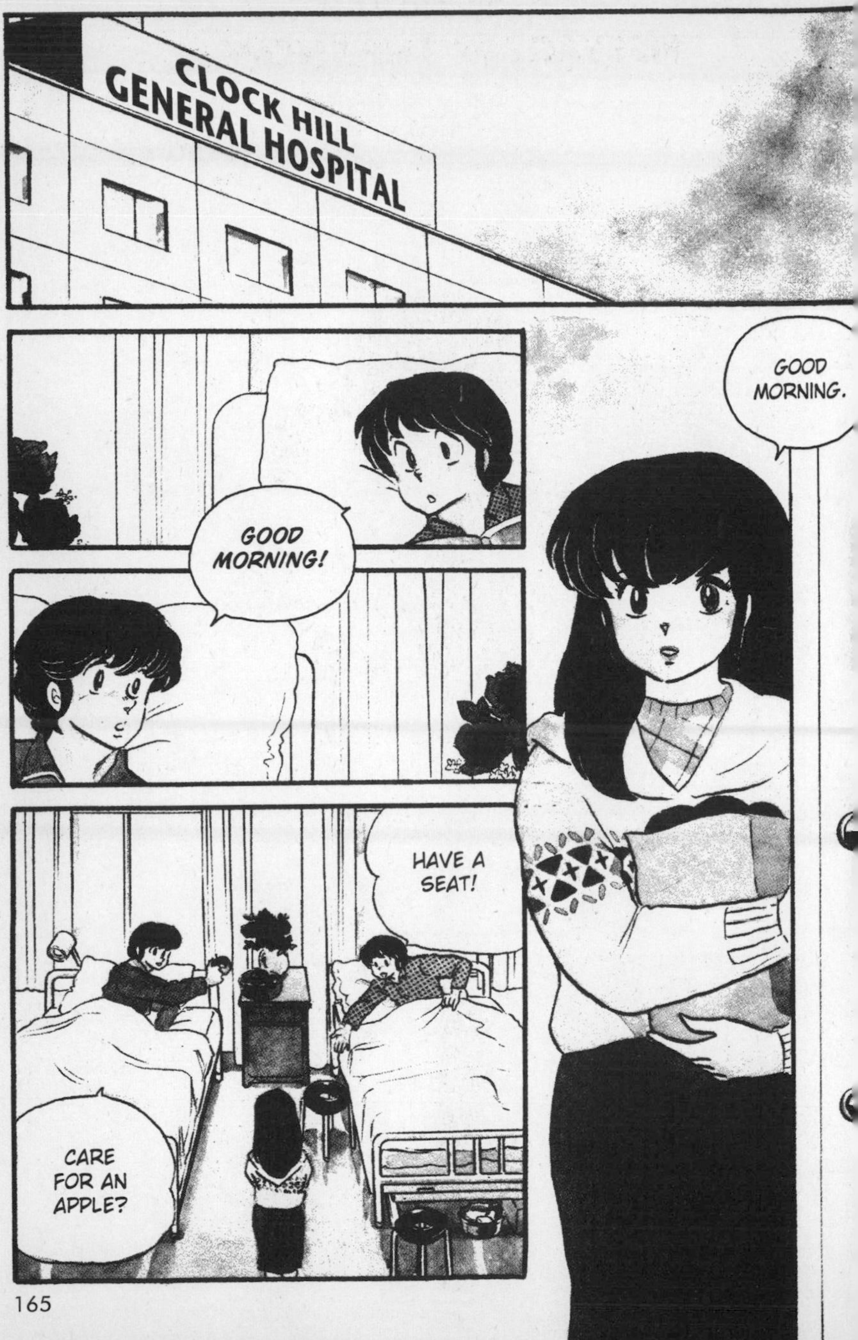
CLOCK HILL GENERAL HOSPITAL
GOOD MORNING.
GOOD MORNING!
HAVE A SEAT!
CARE FOR AN APPLE?

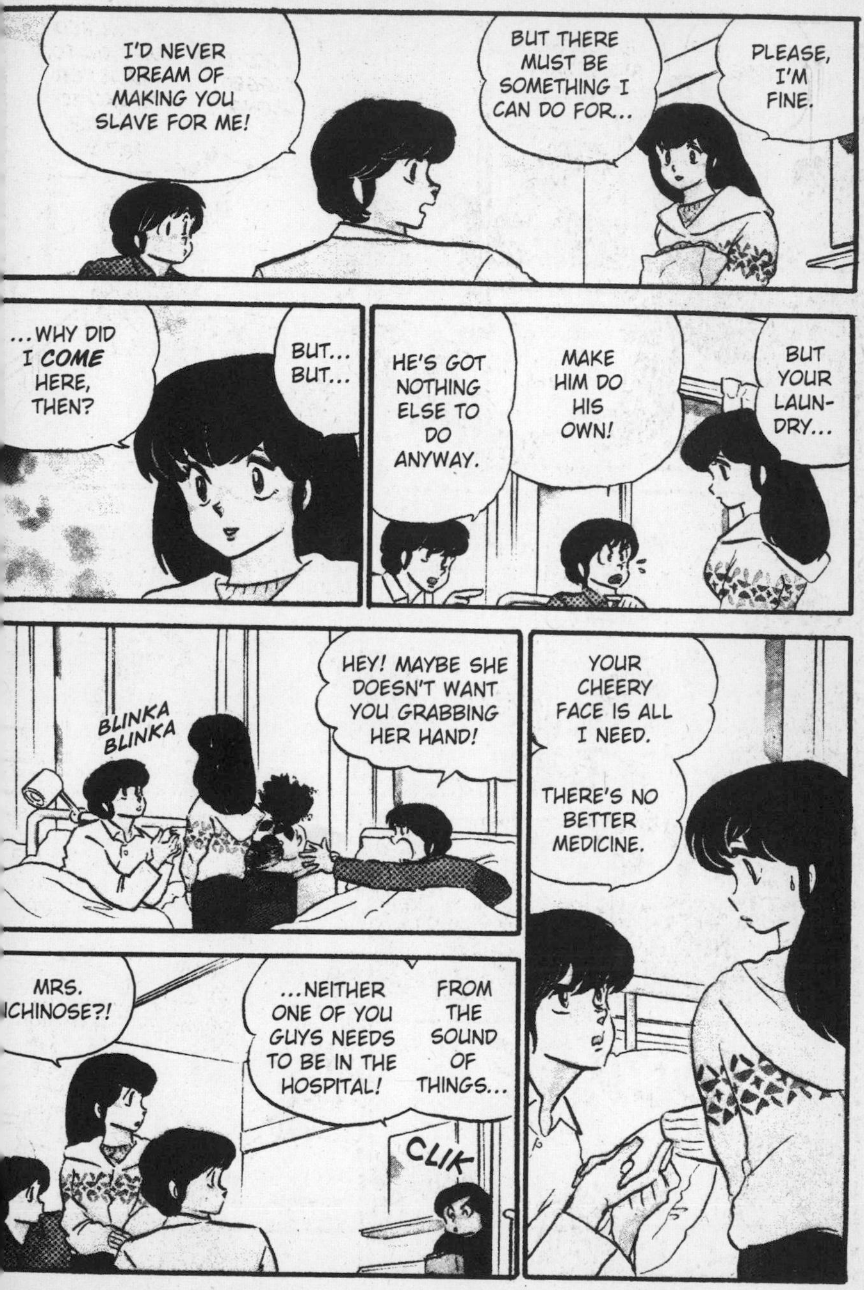
PLEASE, I'M FINE.
BUT THERE MUST BE SOMETHING I CAN DO FOR...
I'D NEVER DREAM OF MAKING YOU SLAVE FOR ME!
BUT YOUR LAUN-DRY...
MAKE HIM DO HIS OWN!
HE'S GOT NOTHING ELSE TO DO ANYWAY.
BUT... BUT...
...WHY DID I COME HERE, THEN?
YOUR CHEERY FACE IS ALL I NEED.
THERE'S NO BETTER MEDICINE.
HEY! MAYBE SHE DOESN'T WANT YOU GRABBING HER HAND!
BLINKA BLINKA
FROM THE SOUND OF THINGS...
...NEITHER ONE OF YOU GUYS NEEDS TO BE IN THE HOSPITAL!
MRS. ICHINOSE?!
CLIK

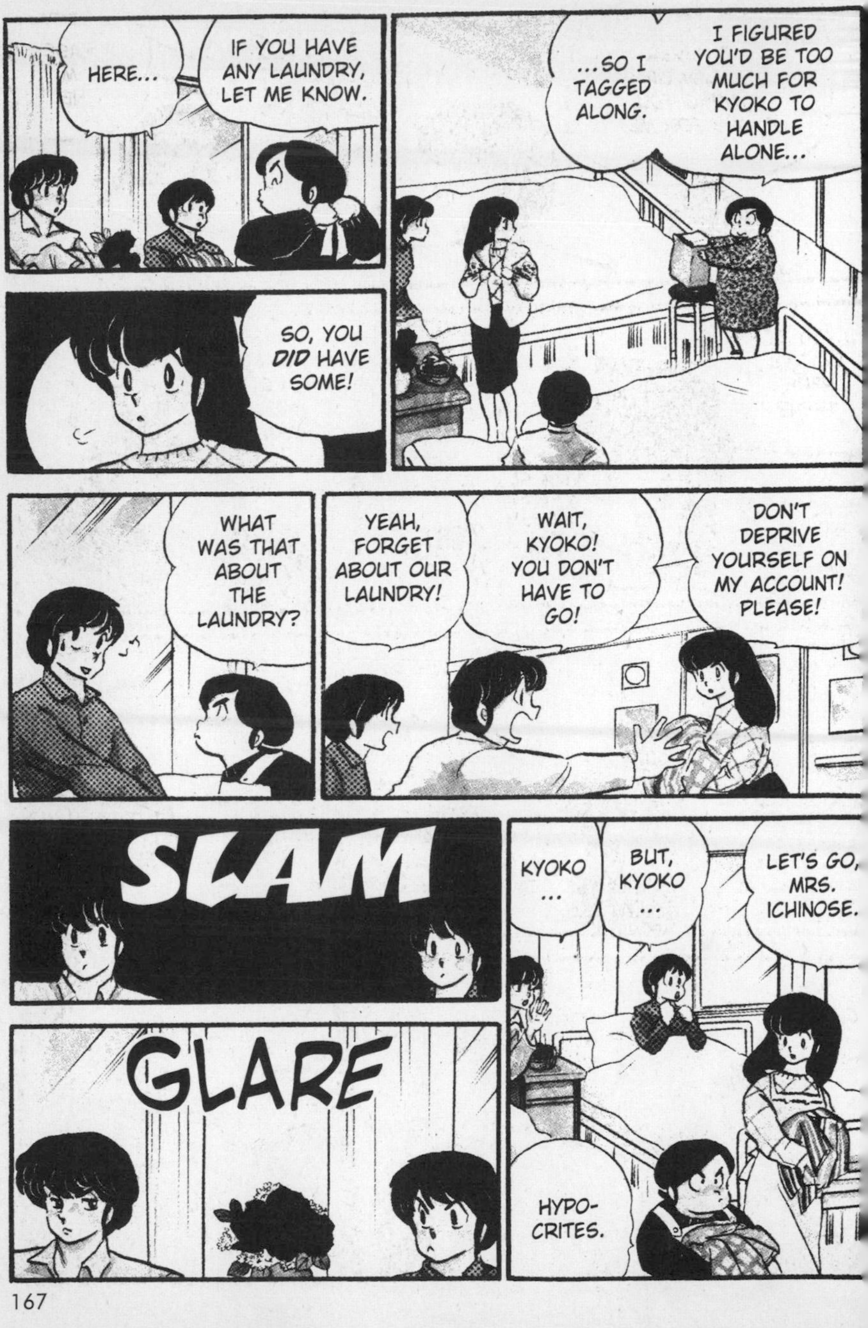
I FIGURED YOU'D BE TOO MUCH FOR KYOKO TO HANDLE ALONE...
...SO I TAGGED ALONG.
IF YOU HAVE ANY LAUNDRY, LET ME KNOW.
HERE...
SO, YOU DID HAVE SOME!
DON'T DEPRIVE YOURSELF ON MY ACCOUNT! PLEASE!
WAIT, KYOKO! YOU DON'T HAVE TO GO!
YEAH, FORGET ABOUT OUR LAUNDRY!
WHAT WAS THAT ABOUT THE LAUNDRY?
LET'S GO, MRS. ICHINOSE.
BUT, KYOKO ...
KYOKO ...
HYPOCRITES.
SLAM
GLARE

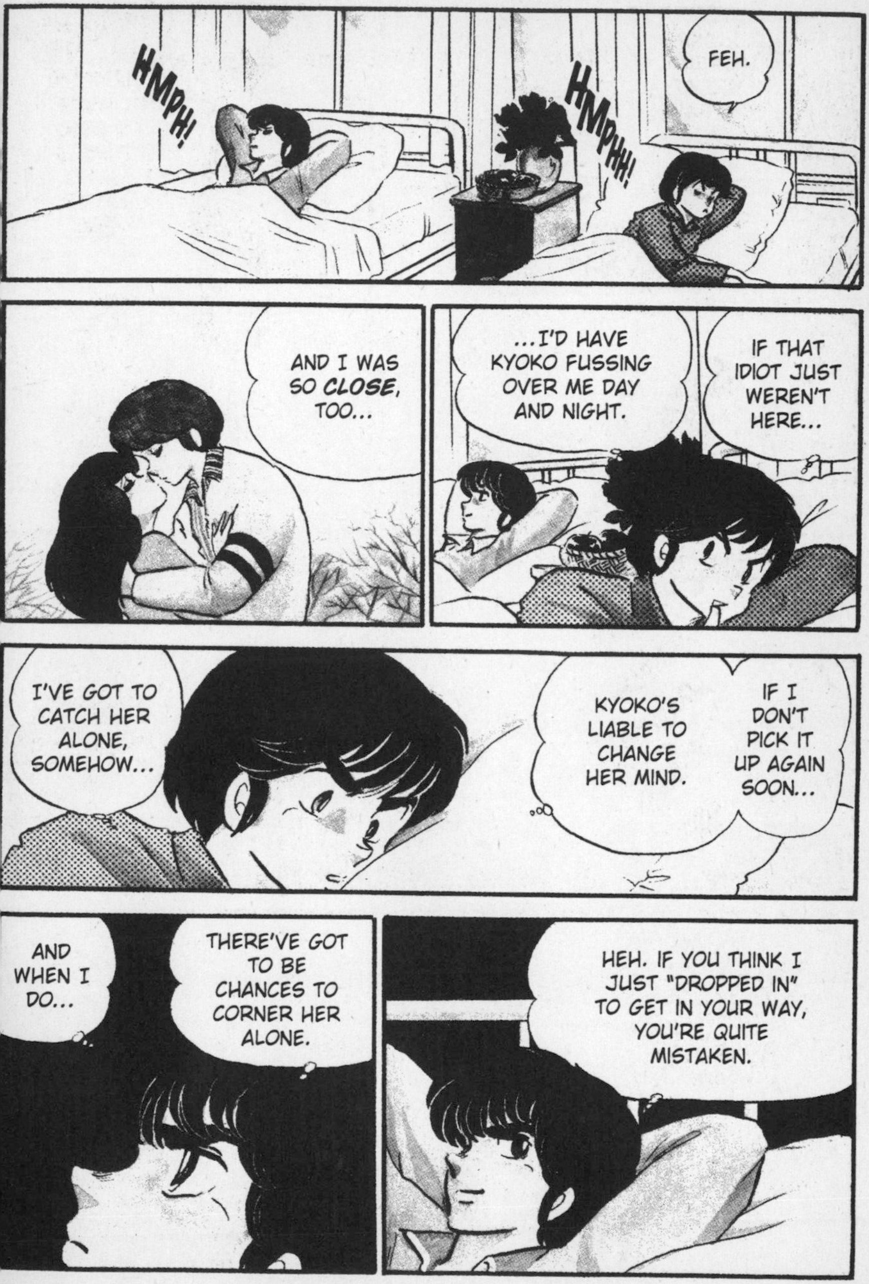
FEH.
HMPHH!
HMPH!
IF THAT IDIOT JUST WEREN'T HERE...
...I'D HAVE KYOKO FUSSING OVER ME DAY AND NIGHT.
AND I WAS SO *CLOSE*, TOO...
IF I DON'T PICK IT UP AGAIN SOON...
KYOKO'S LIABLE TO CHANGE HER MIND.
I'VE GOT TO CATCH HER ALONE, SOMEHOW...
HEH. IF YOU THINK I JUST "DROPPED IN" TO GET IN YOUR WAY, YOU'RE QUITE MISTAKEN.
THERE'VE GOT TO BE CHANCES TO CORNER HER ALONE.
AND WHEN I DO...

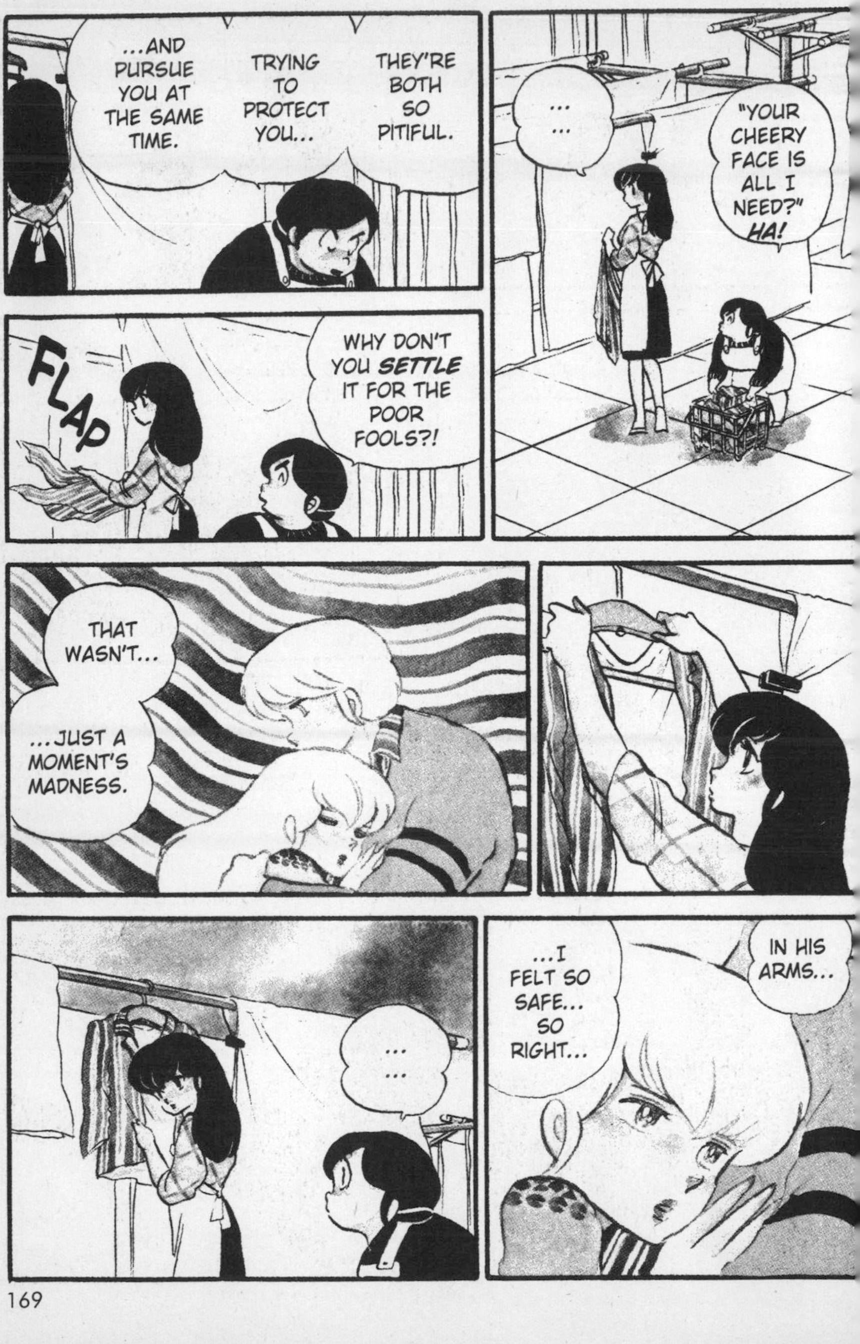
"YOUR CHEERY FACE IS ALL I NEED?" HA!
... ...
THEY'RE BOTH SO PITIFUL.
TRYING TO PROTECT YOU...
...AND PURSUE YOU AT THE SAME TIME.
WHY DON'T YOU SETTLE IT FOR THE POOR FOOLS?!
FLAP
THAT WASN'T...
...JUST A MOMENT'S MADNESS.
IN HIS ARMS...
...I FELT SO SAFE... SO RIGHT...
... ...

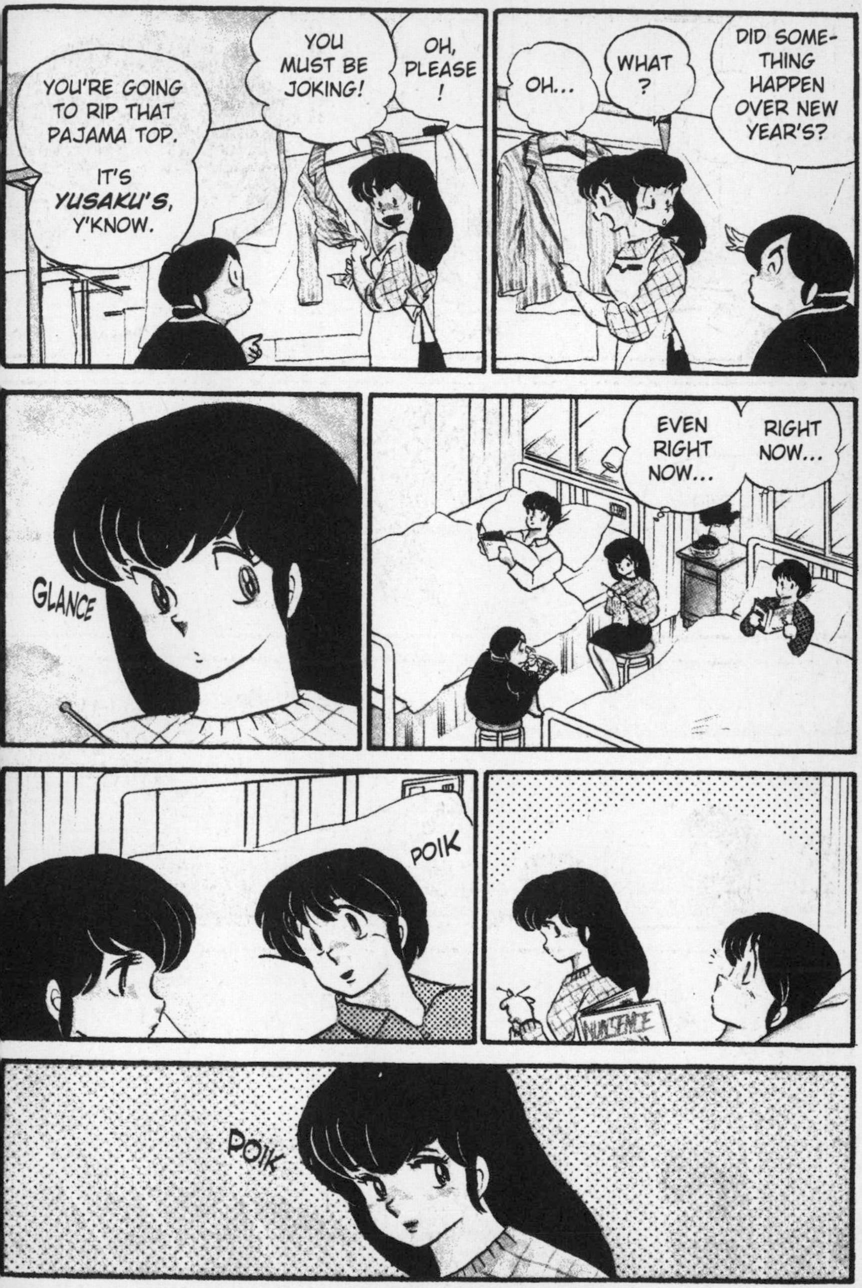
DID SOME-THING HAPPEN OVER NEW YEAR'S?
WHAT ?
OH...
OH, PLEASE !
YOU MUST BE JOKING!
YOU'RE GOING TO RIP THAT PAJAMA TOP.
IT'S YUSAKU'S, Y'KNOW.
RIGHT NOW...
EVEN RIGHT NOW...
GLANCE
NUISENCE
POIK
POIK

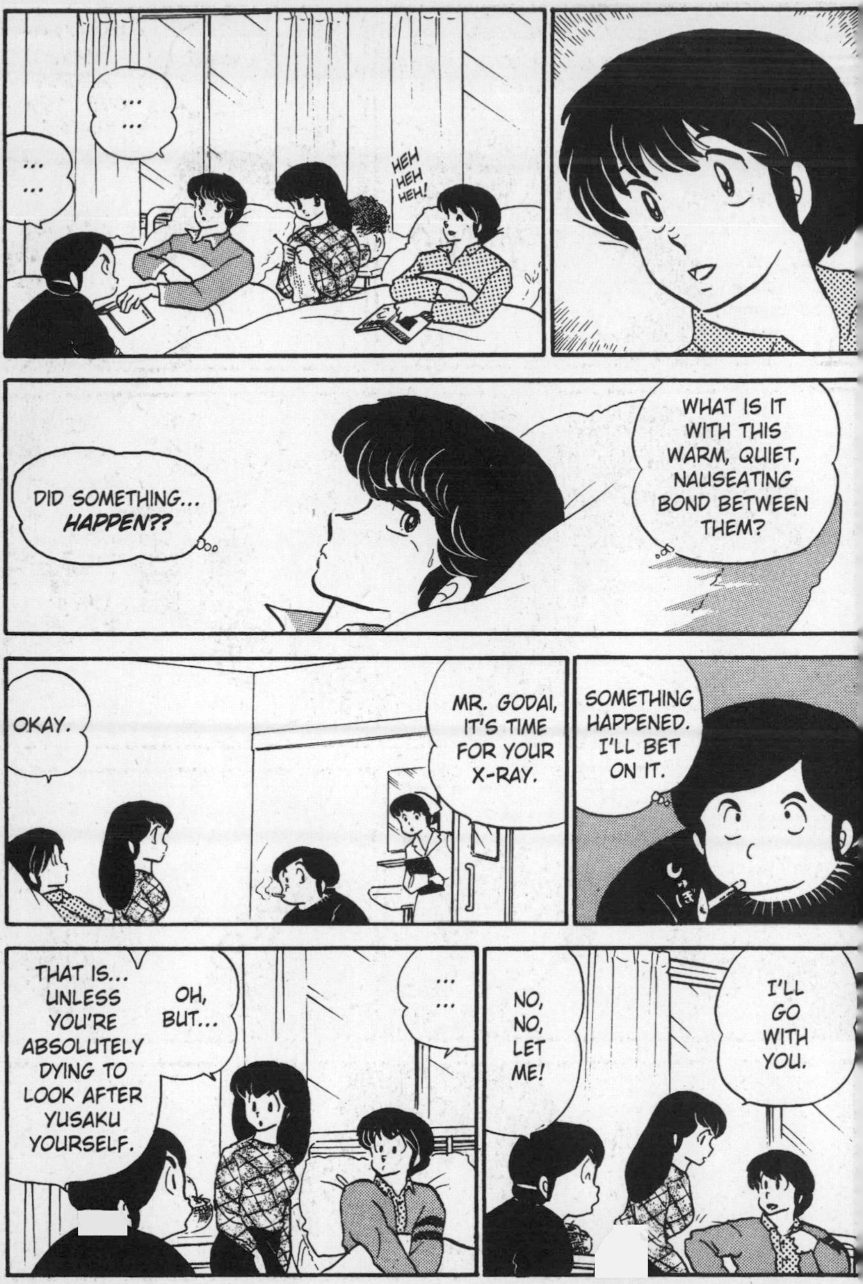
... ...
HEH HEH HEH!
... ...
WHAT IS IT WITH THIS WARM, QUIET, NAUSEATING BOND BETWEEN THEM?
DID SOMETHING... *HAPPEN??*
SOMETHING HAPPENED. I'LL BET ON IT.
MR. GODAI, IT'S TIME FOR YOUR X-RAY.
OKAY.
I'LL GO WITH YOU.
NO, NO, LET ME!
... ...
OH, BUT...
THAT IS... UNLESS YOU'RE ABSOLUTELY DYING TO LOOK AFTER YUSAKU YOURSELF.

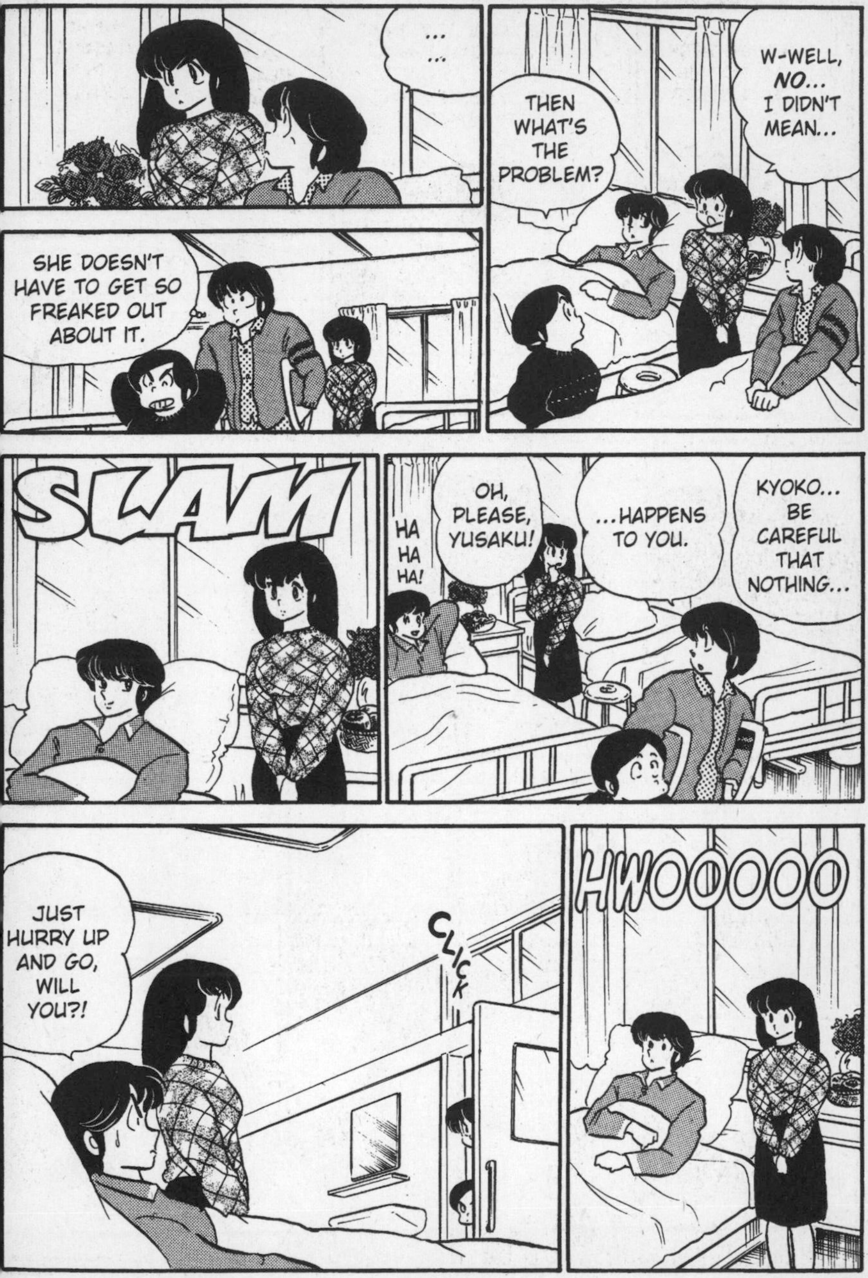
W-WELL, NO... I DIDN'T MEAN...
THEN WHAT'S THE PROBLEM?
... ...
SHE DOESN'T HAVE TO GET SO FREAKED OUT ABOUT IT.
KYOKO... BE CAREFUL THAT NOTHING...
...HAPPENS TO YOU.
OH, PLEASE, YUSAKU!
HA HA HA!
SLAM
HWOOOOO
CLICK
JUST HURRY UP AND GO, WILL YOU?!

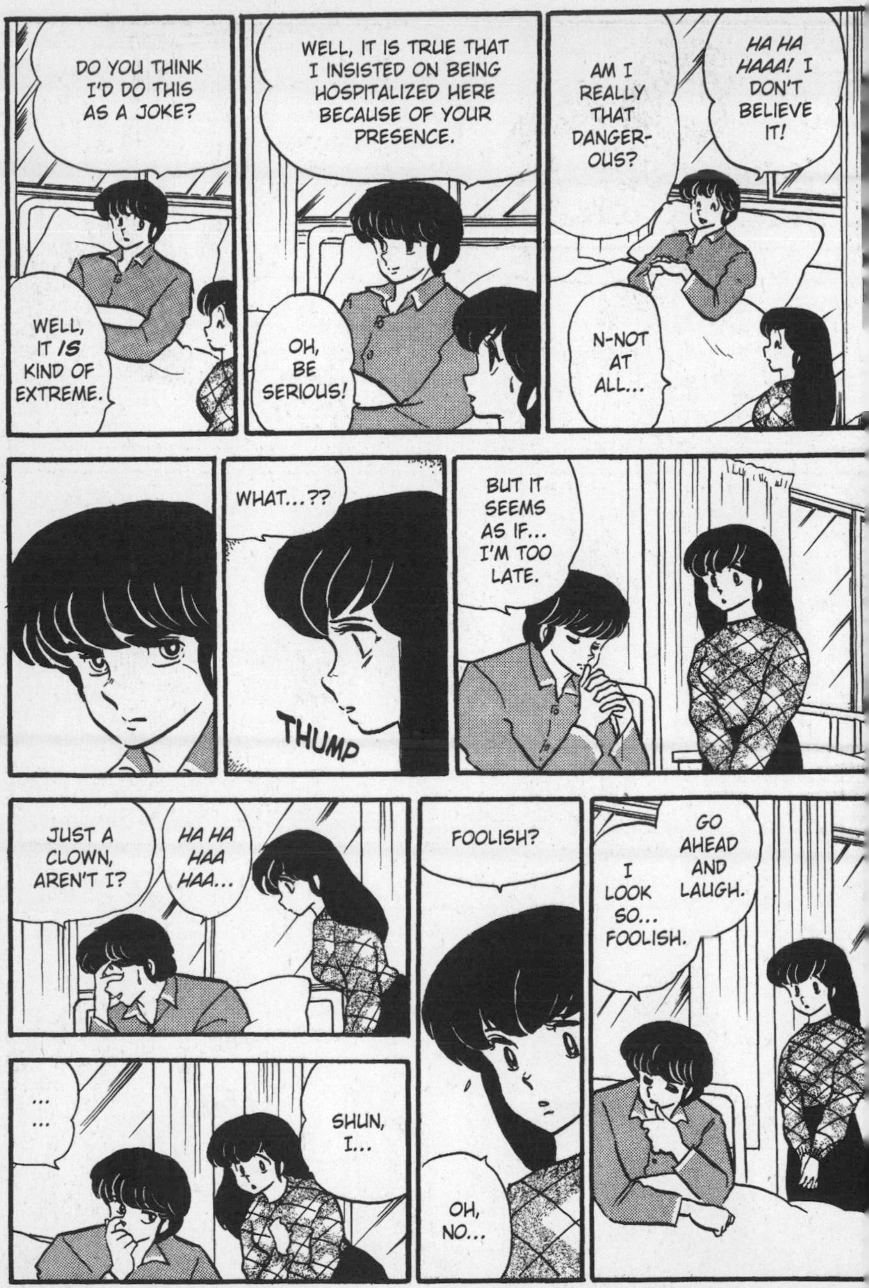
HA HA HAAA! I DON'T BELIEVE IT!
AM I REALLY THAT DANGER-OUS?
N-NOT AT ALL...
WELL, IT IS TRUE THAT I INSISTED ON BEING HOSPITALIZED HERE BECAUSE OF YOUR PRESENCE.
OH, BE SERIOUS!
DO YOU THINK I'D DO THIS AS A JOKE?
WELL, IT *IS* KIND OF EXTREME.
BUT IT SEEMS AS IF... I'M TOO LATE.
WHAT...??
THUMP
GO AHEAD AND LAUGH.
I LOOK SO... FOOLISH.
FOOLISH?
OH, NO...
HA HA HAA HAA...
JUST A CLOWN, AREN'T I?
SHUN, I...
... ...

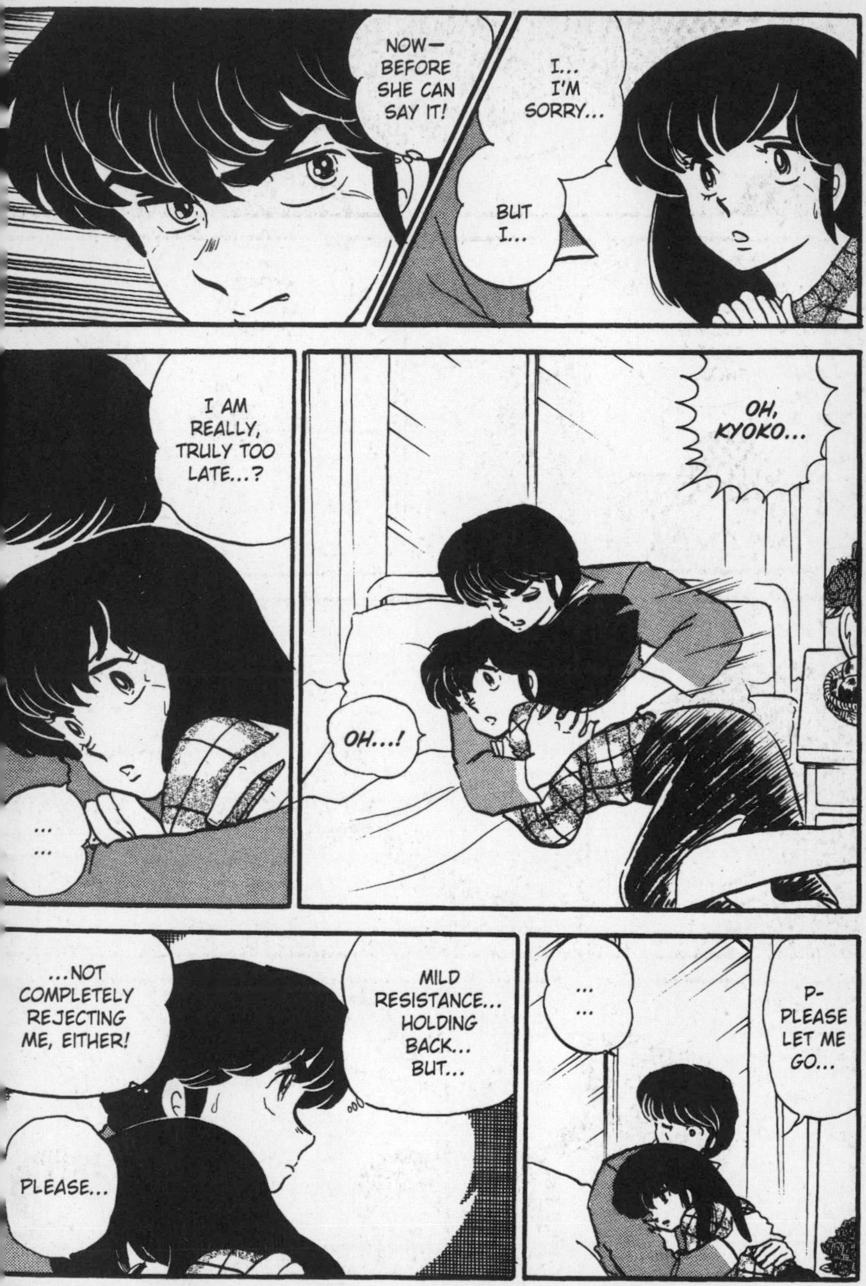
I... I'M SORRY...
BUT I...
NOW— BEFORE SHE CAN SAY IT!
OH, KYOKO...
OH...!
I AM REALLY, TRULY TOO LATE...?
... ...
P-PLEASE LET ME GO...
... ...
MILD RESISTANCE... HOLDING BACK... BUT...
...NOT COMPLETELY REJECTING ME, EITHER!
PLEASE...

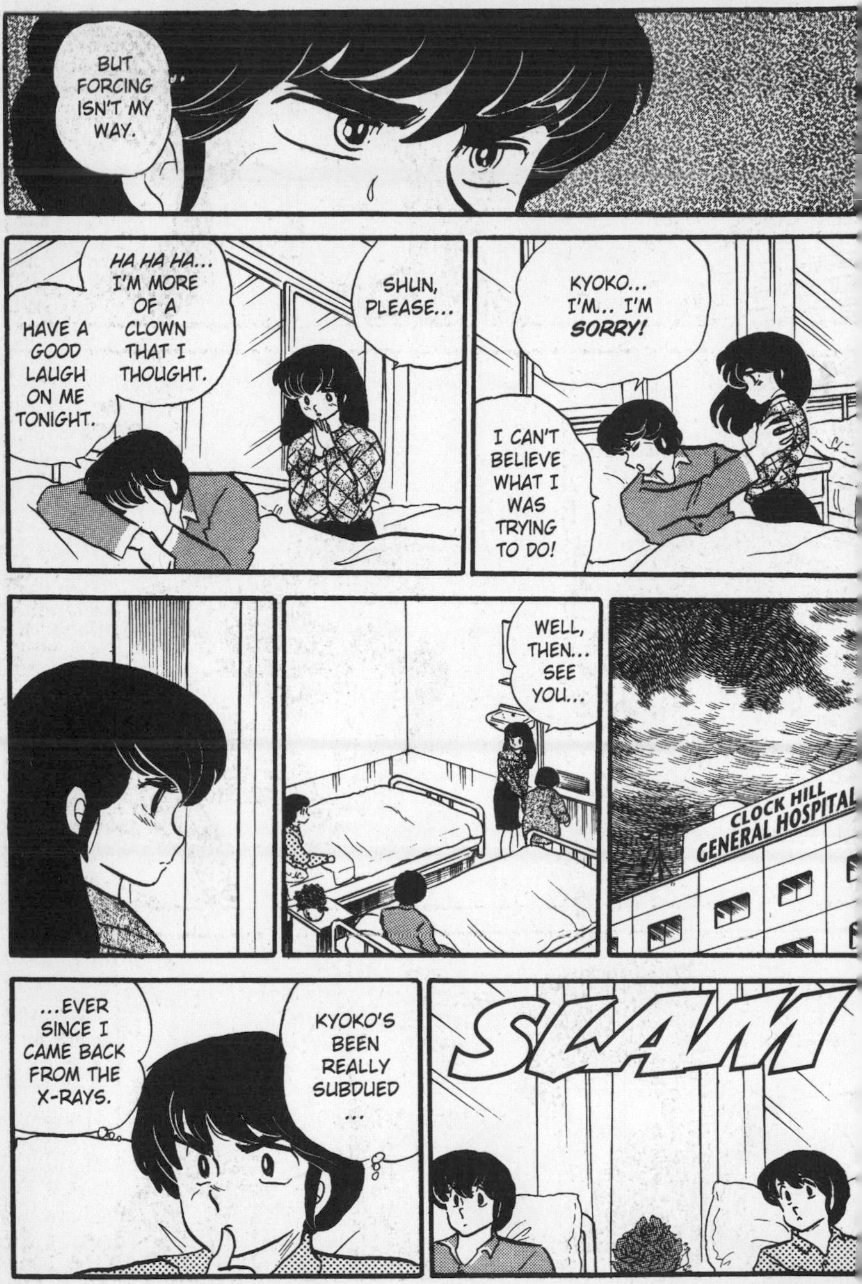
BUT FORCING ISN'T MY WAY.
KYOKO... I'M... I'M *SORRY!*
I CAN'T BELIEVE WHAT I WAS TRYING TO DO!
SHUN, PLEASE...
HA HA HA... I'M MORE OF A CLOWN THAT I THOUGHT.
HAVE A GOOD LAUGH ON ME TONIGHT.
CLOCK HILL GENERAL HOSPITAL
WELL, THEN... SEE YOU...
SLAM
KYOKO'S BEEN REALLY SUBDUED ...
...EVER SINCE I CAME BACK FROM THE X-RAYS.

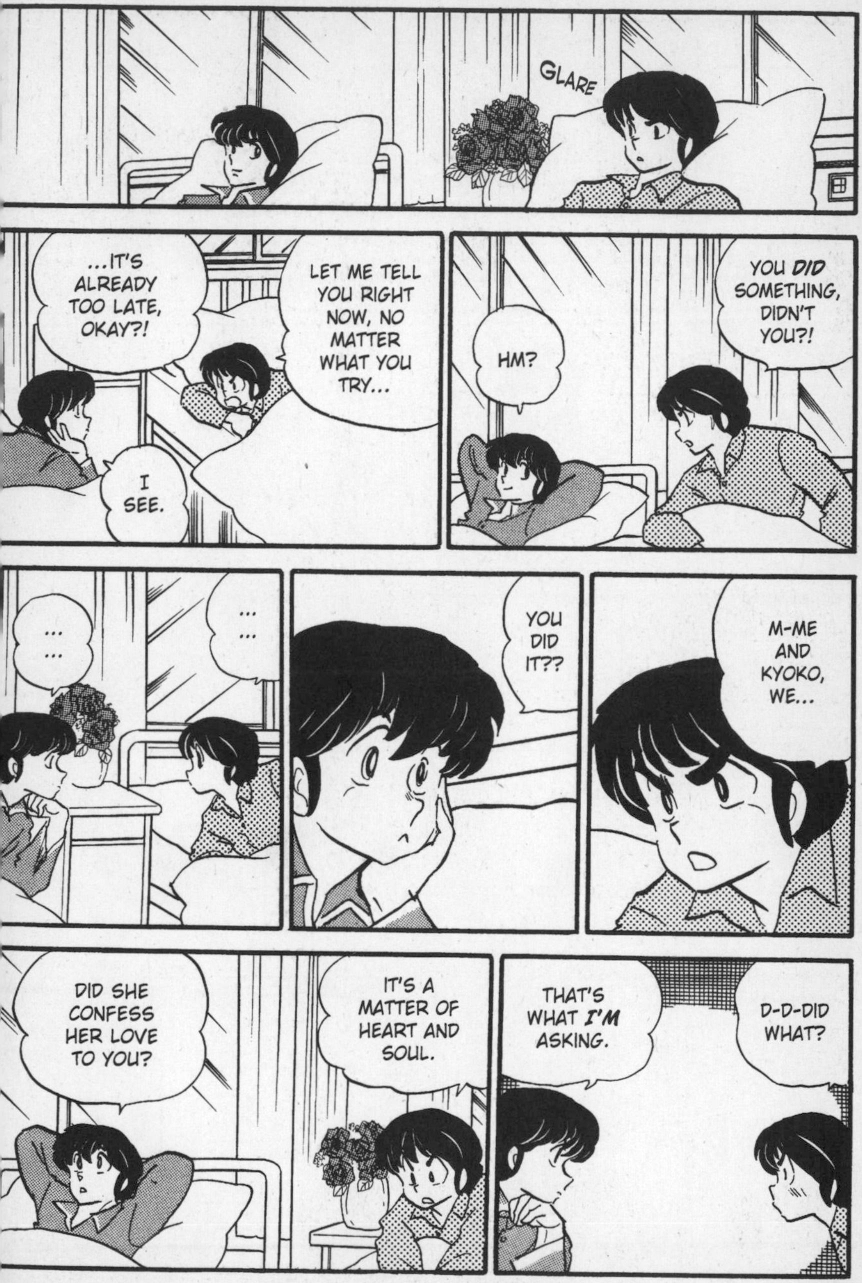
GLARE
YOU *DID* SOMETHING, DIDN'T YOU?!
HM?
LET ME TELL YOU RIGHT NOW, NO MATTER WHAT YOU TRY...
...IT'S ALREADY TOO LATE, OKAY?!
I SEE.
M-ME AND KYOKO, WE...
YOU DID IT??
... ...
... ...
D-D-DID WHAT?
THAT'S WHAT *I'M* ASKING.
IT'S A MATTER OF HEART AND SOUL.
DID SHE CONFESS HER LOVE TO YOU?

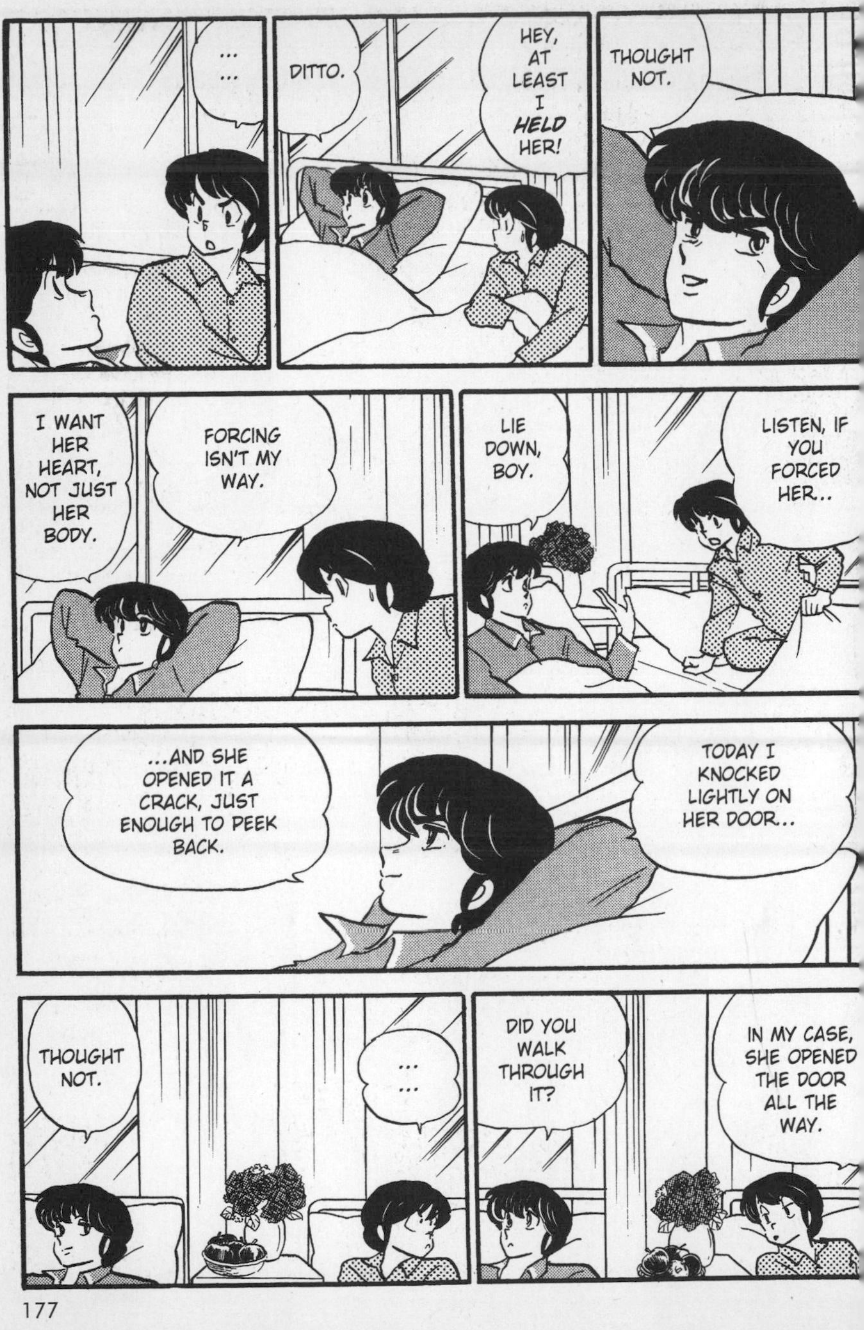
THOUGHT NOT.
HEY, AT LEAST I HELD HER!
DITTO.
... ...
LISTEN, IF YOU FORCED HER..
LIE DOWN, BOY.
FORCING ISN'T MY WAY.
I WANT HER HEART, NOT JUST HER BODY.
TODAY I KNOCKED LIGHTLY ON HER DOOR...
...AND SHE OPENED IT A CRACK, JUST ENOUGH TO PEEK BACK.
IN MY CASE, SHE OPENED THE DOOR ALL THE WAY.
DID YOU WALK THROUGH IT?
... ...
THOUGHT NOT.

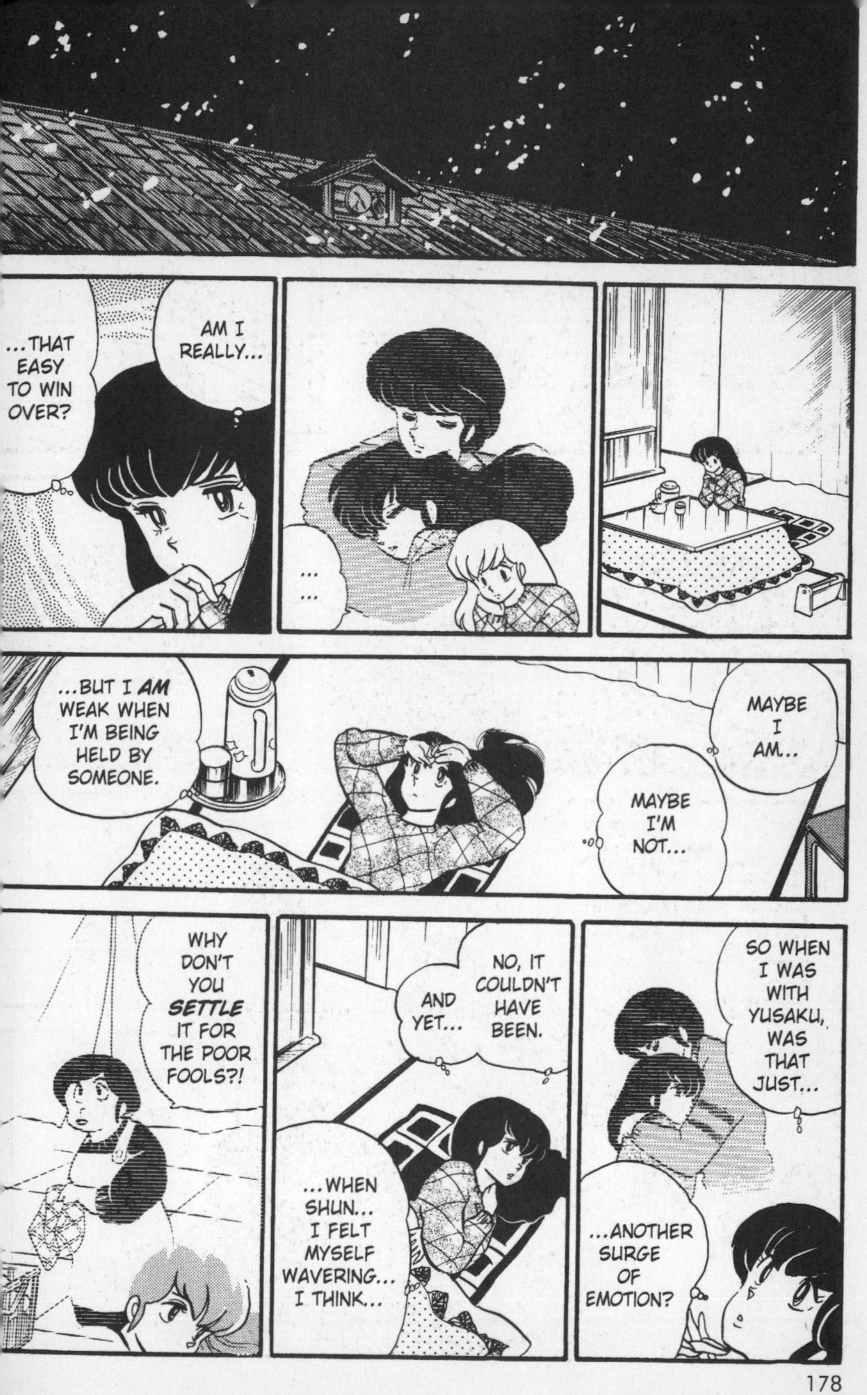
... ...
AM I REALLY...
...THAT EASY TO WIN OVER?
MAYBE I AM...
MAYBE I'M NOT...
...BUT I *AM* WEAK WHEN I'M BEING HELD BY SOMEONE.
SO WHEN I WAS WITH YUSAKU, WAS THAT JUST...
...ANOTHER SURGE OF EMOTION?
NO, IT COULDN'T HAVE BEEN.
AND YET...
...WHEN SHUN... I FELT MYSELF WAVERING... I THINK...
WHY DON'T YOU *SETTLE* IT FOR THE POOR FOOLS?!

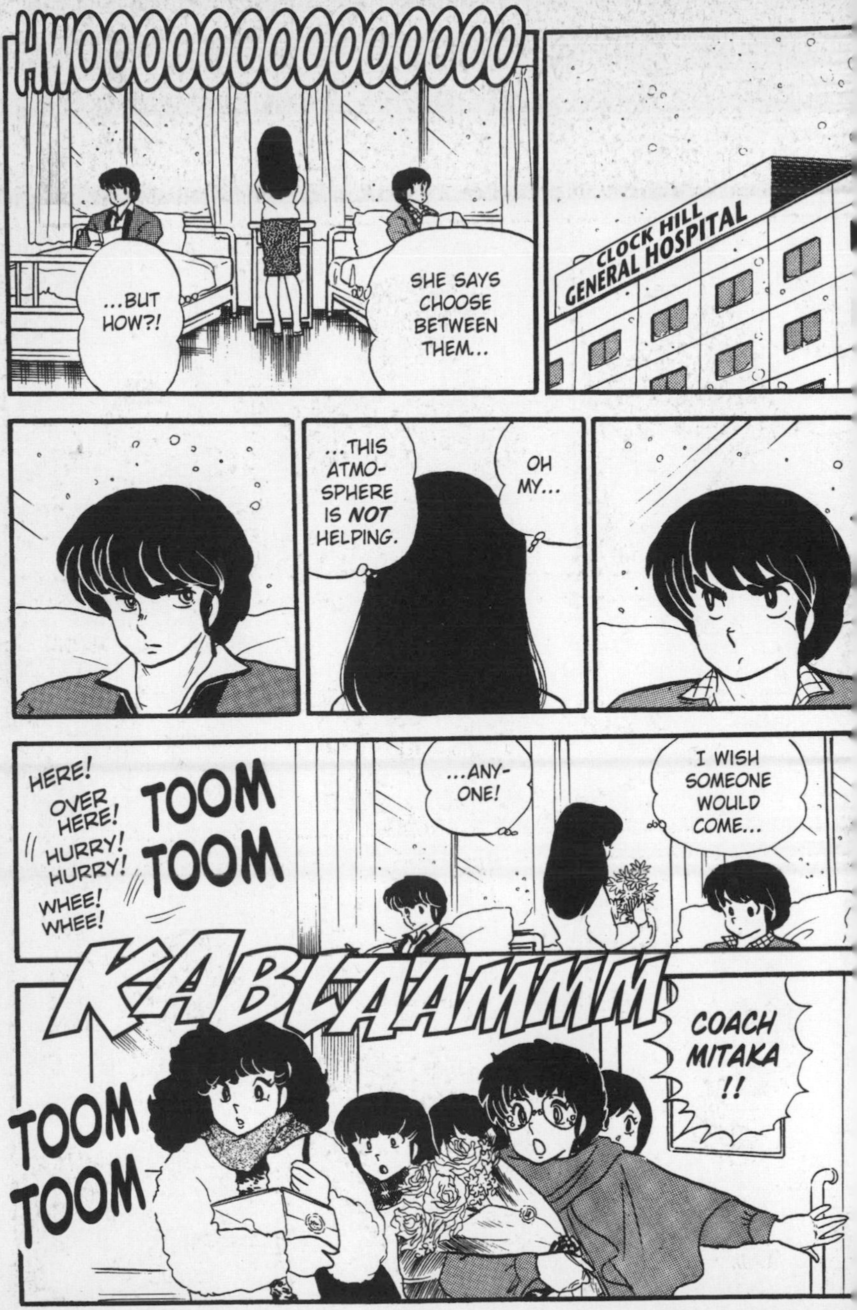
CLOCK HILL
GENERAL HOSPITAL
HWOOOOOOOOOOOOO
SHE SAYS CHOOSE BETWEEN THEM...
...BUT HOW?!
OH MY...
...THIS ATMOSPHERE IS *NOT* HELPING.
I WISH SOMEONE WOULD COME...
...ANYONE!
TOOM TOOM
HERE!
OVER HERE!
HURRY! HURRY!
WHEE! WHEE!
KABLAAMMMM
COACH MITAKA!!
TOOM TOOM

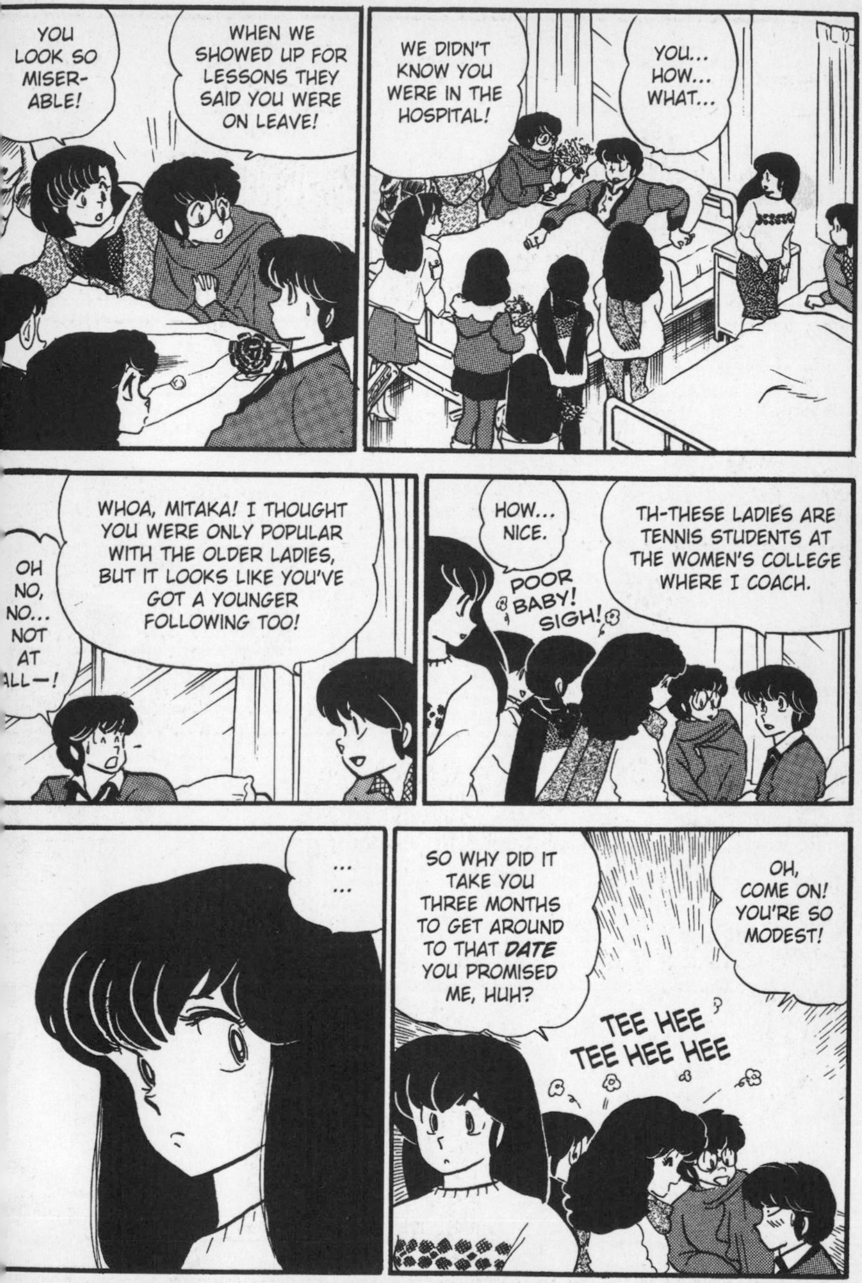
YOU... HOW... WHAT...
WE DIDN'T KNOW YOU WERE IN THE HOSPITAL!
WHEN WE SHOWED UP FOR LESSONS THEY SAID YOU WERE ON LEAVE!
YOU LOOK SO MISER-ABLE!
TH-THESE LADIES ARE TENNIS STUDENTS AT THE WOMEN'S COLLEGE WHERE I COACH.
HOW... NICE.
POOR BABY!
SIGH!
WHOA, MITAKA! I THOUGHT YOU WERE ONLY POPULAR WITH THE OLDER LADIES, BUT IT LOOKS LIKE YOU'VE GOT A YOUNGER FOLLOWING TOO!
OH NO, NO... NOT AT LL—!
OH, COME ON! YOU'RE SO MODEST!
SO WHY DID IT TAKE YOU THREE MONTHS TO GET AROUND TO THAT *DATE* YOU PROMISED ME, HUH?
TEE HEE TEE HEE HEE
... ...

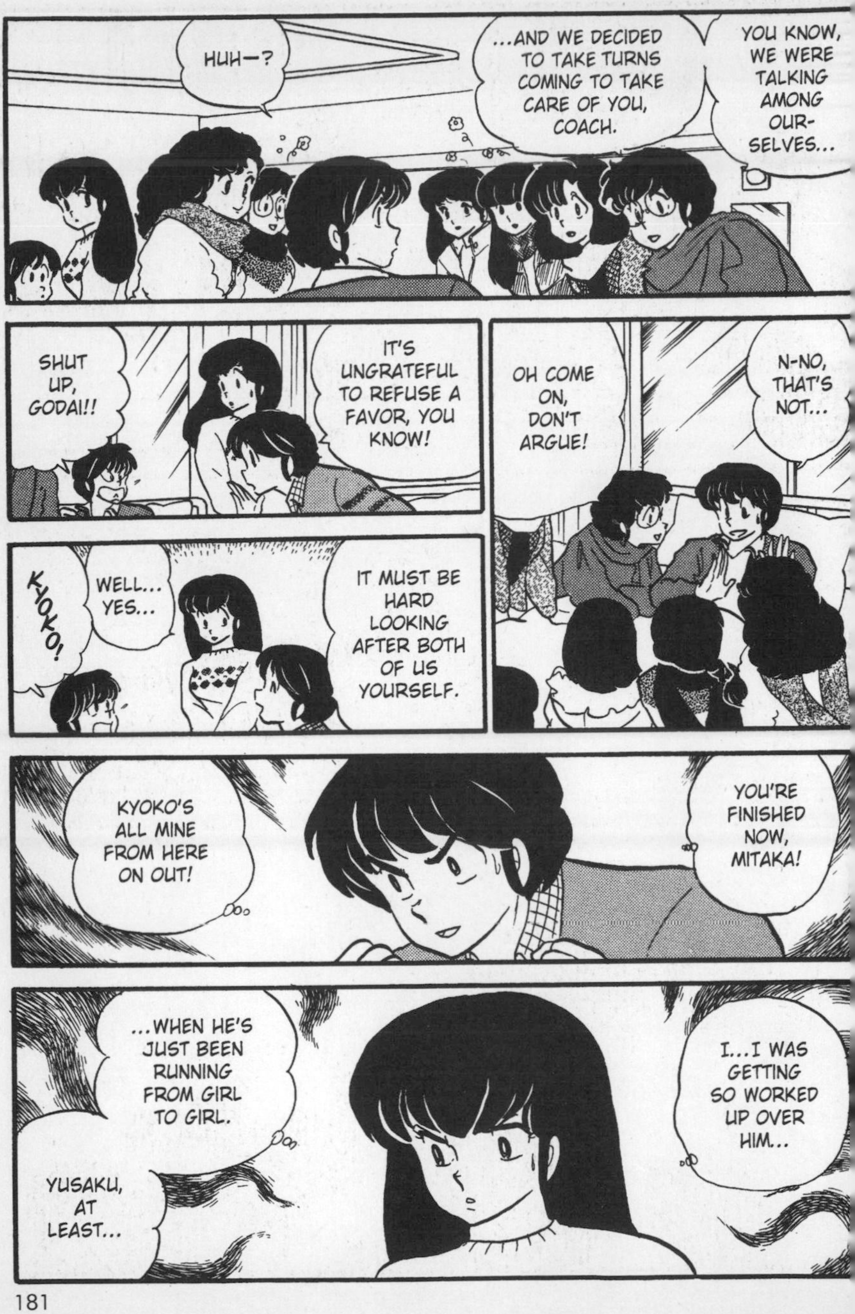
YOU KNOW, WE WERE TALKING AMONG OUR-SELVES...
...AND WE DECIDED TO TAKE TURNS COMING TO TAKE CARE OF YOU, COACH.
HUH—?
N-NO, THAT'S NOT...
OH COME ON, DON'T ARGUE!
IT'S UNGRATEFUL TO REFUSE A FAVOR, YOU KNOW!
SHUT UP, GODAI!!
IT MUST BE HARD LOOKING AFTER BOTH OF US YOURSELF.
WELL... YES...
KYOKO!
YOU'RE FINISHED NOW, MITAKA!
KYOKO'S ALL MINE FROM HERE ON OUT!
I...I WAS GETTING SO WORKED UP OVER HIM...
...WHEN HE'S JUST BEEN RUNNING FROM GIRL TO GIRL.
YUSAKU, AT LEAST...

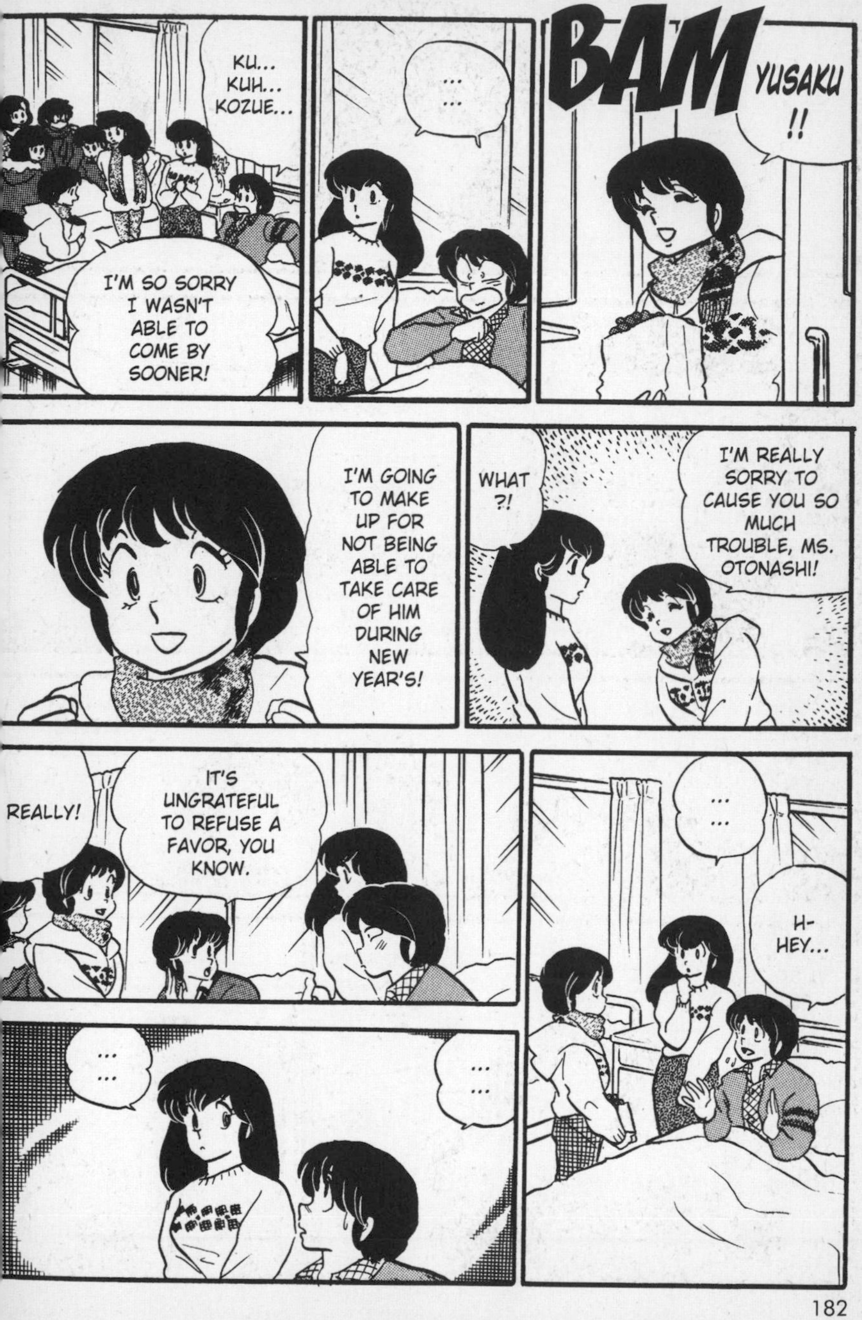
BAM
YUSAKU !!
... ...
KU... KUH... KOZUE...
I'M SO SORRY I WASN'T ABLE TO COME BY SOONER!
I'M REALLY SORRY TO CAUSE YOU SO MUCH TROUBLE, MS. OTONASHI!
WHAT ?!
I'M GOING TO MAKE UP FOR NOT BEING ABLE TO TAKE CARE OF HIM DURING NEW YEAR'S!
... ...
H- HEY...
IT'S UNGRATEFUL TO REFUSE A FAVOR, YOU KNOW.
REALLY!
... ...
... ...

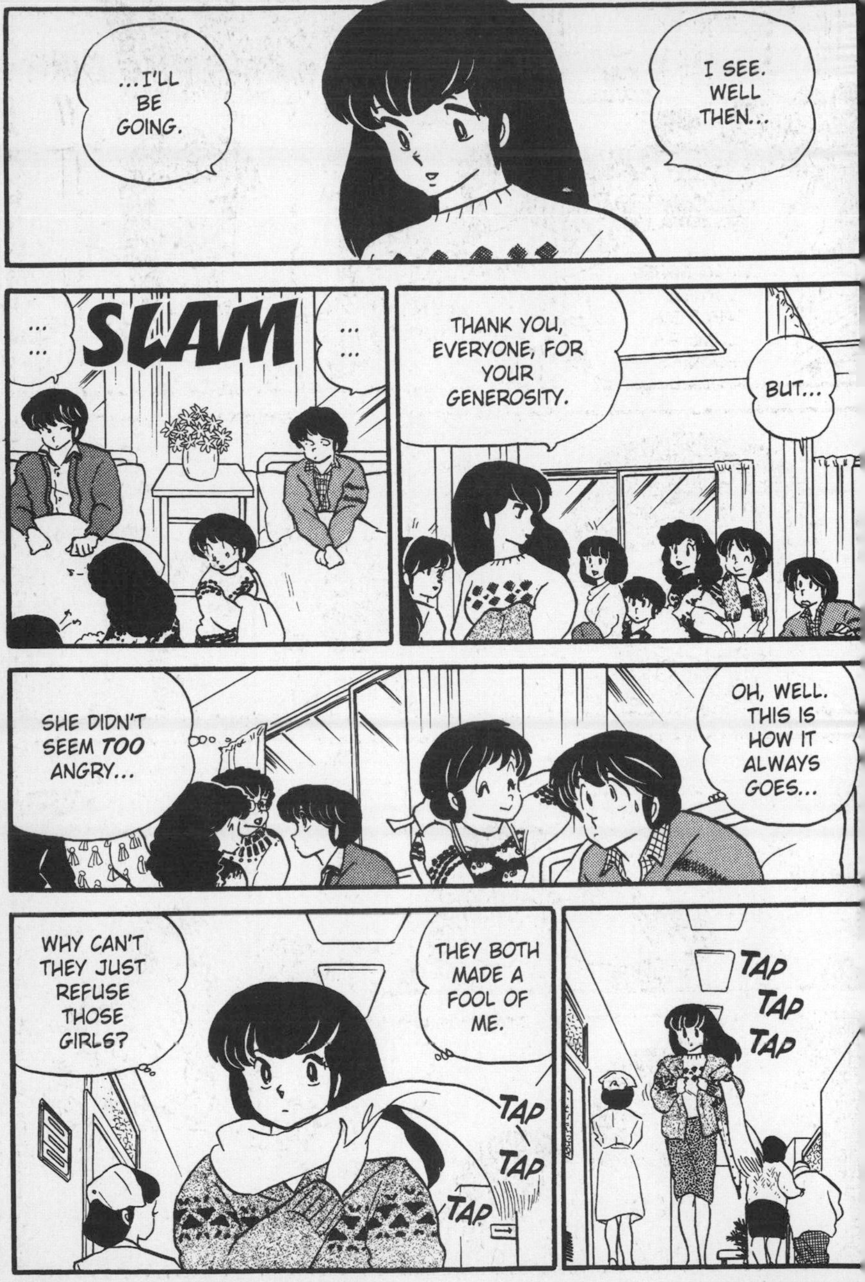
I SEE. WELL THEN...
...I'LL BE GOING.
THANK YOU, EVERYONE, FOR YOUR GENEROSITY.
BUT...
... ...
SLAM
... ...
OH, WELL. THIS IS HOW IT ALWAYS GOES...
SHE DIDN'T SEEM *TOO* ANGRY...
TAP TAP TAP
THEY BOTH MADE A FOOL OF ME.
WHY CAN'T THEY JUST REFUSE THOSE GIRLS?
TAP TAP TAP

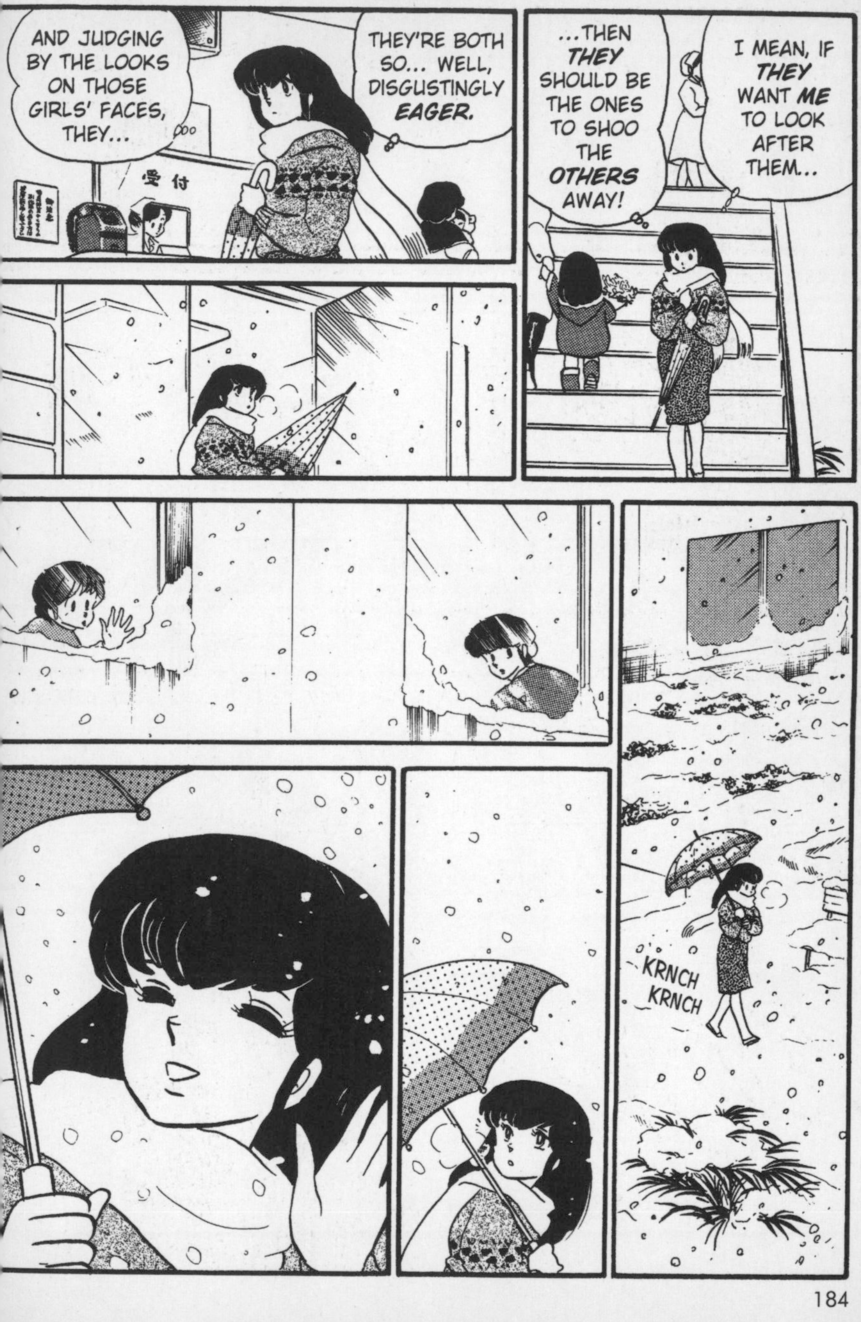
I MEAN, IF THEY WANT ME TO LOOK AFTER THEM...
...THEN THEY SHOULD BE THE ONES TO SHOO THE OTHERS AWAY!
THEY'RE BOTH SO... WELL, DISGUSTINGLY EAGER.
AND JUDGING BY THE LOOKS ON THOSE GIRLS' FACES, THEY...
受付
KRNCH KRNCH

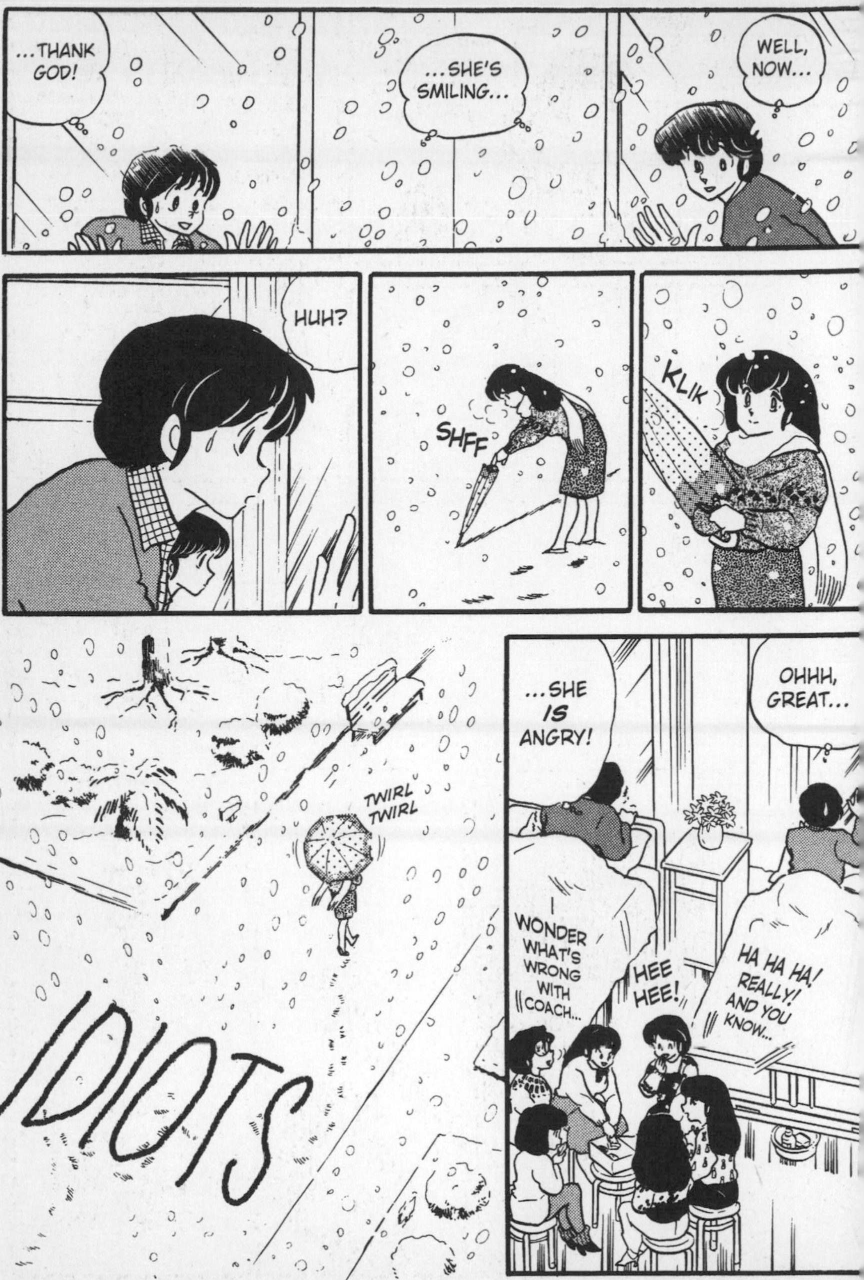
WELL, NOW...
...SHE'S SMILING...
...THANK GOD!
KLIK
SHFF
HUH?
OHHH, GREAT...
...SHE IS ANGRY!
HA HA HA! REALLY! AND YOU KNOW...
HEE HEE!
I WONDER WHAT'S WRONG WITH COACH...
TWIRL TWIRL
IDIOTS

PART NINE
MENDING A BREAK

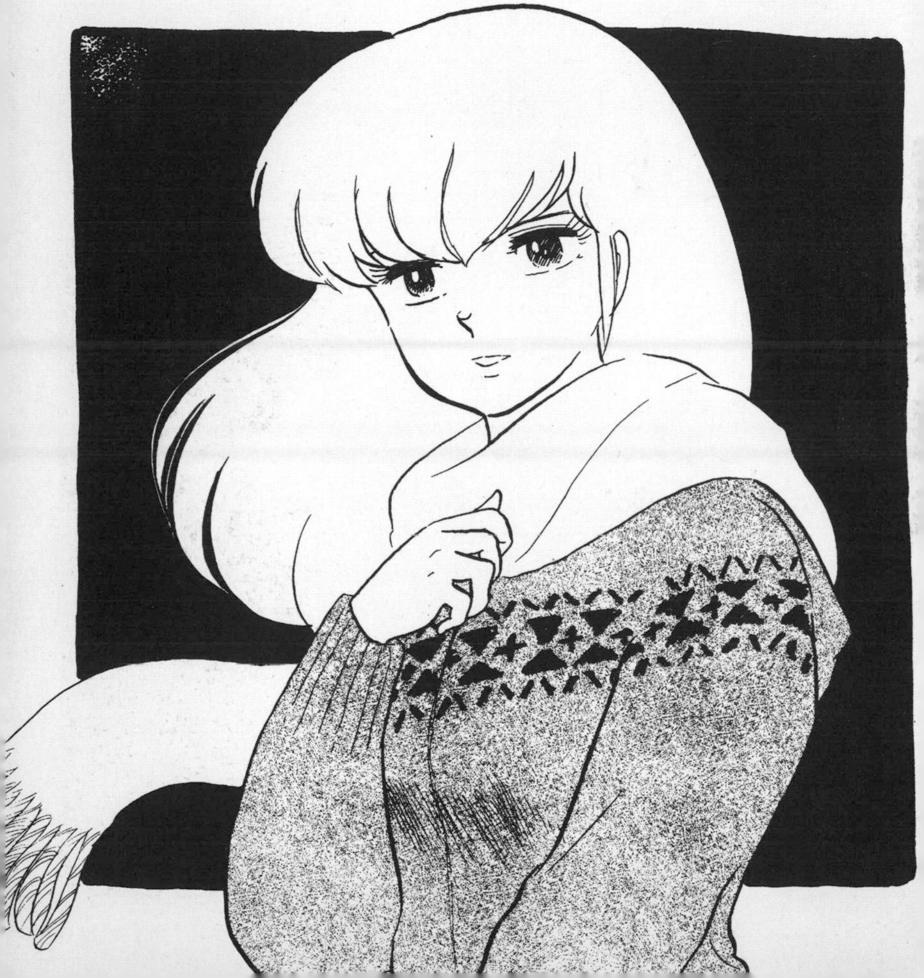

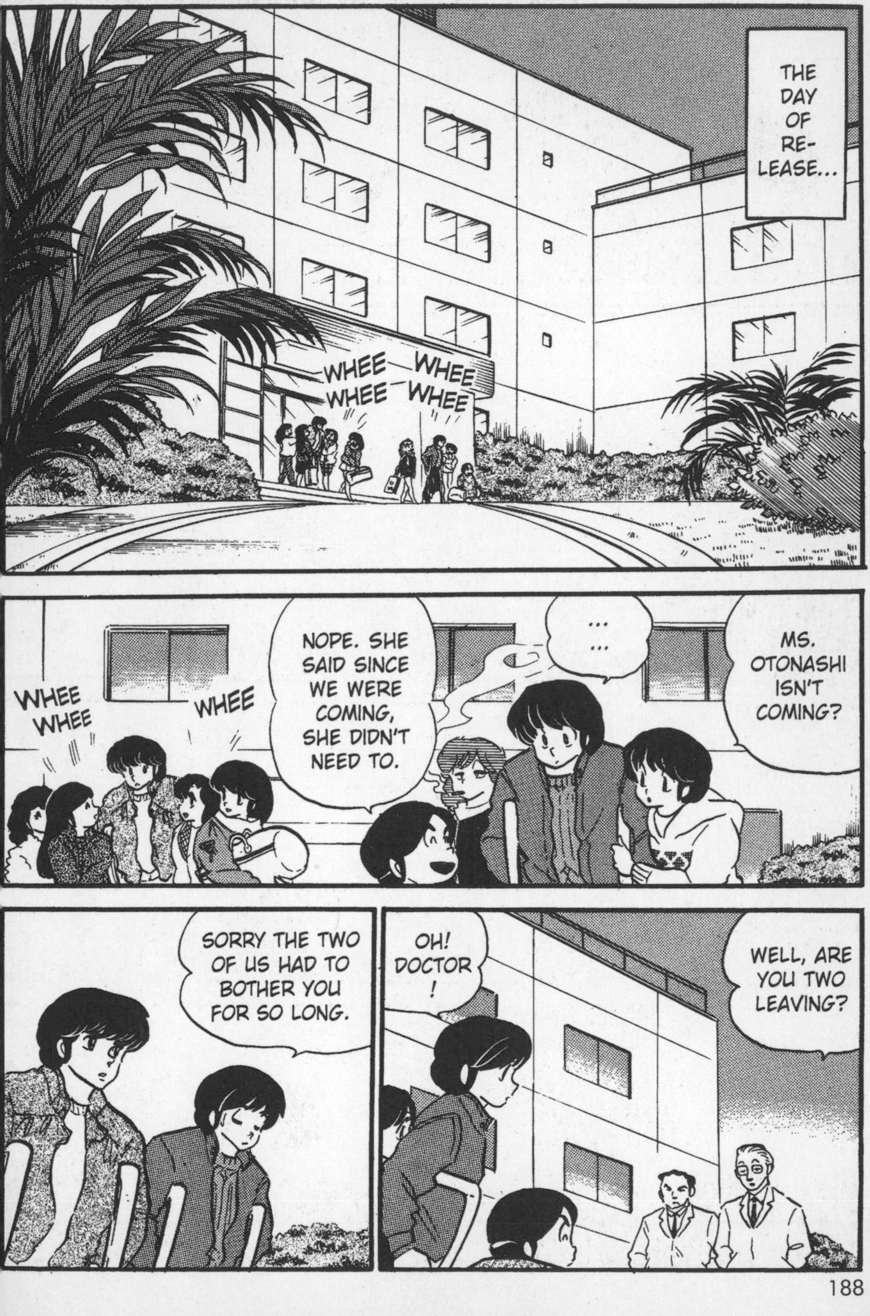
THE DAY OF RE-LEASE...
WHEE WHEE
WHEE WHEE
MS. OTONASHI ISN'T COMING?
... ...
NOPE. SHE SAID SINCE WE WERE COMING, SHE DIDN'T NEED TO.
WHEE
WHEE WHEE
WELL, ARE YOU TWO LEAVING?
OH! DOCTOR!
SORRY THE TWO OF US HAD TO BOTHER YOU FOR SO LONG.

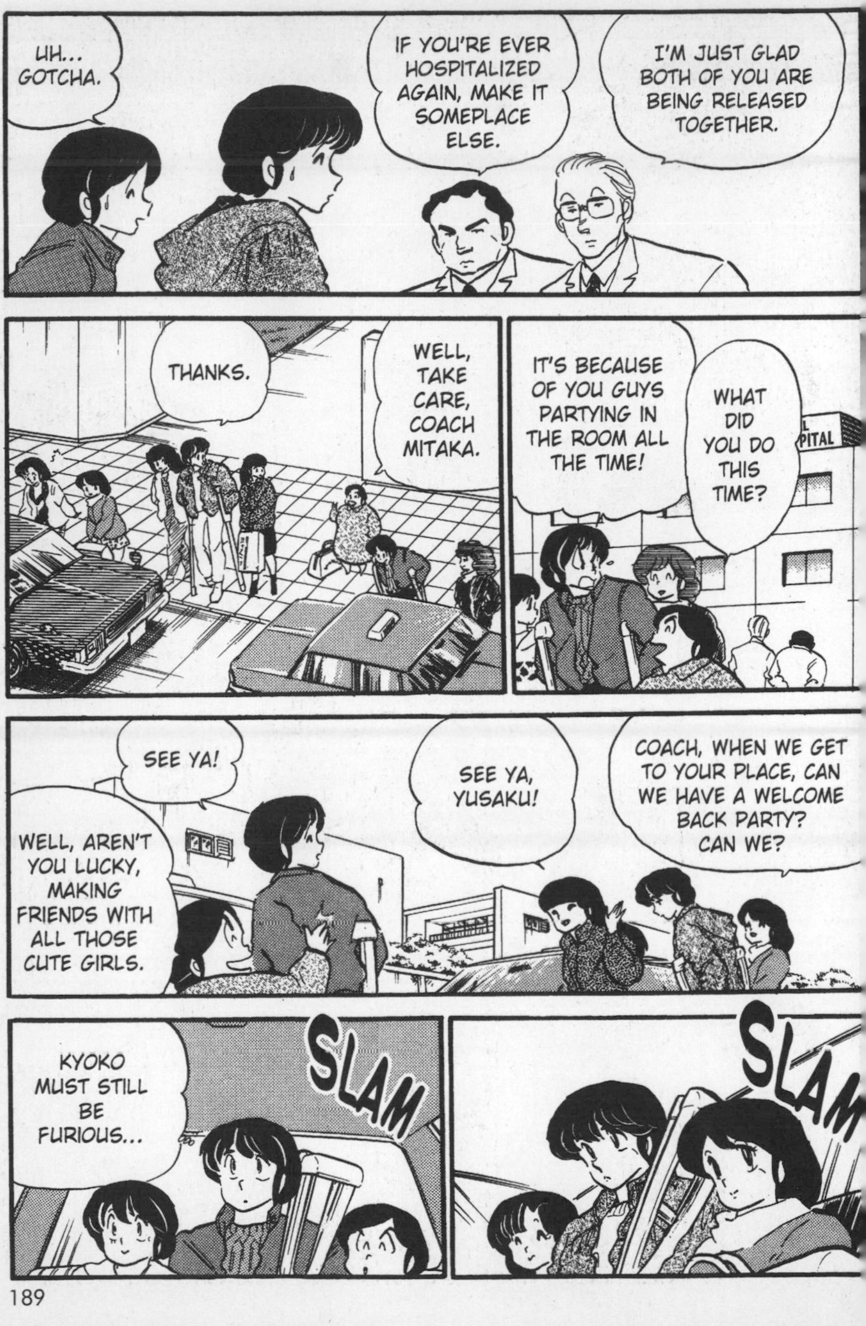
I'M JUST GLAD BOTH OF YOU ARE BEING RELEASED TOGETHER.
IF YOU'RE EVER HOSPITALIZED AGAIN, MAKE IT SOMEPLACE ELSE.
UH... GOTCHA.
WHAT DID YOU DO THIS TIME?
IT'S BECAUSE OF YOU GUYS PARTYING IN THE ROOM ALL THE TIME!
WELL, TAKE CARE, COACH MITAKA.
THANKS.
COACH, WHEN WE GET TO YOUR PLACE, CAN WE HAVE A WELCOME BACK PARTY? CAN WE?
SEE YA, YUSAKU!
SEE YA!
WELL, AREN'T YOU LUCKY, MAKING FRIENDS WITH ALL THOSE CUTE GIRLS.
SLAM
SLAM
KYOKO MUST STILL BE FURIOUS...

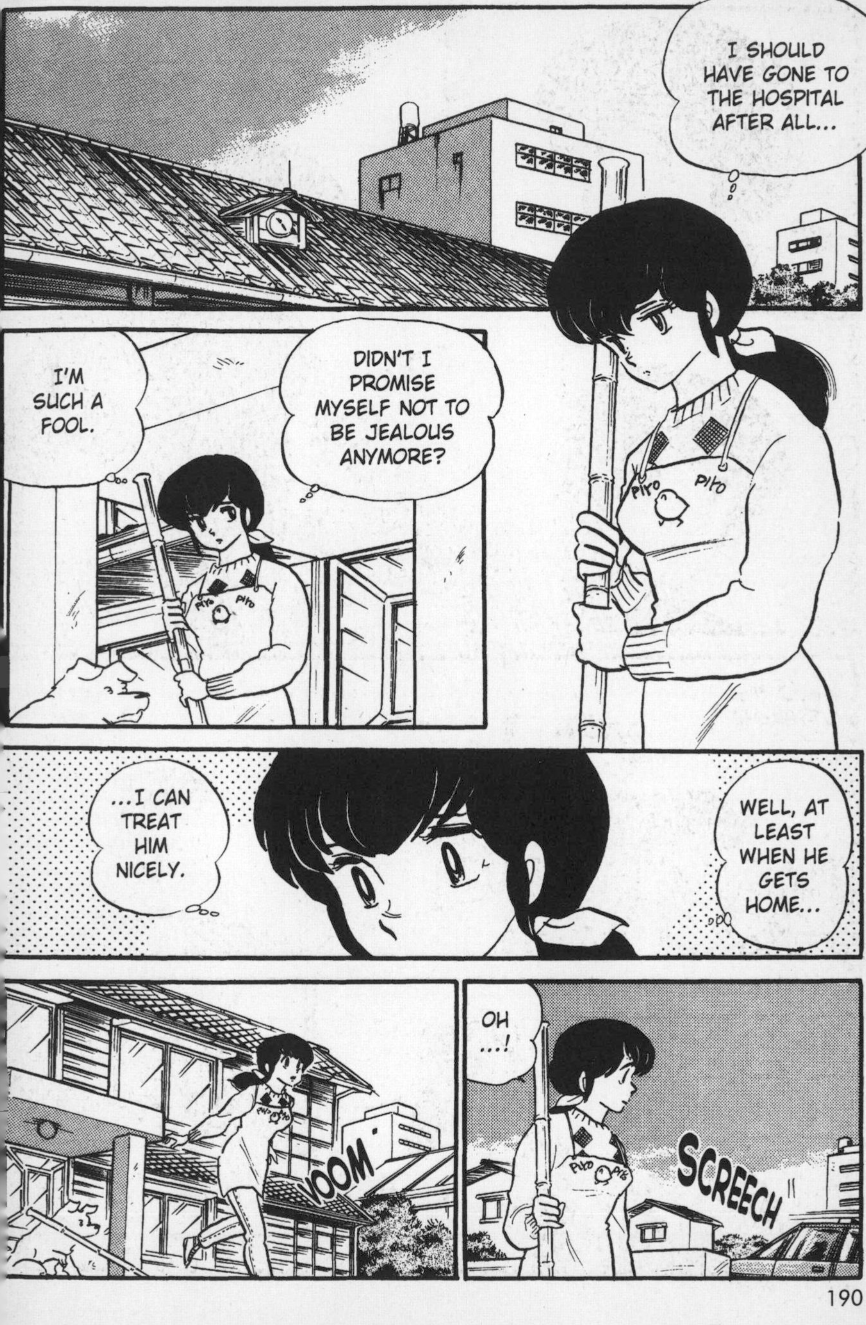
I SHOULD HAVE GONE TO THE HOSPITAL AFTER ALL...
DIDN'T I PROMISE MYSELF NOT TO BE JEALOUS ANYMORE?
I'M SUCH A FOOL.
WELL, AT LEAST WHEN HE GETS HOME...
...I CAN TREAT HIM NICELY.
OH ...!
SCREECH
VOOM

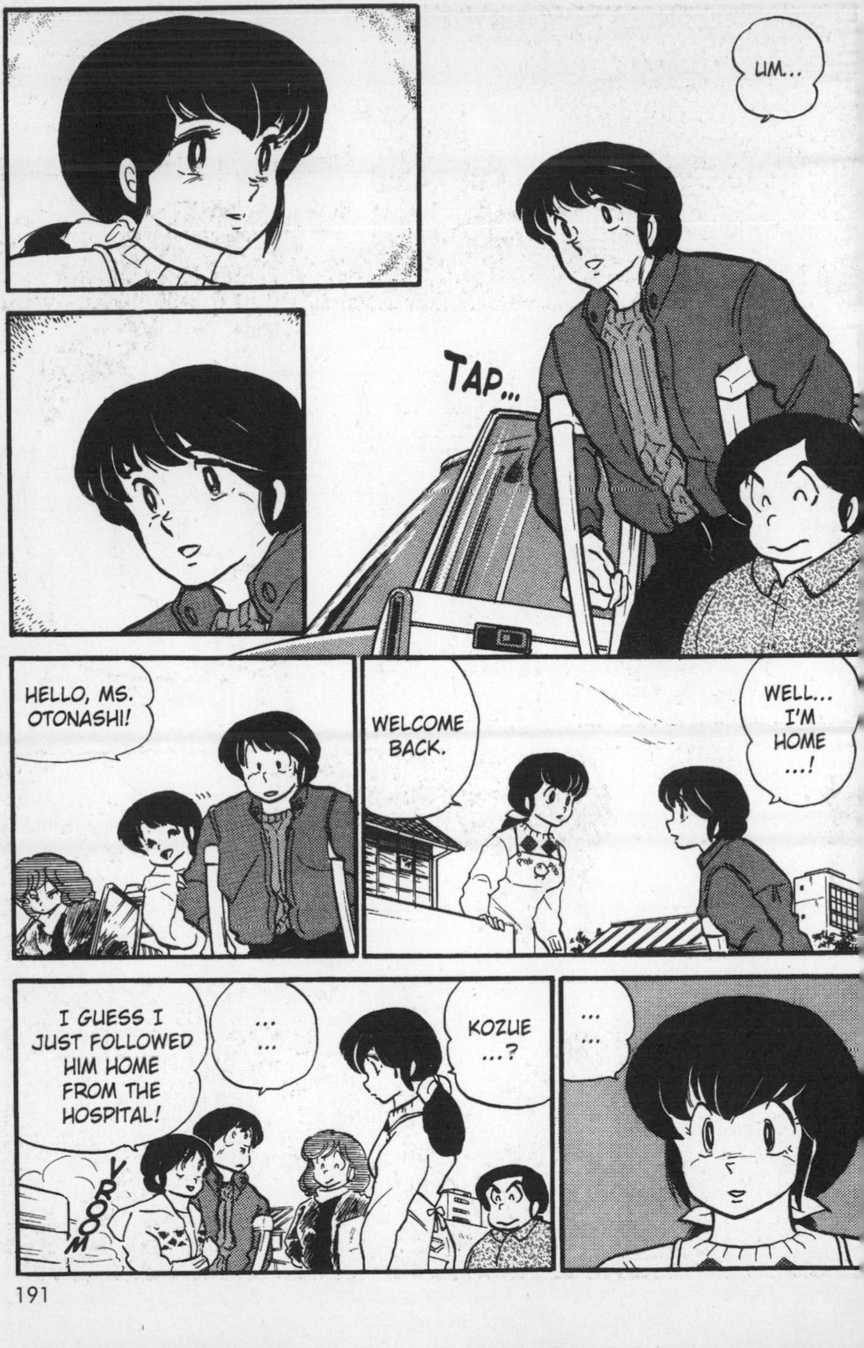
UM...
TAP...
WELL... I'M HOME ...!
WELCOME BACK.
HELLO, MS. OTONASHI!
... ...
KOZUE ...?
... ...
I GUESS I JUST FOLLOWED HIM HOME FROM THE HOSPITAL!
VROOM

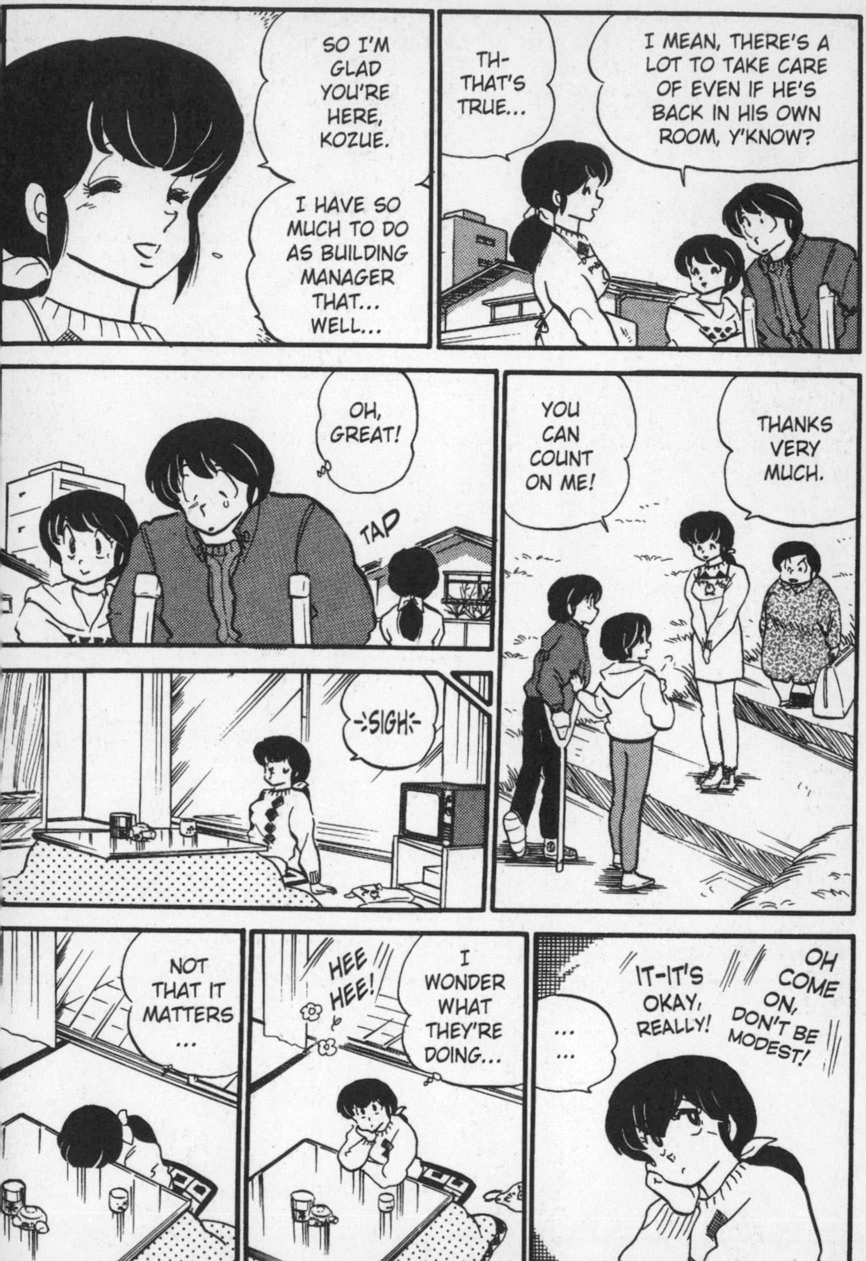
I MEAN, THERE'S A LOT TO TAKE CARE OF EVEN IF HE'S BACK IN HIS OWN ROOM, Y'KNOW?
TH- THAT'S TRUE...
SO I'M GLAD YOU'RE HERE, KOZUE.
I HAVE SO MUCH TO DO AS BUILDING MANAGER THAT... WELL...
THANKS VERY MUCH.
YOU CAN COUNT ON ME!
OH, GREAT!
TAP
-SIGH-
OH COME ON, DON'T BE MODEST!
IT-IT'S OKAY, REALLY!
......
I WONDER WHAT THEY'RE DOING...
HEE HEE!
NOT THAT IT MATTERS ...

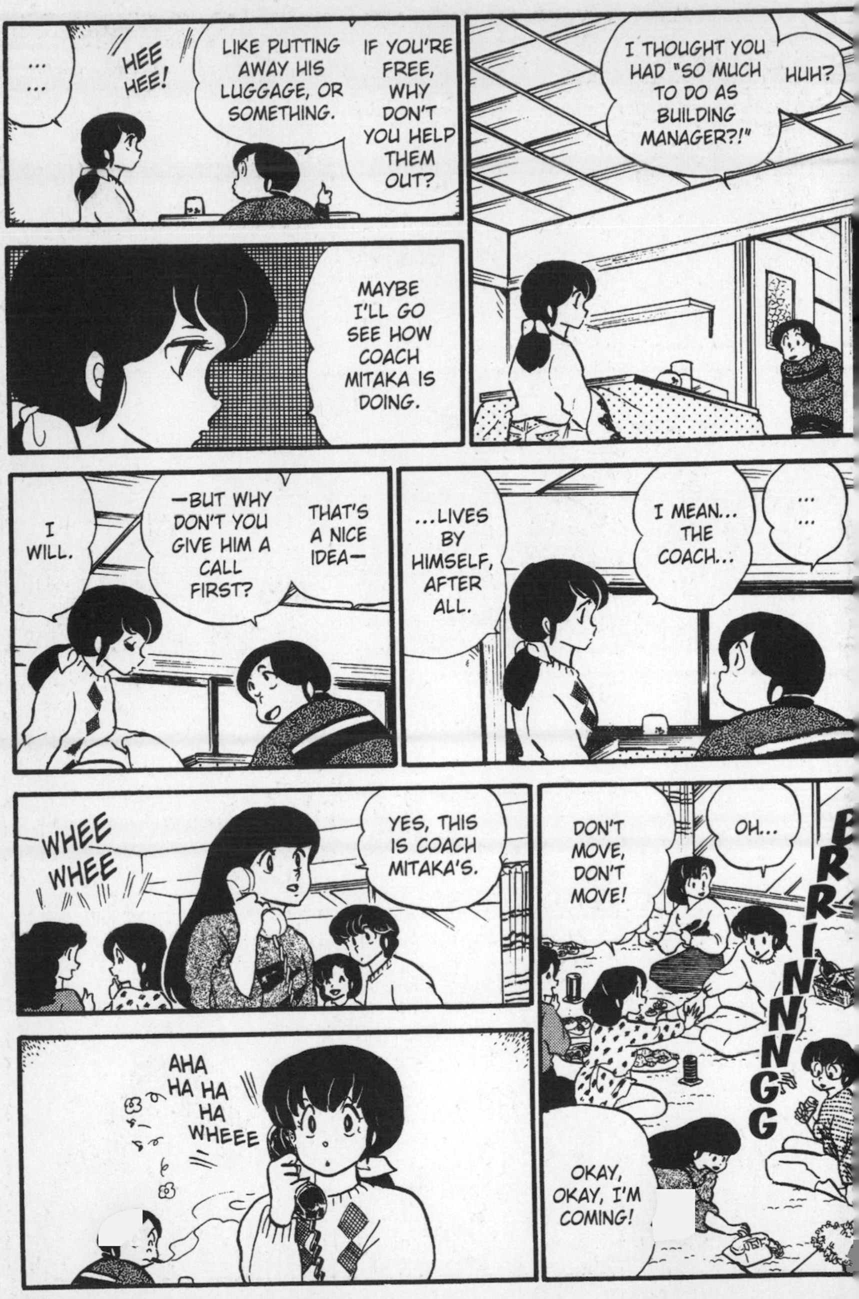
HUH?
I THOUGHT YOU HAD "SO MUCH TO DO AS BUILDING MANAGER?!"
IF YOU'RE FREE, WHY DON'T YOU HELP THEM OUT?
LIKE PUTTING AWAY HIS LUGGAGE, OR SOMETHING.
HEE HEE!
... ...
MAYBE I'LL GO SEE HOW COACH MITAKA IS DOING.
... ...
I MEAN... THE COACH...
...LIVES BY HIMSELF, AFTER ALL.
THAT'S A NICE IDEA—
—BUT WHY DON'T YOU GIVE HIM A CALL FIRST?
I WILL.
BRRRINNNNGG
OH...
DON'T MOVE, DON'T MOVE!
OKAY, OKAY, I'M COMING!
YES, THIS IS COACH MITAKA'S.
WHEE WHEE
AHA HA HA HA WHEEE

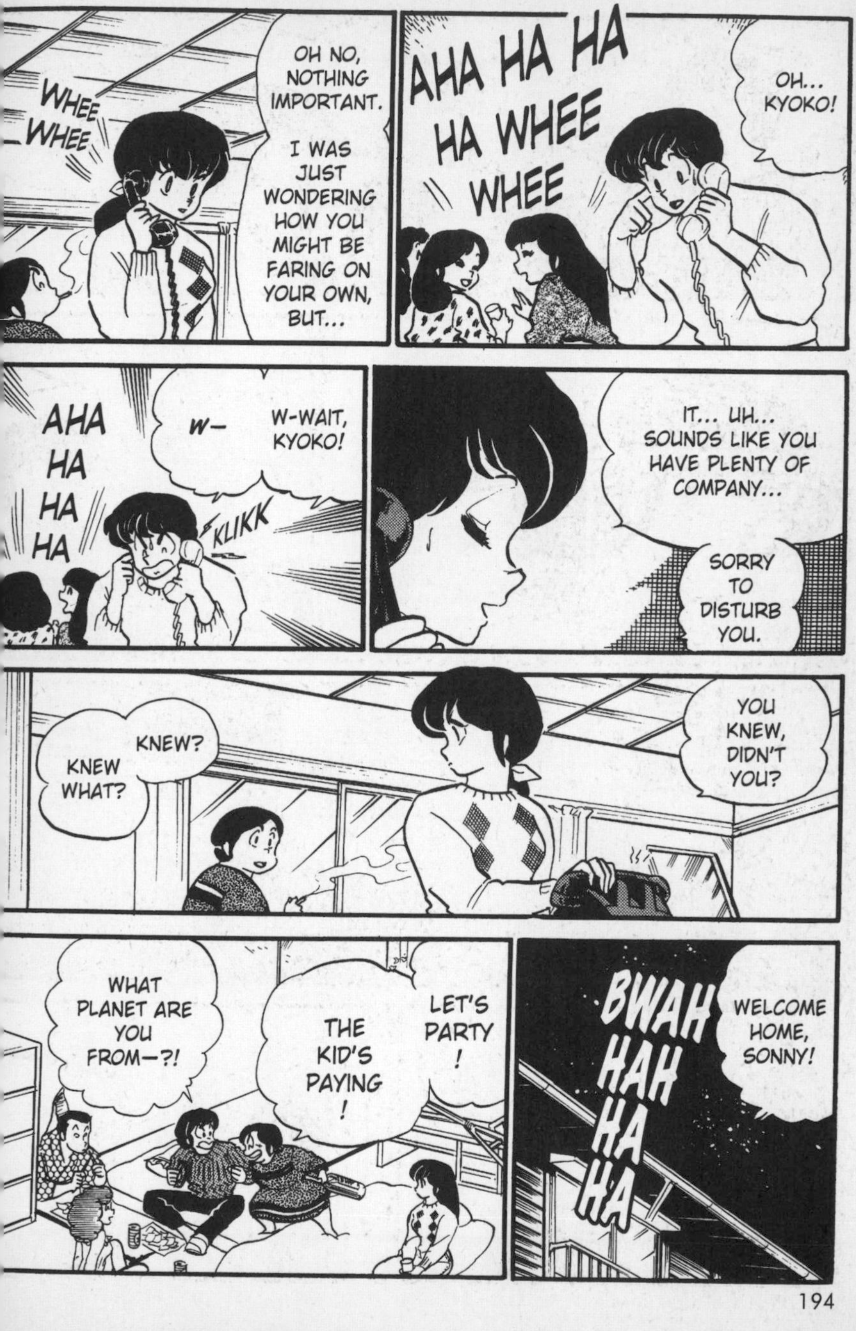
OH... KYOKO!
AHA HA HA HA WHEE WHEE
OH NO, NOTHING IMPORTANT.
I WAS JUST WONDERING HOW YOU MIGHT BE FARING ON YOUR OWN, BUT...
WHEE WHEE
IT... UH... SOUNDS LIKE YOU HAVE PLENTY OF COMPANY...
SORRY TO DISTURB YOU.
W-WAIT, KYOKO!
W—
KLIKK
AHA HA HA HA
YOU KNEW, DIDN'T YOU?
KNEW?
KNEW WHAT?
WELCOME HOME, SONNY!
BWAH HAH HA HA HA
LET'S PARTY!
THE KID'S PAYING!
WHAT PLANET ARE YOU FROM—?!

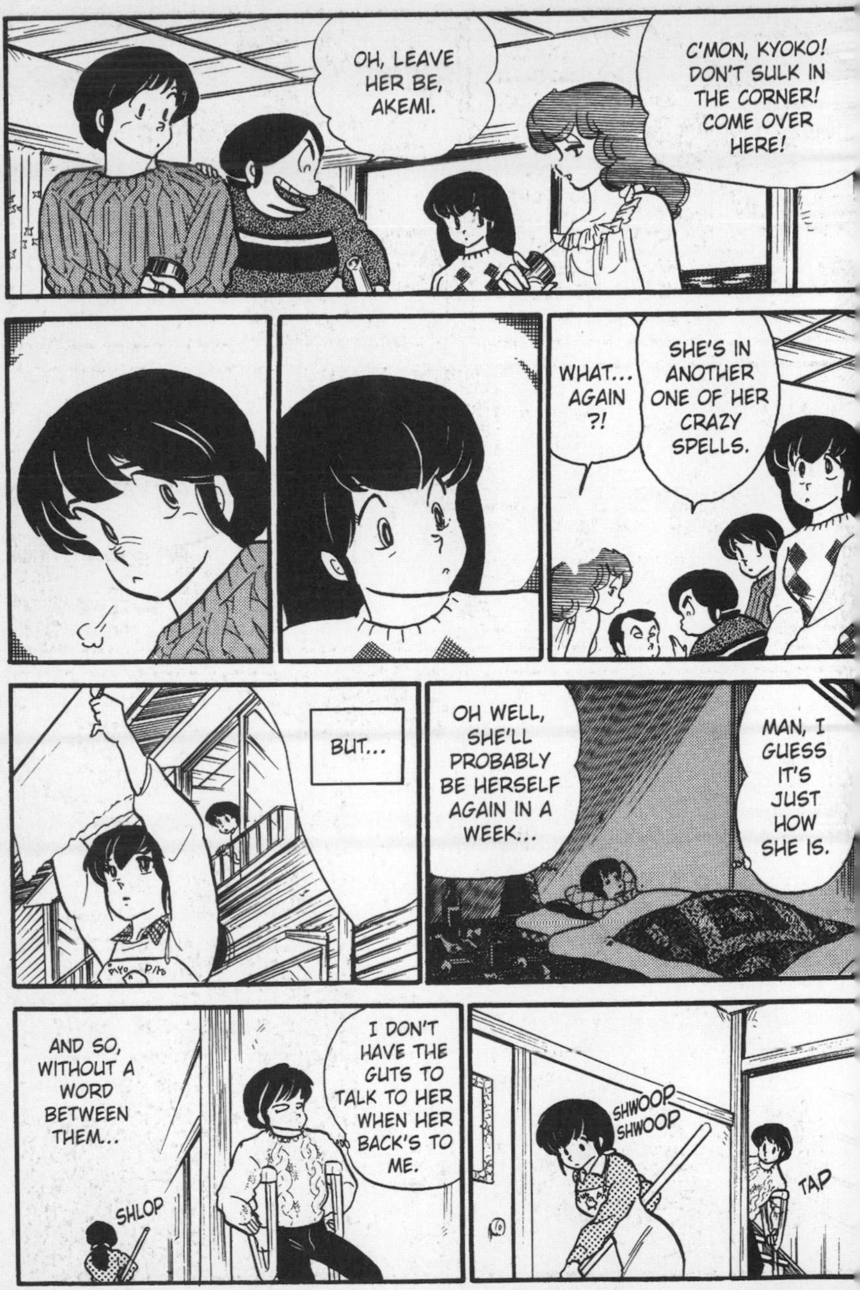
C'MON, KYOKO! DON'T SULK IN THE CORNER! COME OVER HERE!
OH, LEAVE HER BE, AKEMI.
SHE'S IN ANOTHER ONE OF HER CRAZY SPELLS.
WHAT... AGAIN ?!
MAN, I GUESS IT'S JUST HOW SHE IS.
OH WELL, SHE'LL PROBABLY BE HERSELF AGAIN IN A WEEK...
BUT...
SHWOOP SHWOOP
TAP
AND SO, WITHOUT A WORD BETWEEN THEM...
I DON'T HAVE THE GUTS TO TALK TO HER WHEN HER BACK'S TO ME.
SHLOP

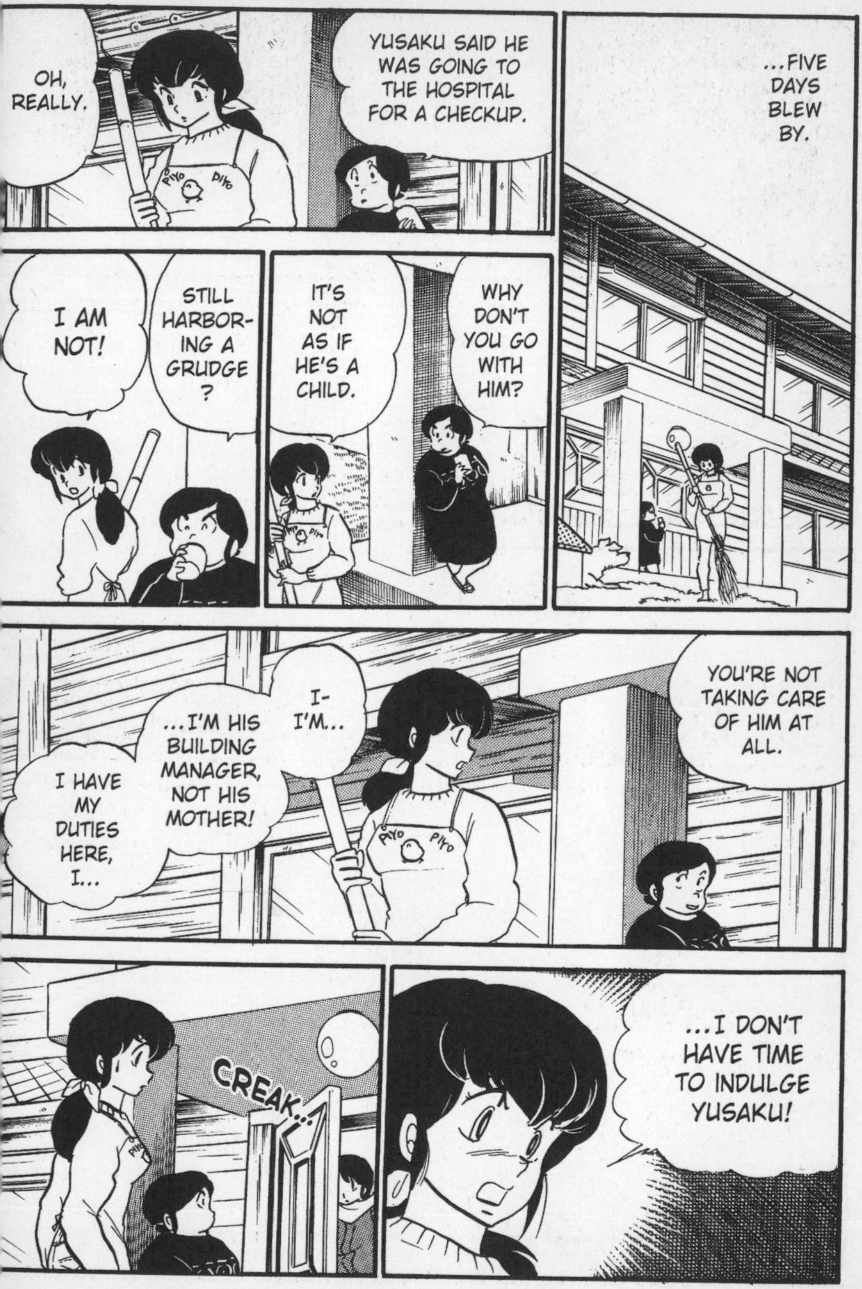
...FIVE DAYS BLEW BY.
YUSAKU SAID HE WAS GOING TO THE HOSPITAL FOR A CHECKUP.
OH, REALLY.
WHY DON'T YOU GO WITH HIM?
IT'S NOT AS IF HE'S A CHILD.
STILL HARBOR-ING A GRUDGE?
I AM NOT!
YOU'RE NOT TAKING CARE OF HIM AT ALL.
I- I'M...
...I'M HIS BUILDING MANAGER, NOT HIS MOTHER!
I HAVE MY DUTIES HERE, I...
...I DON'T HAVE TIME TO INDULGE YUSAKU!
CREAK...

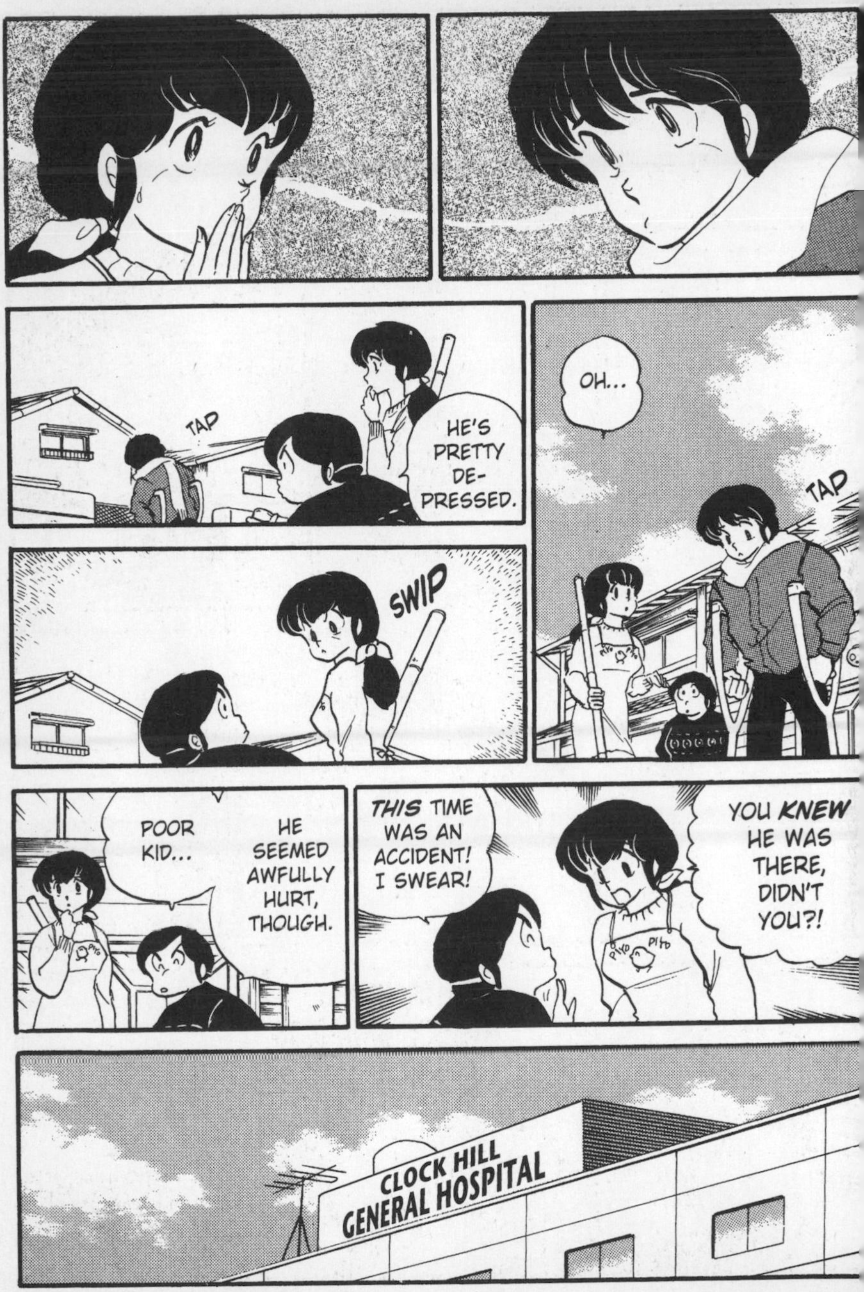
OH...
TAP
HE'S PRETTY DE-PRESSED.
TAP
SWIP
YOU KNEW HE WAS THERE, DIDN'T YOU?!
THIS TIME WAS AN ACCIDENT! I SWEAR!
HE SEEMED AWFULLY HURT, THOUGH.
POOR KID...
CLOCK HILL GENERAL HOSPITAL

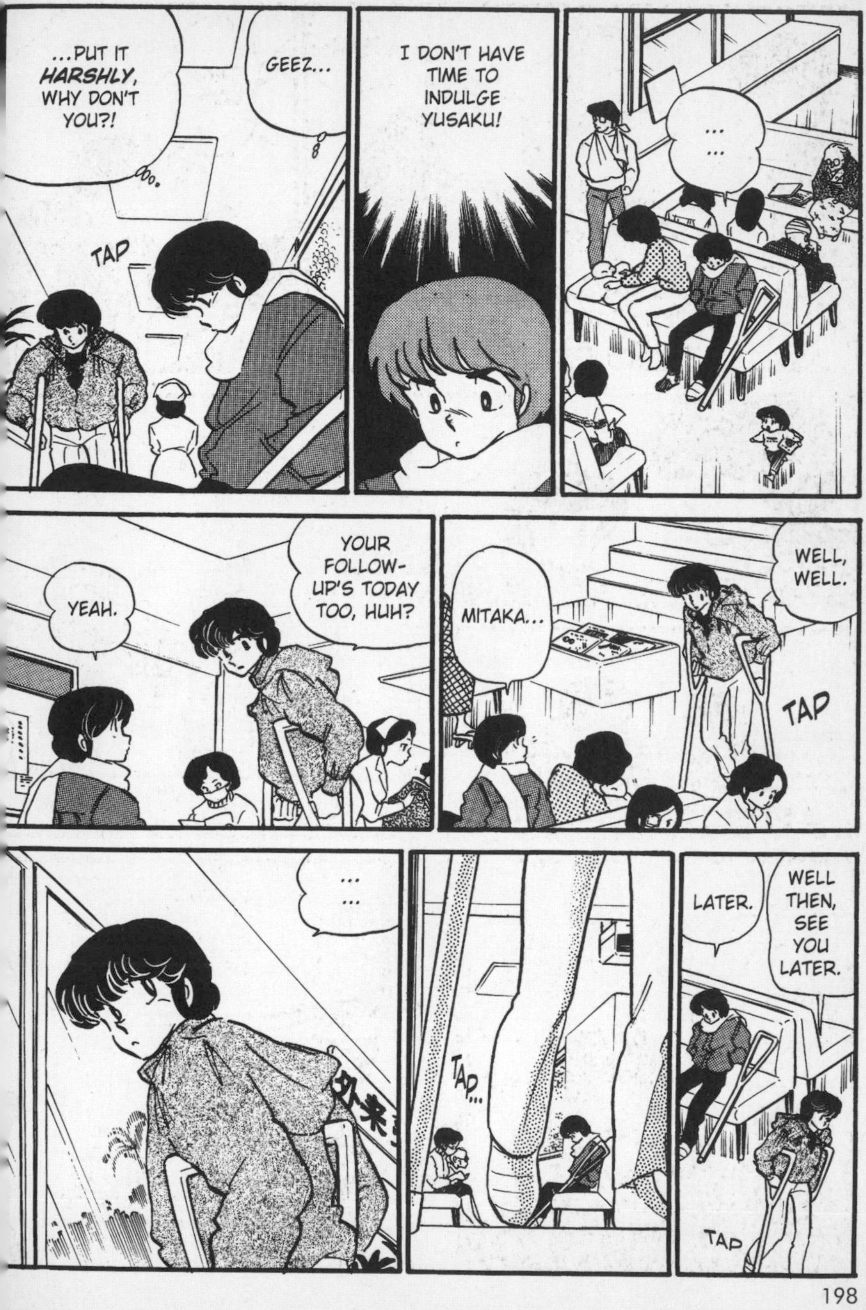

... ...
I DON'T HAVE TIME TO INDULGE YUSAKU!
GEEZ...
...PUT IT HARSHLY, WHY DON'T YOU?!
TAP
WELL, WELL.
MITAKA...
TAP
YOUR FOLLOW-UP'S TODAY TOO, HUH?
YEAH.
WELL THEN, SEE YOU LATER.
LATER.
TAP
TAP...
... ...

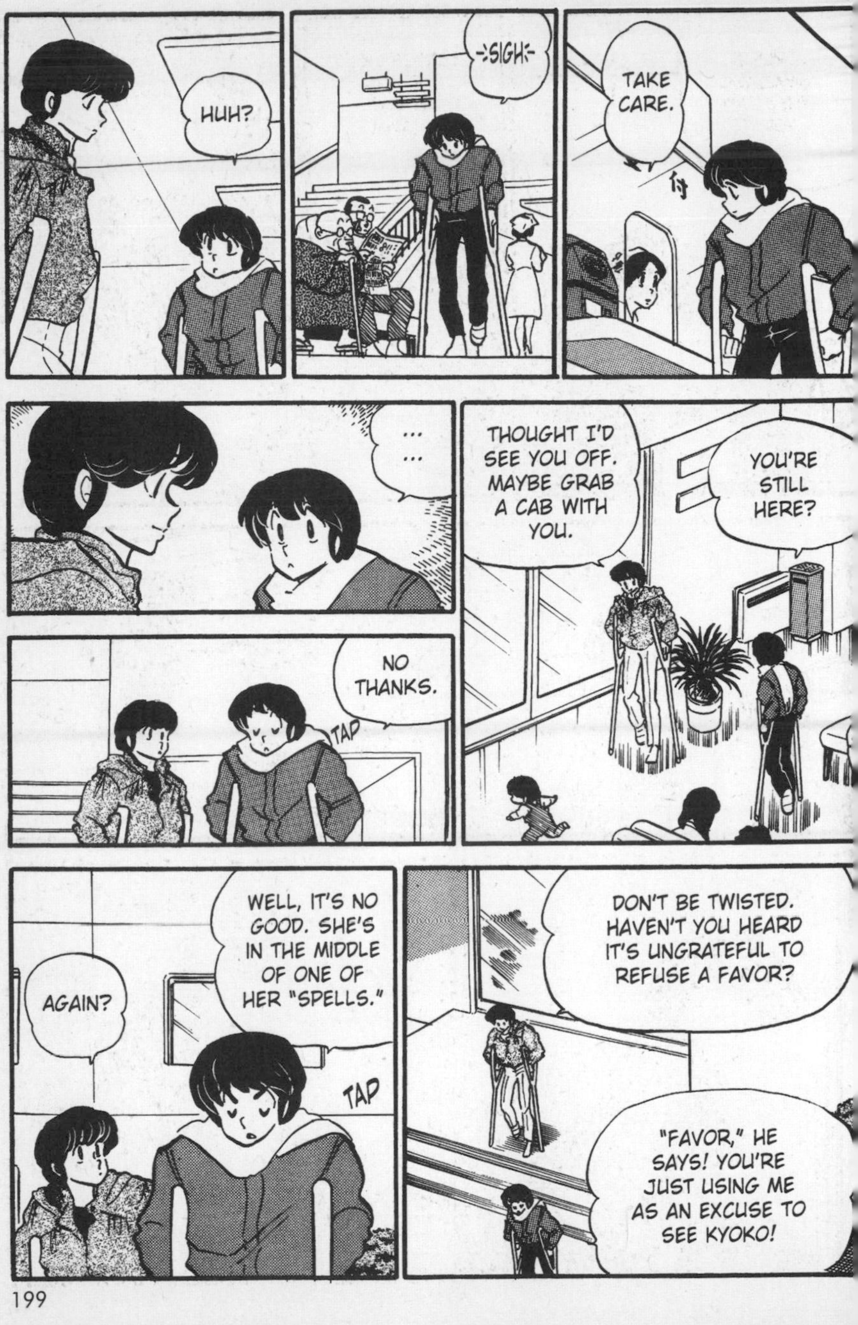
TAKE CARE.
-SIGH-
HUH?
YOU'RE STILL HERE?
THOUGHT I'D SEE YOU OFF. MAYBE GRAB A CAB WITH YOU.
……
NO THANKS.
TAP
DON'T BE TWISTED. HAVEN'T YOU HEARD IT'S UNGRATEFUL TO REFUSE A FAVOR?
"FAVOR," HE SAYS! YOU'RE JUST USING ME AS AN EXCUSE TO SEE KYOKO!
WELL, IT'S NO GOOD. SHE'S IN THE MIDDLE OF ONE OF HER "SPELLS."
AGAIN?
TAP

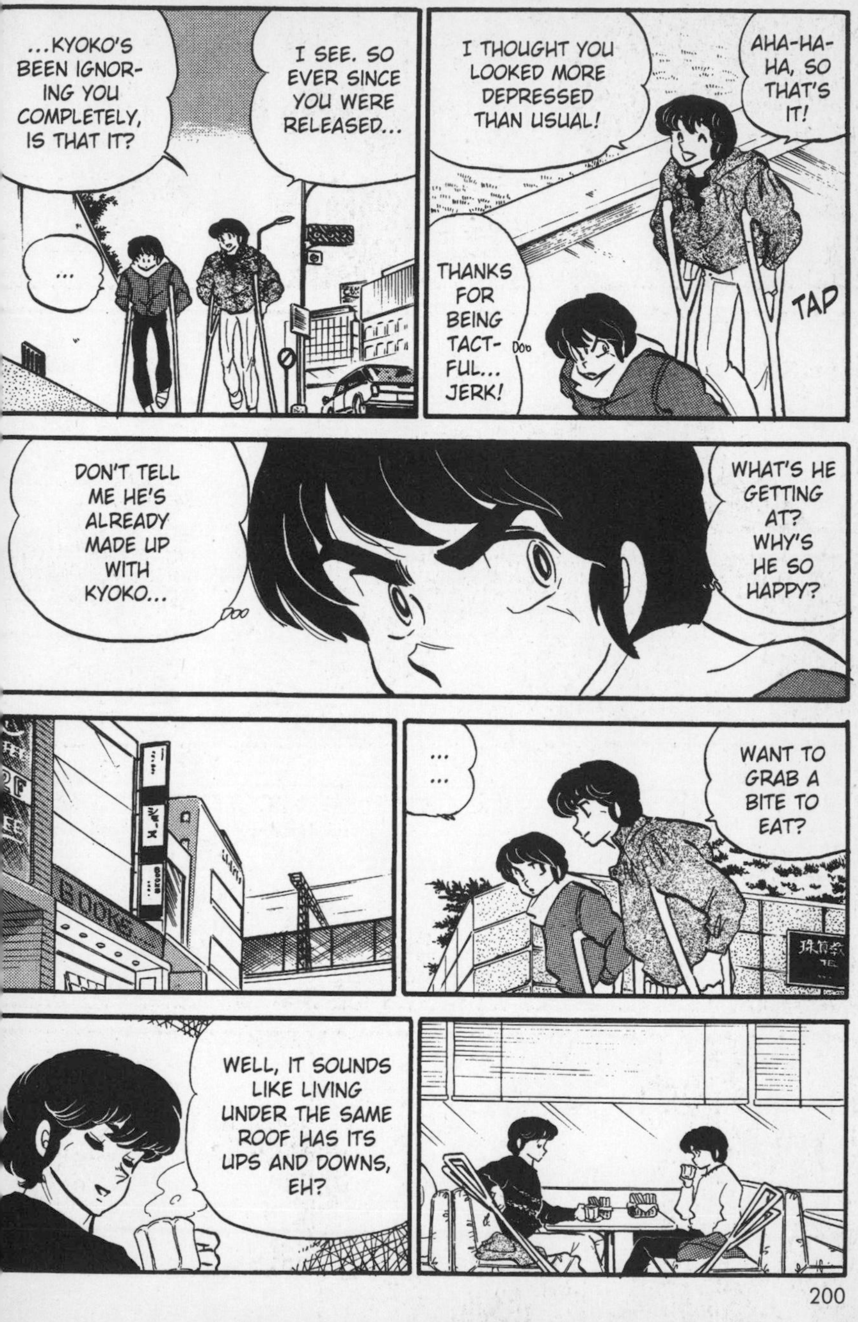
AHA-HA, SO THAT'S IT!
I THOUGHT YOU LOOKED MORE DEPRESSED THAN USUAL!
TAP
THANKS FOR BEING TACT-FUL... JERK!
I SEE. SO EVER SINCE YOU WERE RELEASED...
...KYOKO'S BEEN IGNOR-ING YOU COMPLETELY, IS THAT IT?
...
WHAT'S HE GETTING AT? WHY'S HE SO HAPPY?
DON'T TELL ME HE'S ALREADY MADE UP WITH KYOKO...
WANT TO GRAB A BITE TO EAT?
... ...
2F
BOOKS
WELL, IT SOUNDS LIKE LIVING UNDER THE SAME ROOF HAS ITS UPS AND DOWNS, EH?

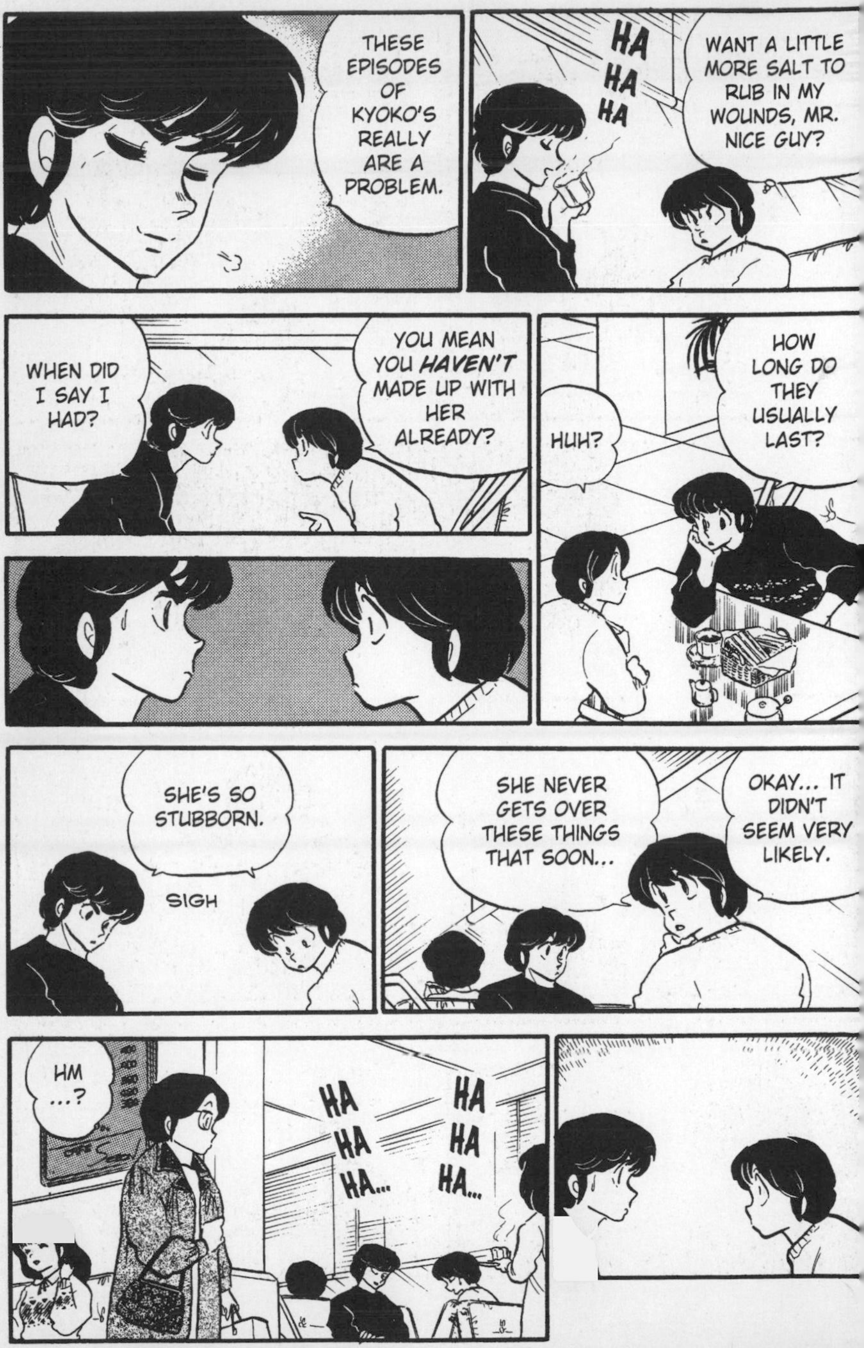
HA
HA
HA
WANT A LITTLE MORE SALT TO RUB IN MY WOUNDS, MR. NICE GUY?
THESE EPISODES OF KYOKO'S REALLY ARE A PROBLEM.
HOW LONG DO THEY USUALLY LAST?
HUH?
YOU MEAN YOU ***HAVEN'T*** MADE UP WITH HER ALREADY?
WHEN DID I SAY I HAD?
OKAY... IT DIDN'T SEEM VERY LIKELY.
SHE NEVER GETS OVER THESE THINGS THAT SOON...
SHE'S SO STUBBORN.
SIGH
HA
HA
HA...
HA
HA
HA...
HM ...?

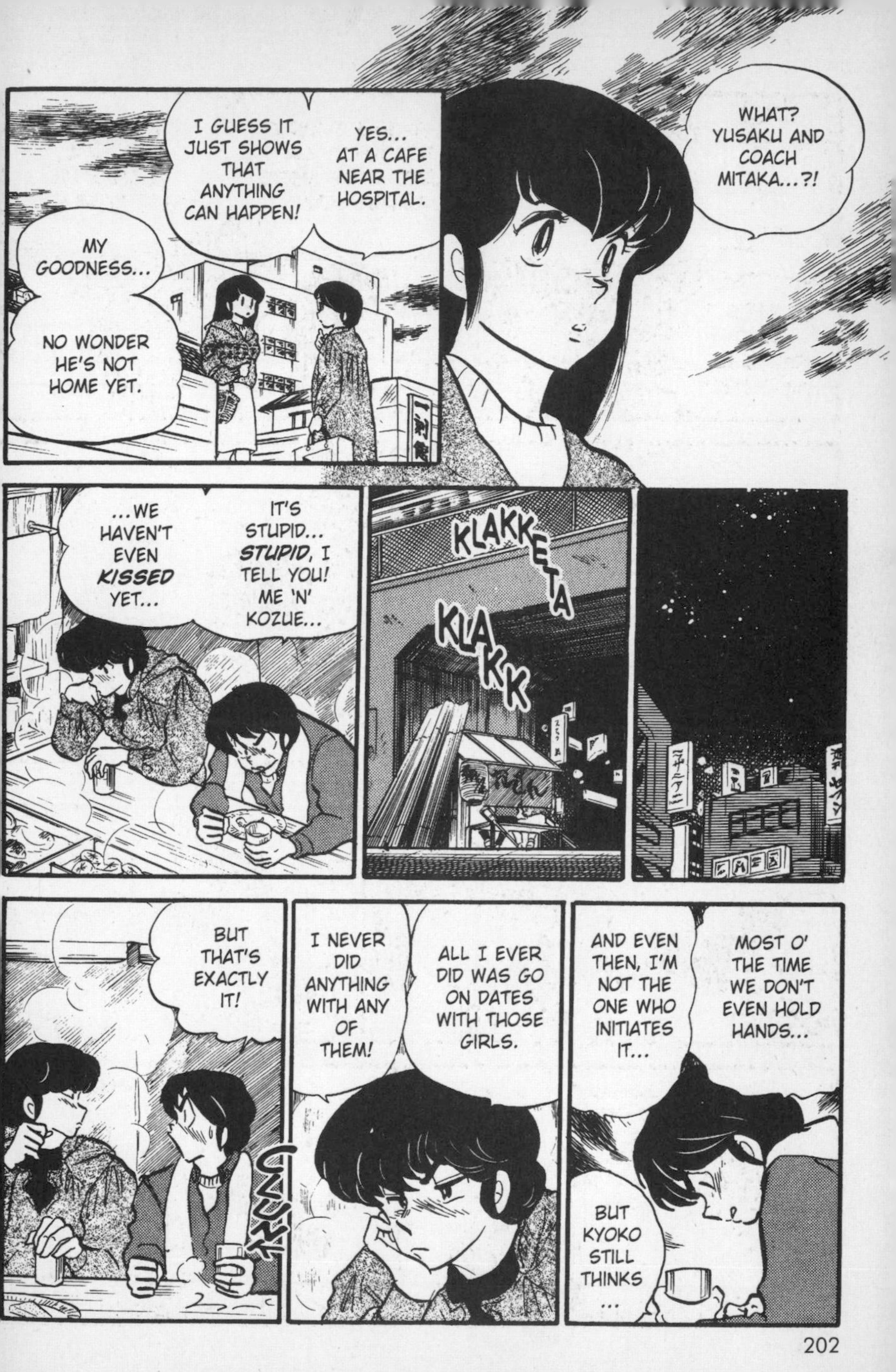
WHAT? YUSAKU AND COACH MITAKA...?!
YES... AT A CAFE NEAR THE HOSPITAL.
I GUESS IT JUST SHOWS THAT ANYTHING CAN HAPPEN!
MY GOODNESS...
NO WONDER HE'S NOT HOME YET.
KLAKKETA
KLAKK
IT'S STUPID... *STUPID*, I TELL YOU! ME 'N' KOZUE...
...WE HAVEN'T EVEN *KISSED* YET...
MOST O' THE TIME WE DON'T EVEN HOLD HANDS...
AND EVEN THEN, I'M NOT THE ONE WHO INITIATES IT...
BUT KYOKO STILL THINKS ...
ALL I EVER DID WAS GO ON DATES WITH THOSE GIRLS.
I NEVER DID ANYTHING WITH ANY OF THEM!
CLUNK
BUT THAT'S EXACTLY IT!

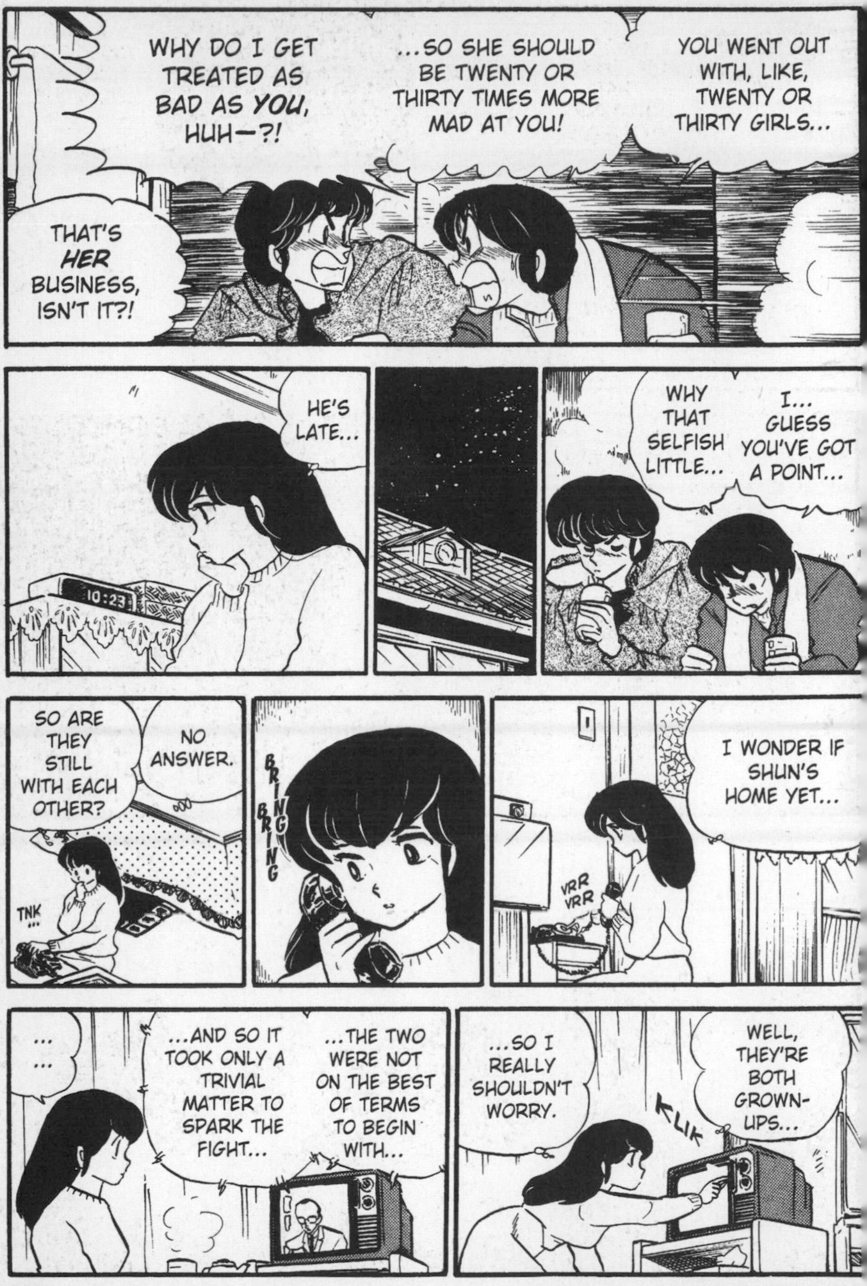
YOU WENT OUT WITH, LIKE, TWENTY OR THIRTY GIRLS...
...SO SHE SHOULD BE TWENTY OR THIRTY TIMES MORE MAD AT YOU!
WHY DO I GET TREATED AS BAD AS *YOU*, HUH—?!
THAT'S *HER* BUSINESS, ISN'T IT?!
I... GUESS YOU'VE GOT A POINT...
WHY THAT SELFISH LITTLE...
HE'S LATE...
I WONDER IF SHUN'S HOME YET...
VRR VRR
BRING BRING
NO ANSWER.
SO ARE THEY STILL WITH EACH OTHER?
TNK...
WELL, THEY'RE BOTH GROWN-UPS...
KLIK
...SO I REALLY SHOULDN'T WORRY.
...THE TWO WERE NOT ON THE BEST OF TERMS TO BEGIN WITH...
...AND SO IT TOOK ONLY A TRIVIAL MATTER TO SPARK THE FIGHT...
... ...

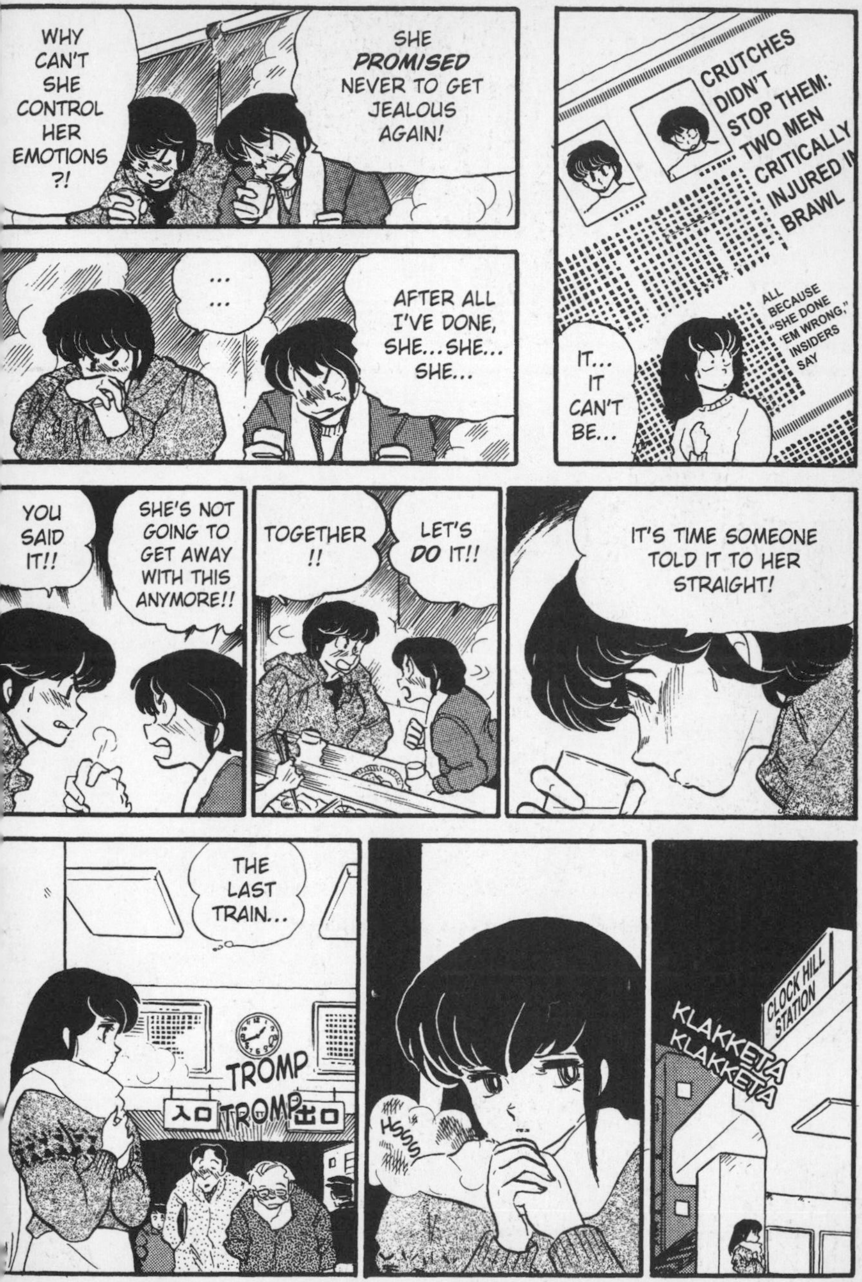
CRUTCHES DIDN'T STOP THEM: TWO MEN CRITICALLY INJURED IN BRAWL
ALL BECAUSE "SHE DONE 'EM WRONG," INSIDERS SAY
IT... IT CAN'T BE...
SHE *PROMISED* NEVER TO GET JEALOUS AGAIN!
WHY CAN'T SHE CONTROL HER EMOTIONS ?!
AFTER ALL I'VE DONE, SHE...SHE... SHE...
... ...
IT'S TIME SOMEONE TOLD IT TO HER STRAIGHT!
LET'S *DO* IT!!
TOGETHER !!
SHE'S NOT GOING TO GET AWAY WITH THIS ANYMORE!!
YOU SAID IT!!
CLOCK HILL STATION
KLAKKETA KLAKKETA
HSSSS
THE LAST TRAIN...
TROMP
入口
TROMP
出口

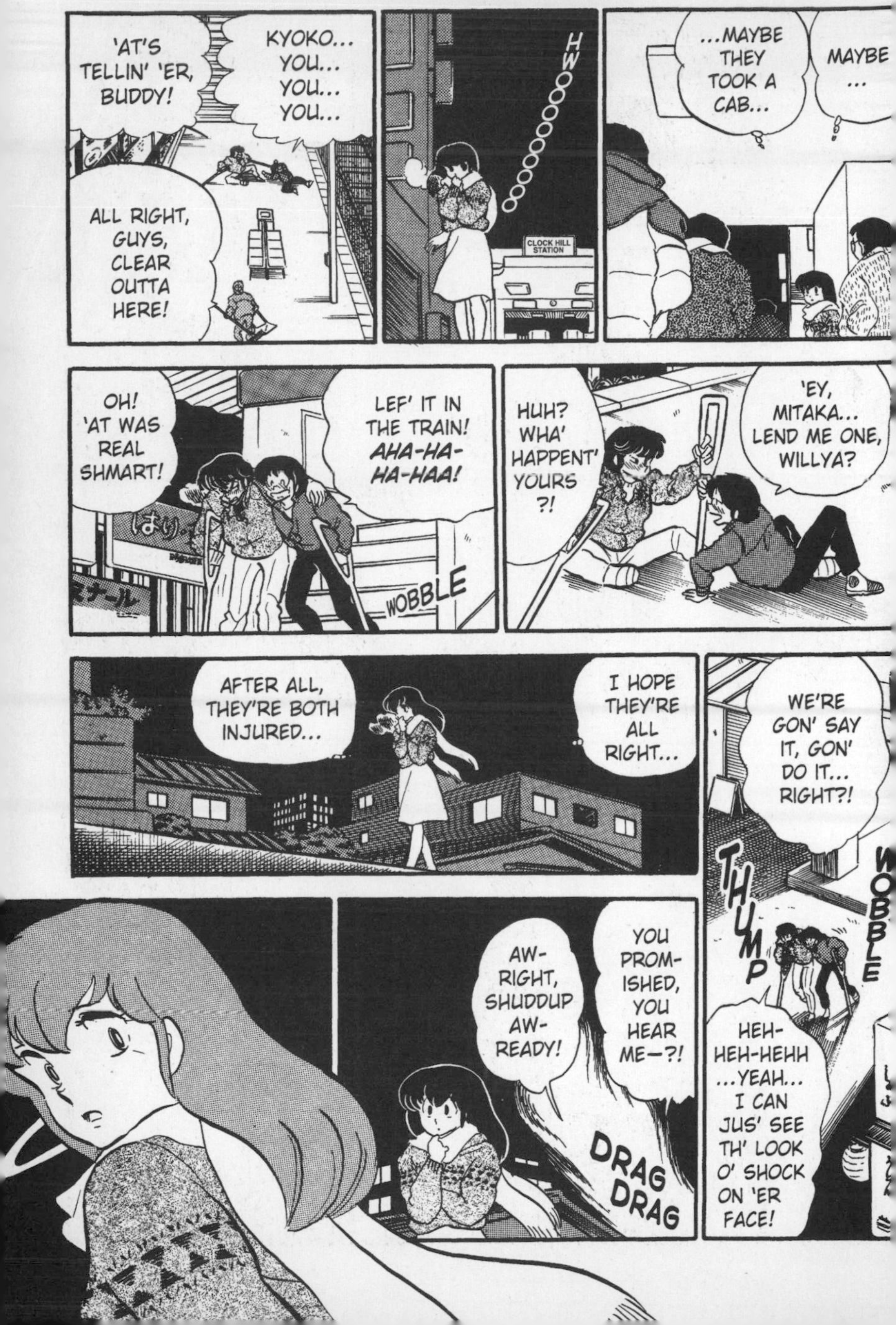
MAYBE ...
...MAYBE THEY TOOK A CAB...
HWOOOOOOOOOOO
CLOCK HILL STATION
KYOKO... YOU... YOU... YOU...
'AT'S TELLIN' 'ER, BUDDY!
ALL RIGHT, GUYS, CLEAR OUTTA HERE!
'EY, MITAKA... LEND ME ONE, WILLYA?
HUH? WHA' HAPPENT' YOURS ?!
LEF' IT IN THE TRAIN! AHA-HA-HA-HAA!
OH! 'AT WAS REAL SHMART!
WOBBLE
WE'RE GON' SAY IT, GON' DO IT... RIGHT?!
WOBBLE
THUMP
HEH-HEH-HEHH ...YEAH... I CAN JUS' SEE TH' LOOK O' SHOCK ON 'ER FACE!
I HOPE THEY'RE ALL RIGHT...
AFTER ALL, THEY'RE BOTH INJURED...
YOU PROMISHED, YOU HEAR ME—?!
AW-RIGHT, SHUDDUP AW-READY!
DRAG DRAG

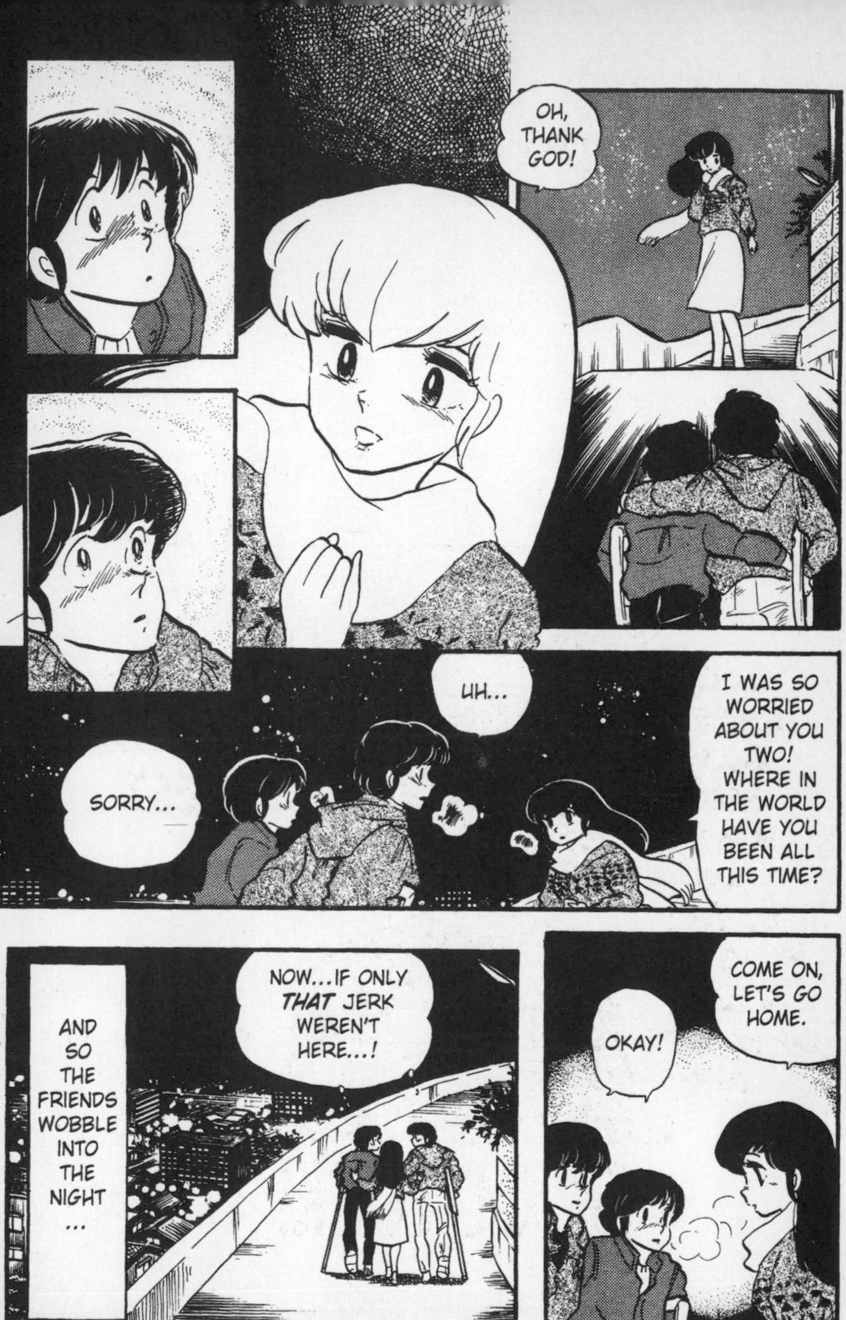
OH, THANK GOD!
I WAS SO WORRIED ABOUT YOU TWO! WHERE IN THE WORLD HAVE YOU BEEN ALL THIS TIME?
UH...
SORRY...
COME ON, LET'S GO HOME.
OKAY!
NOW...IF ONLY *THAT* JERK WEREN'T HERE...!
AND SO THE FRIENDS WOBBLE INTO THE NIGHT...

PART TEN

JUST DO YOUR BEST!

CUT ON DOTTED LINE

JUST CUT OUT, INSERT YOUR NAME, AND CARRY IN YOUR WALLET ON EXAM DAY!

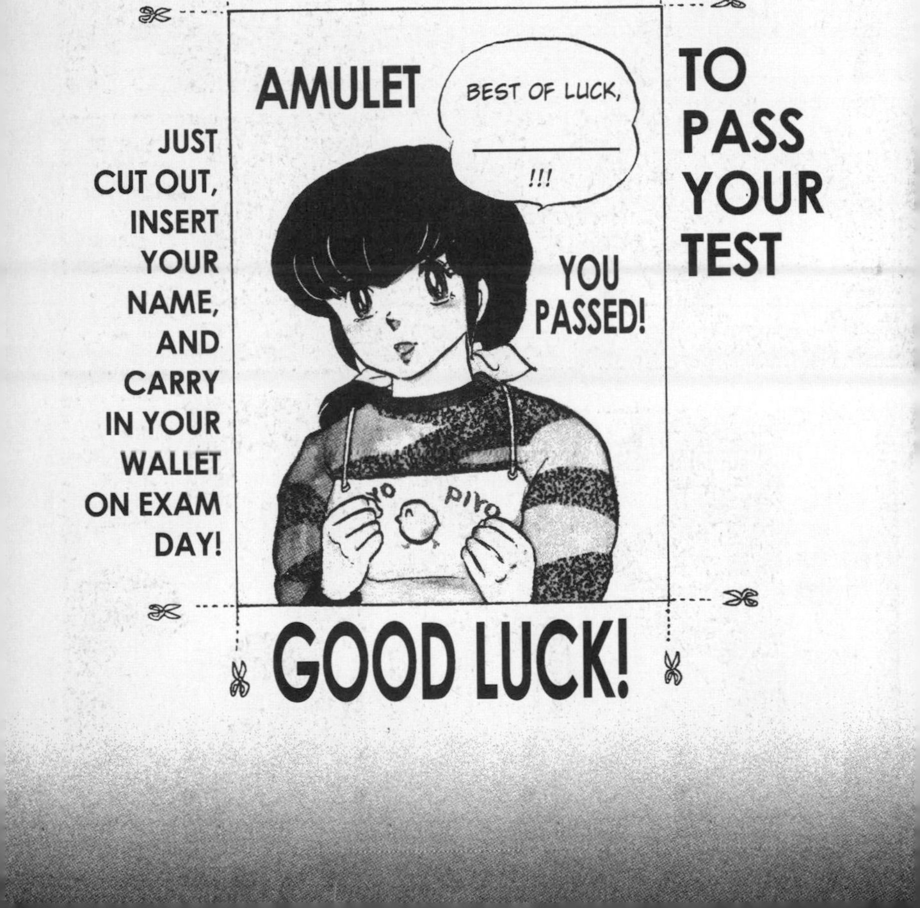
AMULET
BEST OF LUCK, ___________ !!!
YOU PASSED!

TO PASS YOUR TEST

GOOD LUCK!

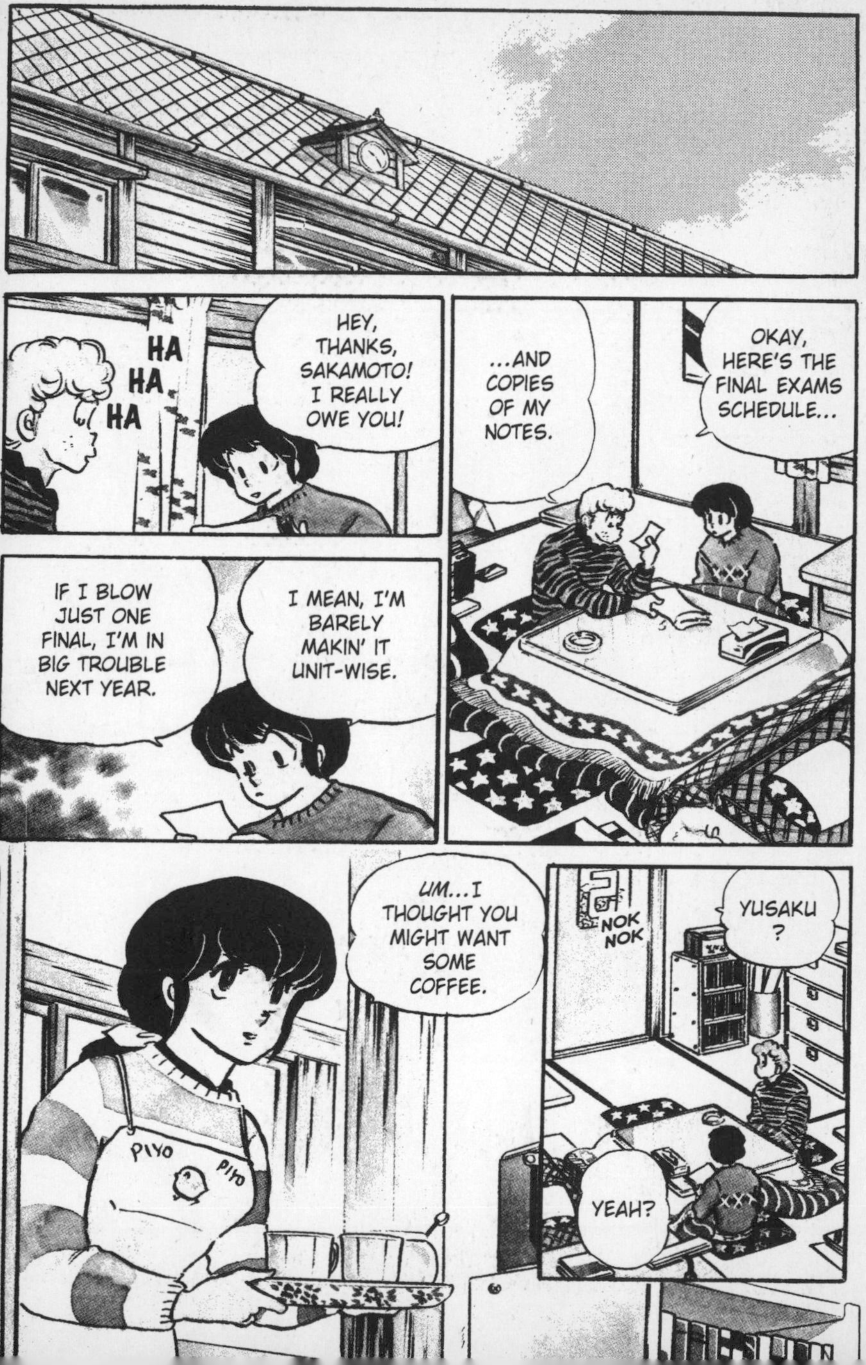
OKAY, HERE'S THE FINAL EXAMS SCHEDULE...
...AND COPIES OF MY NOTES.
HEY, THANKS, SAKAMOTO! I REALLY OWE YOU!
HA HA HA
I MEAN, I'M BARELY MAKIN' IT UNIT-WISE.
IF I BLOW JUST ONE FINAL, I'M IN BIG TROUBLE NEXT YEAR.
NOK NOK
YUSAKU?
YEAH?
UM...I THOUGHT YOU MIGHT WANT SOME COFFEE.
PIYO PIYO

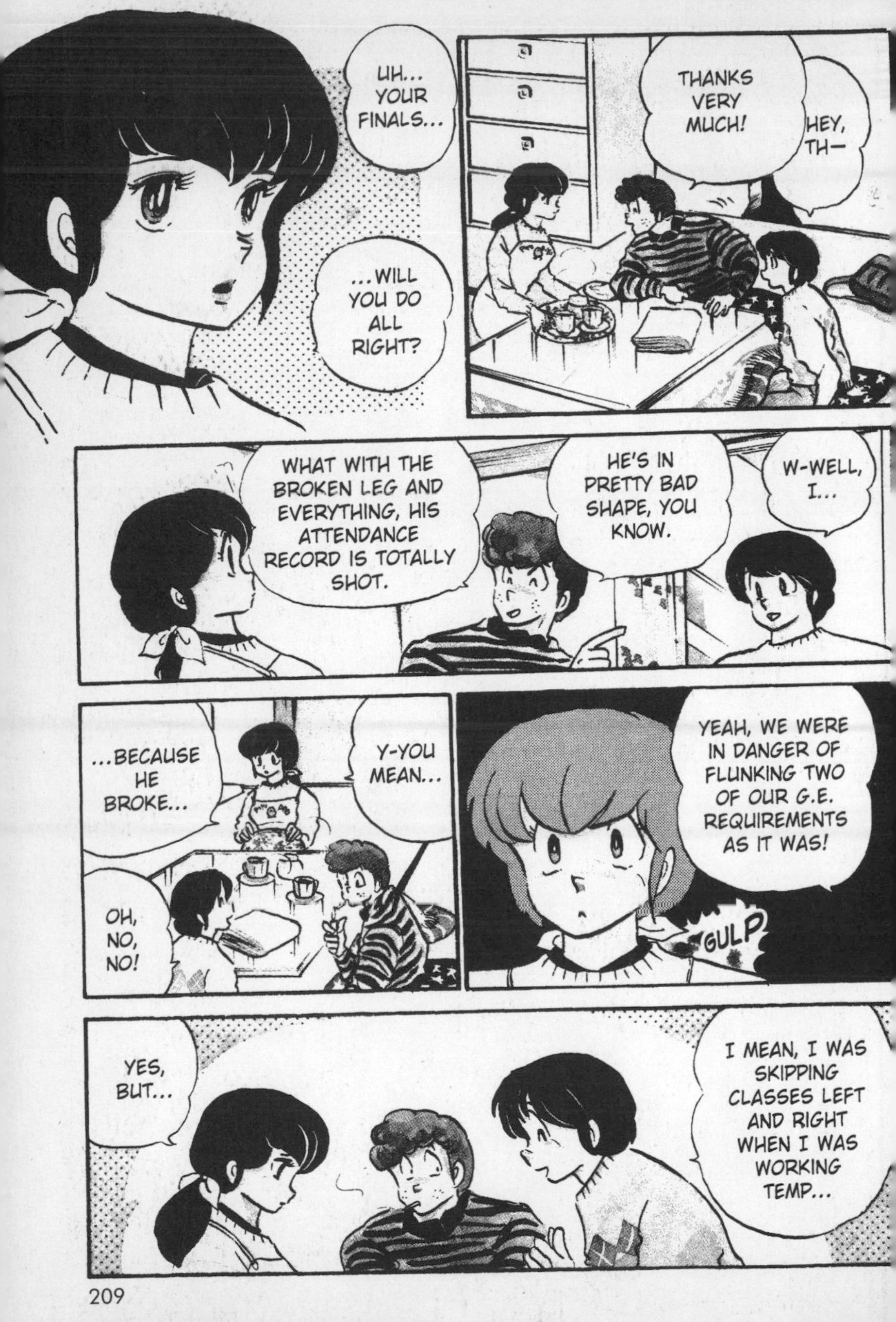
HEY, TH—
THANKS VERY MUCH!
UH... YOUR FINALS...
...WILL YOU DO ALL RIGHT?
W-WELL, I...
HE'S IN PRETTY BAD SHAPE, YOU KNOW.
WHAT WITH THE BROKEN LEG AND EVERYTHING, HIS ATTENDANCE RECORD IS TOTALLY SHOT.
YEAH, WE WERE IN DANGER OF FLUNKING TWO OF OUR G.E. REQUIREMENTS AS IT WAS!
GULP
Y-YOU MEAN...
...BECAUSE HE BROKE...
OH, NO, NO!
I MEAN, I WAS SKIPPING CLASSES LEFT AND RIGHT WHEN I WAS WORKING TEMP...
YES, BUT...

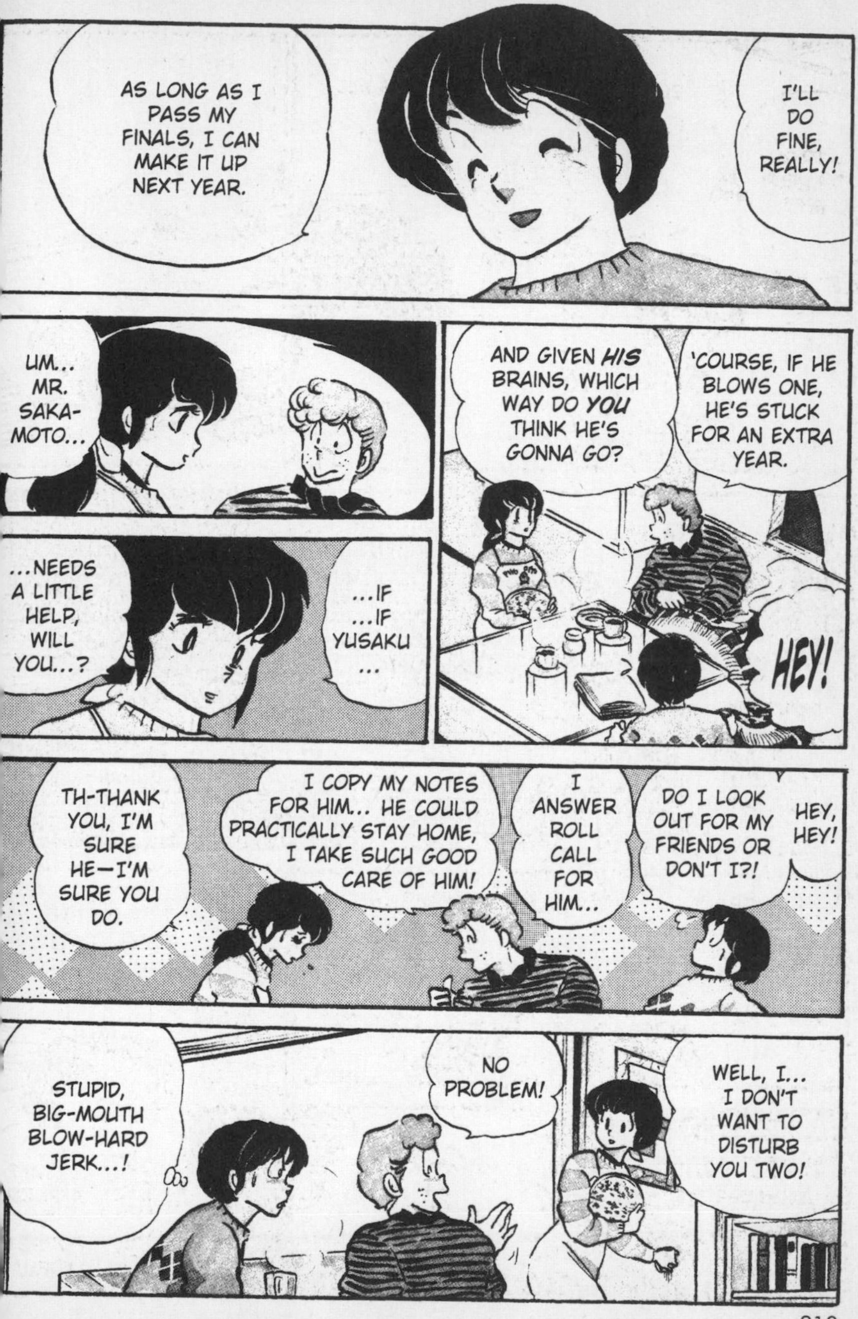
I'LL DO FINE, REALLY!
AS LONG AS I PASS MY FINALS, I CAN MAKE IT UP NEXT YEAR.
'COURSE, IF HE BLOWS ONE, HE'S STUCK FOR AN EXTRA YEAR.
AND GIVEN **HIS** BRAINS, WHICH WAY DO **YOU** THINK HE'S GONNA GO?
HEY!
UM... MR. SAKA-MOTO...
...IF ...IF YUSAKU ...
...NEEDS A LITTLE HELP, WILL YOU...?
HEY, HEY!
DO I LOOK OUT FOR MY FRIENDS OR DON'T I?!
I ANSWER ROLL CALL FOR HIM...
I COPY MY NOTES FOR HIM... HE COULD PRACTICALLY STAY HOME, I TAKE SUCH GOOD CARE OF HIM!
TH-THANK YOU, I'M SURE HE—I'M SURE YOU DO.
WELL, I... I DON'T WANT TO DISTURB YOU TWO!
NO PROBLEM!
STUPID, BIG-MOUTH BLOW-HARD JERK...!

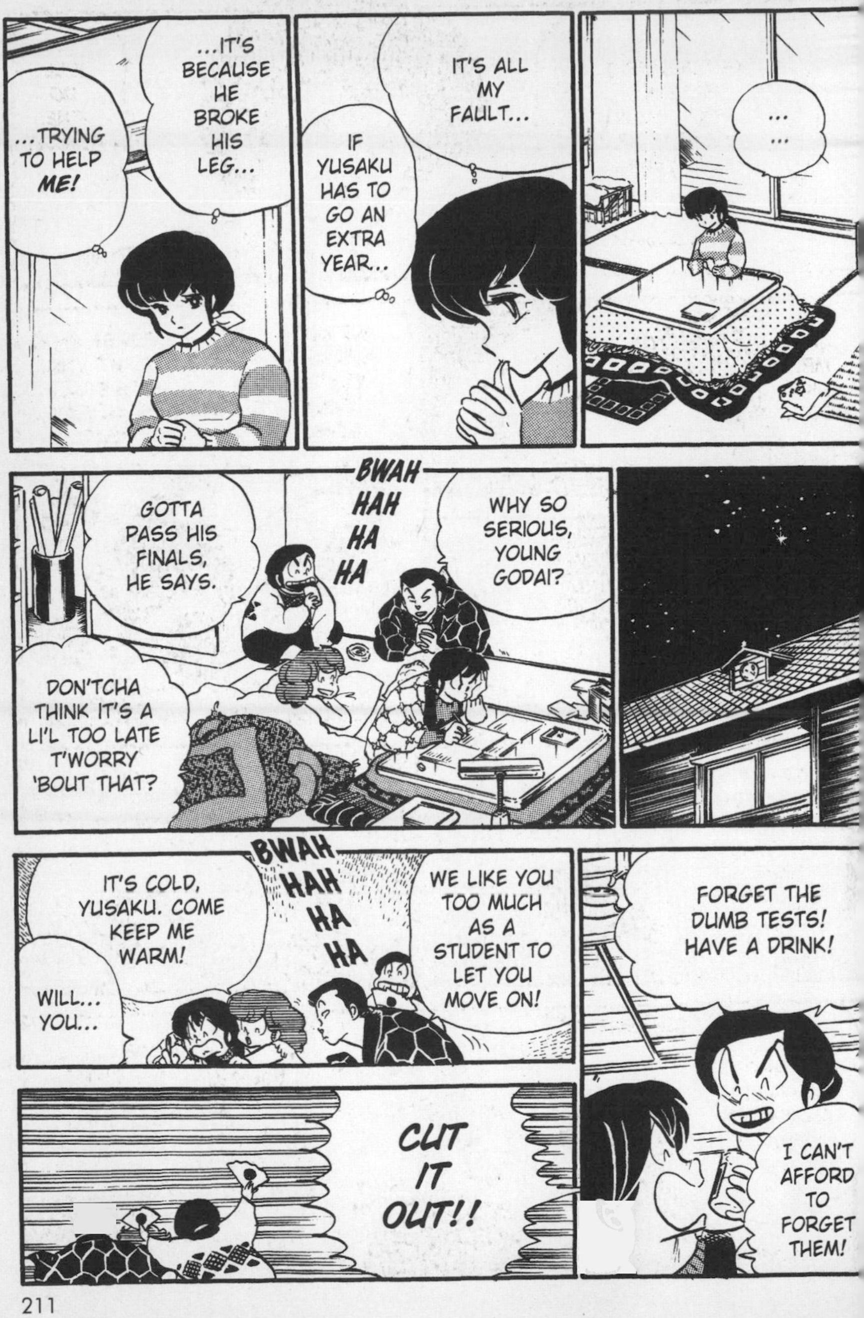
... ...
IT'S ALL MY FAULT...
IF YUSAKU HAS TO GO AN EXTRA YEAR...
...IT'S BECAUSE HE BROKE HIS LEG...
...TRYING TO HELP ME!
WHY SO SERIOUS, YOUNG GODAI?
BWAH HAH HA HA
GOTTA PASS HIS FINALS, HE SAYS.
DON'TCHA THINK IT'S A LI'L TOO LATE T'WORRY 'BOUT THAT?
FORGET THE DUMB TESTS! HAVE A DRINK!
I CAN'T AFFORD TO FORGET THEM!
WE LIKE YOU TOO MUCH AS A STUDENT TO LET YOU MOVE ON!
BWAH HAH HA HA
IT'S COLD, YUSAKU. COME KEEP ME WARM!
WILL... YOU...
CUT IT OUT!!

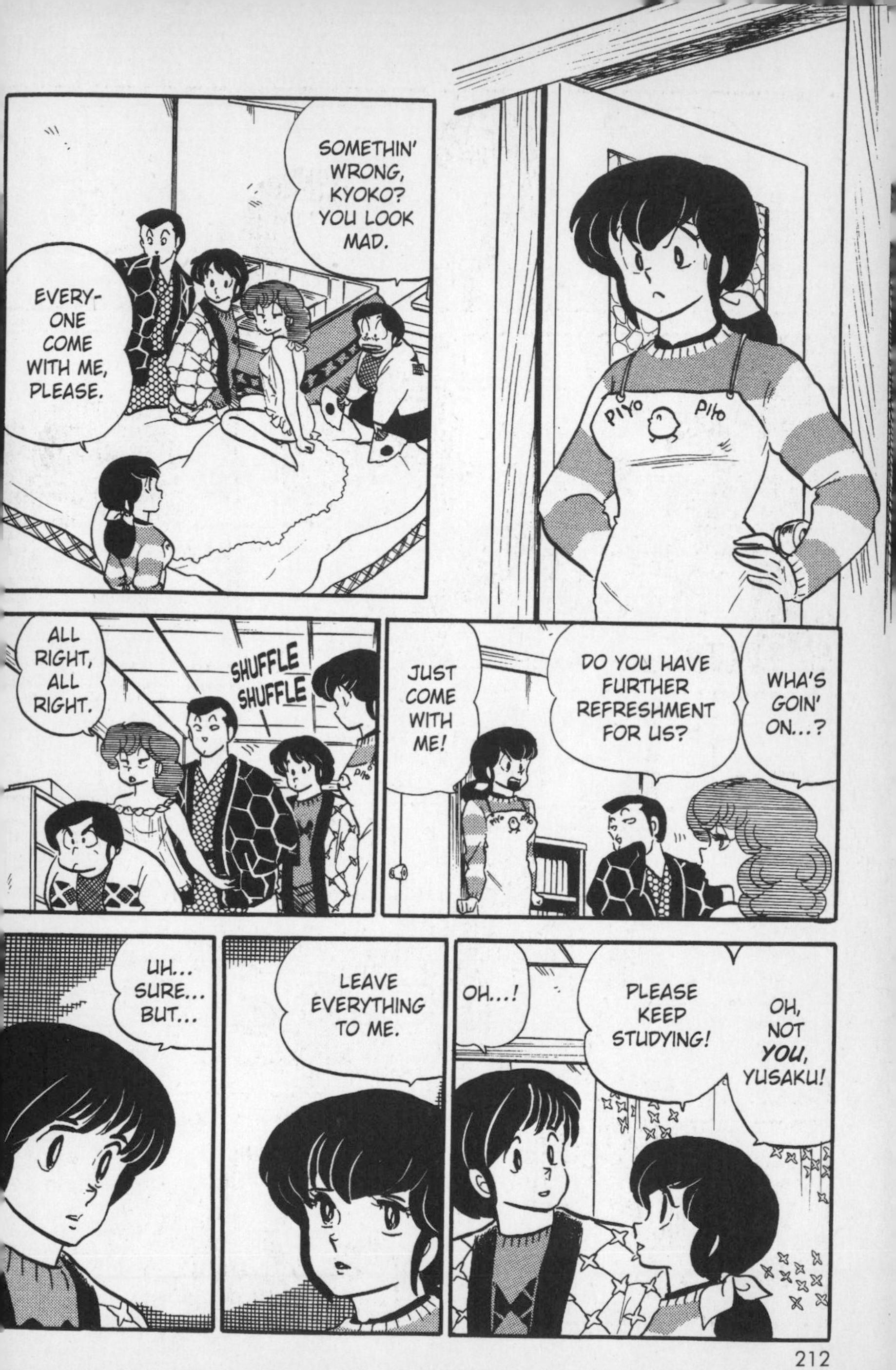
SOMETHIN' WRONG, KYOKO? YOU LOOK MAD.
EVERY-ONE COME WITH ME, PLEASE.
WHA'S GOIN' ON...?
DO YOU HAVE FURTHER REFRESHMENT FOR US?
JUST COME WITH ME!
SHUFFLE SHUFFLE
ALL RIGHT, ALL RIGHT.
OH, NOT *YOU*, YUSAKU!
PLEASE KEEP STUDYING!
OH...!
LEAVE EVERYTHING TO ME.
UH... SURE... BUT...

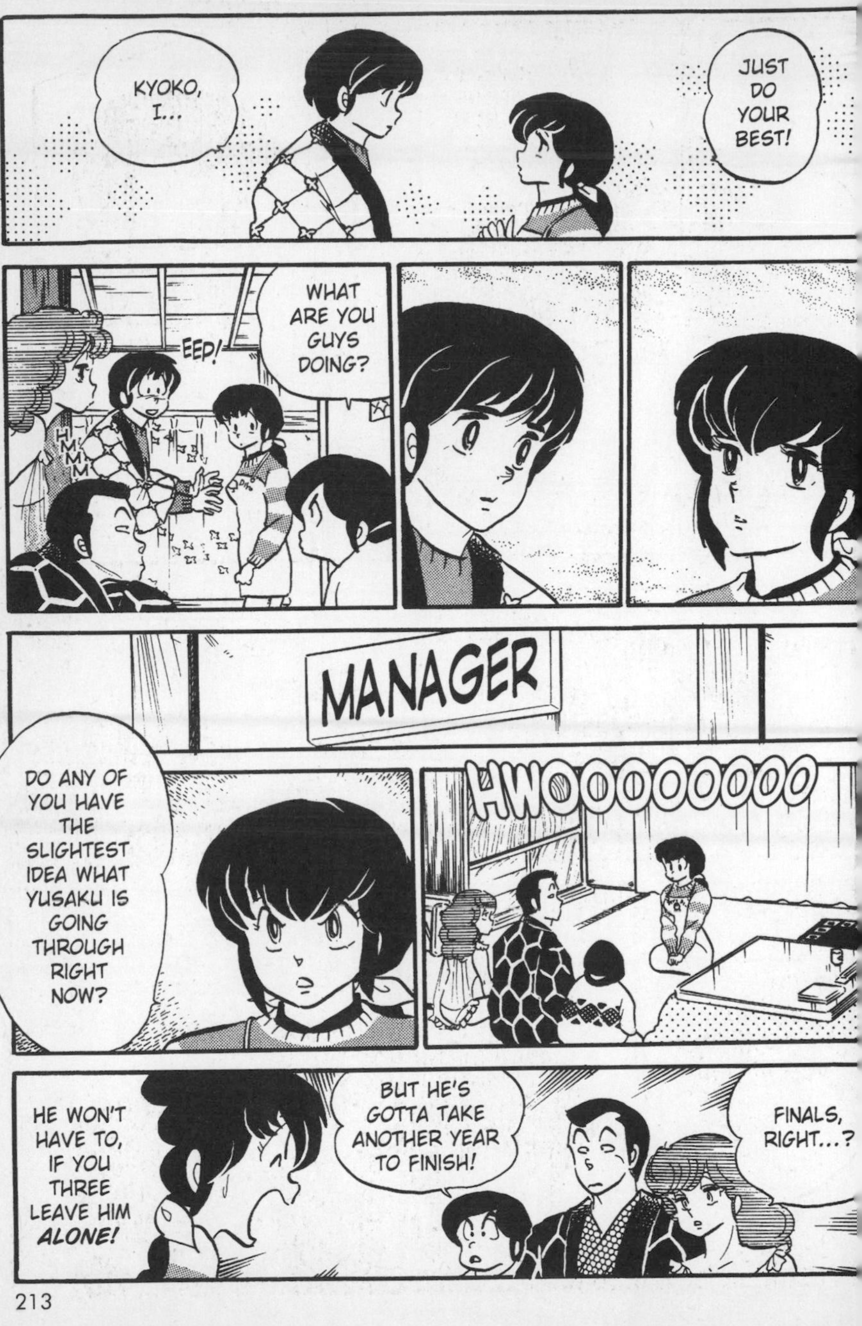
JUST DO YOUR BEST!
KYOKO, I...
WHAT ARE YOU GUYS DOING?
EEP!
HMMM
MANAGER
HWOOOOOOOO
DO ANY OF YOU HAVE THE SLIGHTEST IDEA WHAT YUSAKU IS GOING THROUGH RIGHT NOW?
FINALS, RIGHT...?
BUT HE'S GOTTA TAKE ANOTHER YEAR TO FINISH!
HE WON'T HAVE TO, IF YOU THREE LEAVE HIM *ALONE!*

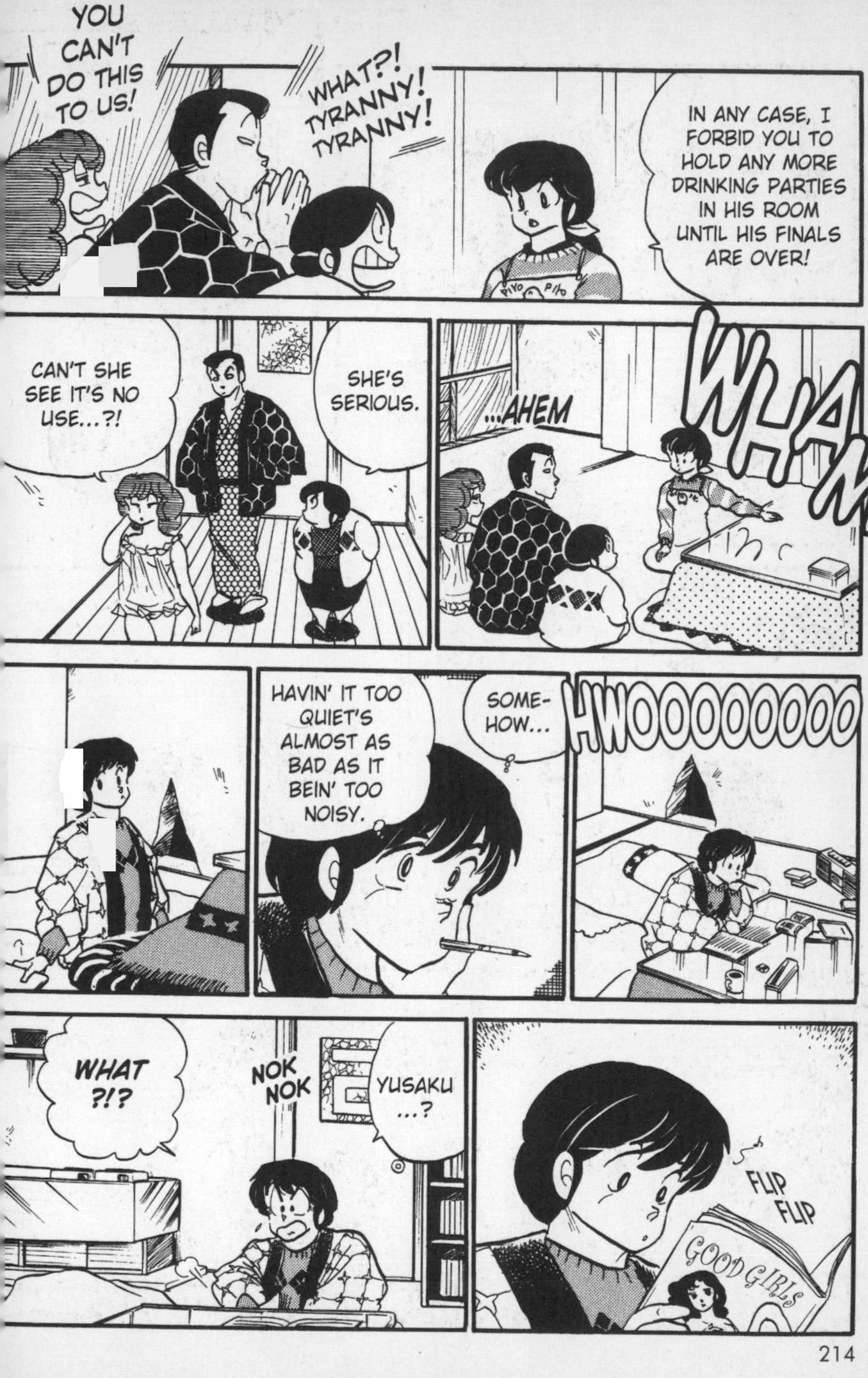
IN ANY CASE, I FORBID YOU TO HOLD ANY MORE DRINKING PARTIES IN HIS ROOM UNTIL HIS FINALS ARE OVER!
WHAT?! TYRANNY! TYRANNY!
YOU CAN'T DO THIS TO US!
WHAM
...AHEM
SHE'S SERIOUS.
CAN'T SHE SEE IT'S NO USE...?!
HWOOOOOOOO
SOME-HOW...
HAVIN' IT TOO QUIET'S ALMOST AS BAD AS IT BEIN' TOO NOISY.
FLIP FLIP
GOOD GIRLS
YUSAKU ...?
NOK NOK
WHAT ?!?

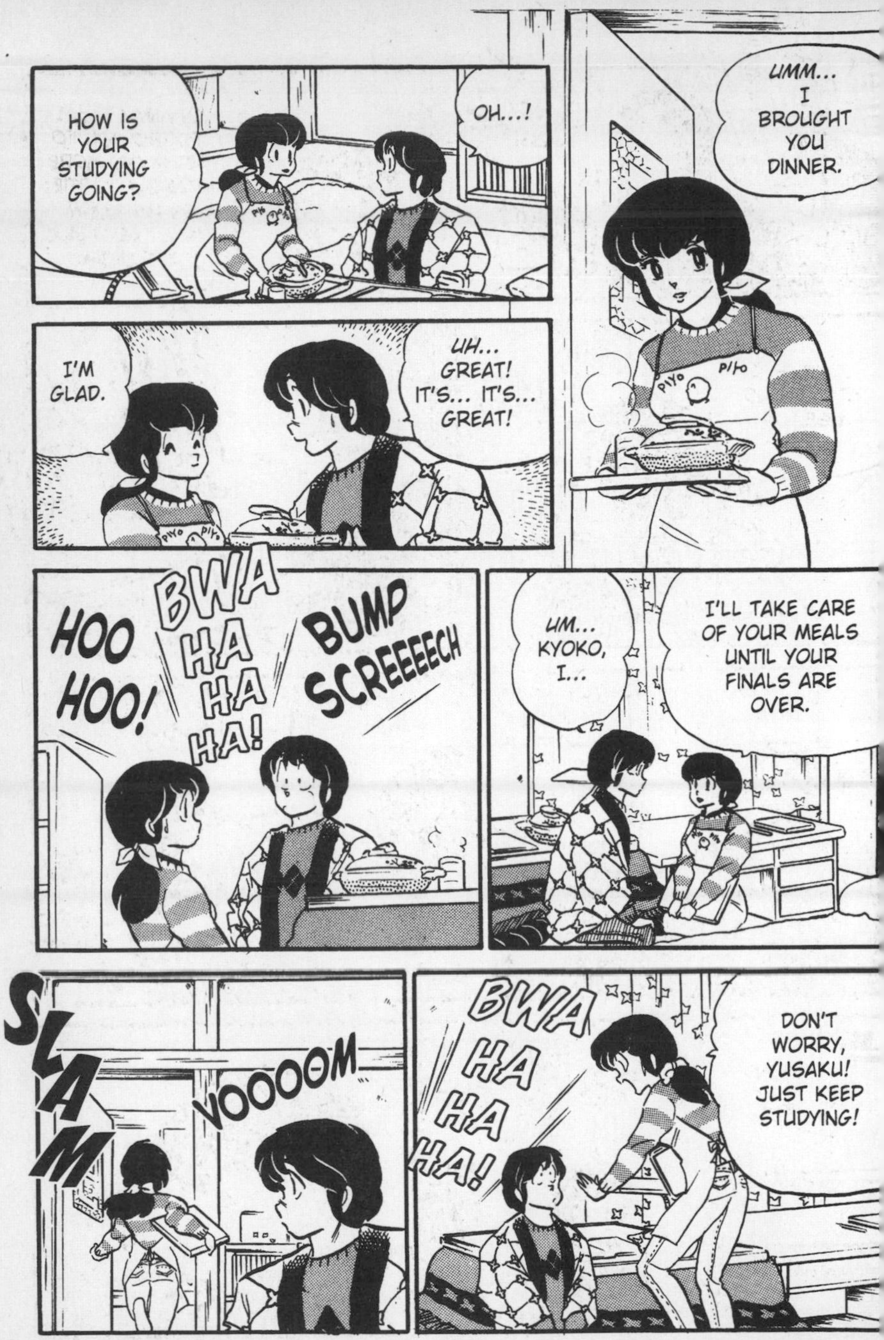
UMM... I BROUGHT YOU DINNER.
OH...!
HOW IS YOUR STUDYING GOING?
UH... GREAT! IT'S... IT'S... GREAT!
I'M GLAD.
I'LL TAKE CARE OF YOUR MEALS UNTIL YOUR FINALS ARE OVER.
UM... KYOKO, I...
BUMP
SCREEEECH
BWA HA HA HA!
HOO HOO!
DON'T WORRY, YUSAKU! JUST KEEP STUDYING!
BWA HA HA HA!
VOOOOM
SLAM

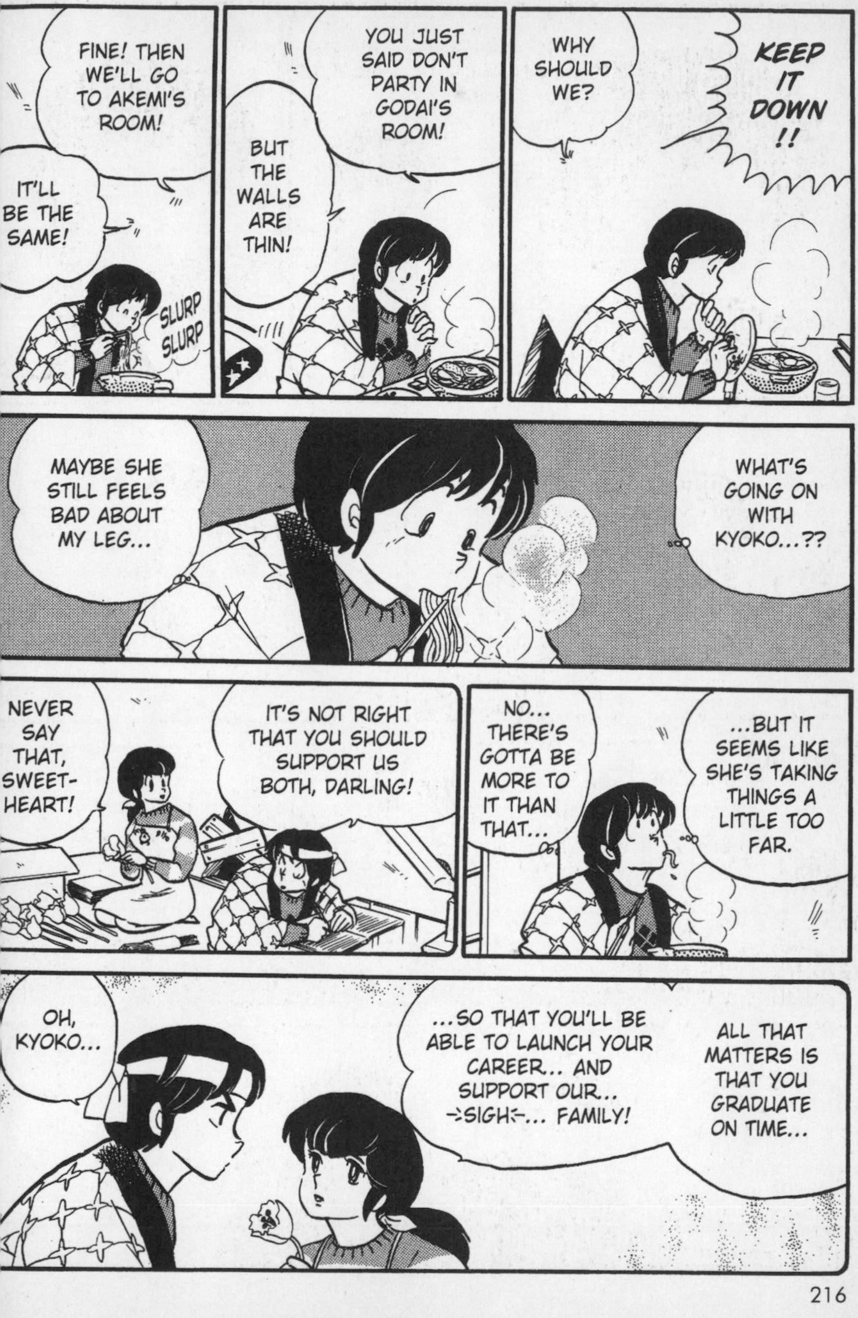
KEEP IT DOWN!!
WHY SHOULD WE?
YOU JUST SAID DON'T PARTY IN GODAI'S ROOM!
BUT THE WALLS ARE THIN!
FINE! THEN WE'LL GO TO AKEMI'S ROOM!
IT'LL BE THE SAME!
SLURP SLURP
WHAT'S GOING ON WITH KYOKO...??
MAYBE SHE STILL FEELS BAD ABOUT MY LEG...
...BUT IT SEEMS LIKE SHE'S TAKING THINGS A LITTLE TOO FAR.
NO... THERE'S GOTTA BE MORE TO IT THAN THAT...
IT'S NOT RIGHT THAT YOU SHOULD SUPPORT US BOTH, DARLING!
NEVER SAY THAT, SWEET-HEART!
ALL THAT MATTERS IS THAT YOU GRADUATE ON TIME...
...SO THAT YOU'LL BE ABLE TO LAUNCH YOUR CAREER... AND SUPPORT OUR... ->SIGH<-... FAMILY!
OH, KYOKO...

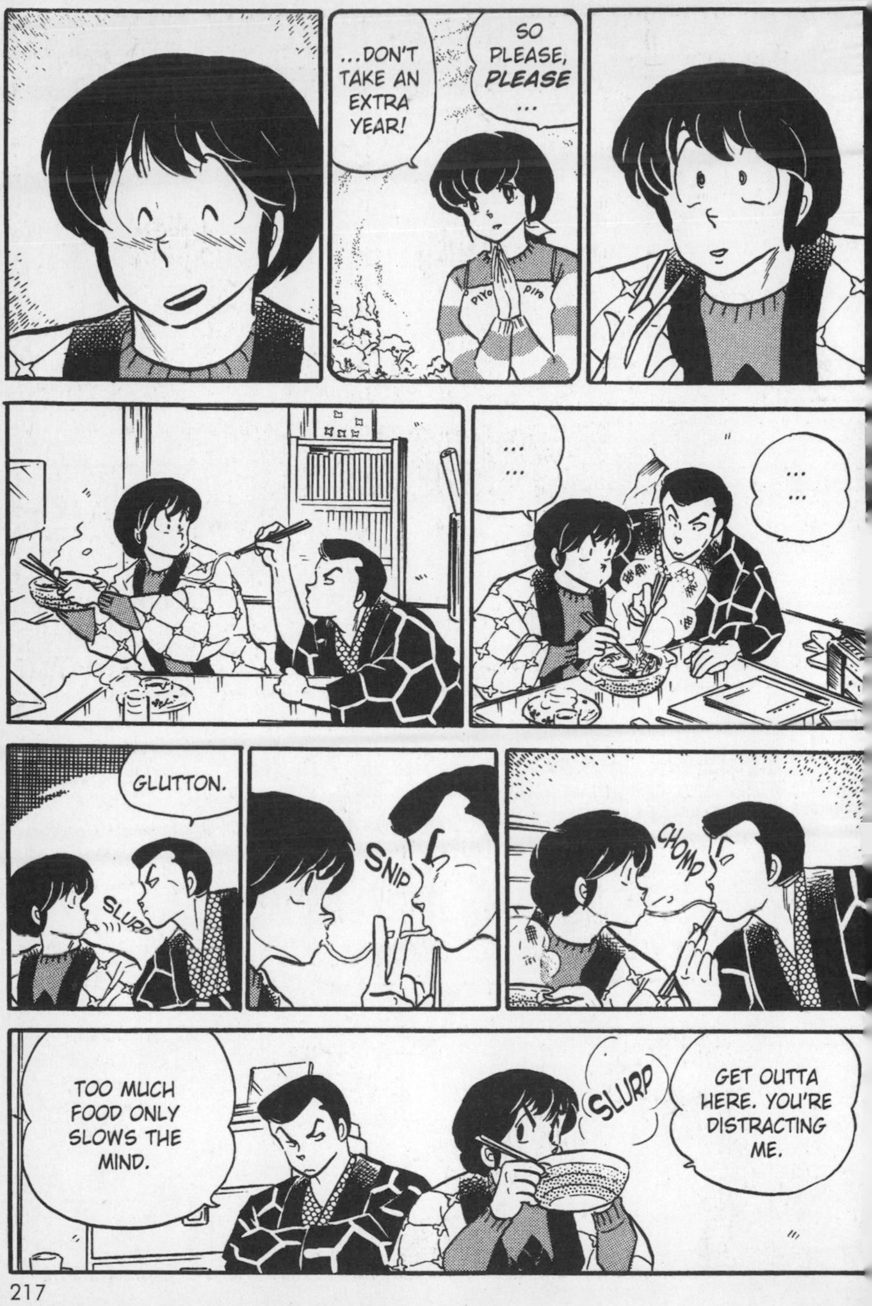
SO PLEASE, PLEASE ...
...DON'T TAKE AN EXTRA YEAR!
PIYO PIYO
... ...
... ...
CHOMP
SNIP
GLUTTON.
SLURP
GET OUTTA HERE. YOU'RE DISTRACTING ME.
SLURP
TOO MUCH FOOD ONLY SLOWS THE MIND.

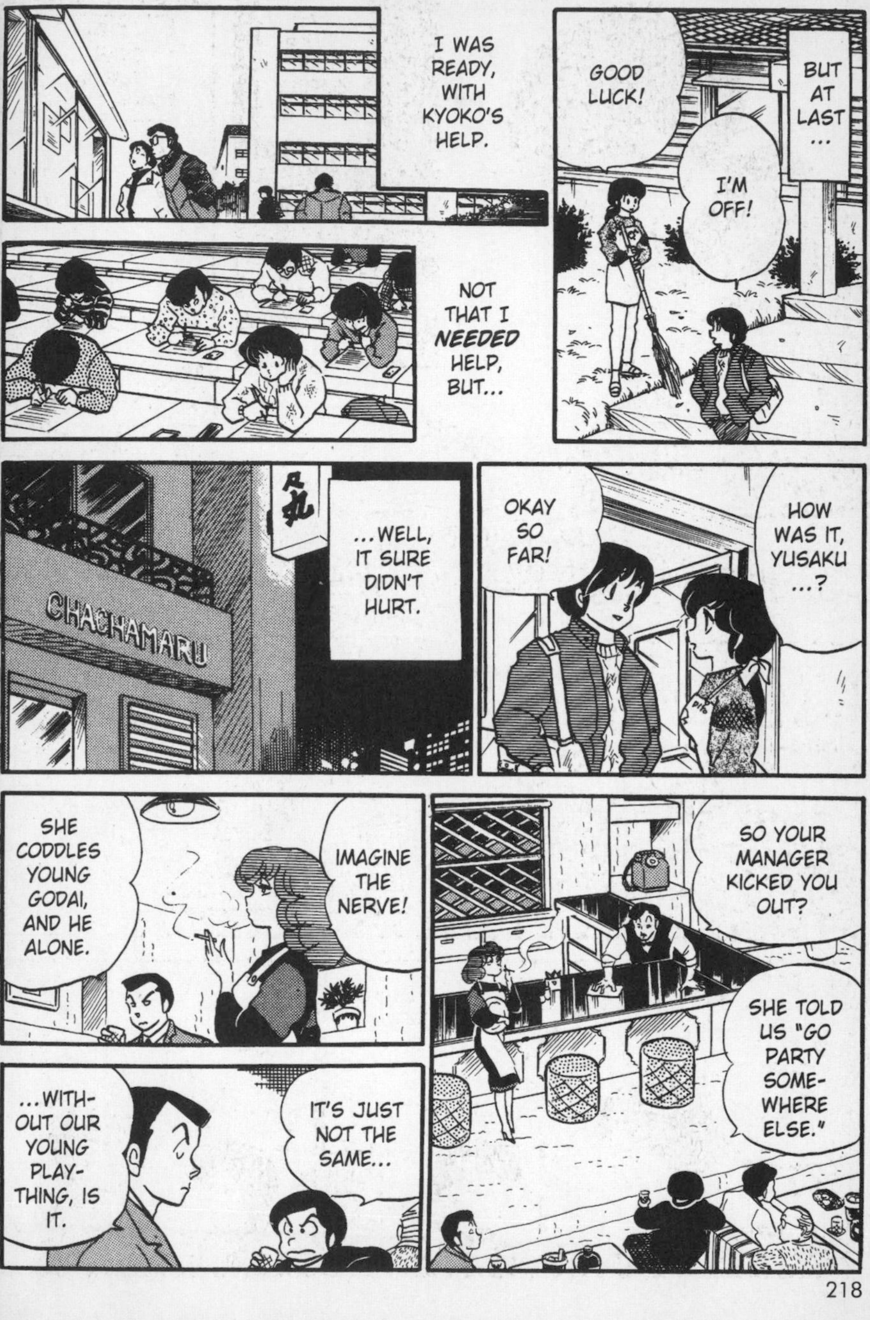
BUT AT LAST...
GOOD LUCK!
I'M OFF!
I WAS READY, WITH KYOKO'S HELP.
NOT THAT I *NEEDED* HELP, BUT...
HOW WAS IT, YUSAKU...?
OKAY SO FAR!
...WELL, IT SURE DIDN'T HURT.
CHACHAMARU
SO YOUR MANAGER KICKED YOU OUT?
SHE TOLD US "GO PARTY SOME-WHERE ELSE."
IMAGINE THE NERVE!
SHE CODDLES YOUNG GODAI, AND HE ALONE.
IT'S JUST NOT THE SAME...
...WITH-OUT OUR YOUNG PLAY-THING, IS IT.

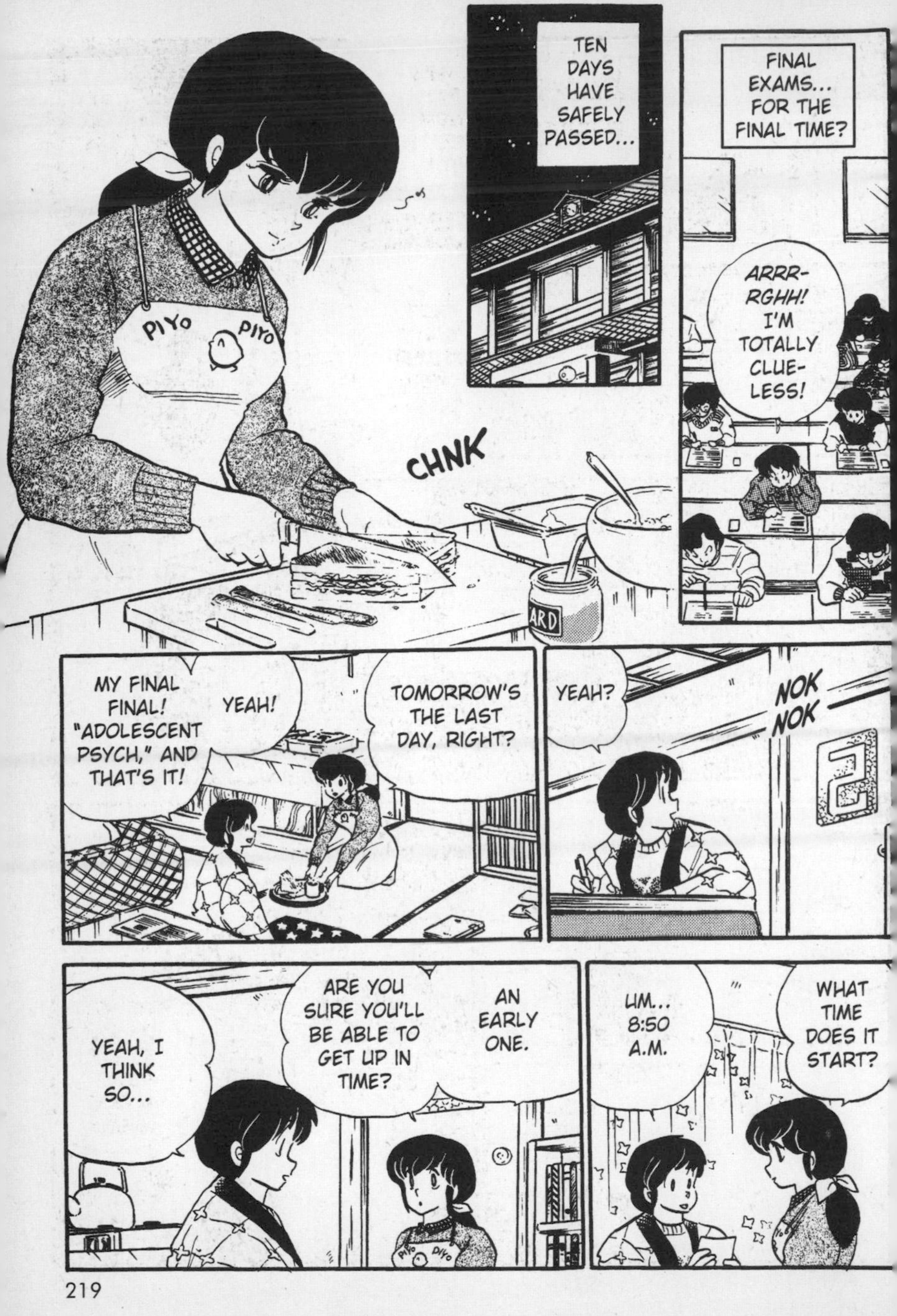
FINAL EXAMS... FOR THE FINAL TIME?
ARRR-RGHH! I'M TOTALLY CLUE-LESS!
TEN DAYS HAVE SAFELY PASSED...
CHNK
PIYO PIYO
NOK NOK
YEAH?
TOMORROW'S THE LAST DAY, RIGHT?
YEAH!
MY FINAL FINAL! "ADOLESCENT PSYCH," AND THAT'S IT!
WHAT TIME DOES IT START?
UM... 8:50 A.M.
AN EARLY ONE.
ARE YOU SURE YOU'LL BE ABLE TO GET UP IN TIME?
YEAH, I THINK SO...

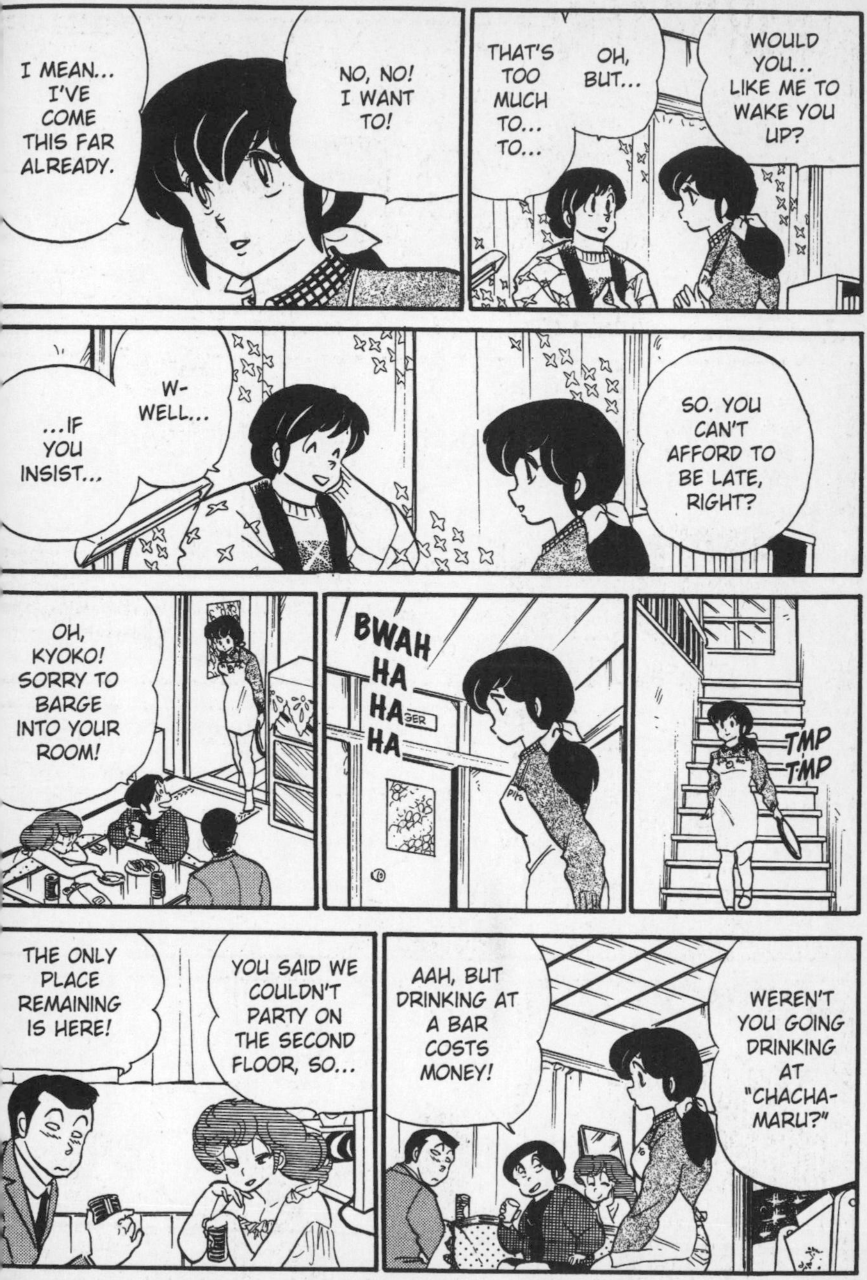
WOULD YOU... LIKE ME TO WAKE YOU UP?
OH, BUT...
THAT'S TOO MUCH TO... TO...
NO, NO! I WANT TO!
I MEAN... I'VE COME THIS FAR ALREADY.
SO. YOU CAN'T AFFORD TO BE LATE, RIGHT?
W- WELL...
...IF YOU INSIST...
TMP TMP
BWAH HA HA HA
OH, KYOKO! SORRY TO BARGE INTO YOUR ROOM!
WEREN'T YOU GOING DRINKING AT "CHACHA-MARU?"
AAH, BUT DRINKING AT A BAR COSTS MONEY!
YOU SAID WE COULDN'T PARTY ON THE SECOND FLOOR, SO...
THE ONLY PLACE REMAINING IS HERE!

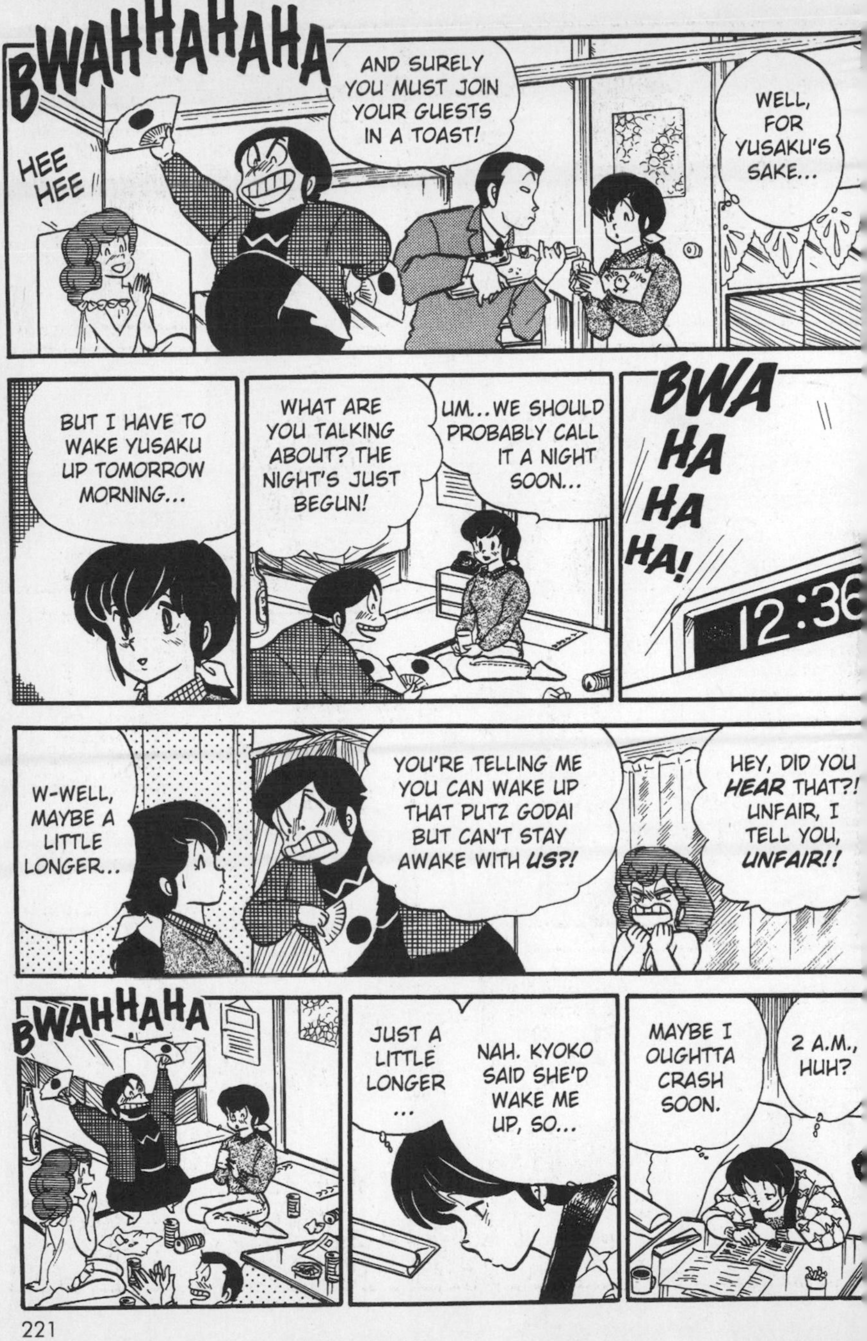
WELL, FOR YUSAKU'S SAKE...
AND SURELY YOU MUST JOIN YOUR GUESTS IN A TOAST!
BWAHHAHAHA
HEE HEE
BWA HA HA HA HA!
12:36
UM...WE SHOULD PROBABLY CALL IT A NIGHT SOON...
WHAT ARE YOU TALKING ABOUT? THE NIGHT'S JUST BEGUN!
BUT I HAVE TO WAKE YUSAKU UP TOMORROW MORNING...
HEY, DID YOU HEAR THAT?! UNFAIR, I TELL YOU, UNFAIR!!
YOU'RE TELLING ME YOU CAN WAKE UP THAT PUTZ GODAI BUT CAN'T STAY AWAKE WITH US?!
W-WELL, MAYBE A LITTLE LONGER...
2 A.M., HUH?
MAYBE I OUGHTTA CRASH SOON.
NAH. KYOKO SAID SHE'D WAKE ME UP, SO...
JUST A LITTLE LONGER ...
BWAHHAHA

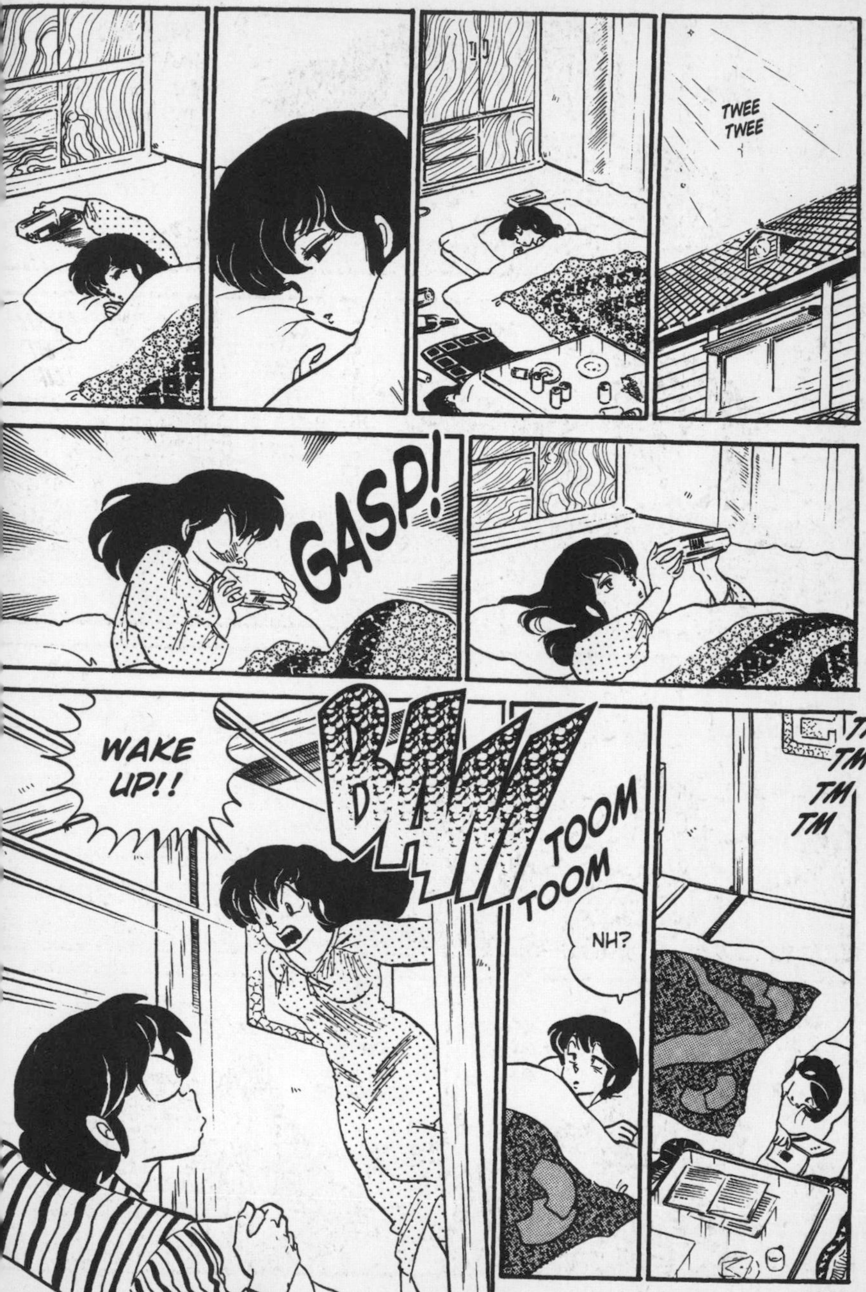
TWEE TWEE
GASP!
TM TM TM TM
NH?
WAKE UP!!
BAM
TOOM TOOM

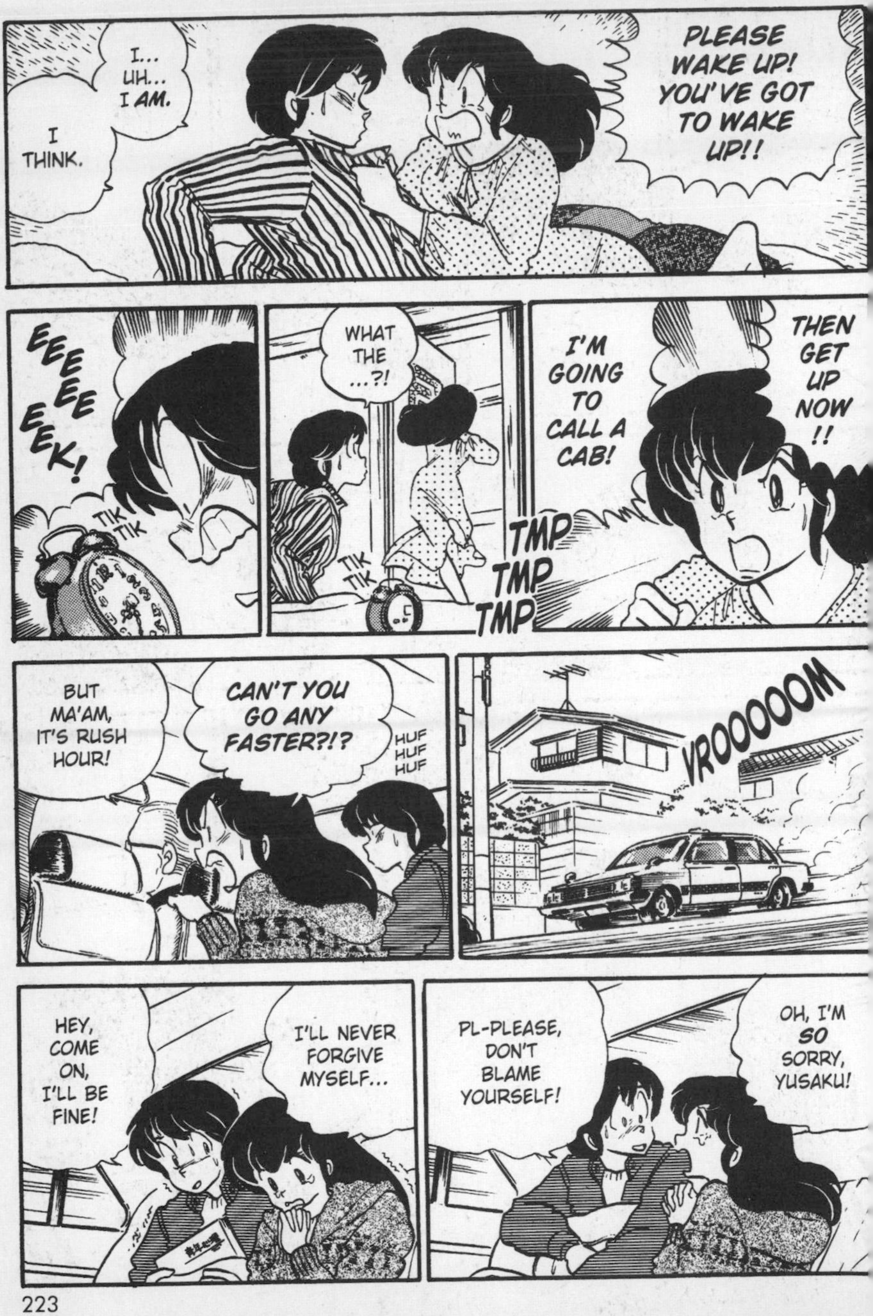
PLEASE WAKE UP! YOU'VE GOT TO WAKE UP!!
I... UH... I AM.
I THINK.
THEN GET UP NOW!!
I'M GOING TO CALL A CAB!
TMP TMP TMP
WHAT THE ...?!
TIK TIK
EEEEEEEK!
TIK TIK
VROOOOOM
CAN'T YOU GO ANY FASTER?!?
HUF HUF HUF
BUT MA'AM, IT'S RUSH HOUR!
OH, I'M SO SORRY, YUSAKU!
PL-PLEASE, DON'T BLAME YOURSELF!
I'LL NEVER FORGIVE MYSELF...
HEY, COME ON, I'LL BE FINE!

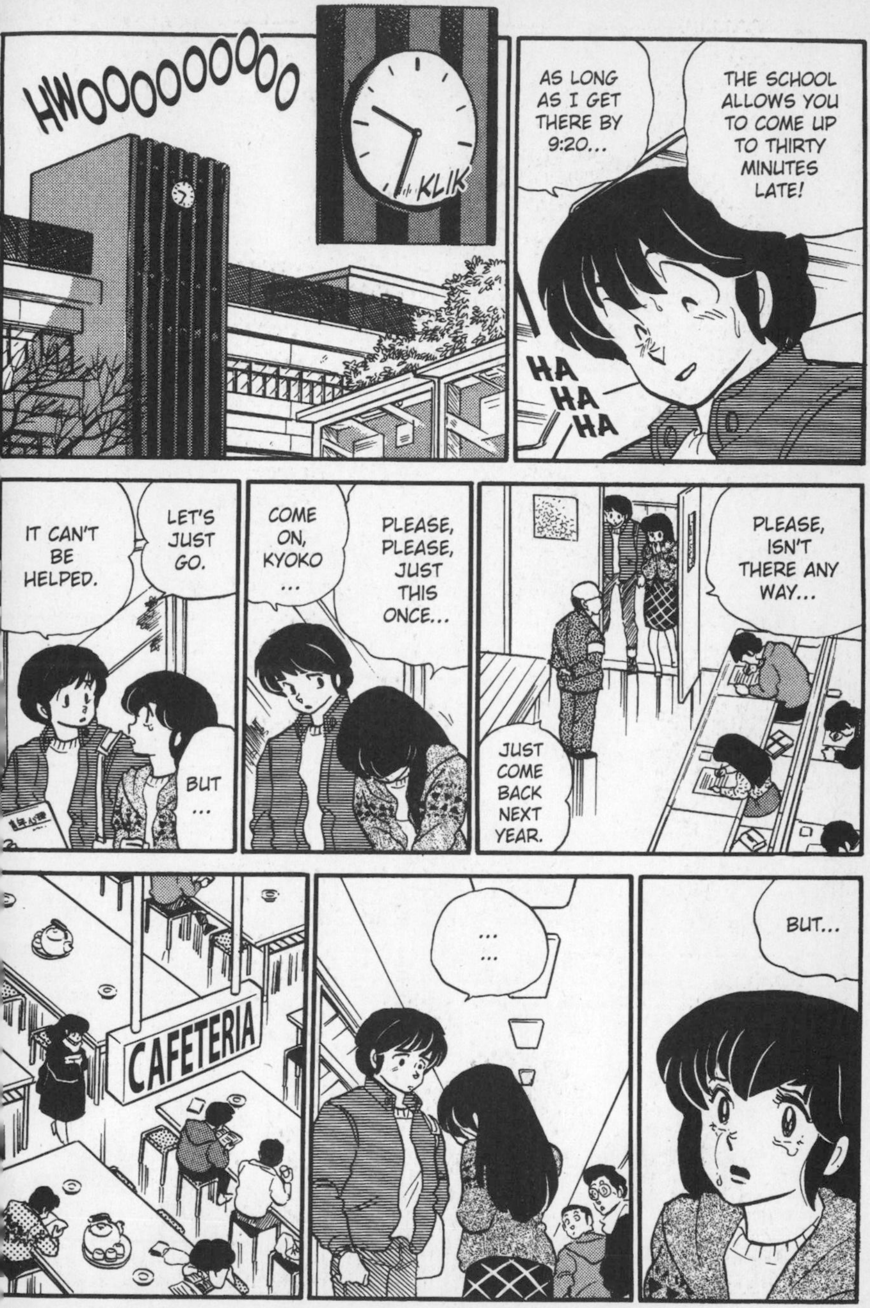
THE SCHOOL ALLOWS YOU TO COME UP TO THIRTY MINUTES LATE!
AS LONG AS I GET THERE BY 9:20...
HA HA HA
KLIK
HWOOOOOOOOO
PLEASE, ISN'T THERE ANY WAY...
JUST COME BACK NEXT YEAR.
PLEASE, PLEASE, JUST THIS ONCE...
COME ON, KYOKO ...
LET'S JUST GO.
IT CAN'T BE HELPED.
BUT ...
BUT...
... ...
CAFETERIA

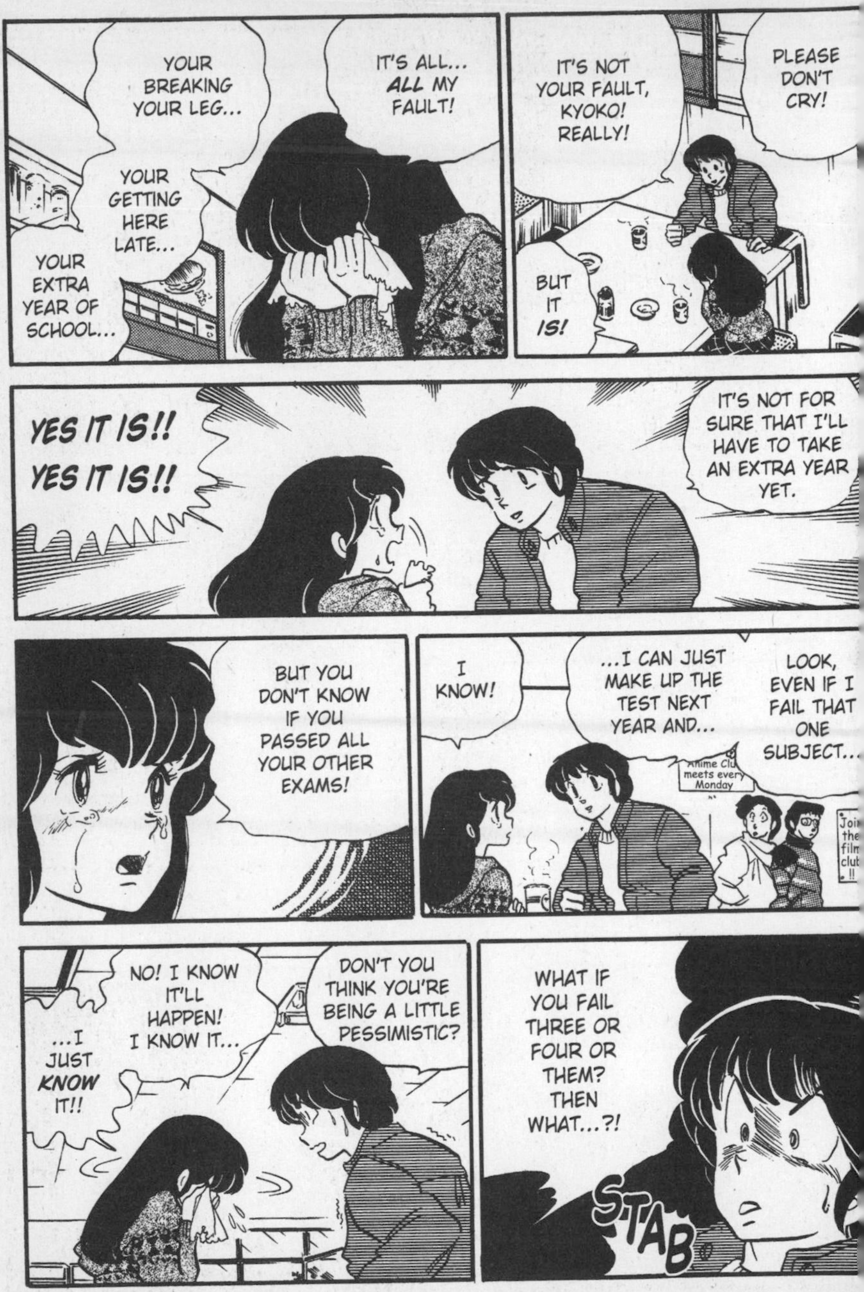
PLEASE DON'T CRY!
IT'S NOT YOUR FAULT, KYOKO! REALLY!
BUT IT IS!
IT'S ALL... ALL MY FAULT!
YOUR BREAKING YOUR LEG...
YOUR GETTING HERE LATE...
YOUR EXTRA YEAR OF SCHOOL...
IT'S NOT FOR SURE THAT I'LL HAVE TO TAKE AN EXTRA YEAR YET.
YES IT IS!! YES IT IS!!
LOOK, EVEN IF I FAIL THAT ONE SUBJECT...
...I CAN JUST MAKE UP THE TEST NEXT YEAR AND...
I KNOW!
Anime Clu meets every Monday
BUT YOU DON'T KNOW IF YOU PASSED ALL YOUR OTHER EXAMS!
WHAT IF YOU FAIL THREE OR FOUR OR THEM? THEN WHAT...?!
STAB
DON'T YOU THINK YOU'RE BEING A LITTLE PESSIMISTIC?
NO! I KNOW IT'LL HAPPEN! I KNOW IT...
...I JUST KNOW IT!!

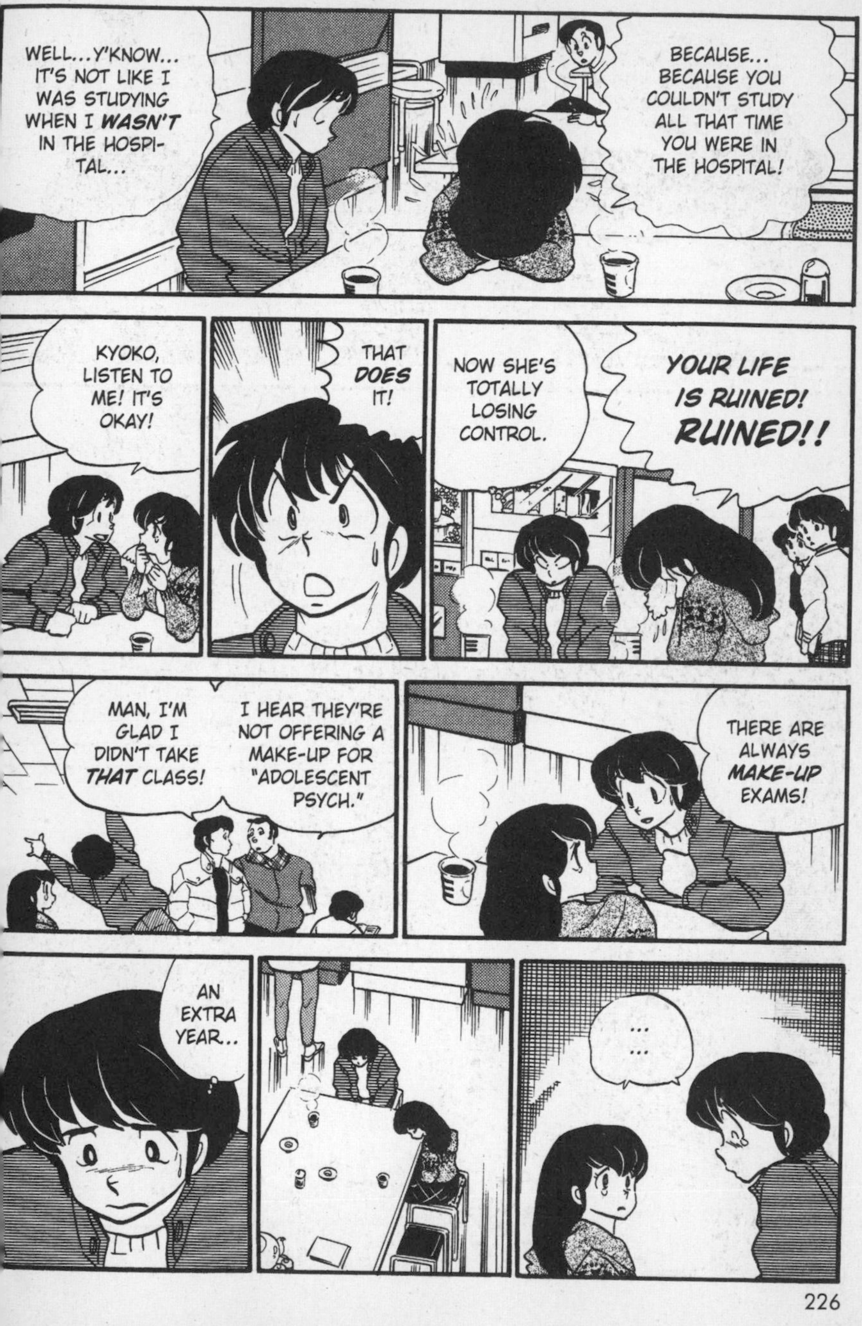
BECAUSE... BECAUSE YOU COULDN'T STUDY ALL THAT TIME YOU WERE IN THE HOSPITAL!
WELL...Y'KNOW... IT'S NOT LIKE I WAS STUDYING WHEN I *WASN'T* IN THE HOSPI-TAL...
YOUR LIFE IS RUINED! RUINED!!
NOW SHE'S TOTALLY LOSING CONTROL.
THAT *DOES* IT!
KYOKO, LISTEN TO ME! IT'S OKAY!
THERE ARE ALWAYS *MAKE-UP* EXAMS!
I HEAR THEY'RE NOT OFFERING A MAKE-UP FOR "ADOLESCENT PSYCH."
MAN, I'M GLAD I DIDN'T TAKE *THAT* CLASS!
... ...
AN EXTRA YEAR...

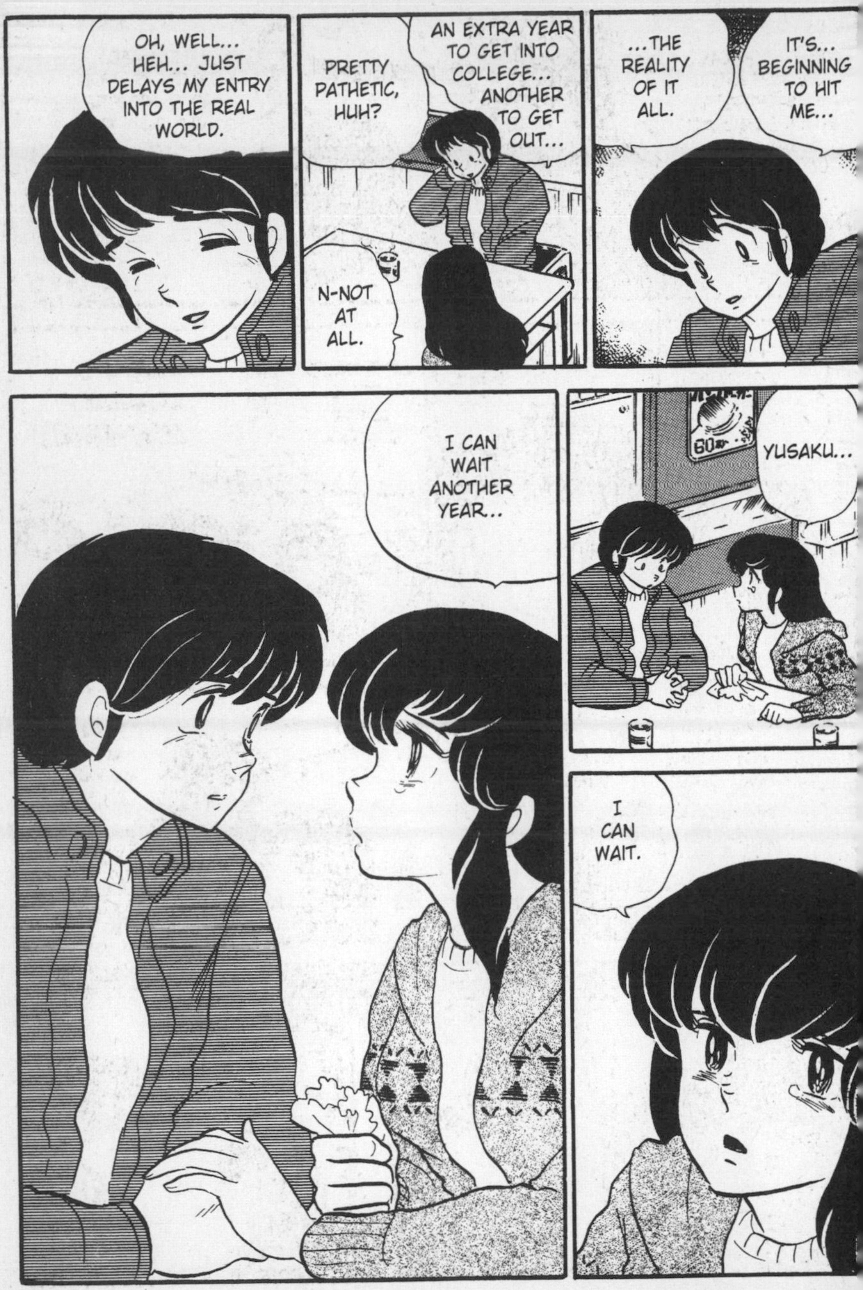
IT'S... BEGINNING TO HIT ME...
...THE REALITY OF IT ALL.
AN EXTRA YEAR TO GET INTO COLLEGE... ANOTHER TO GET OUT...
PRETTY PATHETIC, HUH?
N-NOT AT ALL.
OH, WELL... HEH... JUST DELAYS MY ENTRY INTO THE REAL WORLD.
YUSAKU...
I CAN WAIT.
I CAN WAIT ANOTHER YEAR..

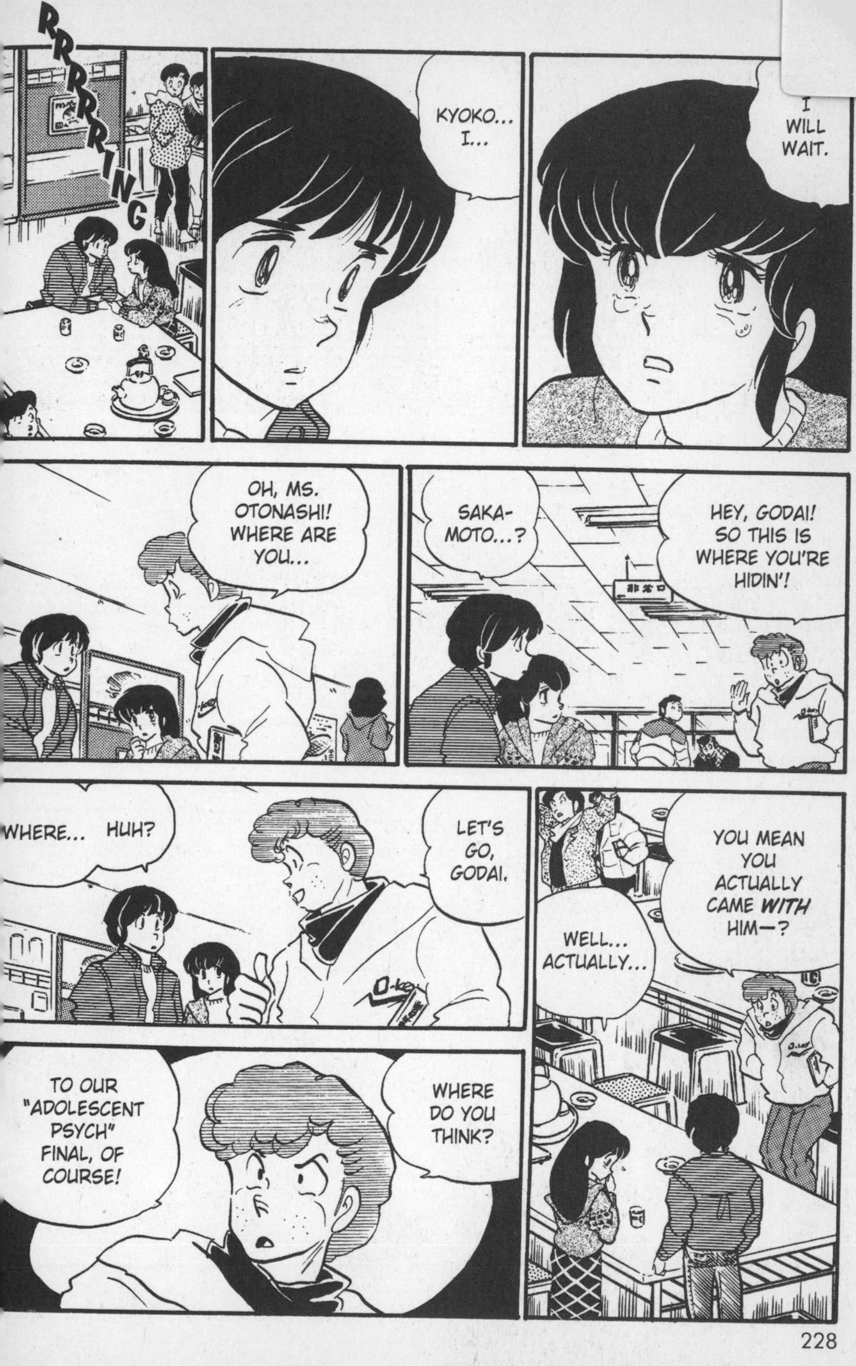
I WILL WAIT.
KYOKO... I...
RRRRRRING
HEY, GODAI! SO THIS IS WHERE YOU'RE HIDIN'!
SAKA-MOTO...?
OH, MS. OTONASHI! WHERE ARE YOU...
YOU MEAN YOU ACTUALLY CAME WITH HIM—?
WELL... ACTUALLY...
LET'S GO, GODAI.
WHERE... HUH?
WHERE DO YOU THINK?
TO OUR "ADOLESCENT PSYCH" FINAL, OF COURSE!

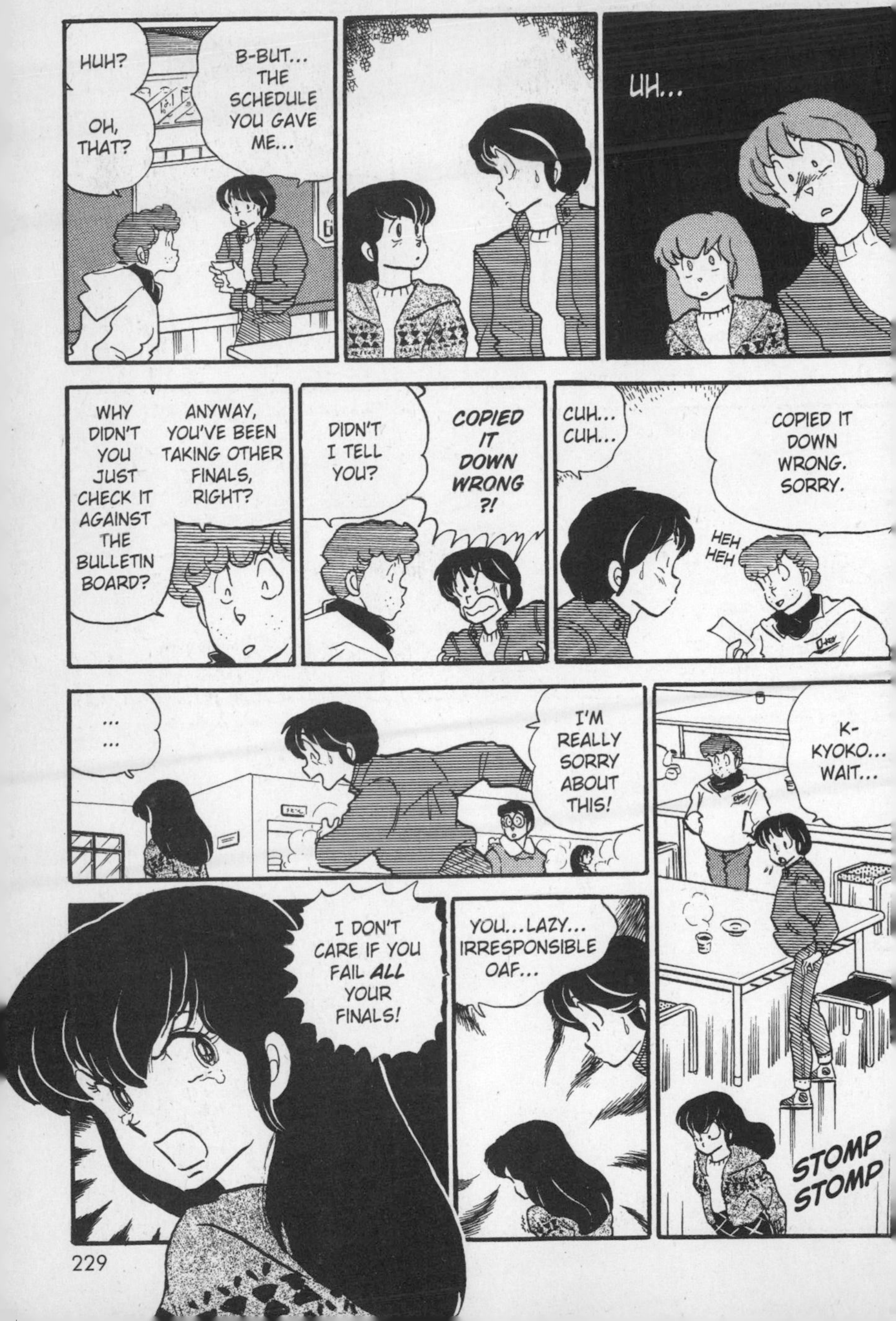
UH...
B-BUT... THE SCHEDULE YOU GAVE ME...
HUH?
OH, THAT?
COPIED IT DOWN WRONG. SORRY.
HEH HEH
CUH... CUH...
COPIED IT DOWN WRONG?!
DIDN'T I TELL YOU?
ANYWAY, YOU'VE BEEN TAKING OTHER FINALS, RIGHT?
WHY DIDN'T YOU JUST CHECK IT AGAINST THE BULLETIN BOARD?
K-KYOKO... WAIT...
STOMP STOMP
I'M REALLY SORRY ABOUT THIS!
... ...
YOU...LAZY... IRRESPONSIBLE OAF...
I DON'T CARE IF YOU FAIL ALL YOUR FINALS!

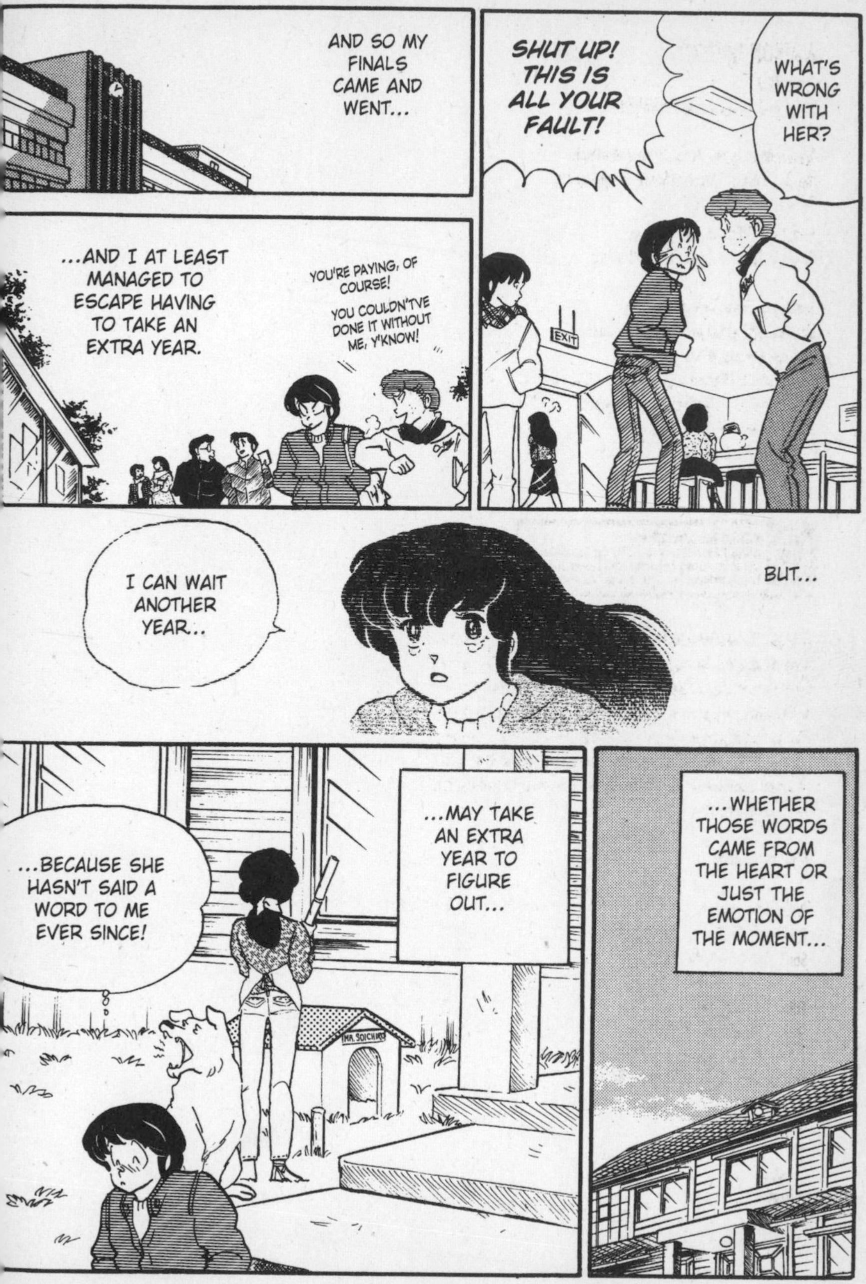
WHAT'S WRONG WITH HER?
SHUT UP! THIS IS ALL YOUR FAULT!
EXIT
AND SO MY FINALS CAME AND WENT...
YOU'RE PAYING, OF COURSE!
YOU COULDN'T'VE DONE IT WITHOUT ME, Y'KNOW!
...AND I AT LEAST MANAGED TO ESCAPE HAVING TO TAKE AN EXTRA YEAR.
BUT...
I CAN WAIT ANOTHER YEAR...
...WHETHER THOSE WORDS CAME FROM THE HEART OR JUST THE EMOTION OF THE MOMENT...
...MAY TAKE AN EXTRA YEAR TO FIGURE OUT...
MR. SOICHIRO
...BECAUSE SHE HASN'T SAID A WORD TO ME EVER SINCE!

MAISON IKKOKU

VOLUME 7
Story and Art by Rumiko Takahashi

Translation/Gerard Jones & Mari Morimoto
Touch-up Art & Lettering/Susan Daigle-Leach
Design/Nozomi Akashi

Editor – 1st Edition/Trish Ledoux
Editor – Editor's Choice Edition/Kit Fox

Managing Editor/Annette Roman
Director of Production/Noboru Watanabe
Editorial Director/Alvin Lu
Sr. Director of Licensing & Acquisitions/Rika Inouye
Vice President of Marketing/Liza Coppola
Vice President of Sales/Joe Morici
Executive Vice President/Hyoe Narita
Publisher/Seiji Horibuchi

PARENTAL ADVISORY
MAISON IKKOKU is rated T+ for Teen Plus.
Contains strong language and sexual themes.
Recommended for older teens (16 and up).

© 1984 Rumiko Takahashi/Shogakukan, Inc. First published by
Shogakukan, Inc. in Japan as "Mezon Ikkoku." New and adapted
artwork and text © 2004 VIZ, LLC. The MAISON IKKOKU logo is a
trademark of VIZ, LLC. All rights reserved. No portion of this book
may be reproduced or transmitted in any form or by any means
without written permission from the copyright holders. The stories,
characters, institutions and incidents mentioned in this publication
are entirely fictional.

Printed in Canada

Published by VIZ, LLC
P.O. Box 77010
San Francisco, CA 94107

Editor's Choice Edition
10 9 8 7 6 5 4 3 2 1
First printing, September 2004
First English edition published 1996

www.viz.com

ABOUT THE ARTIST

Rumiko Takahashi, born in 1957 in Niigata, Japan, is the acclaimed creator and artist of *Maison Ikkoku*, *InuYasha*, *Ranma 1/2* and *Lum * Urusei Yatsura*.

She lived in a small student apartment in Nakano, Japan, which was the basis for the *Maison Ikkoku* series, while she attended the prestigious Nihon Joseidai (Japan Women's University). At the same time, Takahashi also began studying comics at Gekiga Sonjuku, a famous school for manga artists run by Kazuo Koike, author of *Crying Freeman* and *Lone Wolf and Cub*. In 1978, Takahashi won a prize in Shogakukan's annual New Comic Artist Contest and her boy-meets-alien comedy *Lum * Urusei Yatsura* began appearing in the weekly manga magazine *Shonen Sunday*.

Takahashi's success and critical acclaim continues to grow, with popular titles including *Ranma 1/2* and *InuYasha*. Many of her graphic novel series have also been animated, and are widely available in several languages.

EDITOR'S RECOMMENDATIONS

More manga!
More manga!

Fans of

maison ikkoku

should also read:

©1988 Rumiko
Takahashi/Shogakukan, Inc.

RANMA 1/2

Rumiko Takahashi's gender-bending comedy series is the tale of a father and son who fall into cursed springs in China, and their lives are transformed, literally. When they get wet, the father turns into a panda and the son, Ranma, turns into a girl. Comic situations ensue as they try and keep their friends and family, especially Ranma's fiancé and her family, from finding out their secret.

© 1997 Tokihiko
Matsuura/Shogakukan, Inc.

TUXEDO GIN

In Tokihiko Matsuura's romantic comedy, 17-year-old Ginji Kusanagi meets the girl of his dreams, Minako Sasebo, but is killed in an accident before they go on their first date. Ginji is reincarnated as a penguin, and Minako adopts him as her pet, but she has no idea that he's actually her dearly departed love.

© Saki Hiwatari
1986/HAKUSENSHA, Inc.

PLEASE SAVE MY EARTH

Saki Hiwatari's tale of love, loss and reincarnation is part science fiction, part fantasy. Seven scientists from a distant planet realize they've been reborn on Earth as teenagers when they discover they're all having the same dreams.

INUYASHA™

Rated #1 on Cartoon Network's Adult Swim!

In its original unedited form.

maîson ikkoku™

The beloved romantic comedy of errors—a fan favorite!

Ranma ½™

The zany, wacky study of martial arts at its best!

RANMA 1/2 © 2002 Rumiko Takahashi/Shogakukan • Kitty Film • Fuji TV. MAISON IKKOKU ©1984 Rumiko Takahashi/Shogakukan. © Rumiko Takahashi/Shogakukan • YOMIURI TV • SUNRISE 2000.

Your Favorite Rumiko Takahashi Titles...Now Available From VIZ!

Complete your collection with these Takahashi anime and manga classics!

Get yours today!

www.viz.com

INUYASHA ©1997 Rumiko Takahashi/Shogakukan. MAISON IKKOKU ©1984 Rumiko Takahashi/Shogakukan. RANMA 1/2 ©1988 Rumiko Takahashi/Shogak

Ranma Transformed...Again!!

Ranma ½™

Now you can get your favorite martial artist in your favorite form! A must-have to complete your Ranma 1/2 collection.

$69.95 each

Collect Them Now

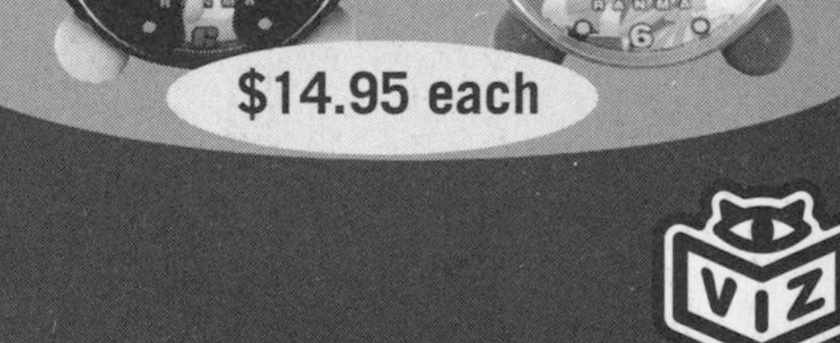

$14.95 each

$29.95 each

Order yours at
store.viz.com

© 2003 RUMIKO TAKAHASHI /
SHOGAKUKAN • KITTY FILM • FUJI TV

No One Said Love Was Easy

What do you do when the boy flirting with you is the object of your friend's desire? Between friendship and love, what will Karin choose?

Experience the roller coaster ride of a girl's first love and first kiss. But this is high school, and living happily ever after isn't on the curriculum!

KARE First Love

Only $9.95!

Start your graphic novel collection today!

©2002 Kaho Miyasaka/Shogakukan, Inc.

shôjo

FRESH FROM JAPAN
日本最新

www.viz.com

editor's
choice

THE STANDARD FOR EXCELLENCE

- Cinderalla
- Collector File
- Dance Till Tomorrow
- Flowers & Bees
- Gyo
- Hansel & Gretel
- Maison Ikkoku*
- Marionette Generation
- Nausicaä of the Valley of the Wind
- No. 5
- Phoenix
- Princess Mermaid
- Saikano*
- Short Cuts
- Vagabond

START YOUR EDITOR'S CHOICE GRAPHIC NOVEL COLLECTION TODAY!

© 2000 Shin Takahashi/Shogakukan, Inc.

www.viz.com

STARTING @ $9.95!

* Also available on DVD from VIZ

COMPLETE OUR SURVEY AND LET US KNOW WHAT YOU THINK!

☐ Please do NOT send me information about VIZ products, news and events, special offers, or other information.

☐ Please do NOT send me information from VIZ's trusted business partners.

Name: _____

Address: _____

City: _____ State: _____ Zip: _____

E-mail: _____

☐ Male ☐ Female   Date of Birth (mm/dd/yyyy): ___/___/___   (Under 13? Parental consent required)

What race/ethnicity do you consider yourself? (please check one)

☐ Asian/Pacific Islander   ☐ Black/African American   ☐ Hispanic/Latino

☐ Native American/Alaskan Native ☐ White/Caucasian   ☐ Other: _____

What VIZ product did you purchase? (check all that apply and indicate title purchased)

☐ DVD/VHS _____

☐ Graphic Novel _____

☐ Magazines _____

☐ Merchandise _____

Reason for purchase: (check all that apply)

☐ Special offer   ☐ Favorite title   ☐ Gift

☐ Recommendation   ☐ Other _____

Where did you make your purchase? (please check one)

☐ Comic store   ☐ Bookstore   ☐ Mass/Grocery Store

☐ Newsstand   ☐ Video/Video Game Store ☐ Other: _____

☐ Online (site: _____)

What other VIZ properties have you purchased/own? _____

_____

PINOLE

How many anime and/or manga titles have you purchased in the last year? How many were VIZ titles? (please check one from each column)

ANIME
☐ None
☐ 1-4
☐ 5-10
☐ 11+

MANGA
☐ None
☐ 1-4
☐ 5-10
☐ 11+

VIZ
☐ None
☐ 1-4
☐ 5-10
☐ 11+

I find the pricing of VIZ products to be: (please check one)
☐ Cheap ☐ Reasonable ☐ Expensive

What genre of manga and anime would you like to see from VIZ? (please check two)
☐ Adventure ☐ Comic Strip ☐ Science Fiction ☐ Fighting
☐ Horror ☐ Romance ☐ Fantasy ☐ Sports

What do you think of VIZ's new look?
☐ Love It ☐ It's OK ☐ Hate It ☐ Didn't Notice ☐ No Opinion

Which do you prefer? (please check one)
☐ Reading right-to-left
☐ Reading left-to-right

A gift from:
Friends of the
Pinole Library

Which do you prefer? (please check one)
☐ Sound effects in English
☐ Sound effects in Japanese with English captions
☐ Sound effects in Japanese only with a glossary at the back

THANK YOU! Please send the completed form to:

NJW Research
42 Catharine St.
Poughkeepsie, NY 12601

All information provided will be used for internal purposes only. We promise not to sell or otherwise divulge your information.

NO PURCHASE NECESSARY. Requests not in compliance with all terms of this form will not be acknowledged or returned. All submissions are subject to verification and become the property of VIZ, LLC. Fraudulent submission, including use of multiple addresses or P.O. boxes to obtain additional VIZ information or offers may result in prosecution. VIZ reserves the right to withdraw or modify any terms of this form. Void where prohibited, taxed, or restricted by law. VIZ will not be liable for lost, misdirected, mutilated, illegible, incomplete or postage-due mail. © 2003 VIZ, LLC. All Rights Reserved. VIZ, LLC, property titles, characters, names and plots therein under license to VIZ, LLC. All Rights Reserved.